T0320869

# An Economic History of Portugal, 1143–2010

A fascinating exploration into the evolution of the Portugese economy over the course of eight centuries, from the foundation of the kingdom in 1143, when political boundaries began to take shape in the midst of the Christian *Reconquista* of the Iberian Peninsula, the formation of an empire, to the integration of the nation in the European Communities and the Economic and Monetary Union. Through six chapters, the authors provide a vibrant history of Portugal's past with a focus ranging from the medieval economy and the age of globalization to war and recovery, the Atlantic economy, the rise of liberalism and patterns of convergence. The book provides a unique long-term perspective of change in a Southern European country and its empire, which responds to the fundamental broader questions about when, how, and why economies expand, stagnate or contract.

Leonor Freire Costa is a tenured assistant professor at the Lisbon School of Economics and Management, University of Lisbon.

Pedro Lains is a research professor at the Instituto de Ciências Sociais, University of Lisbon and a visiting professor at Católica Lisbon School of Business and Economics.

Susana Münch Miranda is a senior researcher at the Institute for History, Leiden University.

# An Economic History of Portugal, 1143–2010

Leonor Freire Costa
*University of Lisbon*

Pedro Lains
*University of Lisbon*

Susana Münch Miranda
*Leiden University*

CAMBRIDGE
UNIVERSITY PRESS

# CAMBRIDGE
## UNIVERSITY PRESS

University Printing House, Cambridge CB2 8BS, United Kingdom

Cambridge University Press is part of the University of Cambridge.

It furthers the University's mission by disseminating knowledge in the pursuit of education, learning and research at the highest international levels of excellence.

www.cambridge.org
Information on this title: www.cambridge.org/9781107035546

First published 2016

Printed in the United States of America by Sheridan Books, Inc.

*A catalogue record for this publication is available from the British Library*

ISBN 978-1-107-03554-6 Hardback

Cambridge University Press has no responsibility for the persistence or accuracy of URLs for external or third-party internet websites referred to in this publication, and does not guarantee that any content on such websites is, or will remain, accurate or appropriate.

# Contents

# Figures

# Maps

# Tables

# Preface

The present book is a substantially revised translation of a book first published in Portugal (*História Económica de Portugal 1143–2010,* Lisbon: Esfera dos Livros, 2011) which was written following the suggestion of a publisher that identified a lacuna for an economic history of Portugal over the period since the foundation of the kingdom, in the twelfth century, to the present times. There are many valuable works that provide a global perspective either for shorter periods of Portuguese economic history, or for longer periods of its political and institutional history, but there certainly was room for a global economic history that covers a wide range of topics, from demographic and institutional developments to the measurement of economic growth and a more formal analysis of factors of growth and structural change. We gladly accepted the challenge because there is a large amount of research from which it is possible to draw a global perspective on the evolution of the Portuguese economy, within its European borders, and regarding its relations with Europe, the empire, and the rest of the world.

When we wrote the first version of the book, we had in mind an international audience, as we were well aware that the economic history of Portugal in the long run can be of interest for students on a wide variety of topics of international reach, such as the making of colonial empires, their consequences for domestic economies and, why economies grow or fall behind. The present English version of the book is the best demonstration of that wider interest in Portugal's economic development. Although we have not changed the manuscript in terms of its main structure, this edition is different from the first in many aspects. Not only have we benefited from recent findings that have clarified our interpretation on the evolution of the Portuguese economy in the long run but we have also stressed further the connections between national and international issues. We hope the international reader will be attracted to the study of this relatively small and peripheral country both because it was the center of an empire for many centuries and it highlights many other issues regarding international economic history.

Our task in writing both versions of the book was rendered possible and in many instances more pleasant thanks to the interactions with many colleagues we have met in Portugal and elsewhere, of whom we would like to mention Cátia Antunes, Rui Pedro Esteves, Joaquim Romero Magalhães, Jaime Reis, and João Paulo Salvado. We would like to thank John Huffstot for his effort in translating the original version of the manuscript of this book, Cláudia Viana for designing the maps, as well as Marta Castelo Branco and Bárbara Direito for their valuable help in the edition of the final manuscript. We would also like to acknowledge valuable comments from three anonymous referees. Finally, we would like to thank the generous grants from Fundação Calouste Gulbenkian, Bank of Portugal, and Luso-American Development Foundation, which rendered possible the work of translation and revision of the original manuscript.

# Introduction

This book is about the evolution of the Portuguese economy during the course of eight centuries, from the foundation of the kingdom, in 1143, when political boundaries began to take shape in the midst of the Christian *Reconquista* of the Iberian Peninsula, to the integration of the nation in the European Communities and the Economic and Monetary Union. While the economy we are interested in responded to external influences across the land and sea borders, its activity also exerted influence on events occurring elsewhere.[1]

The study of the Portuguese economy highlights in a vivid way a number of aspects of European economic history. Indeed, the formation of Portugal as a political unit in 1143 should be seen as part of the broader movement in the Iberian Peninsula, called *Reconquista*, which obtained the statute of Crusade by papal encyclical in 1123. The understanding of the economic forces driving territorial expansion, which ended with the takeover of the Algarve, in 1249, presents a rare opportunity to observe how Christian rulers and settlers managed to conquer and reorganize resources that were once inserted in the Muslim al-Andalus, by then one of the more urbanized and possibly technologically more advanced areas of southern Europe. The *Reconquista* of the Iberian Peninsula spanned 781 years, since the fall of Granada took place in 1491, and thus contributed to expand Europe's cultural, religious, and economic borders while establishing the political and institutional framework of the new Christian kingdom.

Regarding this particular aspect of the first century of Portuguese history, the development of manorial organization in Iberia provides additional evidence for a comparison with the seigneurial regime as it evolved elsewhere in Europe. The rise of a stable and legitimized

---

[1] For Europe, see Broadberry and O'Rourke 2010; Crouzet 2000; Magnusson 2002; Malanima 2009; Persson 2010; and Di Vittorio 2006. See also, for the rest of the world, Findlay and O'Rourke 2007 and Neal and Williamson eds. 2014.

monarchy in the twelfth century went hand in hand with the distribution of land and wealth that defined the balance of power between the king, the nobility, and the Church. This equilibrium needed regular military actions to ensure its sustainability and was accompanied by a dynamic of territorial expansion in order to secure more resources to be distributed. These factors were also the main drivers of the overseas expansion, beginning with the conquest of Ceuta in the northern coast of Africa, in 1415, and the ensuing discoveries. The *Reconquista* and maritime expansion were thus closely linked in their institutional, military, and economic aspects.

The study of the peripheral country that is the focus of the present book provides a unique perspective about European expansion. After Vasco da Gama's first voyage to India (1498), the long-term evolution of the European economy was shaped by the "simultaneous effect of contradictory forces: the forces of decline and the forces of growth" (Malanima, 2009: xiv). Down to a certain point in time, the forces of decline are largely associated with rural areas, and the forces of growth with cities and national, international, or colonial trade, thus defining the regions of the continent which forge ahead or lag behind in different historical moments.

The tension between decline and progress is present in our analysis of the Portuguese economy as will be clear in the book. In the sixteenth century if not in earlier times, the forces of stagnation, or at least of slow growth, in Portugal overweighed the forces of expansion. In fact, the conditions for growth in this region of Europe were less favorable than in the more dynamic axis, located between the northern cities of the Low Countries and the rich plains of Lombardy. That difference became even clearer during the eighteenth century, the period of Europe's "little divergence", and the heyday of the British industrial revolution (Van Zanden 2009). Thus, theories about the causes of industrial and, for that matter, overall economic success, need to be tested in the regions that lagged behind, like Portugal.[2] Yet, despite the undeniable historical level of economic backwardness, the Portuguese economy also made considerable advances, as backwardness and growth are not incompatible concepts.

From the mid-nineteenth century onwards, the Portuguese economy was transformed in a substantial way, albeit not at a pace that allowed it to overcome the gap in the level of income per capita in relation to more advanced countries. The phases of growth and slowdown of the

---

[2] Berend and Rámki 1982; Milward and Saul 1973,1977; Ó Gráda 2001; Prados de la Escosura 1988; Tortella 2000; Pollard 1994; Zamagni 1993. For the eastern European peripheries, see Lampe and Jackson 1982 and Pamuk 2009.

Portuguese economy, as well as those of convergence and divergence vis-à-vis countries that industrialized earlier, are associated with cycles of higher or lower tariff protection, levels of State intervention, and levels of institutional development. This means that the Portuguese experience also provides an excellent lens to observe how these factors interacted in the European economy.[3] As stated in a work on another small peripheral European economy, "the history of any individual country of the West is inseparably connected with the historical development of the West as a whole (. . .) [and that] applies with particular force to a *small* Western country and the *economic* history of such a country."[4]

The long-term analysis we carry out in this book constitutes the ambitious and challenging task of providing a coherent account of the evolution of a national economy and its external and imperial relations during a long period for which quantitative data is scarce, scattered, and sometimes contradictory.[5] We are, however, following the steps of recent work on comparative growth in the long term, which has generated an impressive body of scholarship on convergence and divergence, within Europe or at the world level.[6] In this literature, the main focus is to find large trends in growth and decline and explain them in terms of demographic, political, or institutional change, taking into account information of those different areas that englobe economic activity. In order to grasp economic evolution in such a long period of time, we need to go beyond the standard analysis of macroeconomic variables, for lack of the necessary quantitative information, and integrate institutional developments.[7]

Our approach questions a certain historiographical tradition that somehow dominated earlier interpretations on Portugal's economic growth and was mostly focused on detecting possible consequences of systemic crises, which considered mostly variables such as price levels and scattered information on foreign trade. The influence of this older literature on Portuguese historiography stands out in the notion that the economy was affected by repeated crises, which is based to a large extent on the writings of contemporary observers. By identifying social and institutional constraints, these observers followed a stream of criticism, based on the notion of a national or Iberian decline that shaped their own political agenda. The *arbitristas*, a group of seventeenth-century thinkers and reformers common to Portugal and

---

[3] Berend and Ránki 1982; Broadberry and O'Rourke 2010.
[4] Heckscher, 1954, p. 9 (italics from the original).     [5] Cipolla 2003; Braudel 1982–1984.
[6] Pomeranz 2000; Allen 2001; Broadberry and Gupta 2006; Malanima 2013; Van Zanden 2009.
[7] See North 1981: 3–8; Cipolla 1991.

Spain, are an example of political sensitivity to alterations in the economic environment. These writings were abundantly quoted by a generation of philosophers, historians, and politicians living in the last decades of the monarchy and also by actors of the new republican regime who became profoundly upset with Portugal's backwardness.[8]

This book takes into consideration such qualitative insights that mirror the actors' perspective on lived events, and also recognizes the intellectual legacy left by historians, who provided a broader interpretation of Portuguese economic history by stressing the ups and downs and the causes of the country's falling behind.[9] Our overview relies heavily on the body of literature on Portuguese history and its empire.[10] Although extensive and providing a wide array of information and quantifications, this literature tackles issues and periods that are not usually studied in an economic and integrated perspective. Nevertheless, we believe it is possible to build an intelligible narrative based on information about demographic change, agricultural and industrial outputs, internal and external trade. There will, however, be some room for intellectual doubts in exercises that aim to offer a comprehensive reading of scattered data, especially with regard to medieval or early modern periods for which evidence is often insufficient or even contradictory. Furthermore, our approach adds to this immense literature when it makes use of entirely new results and data sets produced by research projects namely on living standards from 1300 up to 1910.[11] As for the contemporary period, neither scarcity nor scattering of data hinders an in-depth historical investigation. The evolution of the economy in the last two centuries can therefore be based on regular assessments of production, both at the sectorial and at the aggregate levels, and factor productivity.

Economic development is necessarily linked with the development of institutions which provide the framework of formal and informal rules that constrain individual or social choices.[12] An examination of eight centuries of Portuguese history thus needs to identify the bundle of property rights that determined the distribution of resources and output, as well as the fiscal and monetary scope of the decisions taken by the political core, in order to tackle the different paths toward the rise of

[8] Sérgio 1984; Quental 1982.
[9] See Godinho 1955, 1978b; Macedo 1982b. See also Magalhães 1988; Pedreira 1994.
[10] Marques 1973, 1978; Mattoso 1985 and Mattoso ed. 1992–1994; Mata and Valério 2003a; Disney 2009; Ramos, Sousa, and Monteiro 2009; Rodrigues 2008; Freire and Lains, forthcoming; Lains and Silva 2005; Castro 1978; Bethencourt and Curto 2007; Godinho 1982–1984; Magalhães 1988; Hanson 1986; Godinho 1982–1984, Pereira 1983 and their revision in Reis 1993; Bethencourt and Chaudhuri 1998; Costa, Rodrigues, and Oliveira 2014.
[11] Reis, ed. 2008–2010.    [12] North 1990.

modern political institutions.[13] As for contemporary relations between the State and the economy, this book deals with the role of economic policies in constraining or boosting growth.[14]

In the rest of the book, we look into the behavior of variables, such as demography, agriculture, industry, foreign trade, and public finances, to assess the evolution of the Portuguese economy. Not surprisingly, the benchmarks that shape the book's structure are milestones set at the international level, except the year of 1143 that marks the beginning of our story.

The formation of the kingdom in the midst of the Christian *Reconquista* is at the core of Chapter 1 and we argue there that the Portuguese economy in the medieval period was strongly affected by the consequences of changing borders. From 1143 to 1249, economic activity must be seen in the context of the endemic wars against the Muslims. The southward movement allowed the monarch, the nobility, and military orders to take possession of the land, thus expanding the seigneurial regime and its institutional arrangement of wealth and land distribution.[15] At the same time, an ancient tradition of property rights over common land and self-government gave rise to a network of local organizations, based on municipalities (*concelhos*), encouraged either by the Crown or by lay and ecclesiastical lords.[16] The king, the nobility, the Church, and the municipalities were thus the major institutional actors to take possession of the land and derive economic profit from it.

After the end of the *Reconquista*, between *c.* 1250 and the 1340s, population and agricultural output trends became increasingly more aligned with the long cycle of growth in Western Europe.[17] Even though agriculture continued to be the main source of economic change, there is also evidence on the role of commercial activities, both at the domestic level and with the rest of Europe. Within the domestic borders, regular fairs and occasional markets constituted the most important forms of connecting producers to consumers. Externally the kingdom took an increasing part in the burgeoning trade, particularly in the routes that linked northern Europe to the Mediterranean.[18]

---

[13] Hespanha 1982, 1994; Monteiro 2007a. See also Bonney 1995, 1999; Epstein 2000; Schumpeter 1991; Tilly 1990.
[14] Rosas 1994; Corkill 1999.
[15] Castro 1978; Coelho and Homem 1996; Hespanha 1982; Mattoso 1985. See also Ramos, Sousa, and Monteiro 2009.
[16] Coelho and Magalhães 2008; Hespanha 1982. [17] Marques 1987; Rodrigues 2008.
[18] Azevedo 1929; Barros 1956; Marques 1987; Rau 1983.

The phase of demographic and economic expansion from the twelfth century to the thirteenth century was interrupted, like elsewhere in Europe, by the Black Death, certainly one of the worst catastrophes ever to strike the continent. The epidemic wiped out nearly a third of the country's population, dramatically impacting on agricultural output, trade, and manufactures, leading to a demographic and economic crisis that lasted throughout the fourteenth century (Marques 1987). Contemporarily, beginning in 1369, the hostilities with Castile unfolded in several episodes, including the dynastic crisis of 1383–1385 that followed the death of the last member of the House of Burgundy, and which allowed João de Avis, the bastard son of King Pedro, to take the throne as João I. War with the neighboring kingdom lasted until 1411 and put the kingdom's financial resources under tremendous pressure. With the rise to power of the Avis dynasty, a second wave of border expansion took place. The military expedition that captured Ceuta in 1415 was certainly part of the new dynasty's efforts to legitimize its political credibility, both in Portugal and abroad.[19] The addition of Ceuta to the kingdom inaugurated an expansionary phase spanning over a century. Early on during this phase, Portugal colonized islands in the Atlantic, secured its military presence in northern Africa, and undertook a series of long-distance overseas voyages along the west coast of Africa. As early as the 1480s, the goal of reaching India by sea became a priority and was finally accomplished in 1498 with Vasco da Gama's first journey. The second voyage to India (1500) expanded Portugal's area of influence even further, this time to the northeastern shores of South America.

With economic borders that encompassed settlements in three continents, the Portuguese economy showed clear signs of prosperity and after 1500 population grew steadily, in line with the European long-term upward trend and most probably the levels of population and output from the period before the epidemic were attained once again, which was also followed by the growth of commercial relations within the empire.[20] In 1580, Portugal and the other Iberian kingdoms were united under the rule of Filipe II. The dynastic union has been associated since as early as the seventeenth century, with a widespread crisis that put Portugal along a path of decline (Peres 1933, vol. III). Nevertheless, the view that the higher level of integration of the Iberian economies, both within Europe and with the overseas economies, under the rule of the Habsburgs was one of recovery is well established now. Trade across the Cape route was kept active and expanded, while Brazil assumed a leading

[19] Farinha 1998; Godinho 1962; Marques 1998; Thomaz 1994.
[20] Dias 1996; Rodrigues 2008.

position in sugar production between 1580 and 1620, which spurred transatlantic trade to new heights. As a result, the first forty years of the Iberian Union were economically beneficial for Portugal, particularly in terms of its position in the world economy.[21] This conclusion, which we express in Chapter 2, is in line with what we may sense in the literature about European growth in the sixteenth century up to the 1620s. The bulk of this chapter focuses on Portugal's role in the growth of intra-European trade, which is assessed by taking into consideration the relative contribution of each Portuguese colonial specialization. The development of a maritime empire in the sixteenth century ensured a new intermediary role to Portuguese shores, competing with Mediterranean outlets that traditionally had connected Europe to the Middle East and Asia.[22] Domestically, some economic sectors were positively affected, especially shipbuilding. Furthermore, the empire provided the crown's finances with new resources, both through customs duties and through monopoly rights over businesses within the empire directly exploited by the crown or by private groups of merchants. The imperial dimension of the economy thus represented a new level of openness and a greater integration of Portugal in European flows.

Meanwhile, a set of reforms changed the structure of the crown's revenues, but domestic resources continued to be redistributed among the nobility and the Church through fiscal arrangements established since the *Reconquista*. This was a significant mechanism that ensured a social pact that held the kingdom together, and was challenged during the last twenty years of the Habsburg rule. The 1640 coup that restored Portugal's independence from Spain can be explained by the challenges to this fiscal equilibrium brought about by Habsburg rule rather than by the loss of overseas territories due to the international conflicts in which Portugal was involved during the Iberian Union. The hostilities increased in intensity during Philip IV's reign (1621–1665), involving the Habsburg monarchy in the Thirty Years' War (1618–1648), while warfare with the United Provinces resumed after 1621. Chapter 3 opens with this moment, also taken as a turning point in Portugal's economic history.[23]

Portuguese Asia, whose revenue clearly outweighed that derived from other overseas possessions, was increasingly threatened by the encroachment of the maritime trading companies of the United Provinces and Great Britain. The conflict with the Dutch resulted in the loss of

---

[21] Boyajian 1993; Subrahmanyam 1993; Cortesão 1940a and 1940b; Costa 2002a, 2002b; Mauro 1983; Moreira 1990; Polónia 2007; Schwartz 1985; Silva 1988.
[22] Bethencourt and Curto, eds. 2007; Disney 2009; Godinho 1982–1984; Goris 1925; Rau 1971; Subrahmanyam 1993; Torrão 1991; Vieira 2002; Vogt 1979.
[23] Oliveira 1971–1972; Oliveira 1990; Schaub 2001.

settlements in Asia and Brazil whilst, on the domestic front, apart from the rise of taxation, indicators such as demography and agricultural output point to a phase of stagnation from the late 1620s onwards. This is different than what was happening in the Dutch Republic and England, where signs of prosperity in the second half of the seventeenth century confirm the erosion of Portugal's position vis-à-vis European Atlantic powers.[24] Social and political unrest favored a political conspiracy led by the aristocracy that put an end to Habsburg rule.[25] Political independence came in a period of relative economic stagnation and the War of Restoration that followed determined fiscal innovations that had long-lasting effects.[26] In 1641, a universal income tax of 10 percent, the *décima*, was introduced, legitimized on the need for a collective effort to pay for independence and defense of the kingdom. Despite its origins, it continued to be collected after the war ended until well into the liberal period, in the nineteenth century. The *décima* was unparalleled in Europe, where the rise of the state's revenue was mainly based on indirect taxes.[27]

The conflict spanned over almost three decades, and population growth was thus constrained, while agriculture was hit by a succession of poor harvests. In 1668, peace with Spain was finally signed, but Portugal's economy took a long time to recover, and foreign trade remained stagnant until well into the first quarter of the eighteenth century (Rau 1954). However, agricultural output apparently recovered after around the 1680s and the population resumed growth most probably after around 1700.[28] Such signs of positive evolution of the domestic economy occurred in the midst of monetary devaluation and inflation, which probably had significant effects on the distribution of income and on other matters such as the real interest rate of public debt bonds. Reacting to what contemporary actors viewed as a critical shortage of financial resources, foreign trade contraction, and outflows of bullion to offset the trade deficit, the State foresaw the introduction of import-substitution policies.[29] Industrial improvements, together with rising population and investment in the primary sector, at least in certain regions of the country, suggest some degree of economic recovery on the eve of the war of the Spanish Succession (1702–1713).[30]

---

[24] Magalhães 1988; Santos 2003.
[25] For a theoretical approach on this event, from a broader perspective of revolutions and their respective linkages to economic and demographic variables, see Goldstone 1991. Specifically for the Portuguese case, see Oliveira 2002; Costa and Cunha 2006.
[26] Hespanha 2004; Mata 2012.
[27] Bonney and Ormrod 1999: 18. See also Yun-Casalilla and O'Brien 2012, where the case of Portugal is considered.
[28] Amorim 1997; Magalhães 1988; Oliveira 1979, 1980; Oliveira 1990; Santos 2003.
[29] Hanson 1986; Macedo 1982b.    [30] Godinho 1990; Pedreira 1994.

The war put in check the diplomatic links inherited from the times of the Restoration where France had a leading role and, in 1703, Portugal joined the Grand Alliance of England, the Dutch Republic, and the Holy Roman Empire. Chapter 4 begins at this new international order which favored the kingdom's interests in the Atlantic and steered the diplomatic decision of signing a commercial treaty with England in 1703 (known in Portugal as the Methuen Treaty), with relevant economic implications for both parties (Francis 1966). The English wool industry gained easier access to Portuguese markets from then on, while Portuguese wine was taxed in England at a rate one-third lower than that levied on French wines.

The eighteenth century thus started with a positive tone in Europe, at least from the point of view of demographic growth. In the Portuguese case, however, the population fell until around 1730 as a result of unprecedented migration flows to Brazil driven by the gold mining rush.[31] Portugal's trade surplus with the colony ensured inflows of gold as a result of re-exports of European commodities, especially British cloth, which was paid for mostly with gold in the colony. In turn, the abundant bullion that entered the British economy increased the demand and thus exports of wine to the British market experienced an upsurge.[32] The growth of the foreign sector was nevertheless accompanied by successive trade deficits, as imports of both manufactures and foodstuffs were not matched by exports, and the deficits had to be covered by the export of gold.[33] Yet, gold inflows from Brazil clearly exceeded outflows from Europe.[34] Colonial trade thus raised the levels of money supply in Portugal, and this level of liquidity positively affecting the royal treasury must have contributed to the issuing of public debt at decreasing interest rates.[35]

In 1755, a terrible earthquake occurred in Lisbon and in other parts of the country, particularly in the south which had very important consequences at the political and the economic levels (Araújo et al. 2007). The aftermath of this disaster saw the rise of marquis of Pombal, Carvalho e Melo, who led the centralization of the state and a higher degree of economic intervention.[36] The minister's actions went far beyond the context of the catastrophe. He changed the institutional framework of the Portuguese agricultural economy with the creation of the first demarcated wine region, in order to limit and control the production and quality of the wine.[37] Alongside the colonial companies that emerged with Pombal policies, this institutional framework for wine

---

[31] Godinho 1978b; Rodrigues 2008; Serrão 1982, 1993b.
[32] Sideri 1978; Schneider 1980.    [33] Fisher 1971; Meneses 2001; Morineau 1985.
[34] Costa, Rocha, and Sousa 2013; Morineau 1985.    [35] Azevedo 1973; Gomes 1883.
[36] Maxwell 1995; Monteiro 2008.    [37] Martins 1990; Sousa 2008.

production and trade became a bone of contention with Great Britain, and gave rise to the notion that Pombal's government was driven by the aim of nationalization of Portuguese colonial and foreign trade.[38] Apart from the nationalistic implications, which in fact were not a cornerstone of Pombal's policy, his government enhanced the wealth of the elite who dominated colonial commerce, industry, and state financial affairs.[39]

The extent to which the institutional changes put forth by Pombal's government had long-term results is not entirely clear. Doubts remain on the country's economic performance in the late decades of the eighteenth century because the evidence is somewhat contradictory, particularly from the 1790s on. On the one hand, Portugal strengthened its economic ties with the Atlantic system after the Seven Year war (1754–1763), which diversified the country's trade relations with positive consequences on the trade balance.[40] On the other hand, the involvement in ongoing international conflicts increased public expenditure, along with budget deficits, so that in the 1790s, Portugal resorted to issuing paper currency for the first time. This monetary innovation led to rising prices and inflation penalized all stakeholders in the agricultural sector, but wages were also hit.[41] There is evidence that the standard of living on the eve of Napoleon's invasion were lower than those in the middle of the century.[42]

These events marked a new era of Portugal's economic history, which we analyze in Chapter 5. In the following years, soon after the royal court was settled in Rio de Janeiro, the government declared the end of Portugal's trade monopoly with Brazil, in 1808, and a substantial reduction of tariffs levied on the British, in 1810.[43] Political and military instability ultimately led to the 1820 coup that put an end to the absolutist monarchy and to a liberal Constitution. In 1822, Brazil became independent. Stability returned only in 1851, when a new coup appeased the political and military conflicts. And the new set of liberal institutions was only in place well into the third quarter of the century. The slow and troubled political change that we observe in the first half of the nineteenth century was accompanied by the first steps of the Portuguese economy toward industrialization, growth of foreign trade, transformations in the agricultural sector, and increasing levels of urbanization. Portugal started the century as a backward country in the European context, and remained so by the end of the century. But backwardness, or divergence, did not mean an absence of change, and this is one of the most relevant lessons of the experience of this country in the nineteenth century. The century

---

[38] Carreira 1983b, 1988; Marcos 1997; Pedreira 1994.
[39] Madureira 1997; Pedreira 1995    [40] Alexandre 1993; Pedreira 1994; Serrão 1993b.
[41] Cardoso and Lains, eds. 2010; Silva 2005; Silveira 1987.
[42] Costa, Palma, and Reis 2015.    [43] Alexandre 1993; Pedreira 1994.

between the Vienna Congress and the beginning of World War I was relatively peaceful in Europe and elsewhere in the world, allowing for the expansion of international trade, capital flows, and migration. As globalization proceeded, the conditions for industrialization and general economic growth changed considerably, representing both challenges and risks to participating countries. Challenges derived from the fact that new technologies and methods of production were available worldwide and could be imported to more backward countries; and the risks derived from the fact that the world was getting ever more competitive. Looking at what happened in the Portuguese economy in these circumstances highlights the type of possible responses to the new international economic order.

In backward countries like Portugal, one major feature of the liberal century was the creation and consolidation of state institutions that secured the rule of law, allowed for the building of urban and transport infrastructure, and catered for crucial social needs in health and education. These new tasks had to be financed either by raising taxes or by raising domestic or external debt. In the context of expanding financial markets and access to foreign sources of capital, resorting to foreign lending became a major mechanism used by the state to find financing. Ultimately, this became the Achilles heel of the liberal period in Portugal, as well as in other parts of the European periphery.[44] In 1891, due to a financial crisis that led to a partial default, foreign borrowing came to a halt, but the economy recovered shortly after that, and in the two remaining decades industrialization, agricultural change, and general albeit modest economic growth continued.[45] The evaluation of growth trends for the second half of the century is based on quantitative information on output and input growth in agriculture and industry, providing a clear picture of the transformations of the Portuguese economy up to 1914.

World War I had a very significant impact on the international economy and thus both directly and indirectly influenced the countries that were deeply involved in commercial exchanges with the rest of the world, like Portugal. Yet, following the positive trends that marked the previous century, the Portuguese economy again responded positively, this time to an international environment where trade, financial transactions, and emigration were declining.[46] This response is also well documented quantitatively and the quality of the data increases as we move along the twentieth century, analyzed in Chapter 6. Moreover, in the interwar

[44] Cardoso and Lains, eds. 2010; Esteves 2003; Mata 1993.
[45] Lains 2003c; Reis 1993.    [46] Lains 2007; Valério 1994.

period, the rate of growth of the Portuguese economy was higher than that of most European powers, and the gap in living standards was slightly reduced. State protection to the domestic economy took many forms in the interwar period, in Portugal as elsewhere. Import tariffs, subsidized prices, protection of investment, and public investment in infrastructure, namely roads, railways, urban facilities, irrigation, and electricity production, were all part of state protection to the domestic economy.[47] Understanding this positive response depends on the thorough survey of many aspects of the economic and political environment proposed in this book. That survey clearly shows how, once again, Portugal was increasingly becoming part of the European story of industrialization, economic growth, and, to a certain extent, convergence of levels of income per capita.

In addition to its tremendous humanitarian consequences, World War II was very disruptive of the international economic order. Yet, contrary to what happened after the previous war, this time the United States and its European allies responded differently to the challenge of economic recovery. The main difference was that Western governments, after a period of hesitation, took on as their responsibility not only the recovery of the national economies, but also of the international economy. Portugal did not engage in warfare, but it fully engaged in the plans for recovery of international trade and flows of capital and people, and greatly benefitted from this engagement. In fact, although it was a dictatorship, Salazar's government joined the leading international organizations that were propelling the international economy. Opening to the outside went hand in hand with economic policies of market regulation and income redistribution leading for instance to sustained growth and social fairness. Alongside other European countries, Portugal enjoyed a strong growth during these years, marked by economic and financial stability, but tainted by the absence of democracy and by war in the colonies.[48]

The end of the era of "coordinated capitalism" caused by the end of the Bretton Woods system, in 1971, and the 1973 oil crisis, coincided with the end of Portugal's dictatorship.[49] The pressure from increasing competition from the rest of the world was felt all over Europe, which entered a period of recession that was reversed only by the mid 1980s, a period that coincided with the enlargement of the European Communities to Portugal and Spain, in 1986, and ultimately with the creation of the European Union in 1992. These events opened a period of relative

---

[47] For more on European economic history, see Broadberry and O'Rourke's, eds. 2010.
[48] Lains and Silva, eds. 2005, vol. 3.     [49] Eichengreen 2007. See also Neal 2007.

optimism for European growth and convergence, which was, however, halted with the 2008 euro crisis. Whatever lessons we will learn from the latter crisis, we need to conclude that for the Portuguese economy the integration in the wide world depends on integration with Europe, which is both inevitable and historically has brought many economic and political advantages.

# 1 The medieval economy, 1143–1500

Portugal became an independent kingdom in the twelfth century, and just over one hundred years later had established the borders it still has today. Portugal's nationhood was determined not by geography, linguistic issues, or any preexisting political structure. The kingdom's emergence as a distinct entity in the Iberian Peninsula was pivoted on a series of political and military events seeking the reclamation of land occupied by Muslims after their invasion in Iberia in 711–716. The *Reconquista* of the al-Andalus, as Muslims called their conquests in Iberia, is key to understanding the emergence of Portugal as a state. It brought back into Christianity lands that were among the most prosperous in Medieval Europe. At the end of the tenth century, stretching from the river Douro to Gibraltar, al-Andalus had an abundant and diversified agricultural produce, which also enjoyed the reputation of being the most technically sophisticated of the time. Of an estimated population of 10 million, 10 percent lived in cities. It was the western-most part of the Islamic world, which was described at the time as being a series of urban centers, connected by trade routes, lubricated by precious metals, and closely linked to the sub-Saharan empires of Ghana, Mali, and Songhai (Findlay and O'Rourke 2007: 48–59). The al-Andalus "represented a kind of El Dorado or Promised Land" whose resources provided a powerful incentive to the Christian kingdoms of the northern Iberian Peninsula (Chalmeta 1994: 756). Muslim Portugal was part of "Gharb al-Andalus," the western al-Andalus, and evidence suggests that it was notably from the lower valley of the Tagus to the south that Muslim occupation was more dense and urbanized.

The making of a political entity through conquest of land and capture of resources from the western al-Andalus determined the balance of power among the Crown, the nobility, and the Church, which were the three prominent institutions called to organize new settlements and the exploitation of endowments. The partition of wealth among these entities fostered warfare, not only within the borders, but also, and mainly, beyond frontiers. Thereby the main stages of the *Reconquista* that pushed the frontiers further to the south and the capture of Ceuta in 1415 that opened up the European expansion are events having common ultimate factors, namely the king's need of legitimizing his rule by redistributing resources and jurisdictional powers that were pegged to the exploitation of land. In this chapter we provide an overview of the social distribution of land and power and how it shaped the institutional framework of productive sectors. The cornerstone of the analysis is the historical notion that throughout the first centuries of the kingdom's history, after Afonso Henriques had claimed the title of *rex*, the Portuguese economy was shaped by regular moves of frontier. The last of these moves referred to in this chapter, the conquest of Ceuta, paved the way for the making of a maritime empire, which is the event that symbolizes the first milestone of the Iberian Discoveries that were featured through the whole fifteenth century.

## The new kingdom

In the long view, the southward expansion of the *Reconquista* was far from even across time. The frontier lines between the Christian and Muslim territories changed several times, as expansionist bursts alternated with periods of stability and even regression, depending on the political circumstances of the al-Andalus and the balance of power between the Christian kingdoms. By the 850s, the leader of the *Reconquista*, the Christian kingdom of Asturias was expanding to the south, toward the Douro River, incorporating parts of what would be in the future the northern regions of Portugal, notably Minho and Trás-os-Montes. This push of borders was backed by claims of the Asturian kings to the Visigoth inheritance, a claim that aimed to establish them as valid rulers of the Iberian Peninsula. The seizure of the cities of Portucale, at the mouth of the Douro River, in 868, and then Coimbra, in 879, were crucial events that signaled the emergence of the county of Portucale (*condado Portucalense*), as a fiefdom of the kingdom of Asturias. Vímara Peres, the conqueror of Portucale, was granted jurisdiction over the area between the Minho and Douro rivers (Entre-Douro-e-Minho), which was thereby the original core of the future kingdom of Portugal. Lands were repopulated by Christian settlers from the north as well as by Mozarabs, who had previously lived under Muslim rule without converting to Islam.[1] Still, the border with al-Andalus pushed back toward the north, even as far as the Douro, following intense counterattacks by the Muslims in the 900s.

---

[1] Beirante 1993: 281–285; Ramos, Sousa, and Monteiro 2009: 18–19. For a survey in English language, see Disney 2009, vol. 1: 66–67.

The major thrust of the Christian advance took place between 1057 and 1064, with the capture of the earlier episcopal Sees of Lamego, Viseu, and Coimbra and the restoration of the territory between the Douro and Mondego Rivers, about 16,000 km$^2$ or one-fourth of the present-day territory. The Christian successes in the field benefited, no doubt, from the breakup of the Caliphate of Córdoba in 1031 into small principalities that proved incapable of mounting a joint military response. From this time on, the territory was permanently secured by the Christians and it eventually formed the core of the county of Coimbra – one-fourth of the present-day territory (Map 1.1)

Following the successful campaigns, the Asturian kings transferred their base of operations from Oviedo to León, in the *Meseta,* where there emerged first the kingdom of León, and then, in the early eleventh century, the kingdom of León-Castile, through a dynastic union. King Fernando I of León-Castile granted the county of Coimbra to the Mozarab Sisnando Davides, who belonged to his circle of closest councilors. Sisnando was put in charge of ruling the territory and this central region attracted waves of immigrants coming down from the north and new settlements were organized (Amaral 2007: 138–142). In the last quarter of the eleventh century, within the sphere of influence of the kingdom of León-Castile, the lands that are today northern and central Portugal were politically divided between the counties of Portucale and Coimbra, the Douro River marking the border. Their position on the peninsular periphery and their frontier character made them vulnerable to Muslim attack, but also offered conditions to growing autonomy on the part of the two counts vis-à-vis the king of León-Castile. However, any drift toward independence was halted in 1071 with the removal of the count of Portucale. Following this decision, the restoration of the authority of the kings of León-Castile was achieved with the support of the *infanções,* members of the low- and middle-ranked nobility. By taking over local political and judicial power, the *infanções* were in due time responsible for intensifying seigneurialism in the territories of Coimbra and Portucale, which would question León-Castile's ability to keep these territories.[2]

Events at the end of the eleventh century defined the nucleus of the future kingdom of Portugal. The marriage in 1096 between Henry of Burgundy and Teresa, illegitimate daughter of Alfonso VI of León-Castile, who received the county of Portucale as dowry, enabled the unification of Portucale and Coimbra in a single earldom. The fief was hereditary, and thus transmitted to the son of this union, Afonso Henriques. With the support of the low- and middle-ranked nobility,

---

[2] Mattoso 1985, vol. 1: 104–106; Mattoso and Sousa 1993: 165–172.

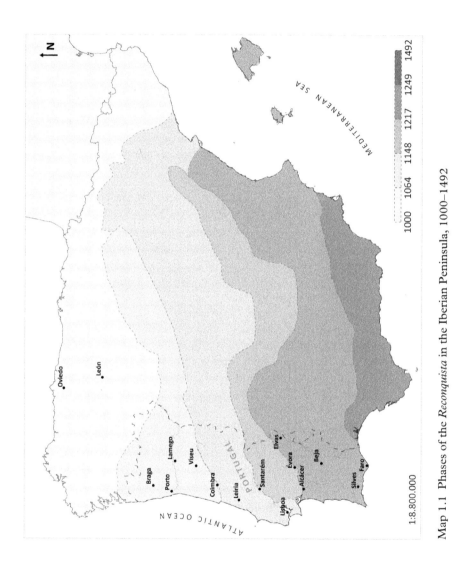

1:8.800.000

Map 1.1  Phases of the *Reconquista* in the Iberian Peninsula, 1000–1492

and capitalizing on an important victory over the Muslim armies at the Battle of Ourique (1139), Afonso Henriques assumed the title *rex* (Ramos, Sousa, and Monteiro 2009: 27–32). By means of the Treaty of Zamora signed in 1143, Alfonso VII of León-Castile probably recognized the new kingdom. The text of the agreement has not survived but it seems likely that Afonso Henriques agreed, in return, not to encroach eastward into the territory which León-Castile claimed as his own and to concentrate instead on pressing southward into the frontier with Gharb al-Andalus (Marques 1985, vol. 1: 133). If so, the treaty contributed to better define the borders between the two Christian kingdoms while also motivating efforts from Afonso Henriques and his successors to stretch the territory of the kingdom further south.

The following 110-year phase of the Portuguese military operations benefitted from the support of international interests wishing to be seen as patrons of the Iberian *Reconquista*. This support came from crusaders and Christian military orders (Templars and Hospitallers) that played a fundamental role in reclaiming land for the "cause of Christianity." In 1147, the capture of both Santarém and Lisbon moved the Portuguese kingdom southward to the Tagus River. The thrust continued over the next century, finally ending in 1249 with the conquest of the Algarve, the last remaining Muslim stronghold. Thereby, the area of the Portuguese kingdom increased by 35 percent, reaching a total of 90,000 km$^2$, not far from the current area of the country, which stands at 92,000 km$^2$ (Map 1.1).

Arising from warfare, by the mid 1100s the kingdom was not only larger, but also much more diverse. As geographers have noted, aside from being a rather well-defined rectangle on the western edge of the Iberian Peninsula, Portugal's regions show remarkable variation. The major north–south division is a diagonal line from the Serra da Estrela and the south bank of the Mondego River. This is joined by a division between the North Atlantic and Trás-os-Montes, which is very different in climate and terrain. Greater uniformity is seen toward the south, far more Mediterranean-like (Ribeiro 1945: 220–236). In addition to the geographical diversity, there are remnants of distinctions related to civilization. These are the indelible legacies of the Muslim presence at the south of the Tagus. The dense nuclei (but more dispersed) settlement pattern that is strongly rooted in the rural areas typical in the country's north and center stands opposed to what prevails in the south. Here the settlement is more concentrated and more urban. After the conquest of Algarve, the colonization of this region grew at a slower pace than the north.

### Lords, communities, and the king

In broad terms, the seigneurial regime was based on the notion that the possession of the land conferred public authority of a military, political, and fiscal nature. Landowning was thus connected to lordship over the common people who were settled on the estates and translated into the dispensing of justice and the collection of dues on the produce of the land in return for protection, Those who possessed land were, hence, recognized as "lords" (*senhores*) by the settlers (Hespanha 1982: 88). In the case of Portugal the *Reconquista* allowed for the expansion of seigneurialism from Minho to the east and to the south, often without intervention of the king (Mattoso and Sousa 1993: 165–172). Against the backdrop of endemic warfare that fairly defines the era, several "lords" induced the people to bend to their power by force. Innumerable manors came into being in this way, not only the earliest ones in Minho, but also those in Trás-os-Montes and Upper Beira, whether by noblemen or by monasteries (Mattoso 1985, vol. 1: 98–99). Another relevant factor that bound the land and men to the "lords" was the assumption that the population living under their rule was exempt from royal tribute. Therefore, the seigneurial rule also expanded by a voluntary process, such as in the case of collective submission of rural communities to a lord of their choosing. The few examples existing in Portugal, the so-called *beetrias* (plebeian lordships) established in the transition zone between Minho and Trás-os-Montes and in the Douro River valley in the 1200s (Castro 1978, vol. 2: 160).

Although the spread of the seigneurial regime could occur without the king's participation, the conflict with the Muslims enforced the king's role. The war was conducted principally in the monarch's name, as was the setting up of the new political and economic environment. Besides assuming the lordship over lands taken from Muslim rule, which passed into his possession as royal manors (*reguengos*), the king encouraged the formation of new lordships, by granting lands to members of the nobility or ecclesiastic institutions. The newly formed lordships enjoyed exemption from the king's jurisdiction, which is to say, royal officials could not enter the lands for the purposes of either meting out justice or collecting taxes. The term *couto* or *terra coutada*, i.e., a seigneurie immune to royal power, provides evidence of these arrangements. The peasant families who settled on these lordships also benefited from royal tax exemptions, a prerogative that attracted other settlers to these newly conquered territories. In Beira, the central region of Portugal, Afonso Henriques awarded vast tracts to the monastery of Santa Cruz of Coimbra and to the bishop of Coimbra. Still, laymen owners were dominant in the area around Coimbra, as a regional study has proved (Durand 1982). Further to the south, the Templar Knights received *terras coutadas* in the valley of the Zêzere River and around Castelo Branco, and the Cistercian monks of Alcobaça received vast concessions of land immediately following the conquest of Lisbon (1147).[3]

The need to organize the defense in the south of the Tagus called for the participation of the religious and military orders in the redistribution of newly conquered land. Following the definitive conquest of Alcácer do Sal (1217), the Order of Santiago located its seat there and received lands in Western Alentejo, while the monastic brothers of Évora (the origin of the Order of Avis) saw their land grants concentrated in an area of the Upper Alentejo (Mattoso 1985, vol. 1: 98–99).

The spread of seigneurial regime throughout the territory of the kingdom concurred with a second form of settlement, which encouraged the formation of new communities or the strengthening of preexisting communities (*concelhos*). Rooted in Roman or post-Roman organizations, these communities were based on the collective possession and exploitation of land and enjoyed a tradition of self-government (Mattoso 1985, vol. 1: 337–340). The endemic state of war with al-Andalus eventually fostered the emergence of fully developed municipal institutions from these preexisting self-governed communities. The earliest evidence comes from settlement charters (*cartas de povoamento*), which transferred the right to explore the land, and in some cases even awarded full property rights, to a given community.

By means of these charters, a lord (the king, the church, or lay nobility) also granted a group of settlers tax prerogatives and the right of self-government. In exchange, the settlement community paid a joint rent, for which the inhabitants of the *concelho* were collectively responsible (Coelho 1996: 557). The first settlement charters date back to the tenth and eleventh centuries and were granted by the kings of León-Castile to attract populations into the newly conquered areas, such as in the remote regions of Trás-os-Montes. The same system was employed in the already populated areas of Minho and Beira. Here the contract was called *carta de foral* (charter of municipal rights), which enhanced the prerogative of self-government of the community in exchange for the payment of dues on the produce of the land (Coelho 1989: 44, 51). Dating from the late eleventh century, the *cartas de foral* laid down the pattern of the relations between the lord and a given community to be followed for many years (Coelho and Magalhães 2008: 18).

By the early twelfth century, the king's role was paramount for the emergence of fully fledged *concelhos*, with their own governing bodies and

---

[3] Gonçalves 1989: 19; Mattoso 1985, vol. 1: 98.

judiciaries, especially in the regions near the advancing border, where recognition and granting of local autonomy was used as an instrument of settlement (Mattoso and Sousa 1993: 217). In the southern parts of the kingdom, the king vested the *concelhos* with extensive *alfozes* or *termos* (rural surrounding area), to be divided among the peasant households of the community (Rau 1982: 38). By means of these charters, whether on Crown or earlier seigneurial lands, the number of *concelhos* multiplied. By the end of the 1400s, practically all the territory was organized under municipal institutions (Monteiro 1996a: 31).

Just as the number of *concelhos* burgeoned, so too did the power of the landlords, considering the seigneurial rights laid down in the charters. But far from providing a contradiction, municipalities and manors coexisted side by side across the kingdom. The relationship between these two modes of organizing the settlements on newly conquered territory was often one of friction regarding the jurisdictional control over their respective landholdings. A complete description of the distribution of jurisdictional rights underpinned by the *Reconquista* needs to recall that the king kept the jurisdiction over the major urban centers and the lordship of several tracts of newly conquered land which were administered directly as royal manors (*reguengos*). The Crown possessed *reguengos* across the whole kingdom, but most of them were concentrated in the regions of Beira and Estremadura. On the other hand, the Crown's estates were scarce in Minho – a result of the strong presence of landed lords predating the emergence of the kingdom (Castro 1978, vol. 2: 148–150).

The partition of jurisdictional rights among the king, the nobility, and the Church institutions spurred by the *Reconquista* had economic implications. In it resided the partition of income, as the exercise of jurisdictional rights, whether or not attached to landownership, was connected to seigneurial exaction. A careful examination of its distribution among the aforementioned political entities is not possible before 1500, due to lack of records. But assuming 1500 as the final portrait of a trend coming from medieval times, the Crown and royal family controlled a third of the kingdom's total area. In so doing, the king was the direct seigneurial lord of 38 percent of the Portuguese population.[4] Laymen lords were responsible for the largest portion of the population – 46 percent – while Church institutions had the lordship over 16 percent. These numbers conceal the existence of a concentrated structure. Of the 46 percent controlled by the nobility, a handful of titled families, such as Bragança, Aveiro, and Vila Real, concentrated the greatest share of seigneurial control. This group was followed by noble Houses of small and medium

---

[4] Monteiro 1996a: 51–53; Rodrigues 1998: 103.

size possessing less important estates. Of the 16 percent of the population lorded over by the Church, about 10 percent lived on the lands of the military orders of Christ, Avis, and Santiago – mostly to the south of the Tagus. The remaining 6 percent of those living under the jurisdiction of the Church were split between bishoprics and monasteries. Notwithstanding their more limited overall control, some of the most powerful lords were ecclesiastics, on a par in terms of lands and jurisdictions with the laymen lords. Among these were the archbishop of Braga and the monasteries of Alcobaça and Santa Cruz of Coimbra, which controlled a considerable number of manors exempt from royal taxes (*terras coutadas*).

With the major guidelines in place since the late 1400s, this balance of power between the Crown and the seigneurial lords remained largely unchanged throughout the 1500s. The only noteworthy exception occurred in 1551, when the Pope granted King João III with the perpetual control over the masterships of the three military orders (Christ, Avis, and Santiago), which entailed the right of the Crown to dispose of their revenues as reward of services rendered by the nobility. We are unable to offer a breakdown of the wealth going to each of the three entities. Seigneurial exaction attached to jurisdictional rights varied from locale to locale, which would be reflected in the respective amount of revenues. Moreover, the level of revenues ultimately depended on production and population trends, which varied during medieval times, as they did in the rest of Europe (Neto 1993: 168–169).

### The population

Like elsewhere in Medieval Europe, Portugal's population grew until the 1340s, when the Black Death interrupted this trend. Sources to quantify such trends are scarce. Tax and military records provide some information, although they relate only to special and partial segments of the population. Among the earliest sources are the *Inquirições* for 1258 (Crowns' enquiries on seigneuries and communities), the *Rol dos Tabeliães* (list of public notaries) of the *concelhos* (1287–1290), and the *Lista das Igrejas* for 1320–1321. The latter is an assessment of the revenue of ecclesiastical benefices, including the parish churches, following a papal donation that granted a tenth of that revenue to the king of Portugal (Marques 1987: 15–16). Later on, questionnaires carried out throughout the 1300s and the enrolment of archers (*Rol dos besteiros do conto*), which recorded the number of men who were obliged to render military service in times of war, allow an estimation of the size and dispersion of the overall population during the Middle Ages. However, figures derived from these sources are often distinct and do not allow firm conclusions. Most studies suggest that Portugal's demography evolved more or less in tandem with the rest of Europe, that is, steady growth from the 1000s to the early 1300s. If that is true, the *Reconquista* "did not result only from demographic growth, but had a lot to do with it" (Mattoso 1985, vol. 2: 26). The rate of growth varied, having been higher in the eleventh and twelfth centuries and flattening out in the thirteenth century. Long-term growth is reflected in the founding of new settlements and monasteries in Minho in the eleventh and twelfth centuries and in the clearing of newly conquered lands for agriculture in the Lower Mondego and Estremadura in the thirteenth century.[5] Population stood at about 700,000 by the end of the 1200s, and was divided unequally between the northern and southern halves of the kingdom (Mattoso and Sousa 1993: 245). The Minho, the Douro valley, and Upper Beira had a greater number of inhabitants. Here settlement was disperse, while in Lower Beira and south of the Tagus, the less populated regions, settlement was more concentrated. Some important urban centers, such as Lisbon and Porto, were along the coast, but the greater part of the population lived further inland. Lisbon had about 10,000 inhabitants at the time of the *Reconquista* (1147). By the end of the 1300s, with 35,000 people, it was far larger than Porto, the second city of the kingdom, with 4,000 – probably about the same as Évora (Ramos, Sousa, and Monteiro 2009: 81).

For the mid 1300s, scholars have fixed the highest bound of total population at 1,500,000 (Marques 1987: 16) and the lowest at 900,000 (Rodrigues 2008: 519). If 700,000 is a plausible figure for the end of the 1200s, and assuming that populations grew within strict limits in early modern societies, a total number close to 900,000 souls just before the outbreak of the Black Death seems credible (see Table 1.1).

The epidemic, originating in Asia Minor, reached the Mediterranean in the autumn of 1347 (Livi-Bacci 1999: 116–117). It spread from south to north, ravaging Portugal in 1348 and 1349. In the sixty years that followed, a chain of new outbreaks progressed through Europe, wiping out a third of the Continent's population, which hit its low point around 1400. Over the next century, the plague became endemic and continued to claim victims in cyclical outbreaks (Livi-Bacci 1999: 116–118). The lack of data mentioned earlier prevents us from accurately quantifying the loss of life in Portugal resulting from the Black Death, as well as from pinpointing the exact regions that were hardest hit, but it is fairly certain that the entire kingdom was affected, probably the worst affected were the most

---

[5] Coelho 1989: 41–42; Mattoso 1985, vol 1: 194–196.

Table 1.1 *Portugal: population estimates,*
*1100–1500*

| 1100 | 495,000 |
|------|---------|
| 1200 | 643,500 |
| 1300 | 700,000 |
| 1340 | 900,000 |
| 1500 | 906,000 |

*Sources:* Palma and Reis 2016; Rodrigues
2008: 519.

densely populated areas – taking a third or more of the people, varying
from place to place.[6]
Following this setback, demographic stagnation characterizes fifteenth-
century Europe. Far from bouncing back quickly, populations in the 1400s
showed volatile swings resulting from suppressed birth rates, periodic
spikes in death rates, and economic hardship. Food scarcities were common in medieval agrarian economies, due to their vulnerability to extreme
climatic conditions. However, famines that occurred during these years
should be seen as evidence of temporary disruption of family-based farming units and their productive cycles resulting from the catastrophic death
tolls and the subsequent loss of labor. If Portugal's population figures
reflected a European pattern, the sudden contraction in the mid 1300s
was followed by a slow recovery starting in the early 1360s (seen, for
example, in the territories south of the Tagus (Boissellier 2003:
133–138), marked however by ebbs and flows throughout most of the
1400s.
Several causes explain this long-term cyclical evolution. Recurring outbreaks of the plague, although less virulent, is one of them, as were the five
Castilian invasions (1369–1370, 1372–1373, 1381–1382, 1384, and
1385). In addition, from the late 1300s to the end of the 1400s, frequent
food crises exacerbated by weak market infrastructures took their toll
(Marques 1978: 263–281). Other variables that are especially sensitive
to socioeconomic contexts, namely marriage and birth rates, probably
contributed to the difficult demographic catch up although this is difficult
to assess, considering the lack of parochial records in Portugal prior to the
sixteenth century. Under critical circumstances, we should not be surprised that the challenges facing the rural population drove birthrates to
fall, just as it is known elsewhere in Europe, such as in England and

[6] Marques 1987: 21; Rodrigues 2008: 113.

Flanders (de Vries 1994b: 39–40). The slow recovery of the population still allowed for a high land–labor ratio with repercussions on the structure of land ownership and farming production. Scarcity of labor, return of cultivated land to pasture or hunting reserves, and constant depopulation – even into the mid 1400s (as seen in Minho, Trás-os-Montes, and Lower Mondego) – point to a persistent imbalance between population and resources, consistent with a "frontier economy" (Henriques 2014a: 2).

## The manorial system

Throughout the *Reconquista*, from 1147 to 1249, the king awarded vast tracts of the newly conquered land to the nobility and ecclesiastical institutions, notably the military orders, assuring them a source of wealth and reinforcing their social status. These land grants formed new seigneuries or manors and were essential to promote the settlement of population. At the same time, they became the main administrative, military, and judicial unit of the territory. As such, the common features of seigneurialism that prevailed in the rural world throughout Europe expanded into the former territories of al-Andalus and shaped a similar framework of property rights.

By the end of the fifteenth century, land ownership was firmly concentrated in the hands of the Crown and royal family, religious institutions, and the nobility, a legacy dating back to the *Reconquista*. The Crown owned several landed estates, known as *reguengos*, scattered across the whole kingdom and claimed either as a right of conquest, or acquired through purchase or exchange. Portions of this mass of resources often changed hands by means of royal donations to various ecclesiastical and lay beneficiaries, while regular confiscations, and other types of acquisition such as swapping also contributed to the fluidity of the Crown's landed property. In the mid 1300s, the amounts of land in the possession of the king and the Church were probably on a par, at least in terms of value, if not quantity. Ecclesiastic institutions held a vast collection of properties spread across the kingdom, most of which had been acquired between the eleventh and the fourteenth centuries through royal donations, purchases, and pious legacies or bequests (*legati pii*). Insofar as the Church was a perennial institution, the properties once acquired could not be sold, thus leading to continual increase of land accumulation. The Crown tried to challenge this trend by passing disentailing acts from the 1200s onwards, but it was only at the close of the Middle Ages that the conversion of private properties into ecclesiastic patrimony was successfully inhibited. This brought some stability to the collection of properties held by the Church. At any rate, this more stable patrimony was far from static, as monasteries and churches regularly traded landed properties among themselves.

When compared with the Crown and the Church, laymen lords seem to have owned a smaller share of this economic resource, although it is difficult to gauge the amount of land actually controlled by the nobility. Also, their holdings changed hands to a greater degree for many reasons, because of both interventions on the part of the king and the social reproduction strategies of the group. In fact, up until the 1400s the nobility did very little to avoid losing their patrimony by alienation or hereditary partition. High birth rates and equal partitioning of inheritances among heirs combined forces to the breaking down of the estates. The fragmentation of patrimony that ensued would be countered only in the 1400s with the implementation of *morgadios* (entailed estates), which essentially ensured the transmission of the entire estate to the eldest son (primogeniture). But until this institution became widely accepted among the nobility, future generations' material sustenance was systematically jeopardized.

By the end of the 1300s the large-scale laymen estates had already disappeared (Ramos, Sousa, and Monteiro 2009: 97). Biological and political factors also explain the volatility of the patrimony in the hands of the nobility. Family lineages came to an end and it was not uncommon that estates reverted to the Crown simply for this reason. The group was constantly remaking itself, loosing members and receiving new ones, especially during periods of political turmoil when members of the nobility lost their estates due to royal confiscation while newcomers were rewarded with landed properties. Along with the Crown, Church, and nobility, but on a much smaller scale, the municipal institutions also enjoyed property rights according to the terms of concessions within the *cartas de foral*. These included common land, such as *baldios* (wasteland for pasture) and forests managed by municipal councils. These concessions of land gave rise to the formation of landholdings at the *concelho* level for common use. In an agrarian economy, the importance of these commons cannot be overstated. Their use as sources of firewood, timber, beeswax, honey, and as places to graze livestock was of inestimable value.

Among the landowners were also a fair number of commoners, albeit the relative share of the land they controlled was certainly low. Owning small-scale properties, these landowners included urban elites (tradesmen, artisans, and professionals), as well as wealthy rural residents who could afford implements and cattle.[7] Given that they were held in full

---

[7] Beirante 1981: 89–105; Magalhães 1970: 228–229; Rodrigues and Duarte 1998: 83–85.

ownership, these lands could be sold, transferred, or divided among heirs, and often changed hands. These transactions gained intensity during periods of poor harvest and economic downturn, thus serving the social mobility of urban elites or royal officials who saw landownership as a means to achieve higher social status (Marques 1987: 90). For jurisdictional purposes, however, any free holding fell under the seigneurial regime, as the owners had to pay a quit-rent in lieu of military service.

The socioeconomic system in Portugal, as in the rest of Europe, favored the landed classes, who were able to siphon off a significant part of agricultural output, either through the collection of seigneurial dues or through the use of various modes of land exploitation, by which property rights were transacted. The main features of these modes of exploitation were being set up since the middle of the twelfth century and are closely linked to the gradual dissolution of serfdom in most of Western Europe. The seigneurial reserves, directly exploited by the lord, receded, as they were increasingly leased out to peasant households, which would become the major locus of production in rural Europe.[8]

In the case of Portugal, the shift to peasant tenure can be traced back to the twelfth and thirteenth centuries. As the *Reconquista* brought new lands to be ploughed and since there were no restrictions to peasant mobility, the high land–labor ratio of a frontier economy was not exclusive to the southern part of the kingdom.[9] Hence, as labor was scarce relative to land, slavery and serfdom were already waning in the thirteenth century. By then, ecclesiastic and lay lords fragmented their reserves, called *quintas* or *granjas*, into smaller farming plots and leased them out to peasant families. From north to south in the kingdom, the so-called *casal* (pl. *casais*) formed as the major unit for land occupation, farm labor, and taxation. The *casal* was mostly a small-scale production unit, drawing upon the domestic household for labor and often comprising a dwelling and several plots of land, devoted to a variety of crops in order to provide the needs of the peasant family.[10]

With the extreme labor scarcity brought about by the Black Death, the seigneurial reserves withdrew even further, as the leasing out of landholding expanded. The monastery of São Salvador of Grijó provides a good example. In the second half of the 1300s, the majority of its seigneurial lands were divided and ploughed by *casais*, whilst the demesne occupied a much smaller area (Amaral 1994: 37, 69). Even though during the 1400s seigneurial lords kept a few properties under direct

---

[8] Duby 1977, vol. 2: 95–123; Persson 2014: 235–238.
[9] Henriques 2014a; Viana 2007.
[10] Castro 1978, vol. 2: 183; Gonçalves 1989: 169; Marques 1987: 79, 2008.

administration, by the transition to the early modern period the percentage of agricultural activity apportioned to the direct exploitation of the seigneurial class was far less than that developed by the *casais*.[11] Farming was mostly carried out by the peasant household, whether through labor services (*jeiras*), in the form of three or four days of work per year performed on the demesnes, or on peasant-managed plots for which rent was paid to the landlord following a leasehold agreement.[12]

Throughout medieval times, access to land exploitation was in fact regulated by agrarian contracts, which could be either collective or individual. The first one, the "collective" or "generic" type, was used mostly in the eleventh and twelfth centuries as a device for settlement and reoccupation of lands taken from the Muslims and took the form of a charter of municipal rights (*cartas de foral*). Granted by the landlord (king, Church, or nobility) to a whole community, which pledged to settle and build a village (*vila*), these settlement charters were common in Trás-os-Montes and some parts of Beira (Serrão 1993b: 85). In return for property rights thus transferred, the landowner claimed several payments, the so-called *direitos de foral* to be borne by the community. They comprised the equivalent of ground rent as well as seigneurial dues. By the early fourteenth century, collective contracts were no longer granted, but the payments due by the *concelhos* of Trás-os-Montes and part of Beira to their respective lords never ceased to convey the original collective agreement (Monteiro 2005a: 70–71).

Upon conclusion of the *Reconquista*, individual contracts became a more regular arrangement. Though simple in name and principle, there was tremendous variety with regard to the land and its use. It is possible, nevertheless, to outline their general features. From the wide range of individual contracts and respective tenures, two were among the most used: the perpetual or long-term tenure, through emphyteusis, and the short-term farm lease. Known elsewhere in Western Europe since pre-Roman times, a contract in emphyteusis (*enfiteuse, aforamento*) divested the owner of his full ownership rights, given the fact that the property was split into two domains.[13] While the landlord kept the direct domain, the useful domain was transferred to the tenant (*foreiro*), either in perpetuity (*aforamento* or *prazo enfateusim*) or for a number of lives (*emprazamento*).[14] On condition of paying an annual ground rent (*foro*),

---

[11] Marques 1987: 76–77; Rodrigues and Duarte 1998: 88–89.
[12] On labor services, see Durand 1982: 375–377; Gonçalves 1989: 144.
[13] Based upon Roman Law, emphyteutic contracts were widely used in continental Europe under several different forms. See Clavero 1986; Congost 2003.
[14] The most common form of *emprazamento* involved three lives (the tenant's, his wife's, and an heir's), although cases of two or four lives were not unknown.

the *foreiro* acquired a limited array of property rights, which comprised the right to dispose of the useful domain, both during his lifetime and after his death, by means of a will (Serrão 1993b: 85, 2000: 426–427). The tenant could sell, lease out, and even sub-emphyticate the landholding (*subenfiteuse*) provided he obtained the consent of the landlord and paid a fine, (Serrão 2000: 563–564). This particular type of arrangement could thus create several layers of domains over the same plot of land. As a typical form of the so-called "imperfect" property, emphyteutic contracts satisfied conditions for both landowner and tenant: the former guaranteed a source of income with very little risk, while the latter received mitigated property rights and long-term conditions of farming a land, in return for the investment in labor and capital. As such, these agreements tended to be employed for plots of land that still needed to be cleared in order to be used for agricultural purposes.[15]

Plural and layered property rights over the same plot of land are absent in farm lease agreements (*arrendamentos*). Tenants acquired the right to farm the land for a relatively short duration (from two to nine years) and the landowner retained a greater range of property rights. These agreements tended to be used for farms of large and medium size, as in the case of *casais* or other farming ventures which comprised costly infrastructures and addressed a range of crops and activities that assured higher revenues. From the point of view of income, farm leases seem to have been more advantageous to the property owner, considering that the rent could be renegotiated at the end of every contract term. Contemporary documents, however, amply record cases of land being overworked to the point of depletion because of the short duration of the contract. Long-term tenants, on the other hand, could be more trusted to respect the ecological limits of their land holdings.[16] Hence, empytheutic contracts, the most common form of land access, and farm lease agreements coexisted since the Middle Ages, characterizing the legal framework for land tenure until the nineteenth century. Among their practical implications are the fragmentation of property rights and the complex social and economic relations woven over the same plot of land. As a consequence, farming resources came to be shared by numerous social agents.

Agricultural output was subject to seigneurial, fiscal, and rent exploitation, the burden of which varied markedly, according to the size and type of the land holding, to the obligations determined by the agrarian contract, as well as by customary forms of taxation. Landholders paid several fees to the

---

[15] Gil 1965: 101; Gonçalves 1989: 190; Marreiros 1996b: 458; Rodrigues and Duarte 1998: 93.
[16] Magalhães 1993: 252; Serrão 2000: 560.

landowner; the largest and most important one was the yearly rent for the use of the land, called *foro* or *renda*, according to the type of tenancy. This was either a fixed portion of the land's production (especially grains, wine, and olive oil) or a variable percentage of the harvest. The landholder also paid seigneurial dues, typically comprised in the charters of municipal rights. They could include payments over particular produce or animals (*direituras* or *miunças*), labor services performed at the demesne (*corveias*), toll payments, fines, and the collection of fees for the mandatory use of seigneurial monopolies, such as ovens, mills, and olive oil presses (banal rights).[17] Farm production was further taxed by the Church, in the form of the tithe, which was instituted in Portugal from the 1200s on. Showing great variation across regions and, contrary to what its name suggests, this tax did not necessarily exact one-tenth of the gross farm produce, but an amount ranging between a seventh and a twentieth in the late 1400s (Rodrigues and Duarte 1998: 101).

Estimates for other areas of Western Europe at the close of the Middle Ages suggest that the seigneurial and ecclesiastical dues combined absorbed, on average, a fourth to a third of the gross product of land (Duplessis 1997: 23). While generalizations to Portugal cannot be made, it has been suggested that the rural families had to turn over a third to a half of their production by means of rents and taxes.[18] On top of this there were operational expenses and the need to save some of the grain in order to seed the next crop (20–25 percent of the harvest, considering a seed-to-harvest ratio of 1:4 or 1:5). It seems reasonable to admit that rural families kept for themselves – in the best-case scenario – little more than a third of the fruits of their labor. During times of crisis arising from a succession of poor harvests or greater demands from their seigneurial lord, they may have ended up with a net loss, forcing them to borrow and thus go into debt.[19] Yet, the fragile economic nature of peasant land holdings coexisted with socioeconomic differentiation among rural communities. Different outcomes of the Black Death at a micro level, winds of fortune, and idiosyncratic features of each unit of production allowed for a few processes of capital accumulation (Gonçalves 2010: 53).

### Economic and institutional change

The territorial expansion achieved in the *Reconquista* was accompanied by an increased agricultural output and diversification of economic activities,

---

[17] Castro 1978, vol. 2: 193–202; Marreiros 1996b: 464–468.
[18] Gonçalves 2010: 50–51; Marques 1978: 105.
[19] Durães 2004a: 248–249; Neto 1997: 79–80; Oliveira 1980: 16–18.

as well. The area that comprises today's Portugal took part in the long cycle of economic growth that started around the eleventh century and lasted until the end of the thirteenth. Expansion of the territorial area that came into agricultural use finds evidence in the proliferation of charters of municipal rights and in the clearing of forests and draining of marshlands (Castro 1978, vol. 2: 99). To this extension of farmland, we also find signs of diversification in the produce, as well as greater integration into local markets, spurred mostly by farming "entrepreneurship" on the part of the Cistercian monasteries and military orders.

*Agriculture*

Taking advantage of the favorable environment ensuing from the territorial enlargement and the conquest of urban centers such as Santarém, Lisbon (1147), and Évora (1165), many ecclesiastic landlords pushed for greater production from their land, as in the monasteries of Tarouca and Alcobaça. This will to boost output prompted investments in vine cultivation and the raising of livestock, as well as in improved techniques, such as metal farm implements, ploughs, and a greater use of wind and hydraulic energy. Known in Western Europe since the eleventh century, these techniques slowly penetrated the western limits of the Iberian Peninsula throughout the thirteenth and fourteenth centuries. It seems, however, that three-year crop rotation (in which two of three parcels of land are cultivated while the third is left to lie fallow) was not employed extensively. This may have been influenced by Mediterranean climate conditions, which do not encourage spring crops. As such, it is not surprising that two-year rotation continued to prevail, even throughout the early modern period (Marques 1978: 91–92).

Investment and capital formation in medieval agriculture are hard to quantify. They may not have created conditions for productivity increase, especially when they were allocated to the exploitation of marginal lands as a response to population pressure. In fact, regional studies document cases of new settlements as well as the draining of wetlands in the early 1300s.[20] However, contrary to the common perception that draining operations are evidence of land scarcity, some historians regard them as evidence for an abundance of land relative to labor (Barata and Henriques 2011: 264). This notion of the persistence of a high land–labor ratio, a legacy from the *Reconquista*, is supported by estimates on Portugal's real per capita agrarian output, which may have been larger than that of England and Wales *c.* 1300. Furthermore, recent estimates on the

---

[20] Viana 2007; Rodrigues 1995: 73–75.

composition of agricultural output in Tomar (1316–1326) point to the relevance of pastoral farming (56 percent grain; 17 percent meat; 11 percent wine; 13 percent olive oil; 2 percent other) (Henriques 2014a). With a sparse population, which was about one-quarter that of England in the same period it thus seems reasonable to admit that Portuguese agricultural production was not experiencing diminishing returns. The Malthusian ceiling was apparently far off and, as such, the Black Death should be seen as an exogenous factor for the population's dramatic decrease in the middle of the century.

The rural world underwent a number of changes after the population loss by the mid 1300s. Villages were abandoned and the amount of land under cultivation decreased across Europe, Portugal included, in varying degrees. A large body of literature pertaining to Minho, Trás-os-Montes, and Estremadura provides accounts of *fogos-mortos* ("cold hearths," i.e., deserted farms and *casais*).[21] Thickets, forests, and pastures reclaimed much of the land that had been cleared in the twelfth and thirteenth centuries, although percentages across the kingdom are difficult to assess. Especially acute was the reduction of lands devoted to grain crops, reflecting the falling demand that ran in parallel to the fewer number of mouths to feed. The slow recovery of the rural world following the loss of population caused by the Black Death was driven by activities that simultaneously demanded less labor and fetched higher prices in the market. One such solution was animal husbandry, and there is evidence for the conversion of crop lands into pasture, and for increased planting of vines. In the first half of the 1400s in the Lower Mondego region, for example, diversified production efforts focused on crops that were more demanding in terms of capital investment.[22] Even if the planting of wheat would later regain favor, all indications are that the recovery of the plague was pushed by other sorts of commercialized crops, such as vine, that would further develop in the 1500s around the major urban centers.

### Manufactures

Until the crisis caused by the Black Death, the growth of agricultural output boosted demand for manufactures, within the limits of a peasant economy, mostly orientated to self-consumption. From the eleventh century onwards, in Portugal and all of Western Europe, the textile industry underwent a few technical advancements, especially in the areas of spinning, weaving, and dying while the main features of industrial

---

[21] Amaral 1994: 43–44; Coelho 1986: 69–78; Marques 1988: 278–285; Rodrigues 1995: 65–70; Viana 2007: 170–173.

[22] Coelho 1989: 154–156; Marques 1987: 103–104.

organization were also laid down (Marques 1987: 50–56). This is particularly true for the two leading forms of organization that would last until the modern period: the artisan workshop and the domestic (rural) industry.

An offspring of the city of the Middle Ages, the typical workshop was a small specialized unit of production, aiming to produce for the market. Operated by a skilled craftsman, with the assistance of family members and, often, a few wage laborers, this form of organization relied on relatively low levels of capital investment, albeit higher than those of the domestic industry.[23] It was flexible enough in adapting to market changes, either by resorting to paid labor or by involving other family members whenever it was necessary to hold down fixed costs (Melo 2009: 157–158). In Medieval Portugal, the more technically advanced workshops were in the hands of Moorish, Jewish, and foreign artisans, especially regarding dying and tapestry making, jewelry makers, and makers of metal tools.[24]

The earliest attempts to regulate urban workshops came in the fifteenth century with the *regimentos de corporação de ofícios* (rules for craft association or guilds) (Melo 2009: 405). Throughout the early 1500s craft guilds grew in numbers in the leading Portuguese cities, encouraged by either the king or the *concelhos*, with the aim of supervising the activities, regulating the guild members collectively, and guaranteeing internal uniformity of technical procedures as well as prices. Although the guild corporative organization was formally established in early modern times, recent historical research has proved that informal associations of artisans go back to the late 1300s in Portugal (Melo 2009: 405–407). These associations afforded the workshop masters a range of jointly executable actions and local political influence, which turned out clearer in times of political turmoil such as the dynastic crisis of 1383–1385. In fact, craftsmen already formed a representative political body known as the *Casa dos Vinte e Quatro* within the city council of Lisbon and played an important role in supporting the new dynasty of Avis (Langhans 1949).

Despite this shift of industrial activities into the cities and villages, a considerable amount of the manufacturing activity remained located in the countryside, where peasant families continued a secular tradition of producing non-agricultural goods for consumption. Demand for clothing, dwellings, and farm implements was thus met by local supply, if not by the very household itself. The proliferation of spinning wheels and looms in rural households is nothing more than an echo of this widely

---

[23] Duplessis 1997: 29–33; Malanima 2009: 203–204.
[24] Marques 1987: 120; Tavares 1987: 300–309.

spread form of industrial organization. In some particular areas of the country, the availability of raw materials (flax and wool), and resources (e.g., ample water supply, essential in textile production), encouraged the production of linens and woolens to supply to local markets. This was the case for linens in Minho, while woolen fabrics were produced in Lower Beira as well as in Upper and Lower Alentejo.[25] This form of regional specialization characterized the Portuguese industrial geography since the 1400s and remained throughout the early modern period. The quantification of the share of the industrial output in a markedly rural society is a matter of educated guesses, but the breakdown of occupations and social categories of villages may shed some light on this issue. At the end of the 1400s, in Alenquer, a village in the region of Estremadura, handcraft workers accounted for 14 percent of the population, tenants and rural unskilled workers for 57 percent, whereas the remaining 29 percent inhabitants were noblemen, knights, squires, urban militias, and servants (Godinho 1978b, vol. 2: 22). As this example is of a fairly prosperous community, we should not expect that these proportions were typical of the entire kingdom, but they probably represent well the share of non-agricultural labor.

### Commerce

Once the *Reconquista* and hostilities came to an end, conditions emerged to boost trade and the circulation of money, although many of the transactions continued to be made directly by the producers themselves without resorting to the work of specialized merchants. Starting in the urban centers, where the use of money was more common, monetization of commercial life and payments of fees and taxes due to the Crown, the Church, and noble houses spread out into the countryside. Among the institutions that promoted a higher level of monetized economy was the fair, which differed from the small, local markets. The latter were usually held on a daily or weekly basis to cater the needs for food and perishable goods of a given community, while the fairs regarded transactions of durable goods, such as textiles or agricultural implements. Crucial for the development of commerce, the medieval fairs in Portugal received the support of the king, especially from 1270 on, which took the form of certain privileges granted to merchants, such as the exemption of duties on transported goods. Thus, fairs activated flows of commodities and people at a supra-local scale and these gatherings mobilized producers and middlemen traders from Portugal and foreign

---

[25] Garcia 1986: 331–333; Sequeira 2012: 19–20.

countries as well. Although their frequency varied, fairs were normally an annual event, but examples are known of gatherings that took place twice and/or three times per year. Over time they became more numerous, with some fifty known for the mid 1300s and about thirty more in the 1400s.[26] Regardless of the increasing number of fairs all over the kingdom, by the end of the Middle Ages the infrastructure of communications was based on a road network that dated back in its design and layout to Roman times, which broke down the economic space of Portugal into multiple local markets. This would change very little over the next centuries. Hence, the sea was the kingdom's principal axis, which ran from the mouth of the Guadiana on the southeast border all the way north to the Minho River. Branching off of this main axis and heading inland were a number of roads that varied considerably. In the north, the terrain severely affected inland transportation into the interior regions, and the track that was followed left the northeast area (Trás-os-Montes) isolated, along with part of Inner Beira. South of the Tagus the mostly flat plains encouraged inland transportation, easing the penetration into the interior and helping to overcome the lack of a dense system of rivers (Matos 1980: 15–16).

Connections were always underpinned by favorable natural conditions, meaning water transportation, either by river or by sea, ensured relative higher speed. The river system in the nation's geographic area is not very dense, but did allow for some connections of the coast to the interior. Without any doubt the two most important routes were afforded by the Douro, connecting Porto to Trás-os-Montes and Inner Beira; and the Tagus, which linked Lisbon to the Ribatejo and Lower Beira (Gaspar 1970). Therefore, the sea was the linchpin in the kingdom's communication system.

In fifteenth-century Portugal, coastal trade was intense, joining the littoral into a near single unit. Innumerable ports dotted the coastline, providing regular connections between Lisbon, Valença, Viana do Castelo, Vila do Conde, Aveiro, Salir, Cascais, Setúbal, and many sites in the Algarve (Marques 1987: 130). This intense coastal trade is recorded in royal documents, namely the *Inquirições* (royal inquiries) that defined the seigneurial rights to collect levies on domestic trade. Although these documents do not record the volume of trade or the type of transactions involved, they reveal Portugal's participation in the increasingly complex supra-regional trade routes from the 1200s on. They confirm that Portuguese goods were traded up and down the coast in ports that also conducted foreign trade. For example, the salt

[26] Marques 1987: 44; Rau 1983.

from Setúbal that was often unloaded at Lisbon was not always destined for domestic consumption – some was bound for outward trade. The same can be inferred for goods moving between Porto and Aveiro, other salt-producing areas. Salt was traded in great quantities along with dried fish, and Porto was a favorite location for exporting salt.

Porto, the largest city in the north, picked up strength since the late thirteenth century, responding especially to factors that became significant after the bubonic plague. These factors included economic changes that occurred in Europe's northwestern regions, where the textile industry flourished, while the Hundred Years' War brought England, Flanders, and the cities of the Hanseatic League into Portugal's trade sphere. The range of goods that Portugal exported competed directly with those from France, and the challenges facing that nation involved in the war with England aided Portugal's access to the markets of northern Europe. The products mentioned comprised salt, dried fish, wine, olive oil, dried fruits, leather, wax, and cork, a raw material harvested from cork oak trees, which covered the whole Iberian Peninsula at this time, from north to south.

As it happened with fairs, commerce at a supra-regional level caught the monarchs' regard, who aimed to attract capital and know-how. At the behest of King Edward III of England, Portuguese merchants were granted privileges that encouraged them to set up operations in English ports, triggering a migration that was small but vital in establishing regular commercial links. Similar commercial rights were also granted to Lisbon and Portuguese merchants established at the port of Harfleur in Upper Normandie by French kings, respectively in 1309 and 1340 (Miranda 2014: 123). On the side of Portuguese monarchs, charter-parties were granted to Florentine, Genoese, Flemish, and German communities to attract capital and entrepreneurship (Marques 1987: 150–151). Migrations and products testify to the advantages of Portugal's location – a crossroads between the wealthy and more sophisticated Italian cities, distributors of Asian goods, and northern Europe, which had moved to the fore regarding textile making and bulk trade. From this confluence of trade emerged the chance for Portugal to gain valuable nautical and cartographic knowledge from both directions – Atlantic and Mediterranean – and to overhaul its shipbuilding industry. By the late 1300s there is already iconographic evidence for the Portuguese caravels that would sail west into the Atlantic in the next century on voyages of exploration. The maritime activities that drove the growth of shipbuilding in Portugal called for regular imports of intermediate goods such as hemp, timber for masts, and metals – both iron and non-ferrous ones (Rau 1984: 101).

Flanders, England, and Ireland are mentioned in Portuguese price regulations as the most important overseas sources of textiles. A decree of King Afonso III of 1253 set the selling price of "English scarlet" at 70 *soldos*, the *côvado* (0,70 m) and the *flamenga* at 60, while the Portuguese *burel* (coarse woolen) was sold for 4 *soldos*. Prices of these goods were far higher than those of coarse fabrics woven and worn by most of the Portuguese population, which indicates that long-distance trade was based on luxuries. However, quantities passing through customs could reach significant levels, forcing the re-exportation to Spain (Galicia) when distribution to domestic markets was slow and owners aimed to avoid depreciation of the merchandise deposited in warehouses (Rau 1984). These are scattered references that shed no light on the actual volume at stake, although they refer to cases in which transactions implied capital and the ability of Portuguese merchants to lead interregional transactions.

On the sea lanes that joined Medieval Europe's many coastlines together, the prominent role of Lisbon was already in place by the second half of the 1400s. The longer sojourns of the king and royal court in the city played in favor of its growth and pushed the local demand for commodities supplied by external markets. In many occasions, royal edicts sought to stimulate the capital's supply of wheat both from North Africa and from Europe, in return for salt. The arrangement of exchanging salt for grain dates back to the very earliest days of the kingdom. It continued throughout the entire early modern period and was one of the most important trade programs accounting for Portugal's integration into the European economy, right down to the seventeenth century.

Frequent mention of imported wheat and other cereals in medieval documental sources, whether to barter for salt or not, caught the attention of historians who have elaborated on the chronic failure of the nation's agriculture to feed its growing population. In the words of Oliveira Marques, "it seems possible to characterize the Portuguese Middle Ages, with regard to cereals, as an age spent fighting desperately for self-sufficiency not yet resigned to dependence on foreign trade in order to survive, in contrast to the early modern age that had accepted wheat imports as normal" (Marques 1978: 15). Medieval laws refer to incentives to cultivation, such as granting of *sesmarias* (concession of vacant lands by the Crown); punishment for malingering, and by imposing forced labor, even prior to the Black Death (Rau 1982: 104–141). In any event, the inclusion of grain among the items regularly imported to supply the populations of the port cities, while a larger share of land was allocated to wine and cattle after the Black Death is also a sign of a first step toward a long-term integration of the kingdom's local markets into foreign exchange.

The structure of the foreign trade that developed in the 1200s and became consolidated in the 1300s followed up in the next centuries, despite the fact that the empire soon provided new luxuries to the wealthy European customers. But since medieval times, a number of Portugal's ports became regular shippers of wine and olive oil, raw materials of a forestry nature, and products derived from its maritime activities and fishing. The references to imports of textiles coupled with scarce information on exports of such kind of commodities suggest the superiority the European producers had already achieved and Portugal's inability to compete in the markets for textiles.

### The royal treasury

The setup of a fiscal administration can be traced back to the mid 1200s, when the first steps were taken to provide the king with better means to control his revenue (Henriques 2008: 130–146). Building an institutional network for the purpose of tax and rent collection was a slow process, yet it turned out to be decisive in asserting the royal authority over the kingdom. Key figures in the new territorial network of tax administration were the so-called *almoxarifes*, originally a word used to designate tax-farmers of the southern parts of the kingdom in earlier days. During the reign of King Afonso III (1248–1279), *almoxarifes* were assigned with tax collection and, already as royal officials, their number increased. More importantly, these officials were appointed to the northern parts of Portugal, which allows concluding that a territorial grid covering the kingdom was beginning to take shape. As local treasurers, their responsibilities included both the collection and the disbursement of royal revenues within the territorial boundaries of the *almoxarifado*. In the reign of King Dinis (1279–1325) the network of these financial districts grew denser, covering eventually the whole territory under King Pedro I (1356–1367).

Several revenues passed through the hands of the *almoxarifes*, displaying the main features of what fiscal history has called "domain state" (Bonney and Ormrod 1999: 19). The concept stands for a fiscal regime in which most royal income derives from patrimonial revenues as well as from regalian and jurisdictional rights. In the Portuguese case, the domain revenues collected by the *almoxarifes* comprised rents from the Crown's estates (*reguengos*) and seigneurial levies, enforced by the *cartas de foral* on inhabitants of villages and towns under royal rule. But there were also indirect taxes, such as the *dízima*, levied on imports and exports, secured as a royal entitlement in the second half of the 1200s.[27] In spite of

[27] Castro 1978, vol. 2: 162–164; Pereira 1983: 22–24.

a later evolution toward a "tax state," already signalized in the king's entitlement to the *dízima*, the patrimonial features of the royal revenues would remain in the next centuries through the persistence of a few *almoxarifados* particularly assigned to collect agrarian produce, notably in Estremadura or in Alentejo as late as the 1600s (Hespanha 1994: 102).

The financial and administrative network implied a hierarchical structure designed to link the political center to the territorial grid. From 1273 onwards, the *almoxarifes* reported the collected income to a group of auditors, at the end of their appointments. These auditors cross-checked the accounting books with the proofs of expenditures to verify the legitimacy of the disbursements and assess the net balance of revenues and expenses. In 1296, the audits, previously undertaken by a body of auditors, became a formal and permanent institution justifying the foundation of the *Casa dos Contos de Lisboa*, which acted as a centralized general accounting office.[28] The creation of a head office called *vedor da fazenda* (treasury overseer) in the 1340s added to this financial hierarchical structure and paved the way for the specialization of the royal treasury administration (Henriques 2008: 139–140). The *vedor da fazenda* was in charge of the king's finances, which involved overseeing the collection of revenues, allocating the income to specific ends, and informing the monarch of the state of his treasury. Hence, in sixty years (1280–1340), earlier than in the neighboring kingdom of Castile, the monarchs were able to put together a financial organization at the central and local level.

Notwithstanding the precocious making of a bureaucracy, the royal revenue of the thirteenth and fourteenth centuries remained thwarted by the landed classes and the *concelhos*. As it happened, a portion of the income due to the Crown was in the hands of nobles and ecclesiastic institutions, a result of a redistributive system drawn by the king's need to pay for services or to smooth the potentially conflicted relations with competing bodies, such as the Church or the nobility. In any event, a more effective collection of revenues contributed to the enforcement of the royal power through the accumulation of wealth in the royal treasury. The last wills of the kings shed light on this issue. According to values mentioned in the testaments until the reign of King Afonso IV (1325–1357), the wealth based on liquid assets was truly extraordinary. Sancho I (1185–1211) left an estate of 9,955 marks of pure gold – with 229.5 g to the mark – i.e., 2,285 kg. None of his successors was able to equal this amount. Afonso III (1248–1279) left 405 marks (93 kg) in cash upon his death. King Dinis (1279–1325) bequeathed 2,013 marks (462 kg) of gold to his heirs and Pedro I (1357–1367) 5,009 (1,150 kg) (Henriques 2008: 46). These assets

[28] Henriques 2008: 137; Rau 1951a: 7–9.

were mainly in the form of coin pointing to a relatively high level of monetization, a notion confirmed by the wording of the charters of municipal rights. Both types of sources certainly reflect the fact that the *Reconquista* afforded the occupation of territories previously under Muslim rule, which had been among the most urban and market-oriented within Medieval Europe. Yet, it seems unlikely that the loots of war against either the Muslim or Castile would have been enough to amass such wealth in the form of coin. The values recorded suggest that rents from the Crown's *reguengos* also played their part together with revenue derived from his *regalia* or regalian rights, such as the right to mint coin (Mattoso 1985, vol. 2: 93–94). Therefore, aside from the resources reaped in armed hostilities, a growing population living in an agrarian economy and the setting up of a fiscal administration enabled the kings of Portugal up to King Fernando I (1367–1383) to become the most powerful seigneur in the kingdom.

Information on expenditure is very patchy. Still from the kings' wills it is possible to surmise that considerable wealth was lavished on the royal house itself, and on its retinue of nobles. In addition, there were considerable expenses with dowries and marriages of princes as well as generous gifts to the Church and the Pope, besides the sponsorship of the construction of monasteries. An extra point of interest is that all royal wills mention the payment for the construction of bridges. This was justified by the frequent use of these structures by the royal family and retinue, itself, in its many travels, and by their valuable contribution to the public welfare derived from troop movements. Even if this were the main motivation, the royal sponsorship had positive externalities in the improvement of communications which may have impacted on tax revenues, considering the practice of collecting tolls on bridges. The royal treasury faced rising challenges from 1369 on, when renewed hostilities with Castile brought an inevitable surge in expenditures. The fiscal reforms that ensued confirm that, by then, the economy had reached a high level of monetization and that the Crown made use of the right to mint money to overcome financial shortages.

### War, money, and fiscal innovation

The campaigning of the "Fernandine Wars" (1369–1370, 1371–1372, and 1381–1382) and the dynastic crisis of 1383–1385 brought considerable changes to the structure of the Crown's tax revenues.[29] In 1372, King Fernando imposed the *sisa*, a sales tax in the whole kingdom. This

---

[29] Gonçalves 1964; Godinho 1978b: 52–53.

was not an entirely new tax, in fact, since it had been collected by municipal councils since 1336, whenever the king asked for extraordinary subsidies. Yet, in the context of the second war against Castile, it went from being a temporary and voluntary service rendered by the municipalities to the king, to a permanent tax (Henriques 2014b: 52–56). Between 1382 and 1384, the crucial years that witnessed the change from the Burgundy dynasty to the Avis, the *sisa* raised overall revenues by 41 percent (Henriques 2008: 158). In the following years, its weight in the total royal income, in nominal terms, kept rising. An estimate for the year 1401 suggests that this tax over domestic transactions had become the main source of the Crown's total revenue, accounting for about 74 percent of 81.6 million *libras* (6,936 kg).[30] These receipts display the differences between the Iberian kingdoms and the others of Medieval Europe, where royal income was mostly dependent on direct taxes.[31]

By the mid 1400s, Portugal's unusual quasi-universal taxation reflects the operational advantages of a territorial network composed of twenty-five treasury districts, called *almoxarifados* (Marques 1987: 300). In the late fourteenth century, this territorial organization moved toward greater specialization and hierarchical complexity by the creation of the *contadorias*, a new level of administration designed to exert an intermediate control over a given number of *almoxarifados*. The *contadorias* were headed by a *contador*, who oversaw the regional collection of revenues and the royal agents, which improved the integration of central institutions (*Casa dos Contos* and *vedor da fazenda*) with the *almoxarifados*.[32]

Aside from the positive impact of this administrative network over the Crowns' income, the currency itself proved to be a fiscal source by way of a mint tax (*senhoriagem*), since the striking and issuing of coins was a regalian right (Hespanha 1982: 145). In the 1220s the Portuguese monarchs struck gold coins, though not in abundance – the so-called *morabitinos* – still pegged to the earlier Muslim issues, which circulated in the kingdom side by side with the coins of Castile and León (Godinho 1982–1984, vol. 1: 95). Circa 1260, this system was replaced by the Carolingian system, based on *libras* (pounds), *soldos* (shillings), and *dinheiros* (pennies), with the last two struck in silver and copper, respectively. *Libras* and *soldos* served as units of account, while the *dinheiros* (copper money) were the backbone of the specie in circulation.[33] As the *libra* was already in use in the rest of Europe, its adoption facilitated Portugal's

---

[30] Henriques 2008: 160. In 1401, the metallic content of the *libra* was 0,085 gr. silver.
[31] Bonney 1999; Bonney and Ormrod 1999.
[32] Hespanha 1994: 208, 213; Rau 1951a: 25–26.
[33] 1 *libra* = 20 *soldos* = 240 *dinheiros*. See Marques 1987: 204.

Table 1.2 *Debasement of Portuguese silver*
libras, *1340–1406 (1252–1263 = 100)*

| | |
|---|---|
| 1340* | 158 |
| 1369 | 242 |
| 1385 | 550 |
| 1387 | 3,850 |
| 1391 | 16,866 |
| 1398 | 28,875 |
| 1406 | 10,000 |

*Source:* Castro 1978, table 14: 272–273.

integration into international trade flows, and even improved domestic transactions, due to its ease of use through its multiples and fractions. In 1437, the *libra* was replaced as the standard money of account by the *real*, a denomination that was then uniquely Portuguese, creating a unified monetary area. Switching over to a new and entirely "national" monetary system was not without its difficulties since it was irreconcilable with the system it replaced. Hence, the period of transition was marred by laborious calculations regarding equivalencies (Mattoso and Sousa 1993: 253).

Along with the alteration of monetary systems, the kings of the medieval period resorted frequently to debasements of coinage (*quebras de moeda*). Sometimes, instead of devaluing the currency, an extraordinary tax was enforced in order to stabilize the kingdom's currency, revealing the monarch's reasoning to use debasements to counteract rising expenses (Castro 1978, vol. 2: 270). When implemented, the debasements took the form of lowering the percentage of gold or silver while maintaining the face value of the coin, or leaving the coin's alloy the same but raising the face value. Devaluations occurred with fair regularity throughout the period under analysis here (Table 1.2). The years from 1387 to 1398 were critical in this regard, and corresponded to a long-lasting dynastic war with Castile, which brought to the throne King Pedro I's bastard son, the master of the Avis military order, who took the name João I upon his coronation.

Recurring devaluations accompanied the military conflict with Castile and marked the last quarter of the fourteenth century. This bore a variety of economic, social, and political consequences, the most important of which was perhaps inflation, and its expected effects on the redistribution of income. It is almost certain that the falling value of the currency worked to the detriment of the landed nobility, especially for those who collected rents from short-term leases, in which part or even the totality of the rent was to be paid in cash (i.e., metallic coin) (Castro 1978, vol. 2: 270–278). The financial cycle that must have mostly affected seigneurial income was at the root of a new phase in Portuguese economic history, one which pushed the border further to the south, to North African territories, beginning with the conquest of Ceuta in 1415. The military expedition was executed by the first king of the House of Avis, who claimed the throne after the dynastic crisis in 1383. The lineage of king João I, former master of Avis, is today remembered for the deeds of one of his sons, Prince Henry. The discovery of new lands and maritime routes is his momentous legacy. However, military campaigns in North Africa – and not the early Atlantic exploration – were the driving force of Portugal's first move to the making of a colonial empire.

### The overseas expansion

From its medieval origins until the end of the early modern era, Portugal's polity was shaped by territorial expansion, first within the European borders and then to the outside world. The century from 1147 to 1249 was marked by the *Reconquista* whereas from 1415 to 1500 the Portuguese settled in four Atlantic archipelagos, established trading posts in western Africa, and reached India and South America. The two sorts of territorial expansion are somehow entangled in its driving forces and profoundly shaped many of the economic structures that lasted all the way until the nineteenth century. In 1415 a military expedition conquered the city of Ceuta. A second expedition to North Africa targeted Tangiers in 1437, but the city was only successfully conquered in 1471. Its geostrategic value lasted throughout the early modern era, which justified its being ceded to England as a royal dowry in the 1660s. In addition to Ceuta and Tangiers, the number of North African territories held by the Portuguese Crown grew to eight by 1513. By the 1540s in a juncture of political stress within the kingdom of Fez, King João III opted to abandon four of the garrisons (Safi, Azemmour, al-Qsar al-Saghir, and Asilah). These set-backs did not put an end to further attempts to expand Portuguese settlements. Military operations in northern Africa lasted until 1578, when Portuguese troops were defeated at the battle of al-Ksar al-Kebir, in which King Sebastião was killed. Since he left no successors, this episode eventually led to the annexation of Portugal by the Spanish Habsburgs (1580) (Map 1.2).

If the political fate of Portugal in late sixteenth century is connected to the expansion in North Africa, the Moroccan strongholds ended up

Map 1.2  Portuguese strongholds in North Africa, 1415–1578

having relatively small relevance in commercial and economic terms. In fact, they did not generate considerable revenues for the Portuguese Crown, while the expenses of maintaining and defending the occupation were enormous. The history of the expansion has become mired in a crusader-like image of the overseas undertaking, largely because of its military quality in North Africa – the same as what is applied to the *Reconquista*, which underpinned Portugal's very nationhood. Nonetheless, Portugal's boundaries also advanced due to the opening of sea routes, which provided access to markets outside Europe. Unlike the movement into North Africa, this expansion had considerable economic and cultural impacts in Portugal and throughout the rest of Europe. Europe's stock of knowledge surged forward, laying the groundwork for scientific revolution in geography and astronomy and calling into

question much of Europe's inheritance from Classical Antiquity
(Domingues 2007). In fact, thanks to consecutive breakthroughs in nautical science and cartography, Renaissance Europe came to realize that
the Atlantic Sea stretched far beyond Cape Bojador, that it was possible to
circumnavigate the southern tip of Africa and reach India by sea, and that
a new continent lay to the west across the Atlantic, of which the sacred
texts were totally ignorant (Alegria, Garcia, and Relaño 1998: 26–34).
This radical shift in paradigms was accompanied by the creation of
administrative infrastructures designed to support maritime voyages,
which promoted further improvements in shipbuilding and sailing
technology.

*The European context*

Since there is no clear and single trigger for all of these transformations,
different explanatory hypotheses have been put forward by scholars.
The remarkably different interpretations are due, on the one hand, to
the fact that the stakeholders – social groups and institutions –were many
and diverse, each having their own agenda. On the other hand, the causes
for the overseas expansion varied over time as the whole dynamic process
unfolded. For example, the motivations for Ceuta's conquest in 1415
cannot be explained by the end result of the process, that is to say, as the
first step of a supposed project to reach India.[34] Considering the plurality
of explanations, it should be stressed that certain variables are common to
other dynastic states in the economic context of the Renaissance.
By earlier historiographical accounts, the perception of a Turkish threat
to the trade routes that linked Asia to Europe was considered one of the
motives for European expansion (Bensaúde 1942). Luxury goods and
spices from Asia had to be carried overland, through the territories
belonging to the Ottoman Empire, whose expansion in the fifteenth
century caused interruptions of supply and increased price volatility.
The need to find an alternative route by sea to reach the Asian markets
was thus considered an explanation for the European expansion.
However, this traditional historiographical explanation flies in the face
of the chronological order of actual events. It is well known that the
Portuguese overseas expansion got underway before the fall of
Constantinople (1453), and the rise of Turkish power would thus have
been of negligible importance for a small, sparsely populated kingdom in
Europe's extreme west. In fact, Ceuta's conquest followed by the

---

[34] Cortesão 1940a:13, 1979, vol. 1; Coimbra 1938; Lopes 1938; Peres 1983: 39, 43, 46;
Godinho 2008: 62.

exploration of the western coast of Africa happened three decades before the fall of Constantinople (Godinho 2008: 77, 85–86).

Another traditional explanation emphasized continuity with the prior phase of commercial expansion from the twelfth century to the fourteenth century. Economic development in the medieval period stimulated monetized trade across vast geographic areas, uniting Iberian markets with those on the Brittany coast, Flanders, and England, through regular trade in iron, tin, salt, wine, textiles, and fish. This earlier expansion, which involved Portuguese merchants living in Flanders, England, and elsewhere in Europe, might have driven the discoveries by encouraging overseas trade and by fostering advances in naval design and shipbuilding (Cortesão 1979, vol. I: 130, 2008: 93). Moreover, this first phase of consolidation of supra-regional trade routes strengthened the demand for a universal medium of trade – i.e., coined money – whose scarcity was felt in recurring debasements (Munro 1992: 97–158). In fact, the need for precious metals, mainly gold, to be used for international transactions could have impelled the military occupation of key locations in North Africa, which were deemed plentiful sources of precious metals in Muslim stories of caravan trains crossing the desert from the rich mines of Sudan.[35] Although Portuguese strongholds in North Africa never provided gold riches, it seems that the demand for sources of precious metals is a stronger explanation than the one based on the Turkish threat.[36]

However, the set of arguments stressing the continuity between commercial cycles of medieval expansion neglects the disruptive effects of the Black Death, which have to be taken into account. The sharp plunge in population after 1347 had inevitable consequences on the cost and on the institutional framework of labor, both in Portugal and in the rest of Europe. Notwithstanding the king's repeated enactments to fix wages, Portugal was among the European nations that did not resort to serfdom to deal with the sudden rise of the ratio between fixed resources and labor, unlike what occurred in central Europe. Rising wages and inflation caused by monetary variables adversely affected the income of landowners more than that of the workers (Findlay and O'Rourke 2007: 116–117). According to this perspective, some historians interpret the genesis of European expansion as a response to the crisis in the feudal system, from which would emerge the integration of regional economies, in large economic spaces by way of a market system (Wallerstein 1974–1980, vol. I).

[35] Godinho 2008: 54, summarizing António Sérgio; Cortesão 1979, vol. I: 106.
[36] Godinho 1978b: 115, 2008: 63; Simões 1938: 443.

*Why Portugal?*

If there is no doubt that overseas expansion was a European phenomenon, thereby demanding an explanation focused on a broader context, the fact is that Portugal was at the fore. Historians have thus been looking for specific causes that may have contributed to the Portuguese interest in exploring the Atlantic Ocean. Portugal's geographic location is one of them. At the crossroads of Mediterranean and Atlantic sea lanes, Portugal had accumulated considerable experience and know-how about winds and sea currents by virtue of fishermen and seafarers who ventured out into the seas linking the kingdom to distant shores. However, geography alone is not sufficient to explain the building of an empire. Economic and institutional factors are crucial to understand the context and the dynamics of the expansion. Unlike the *Reconquista*, the new phase of territorial growth occurred in the aftermath of one of the worst demographic recessions. It was not, therefore, a thirst for land or a population pressure over a fixed amount of resources that drove the reconfiguration of the Portuguese economic space. In fact, the use of slaves in deserted or scarcely populated newly found lands (e.g., Atlantic islands) confirms that the lack of free labor in Portugal accompanied this movement of borders. Still, agricultural issues deserve to be considered. As in other European regions, the changes in the countryside following the Black Death included the replacement of much of the grain cultivation with vines and pasture use. Evidence regarding wheat imports to feed Lisbon supports the belief that the Portuguese were hoping to gain access to the wheat fields of Morocco by capturing Ceuta. Even though this was never achieved, the fall of grain production – an outcome of the scarcity of labor – may have been among the motives for expansion (Godinho 1978b: 114).

Besides this set of proximate causes of expansion, other levels of explanation have been brought forward. Portugal bears the features which Fernandez-Armesto (2007: 485–486) called the "small-country's psychosis: the need to grow by conquest." As such, the short answer to the question "why was Portugal first" goes back to the conditions of a kingdom "that came about through internal colonization, spreading into lands to the south of the Douro" (Godinho 2008: 66). The movement of the frontier organized the territory and molded the distribution of power and resources between the Crown and social elites. Any potential imbalance between the Crown and competing powers could only be staved off by appropriating and distributing estates under the "leadership" of the king. The dynastic crisis of the end of the fourteenth century created a challenge to the new king, adding a new, proximate factor to the ultimate causes discussed earlier and leads to a second key issue, "why was Ceuta conquered in 1415?".

The answer goes back to the dynastic crisis of 1383–1385 and to the ensuing warfare, which encouraged the formation of a new nobility. The end of hostilities in 1411, with the signing of the peace treaty with Castile, set up the backdrop to North African conquests. Coming out of the war was a new group of nobles who were expecting to be rewarded, and the Crown's position depended on its ability to pay up. The best way forward for the king was to protract the economy of war and find new resources to redistribute. Portugal's first move overseas was not just the extension of a crusade carried on during the *Reconquista*, but also an attempt to secure new resources in order to strengthen the new dynasty. It forms a social and institutional framework that allows for comparisons to extractive institutional systems (Acemoglu and Robinson 2012).

The landing of the Portuguese expeditionary forces in North Africa in 1415 was a continuation of the *Reconquista*, sanctioned by Papal bulls, improving the nation's geostrategic positioning and security for shipping through the Strait of Gibraltar. The war against the Muslim in North Africa, which lasted throughout the entire Avis dynasty (from King João I to King Sebastião), reveals the importance of this conflict for the reputation of the new royal house, just as the *Reconquista* had been significant for the first dynasty during the medieval period (Farinha 1998: 120). More than any other part of the Portuguese empire, the North African strongholds depended on military services rendered by the nobility, thus deepening the political and social ties between the Crown and the nobility. The north African ventures do not explain the making of an overseas empire, yet the conquest of Ceuta should be reckoned as the first stepping-stone in the building of the empire.

### The making of the empire

Warfare and its spoils were not the only reasons driving Portugal's maritime expansion. Early sailing knowledge of continental coasts, winds, and currents was both a product of the military undertakings and a reaction to it. Discovery and conquest together nourished the expansion of the nation. It was already evident by the time of Prince Henry that these two activities were inextricably intertwined. The occupation of Ceuta provided information about the production centers of the goods arriving there and bolstered the hopes that distant sources of gold could be accessed directly by sea. As it happened, the exploratory voyages southward along the African coast, which were simultaneously opened to plundering, led to the discovery of Atlantic islands. The exploration and settlement of these archipelagos in the space of a single generation were spurred through the use of slave labor obtained in the recently established *feitorias* (royal trading posts) along the West African coast (Arguim). Even into the sixteenth century the efforts to occupy Moroccan outposts continued to return complementarities between these North African possessions and the desired advantages of trade with the *feitorias* further down the African coastline. King Manuel's ambition to take Safi in yet another military expedition is a good example. This city was the source of textiles supplying the slave markets, a clear demonstration that targets of conquest were selected on the basis of needs associated with the exploitation of new territories (Godinho 2008).

Over the length of the 1400s this interplay between offshore war and seafaring exploration changed the character of Portugal's economic space. From conquest came sovereignty over North African fortresses; from discovery of islands, the kingdom's first experience with colonization; from the establishment of *feitorias*, where regular trade was conducted with non-hostile populations, command of trade routes along the West African coast (and later, trade routes to Asia). Empire building called for a three-pronged formula of domination: conquest, discovery-colonization, and monopoly over some trade flows. Each of these levels of sovereignty involved different institutions and social groups.

The Crown secured the participation of noblemen, who served as governors in the Moroccan fortresses, took part in colonization efforts, and captained expeditions of exploration into unknown territories. The legitimacy of these undertakings afforded by Papal bulls, which imparted a "quasi-crusader" nature to them asked for the intervention of the Church. In fact, the spiritual jurisdiction of all the regions conquered by the Portuguese was granted to the Order of Christ, of which Prince Henry was the administrator and governor.[37] From the king's perspective, throughout the first half of the 1400s conquest took priority over discovery, and colonization was always left to seigneurial institutions. During the reign of King Afonso V, the priority given to the military interests in North Africa left the undertaking of exploratory voyages to non-nobles who sought the sources of Sudanese gold. The participation of mercantile business groups grew from then on and was also evident in the efforts to economically exploit the islands of Madeira, the Azores, and Cape Verde. The most significant example of this collaboration is the leasing out of the Crown's monopoly over the Guinea trade to Fernão

[37] Costa 2009; Sousa 1991.

Gomes, a Lisbon-based merchant. From 1468 to 1474, Gomes was entitled to the profits earned on all trade with the Guinea coast in exchange for an annual fee of 200,000 *réis*. His contract also stipulated the exploration of an additional one hundred leagues of African coast each year and, as such, this agreement between a private merchant and the Crown led to the discovery of the islands of São Tomé and Principe and the gold-producing coastal areas of the Gulf of Guinea (Peres 1983: 116). Finding these sources of gold encouraged the Crown to resume direct control over the overseas expansion.

The opening of new markets for gold occurred in a new international context, marked by the Turkish conquest of Constantinople (1453), which had effects on the relative prices of pepper, that is, a ratio of its price to that of wheat. From 1450 to 1500, it rose by 46 percent, revealing the scarcity of pepper relative to an essential good (Williamson and O'Rourke 2002: 446). Therefore, the quest for spices, primarily pepper, fits as a motivation for Portugal's expansion only in this juncture so that the aspiration to reach India by sea became the driving force behind the whole program of exploration in the reign of King João II (1481–1495). While Bartolomeu Dias sailed toward the Cape of Good Hope in 1488, the king dispatched two emissaries to East Africa and India via the Mediterranean. They were to gather information on Asian markets and on the mythical Christian kingdom of Prester John, thought to be a potential ally against Islam (Peres 1983: 193, 247–250). Both means of gathering information paved the way to Vasco da Gama's first voyage (1497–1499), entirely financed by the Crown.

The Crown's plan to reach India rewrote the idea of what the sea was, in general, and the Atlantic Ocean, in particular. It was now seen as a space that could be appropriated, as a territory or as an exclusive resource (Fonseca 2005: 113–115). The Portuguese made use of the juridical notion of *mare clausum* (in the sense of "territorial waters"), which implied property rights over the sea itself sanctioned by a Papal bull (Ferreira 1995: 111–123). The Portuguese monarch sought to enshrine this concept in treaties with Castile, since the neighboring kingdom was also competing for control over Atlantic waters. When Columbus discovered westward land, following his first voyage, the dispute reached new heights and was settled by the Treaty of Tordesillas (1494). Both Portugal and Castile agreed on dividing the newly discovered lands outside Europe along a meridian, which granted rights over what would later become Brazil to Portugal. In fact, six years after the Tordesillas agreement, while heading the second maritime expedition to India, Pedro Álvares Cabral reached the eastern shores of Brazil.

Throughout the first three decades of the 1500s, Brazil provided a few tradable commodities, such as dyewood and exotic animals, whose exploitation was carried out by a system of trading factories, similar to the one established in the western coast of Africa. Given the riches of Asia, the colonization of the new territory was, hence, a postponed enterprise. When in the mid 1530s, King João III finally recognized that a permanent settlement was crucial to guarantee sovereignty claims over the territory, the colonization was handed over to *capitães-donatários*. By royal gift (*doação*), twelve members of the lower nobility received fourteen captaincies, as a hereditary grant (Johnson 1987: 13–14). This division of Brazil into donatary captaincies reproduced the institutional framework set up in the Atlantic archipelagos, which in turn, replicated the features of the seigneurial system enforced during the *Reconquista*. The economic significance of Brazil only took off after the mid 1500s, following the setting up of a plantation economy, based on sugar production.

Giving up control of production is an indicator that the Crown concentrated efforts on maritime routes, which were of paramount importance in securing Asian markets. Therefore, in the Indian Ocean the Crown established an entire administrative structure and a local military force sustained by a fleet of heavy warships – later to become known as *Estado da Índia*. Building and exploiting the *Estado da Índia* as a part of the empire (but with its own, and different, models for administration and dominion) ran hand in hand with an upturn in aggregate production throughout the sixteenth century. The next chapter addresses the contribution of this imperial dimension to the performance of the Portuguese economy.

# 2 The age of globalization, 1500–1620

Fernand Braudel characterized 1480–1620 as the "long sixteenth century" of economic and population growth in Europe (Braudel 1982–1984, vol. 2). In Portugal too, after roughly 1480/1490, the upturn in the population numbers is one of the positive signs of this long-term cycle of prosperity. Growing trends started out from a situation in which low population densities were consistent with a high land–labor ratio typical of a "frontier economy." From what is known about the rest of the Iberian Peninsula, this phase of demographic growth went together with a rise in *per capita* output, recovering to, though not exceeding, the levels that had existed before the Black Death (Álvarez Nogal and Prados de la Escosura 2013). The Portuguese economy may have followed a different path. Recent estimates suggest that output per capita decreased (Palma and Reis 2016). However, while per capita agricultural production declined, the Portuguese intercontinental trade reached its peak years by comprising offshoots in America, Africa, and Asia. Dealings overseas are one of the most studied features of Portugal's economy. The effects of these trade flows on *per capita* gross domestic product (GDP) in European colonial powers remain an open and controversial issue (O'Brien and Prados de la Escosura 1998). Some scholarly insights point to colonial trade as the cause of living standard improvements in the mother country. Although there is no agreement about the significance of that contribution, it is certain that it grew throughout the early modern period and achieved its higher impact in the late eighteenth century.[1] Therefore, during the first hundred-year period of the history of the empire, in which the route of the Cape of Good Hope earned a particular advantage over other imperial resources, the colonial trade had a negligible effect on the GDP, though it fostered sectors like shipbuilding and shipping.

This chapter examines the evolution of domestic production and estimates the contribution of resources provided by the empire. During the period under analysis, roughly from 1480 to 1620, Portugal became

---

[1] Costa, Palma, Reis 2015; Pedreira 1994.

a kingdom integrated in the Habsburg monarchy (1580). The history of the empire points to the relative advantages Portugal reaped from the political union, since it created new opportunities for slave traffic paid with silver, controlled by Portuguese merchants. Silver was at the time the most important item in the Portuguese Cape Route. Hence, and notwithstanding Brazil's leadership in sugar production, the Asian trade reached peak values after 1580. The impact of colonial resources on the Crown's revenue is one of the consequences of the empire that has raised consensus among historians. The following pages describe a long sixteenth century of the Crown's financial prosperity (Godinho 1978b). On the Habsburg kings' perspective, the income afforded by the Portuguese empire allowed them to postpone the most critical escalation of the fiscal burden. As such, during two-thirds of its sixty-year duration, Portugal's loss of political autonomy had little, if any, severe economic drawbacks.

## Demographic trends

In the final decades of the fifteenth century, recovery from the devastations brought about by the Black Death and its successive waves was under way. By 1500 the population had climbed back up to where they had been before the outbreak of the disease, i.e., about 900,000 million (Palma and Reis 2016). This number, which is only an estimate, suggests that at the start of the 1500s Portugal was a country with a fairly small pool of human resources to draw upon, which amounted to less than 2 percent of Western Europe's population. In the Iberian Peninsula, too, the Portuguese were a minority – representing 16 percent of the population (Table 2.1).

After 1500 Portugal's demographic evolution became steadier, in line with the European long-term upward trend. The data published in the *Numeramento de 1527–1532*, the first population count which covered nearly the entire Portuguese mainland, confirm this.[2] Seeking information pertaining to a taxable base, this count is considered trustworthy, despite the vagueness resulting from the choice of the "hearth" (*fogo*) as the unit of account. In 1527 there were 282,708 "hearths" in the kingdom. To estimate a total number of inhabitants, demographic historians have considered different factors of conversion, ranging from 3.85 to 4.6 individuals per hearth, which would point to a total between 1,088,426 and 1,300,457 inhabitants.[3] Using the intermediate factor of 4.3 inhabitants, the kingdom's population is estimated at 1,215,644 (Serrão 1994: 343) (Table 2.2). Assuming this estimate, the average density stood at 13.6 per

---

[2] Galego and Daveau 1986; Dias 1996.    [3] Dias 1998: 16; Rodrigues 2008: 176.

Table 2.1 *European population in 1500*
*(thousand of inhabitants)*

| | |
|---|---|
| Germany | 7,200 |
| Austria | 2,000 |
| Denmark | 600 |
| Spain | 4,800 |
| France | 15,000 |
| British Isles | 3,900 |
| Italy | 10,500 |
| Norway | 300 |
| Northern Low Countries | 950 |
| Southern Low Countries | 1,400 |
| Portugal | 906 |
| Sweden | 550 |
| Switzerland | 650 |

*Sources:* Maddison 2001: 241; Álvarez Nogal and Prados de la Escosura 2007: 330 (data for Spain are for 1530); Palma and Reis 2016; Pfister and Fertig 2010: 5.

Table 2.2 *Regional distribution of the Portuguese population in 1527*

| Comarca (district) | Number of hearths | Population* | Percentage of total population | Density (persons/ km²) | Area (km²) | Percentage of total area |
|---|---|---|---|---|---|---|
| Minho | 55,016 | 236,569 | 19.5 | 32.6 | 7,252 | 8.1 |
| Trás-os-Montes | 35,629 | 153,205 | 12.6 | 13.3 | 11,493 | 12.9 |
| Beira | 67,696 | 291,093 | 24.0 | 19.0 | 15,298 | 17.1 |
| Estremadura | 65,515 | 281,715 | 23.2 | 14.1 | 19,930 | 22.3 |
| Alentejo | 48,934 | 210,416 | 17.3 | 6.9 | 30,319 | 34.0 |
| Algarve | 9,918 | 42,647 | 3.5 | 8.6 | 4,989 | 5.6 |
| Totals | 282,708 | 1,215,644 | 100 | 13.6 | 89,281 | 100 |

* Calculated at 4.3 persons per hearth.
*Sources:* Serrão 1996: 68; Rodrigues 2008: 177–178.

square kilometer, not as low as in Spain (9.9/km²), but clearly below the densities attested for other countries in Western Europe, such as Italy (29.9), England (23.2), or the Netherlands (28.8) (Malanima 2009: 16). Portugal thus appears to have been a scarcely populated country at the dawn of the sixteenth century. However, the comparatively low average density conceals substantial regional differences in population distribution, a carryover of the settlement patterns of earlier centuries.

Of the six territorial units which divided the kingdom for judicial purposes (Map 2.1), the Minho (northwestern region) was by far the most
densely populated. Although accounting for just 8 percent of the kingdom's total area, about a fifth of the country's people lived there. At the
other end of the spectrum, with a far greater area (almost 34 percent of the
total), the Alentejo (south of the Tagus) was the less densely populated
region followed closely by the Algarve. These two regions of the country
displayed a land–labor ratio similar to that of Spain. Between these two
extremes, the northwest and the south, Beira appears as the most balanced
judicial district, despite an irregular intra-regional distribution resulting
from the existence of mountainous areas, such as the Serra da Estrela.

Different levels of urbanization are another feature of Portugal's population distribution, according to the data compiled in 1527–1532.
Restricting the definition of "city" to concentrations of more than 1,000
hearths/homes, that is, 4,000–5,000 inhabitants (considered as the minimum size to allow for any regional dynamism), the percentage of urban
dwellers in Portugal stood at 11.6 percent. This is higher than the
European average in 1500, which stood at about 7–9 percent (Table 2.3)
and even higher than neighboring Spain (9–10 percent) (Dupâquier 1997:
258). The urbanization in Portugal was, however, lower than in the most
advanced urban areas in Europe such as the Northern (20–26 percent) and
Southern Low Countries (30–45 percent) and Italy (15–20 percent).[4]

The urbanization rates were in line with the European pattern, but this
reveals little about significant differences within the country (Table 2.4).
In Beira and Trás-os-Montes, while there were numerous small towns –
none of them was larger than 1,000 hearths/homes –in the Alentejo there
was a greater concentration of cities larger than that size. Reflecting
settlement patterns that went back to the Muslim presence, the majority
of the largest cities were located south of the Tagus River, in contrast to
the northern part of the kingdom, where settlements were traditionally
more dispersed and urban life less important. Nevertheless, the urban
network did not even come close to covering the country in
a homogenous way.

The thirteen urban centers that reached the 1,000-hearth threshold
had differing scales of population concentration. Rivers are a factor for
these differing scales, especially when the river is navigable and allows for
linking the surrounding countryside to distant locations. This accounts in
large part for the locations of Lisbon, Porto, and Santarém (Map 2.2).
The first two cities also served as deep-water ports, thereby linking outward trade directly to the inward-bound river transportation. Lisbon built

---

[4] De Vries 1994b: 15; Livi-Bacci 1999: 57–58.

Map 2.1 Judicial districts, *c.* 1500

Table 2.3 *Urbanization in Europe in 1500 (percent of total population)*

|  | Cities with >5,000 persons | Cities with >10,000 persons |
|---|---|---|
| Germany | 7–9 | 3.2 |
| Scandinavia | 5–8 | 0.9 |
| Spain | 9–10 | 6.1 |
| France | 9–12 | 4.2 |
| England | 7–9 | 3.5 |
| Italy | 15–20 | 12.4 |
| Northern Low Countries | 20–26 | 15.8 |
| Southern Low Countries | 30–45 | 21.1 |
| Portugal | 11.6 | 6.7 |
| Russia | 3–6 | 3–6 |

*Sources:* Dupâquier 1997: 258; Livi-Bacci 1999: 57; Portugal: adapted from Rodrigues 2008: 193; Álvarez Nogal and Prados de la Escosura 2007: 337.

Table 2.4 *Urbanization in Portugal, 1527–1532*

| Comarca (district) | Cities with >1,000 homes | Percentage of total population | Cities with >2,500 homes | Percentage of total population |
|---|---|---|---|---|
| Minho | 2 | 8.0 | 1 | 5.5 |
| Trás-os-Montes | – |  | – |  |
| Beira | – |  | – |  |
| Estremadura | 3 | 24.9 | 1 | 19.9 |
| Alentejo | 6 | 19.2 | 1 | 5.8 |
| Algarve | 2 | 28.9 | – |  |
| Totals | 13 | 11.6 | 3 | 6.7 |

*Sources:* Dias 1998: 18–20; Serrão 1996: 68; Rodrigues 2008: 193.

upon these factors even further by being the seat of the royal court and capital of the kingdom and the empire, which explains its ability to act as a powerful magnet of immigration. In 1527, with 50, 000–60,000 inhabitants, Portugal's capital was the seventh largest city in Europe – larger even than Florence, Genoa, Rome, London, and Antwerp (Clark 2009: 37). Under the stimuli of the *entrepôt* trade, especially with Asia, its population kept growing, reaching about 120,000 inhabitants in the third quarter of the sixteenth century (Rodrigues 2008: 191).

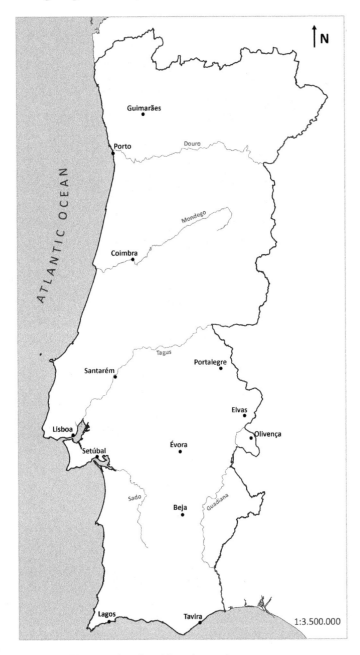

Map 2.2  Rivers and major cities, sixteenth century

In the urban hierarchy, Lisbon was followed, at a substantial distance, by Porto and Évora, with about 12,500 inhabitants each, and Santarém and Elvas counting around 8,000 – an ordering not very different from that which existed during the late Middle Ages, when the border was being drawn between Portugal and the neighboring kingdoms. The threshold of 5,000–6,000 inhabitants still allows to define as townships Guimarães, Coimbra, Portalegre, Setúbal, Beja, Olivença, Tavira, and Lagos, the last two in the Algarve, one of the most urbanized regions of the country until the seventeenth century. The growth of Lagos and Tavira was rooted in their port activities, which were focused on trade links with Andalusia and the Portuguese garrisons in North Africa (Magalhães 1970: 185–189). In Inner Alentejo urban concentration reflected local farming wealth, as well as a traditional Moorish settlement pattern which was not hampered by the military orders' efforts to colonize the region after the *Reconquista*. Here the trade links with Castile also prevailed as an important factor in shaping the size of cities.

Throughout the 1500s the population continued to expand, at a rate that it is still under debate. It has been accepted that a phase of rapid demographic growth persisted until 1580 and was followed by a slowdown, which lasted until the 1620s.[5] A recent estimate narrowed the slowdown to time span between the 1590s and the 1610s (Palma and Reis 2016). Data collected from a few regions illustrate these trends and suggest an average growth rate between 0.4 and 0.8 percent yearly. This is based on the case of Évora (south of the Tagus River), whose figures display falling rates: 0.63 percent from 1527 to 1589; 0.42 percent from 1589 to 1593; and only 0.12 percent thereafter (Santos 2005: 353). One of the most rapidly expanding areas was Beira, as from 1496 to 1527 it had an annual variation above 1 percent, which certainly accounted for the immigration of Jews expelled from Castile in 1492. On the other hand, also north of the Tagus but in the region of Estremadura, the population varied at the modest rate of 0.1 percent per year in the first quarter of the 1500s (Pereira A. S. 2003, vol. 1: 48 and 53). Admitting to an average growth rate of 0.6 percent between 1500 and 1600 – very close to Spain's 0.58 percent – Portugal would have about 1.667 million inhabitants in 1600 (Palma and Reis 2016).

After 1590, the vigorous expansion was hampered by the accumulated effects of mortality crisis. In 1593–1594 and again in 1599, abnormal weather conditions hit Iberia, but were also felt in France, Germany, Italy, and England, causing severe harvest failure. Famines, together

---

[5] Oliveira 1991: 52–56; Rodrigues 2008: 519.

with outbreaks of disease, notably plague in 1603–1604, were responsible for soaring death rates across Western Europe.[6] In Portugal, regions as widely separated as Minho, Trás-os-Montes, Beira, Alentejo, and the Algarve experienced severe mortality crisis.[7] Overall, population declined somewhat by the end of the 1590s and flattened out in the following years. Growth resumed in the late 1610s, when the balance of births and deaths favored the former, if only slightly (Palma and Reis 2016). Until the 1630s, population grew at a slower pace, although there are regional variations in what concerns the time when this positive trend came to a halt. North of the Tagus, for example, population increased up to 1621 whereas stagnation started earlier to the river's south.[8]

If epidemic breakouts mostly explain the shifts in the population of the 1590s, there are other variables to consider. Among them is the European marriage pattern, because of its influence in the number of childbirths. Although it is uncertain whether this marriage pattern was in place as early as 1500 in Portugal, there is evidence that points to its becoming more common to the north of the Tagus after 1550. Here women married later (23–26 years old), and a non-negligible number of persons (more women than men) remained committed to a life of celibacy. Following more closely the behavioral pattern prevailing in the Mediterranean, men and women married younger in the Algarve and Alentejo (Rodrigues 2008: 208).

As for the other variable relevant to demographic evolution, emigration to overseas territories seems to have played only a secondary role in the pace of population growth. As the data available is patchy, estimates for overseas emigration are to be taken as rough orders of magnitude. After a first phase in which emigrants headed out in small numbers (perhaps 500 per year) toward North Africa and the Atlantic islands, from the mid 1500s onwards, the numbers swelled – bound for Asia and Brazil. According to one estimate, some 3,500 persons left the country every year between 1500 and 1580, amounting to 280,000 altogether (Godinho 1978a: 9). However, this educated guess does not add up to another one according to which by 1600, 100,000 Portuguese were living overseas, 30,000 of which in Brazil.[9] It is reasonable to admit thereby, that emigration flows did not hinder population growth of the mother country. In any event, Portugal's population outflows in the 1500s should not be neglected since the economic activities in the empire demanded for

[6] Dupâquier 1997: 20; Campbell 2010.
[7] Amorim 1997b; Oliveira 1971–1972, vol. 1; Santos 2003; Magalhães 1970.
[8] Oliveira 1979: 498–501; Oliveira 1989; Oliveira 1971–1972, vol. 1: 279; Oliveira 1990; Rodrigues 2008; Santos 2003: 192, 203; Magalhães 1988: 19–20.
[9] Johnson 1987: 31; Subrahmanyam 1993: 217–218.

labor and human capital. Even so, it is doubtful whether the empire in this century ever represented the benefits expected from "ghost acreages" which would prevent the economic setbacks stemming from inelastic resources under population pressure, thus delaying the effects of decreasing marginal returns of land.

In the late sixteenth century the downward demographic trend went together with slow improvements in the agricultural sector. Even so, this century of expansion should be remembered for crop diversification due to the introduction of maize, illustrating the exchange of plants that characterized the European expansion.

## Agrarian expansion

The long-term population growth of the sixteenth century pushed up the demand for land, whilst the urban expansion also asked for regular provisions of foodstuffs and raw materials. To understand how these needs were met, we start by looking for signs of enlargement of ploughed areas. We then examine the composition of farming output and its possible linkages to population pressure on resources leading to tenants' choice for grain to the detriment of livestock.

From the last decades of the fifteenth century on, more lands were brought under cultivation. At first, the extension of arable land consisted of reclaiming areas left empty after 1350. Apart from the Minho, where only the hilly areas remained uncultivated, Portugal still had plenty of land that could be put to agricultural use. Throughout the country, landowners, seigneurial lords, and church institutions encouraged the recovery of abandoned farming plots by allowing lower fees for the use of land. In the central region of the country, the monastery of Santa Cruz de Coimbra did so in the early 1500s, as did the Military Order of Santiago in their large holdings in the Alentejo. The latter recognized in 1510 that it was in possession of land that had lain idle for decades and made efforts to bring it back under cultivation (Pereira A.S. 2003, vol. II: 259–261). The expansion of farmland also called for clearing acreages that had never been cultivated, although it is difficult to distinguish between the two (reclaiming of abandoned areas or clearance of new ones), given data ambiguities.[10] In the case of Alcobaça (Estremadura), by the end of the 1400s an estimated 77 percent of the leases and rents for farming applied to newly conquered land (Gonçalves 1989). Although examples of enlargement of arable land can be detected almost everywhere, the main centers of agrarian pressure were located in Beira and

---

[10] Coelho 1989; Devy-Vareta 1986.

Estremadura and included the following regions and subregions: the lower Mondego River and the lower Vouga River; along the Tagus River valley, from Almada to Abrantes and Tomar; and closer to Lisbon, around Sintra and Alenquer. Although less intensely, land clearings also took place further north, around Lamego (Beira); in the southernmost regions of Alentejo – Montemor-o-Novo, Évora, Elvas, Arronches, Olivença, Monsaraz, Mértola; and lastly, in the surroundings of a few urban centers in the Algarve, notably around Lagos.[11]

The expansion of arable land took the form of clearing woodlands, and draining of marshlands, documented for the Estremadura (Mondego valley, Alcobaça) and the Algarve. The clearings led to total deforestation in some regions. By 1530, the edges of the forest near Alcobaça had retreated with the creation of newly found settlements (Gonçalves 1989). In the hilly areas of the northwest, impoverished peasants used the slash-and-burn technique to obtain, albeit for a limited time, new land for the cultivation of rye. After decades of clearings, also related to the intense demand for shipbuilding timber, shortage of wood around the city of Viana do Castelo became obvious in the 1530s (Devy-Vareta 1986). In the Algarve, the recurrent use of slash-and-burn clearings triggered deforestation of the mountains near Tavira. Consequently a prohibition of the use of the mountains ensued in 1561, in order to protect the woodlands and the shipbuilding sector (Magalhães 1970: 41–42).

This extensive growth occurred within the institutional framework that ruled access to land and determined social property relations since the early Middle Ages. Access to land was still regulated by several types of agrarian contracts, which provided the necessary incentive for the takeover of new acreages. This is the case of the emphyteutic contracts, by which limited property rights were transferred to tenants, either in perpetuity or for two or three successive lives. Regional studies confirm that emphyteutic contracts for lives were particularly widespread, as they satisfied conditions for both the landowner and the tenant (see Chapter 1).[12] If these contracts were the most common device to bring more land under cultivation, they were, however, not the only one. Rights of exploitation over plots of land communally owned were regularly transferred to peasant families, by short-term leasing, an arrangement which fostered the replacement of pasture to arable land (Magalhães 1993: 246). Another option comprised the granting of *sesmarias*, i.e., vacant or abandoned land appropriated by the Crown and allocated to

[11] Gonçalves 1989: 247–251; Magalhães 1970: 52–53; Rodrigues 1995: 236; Pereira 2003, vol. 1: 329–330; Silva 2006; Rodrigues 2013.
[12] Gonçalves 1989: 248–249; Rodrigues and Duarte 1998: 91–94; Costa J. 2010: 46–47.

peasants under the condition that it was put under cultivation (Magalhães 1993: 246). Around Óbidos (Estremadura), woodlands were still granted in *sesmaria* in the late 1530s to promote cereal cultivation, although at a much slower rhythm than in the last years of the fifteenth century and the beginning of the sixteenth century (Rodrigues 2013: 110, 153, 544).

In a smaller scale, landowners also played an active role in the extension of arable land by investing in more expensive and technically demanding ventures, such as the drying of marshlands or the clearing of woodlands. Across the country, but especially in the valley of the Mondego River, of the Tagus River or in the vast lands of Alentejo, ecclesiastical institutions and members of the nobility channeled resources for such land reclamations.[13] The king's landed estates (*reguengos*) underwent similar efforts, as well as those in possession of the queen, whose investments in the draining of swamps around Óbidos (Estremadura) are well known (Magalhães 1993: 247). The ambitious engineering work that changed the course of the river Tagus in the years 1543 and 1544, counts among the most expensive investments in agriculture of the time. Designed to protect the farmland in the floodplains around Santarém from the sand brought by the river, the enterprise involved building an artificial riverbed with an extension of 10 km and was paid for by Prince Luís, one of the most influential seigneurial lords of the time (Dias 1984: 68–70). In any event, the expansion of arable land was achieved mostly by peasant families in the form of small increments.

The agrarian expansion responded to a steady rise of the prices of agricultural produce throughout the century, creating incentives to land investments and determining land-use choices (Godinho 1978a: 180). A general pattern of low land rents also marks the first phase of the agrarian upward trend which was particularly evident in areas that were being reclaimed or newly conquered to agriculture. But this trend gave way to higher rents by the 1570s and 1580s, which is consistent with population pressure on resources and increasing demand for food (Rodrigues and Duarte 1998: 100). In 1595, rents in the Alentejo reached their highest peak in a data set that extends into the early nineteenth century (Santos 2005: 370–371). In the recently occupied regions close to Ourém, in Caldas da Rainha (Estremadura), the rent trends display a similar pattern (Rodrigues 2013: 772–773). Signs of increasing output can be found also in the revenues of the archbishoprics, which depended mainly on the tithe, although with different intensity: in the south, the revenue of the archbishopric of Évora grew threefold; the

---

[13] Gil 1965: 41–49; Pereira 2003, vol. 1: 327.

archbishopric of Lisbon, fourfold, and in the northwest, the arch-bishopric of Braga, fivefold.

### The main crops

Regional data for the sixteenth century allows identifying the major features of the composition of agricultural output. Since this information is missing for most of previous centuries, a comprehensive comparison is not possible and we have to rely on circumstantial evidence. Nevertheless, considering the underlying factors encouraging agriculture – population growth, rising prices, and urban expansion – it seems reasonable to assume that a few changes took place.

As elsewhere in Europe, most of the arable land was allocated to cereal production. Taking Estremadura as an example, in Torres Vedras 87–95 percent of the cultivated area was occupied with grain crops (Rodrigues 1995: 253). Among the cereals cultivated in Portugal in the early 1500s (and that were part of the Mediterranean tradition) wheat, millet, rye, and barley were the most common. Of these, wheat was the most widespread, despite the fact that only a few areas met the necessary soil and climate conditions to ensure good yields of this demanding crop. Such was the case of the lands around Beja, of red lands around Lisbon, and the floodplains of the Tagus River. Even in adverse natural endowments (as in the Algarve) wheat was farmed, and this certainly accounts for the overall low productivity, among the lowest in Europe (Marques 1978: 22–23). Both the cultural preference given to bread made of wheat flour and the social significance assigned to its consumption, justified its culti-vation from the north to the south (Magalhães 1993: 258).

In the mountainous area of Trás-os-Montes, and in several areas of Beira (Viseu and Serra da Estrela), rye was the leading grain crop. It was more resistant and better suited to withstand its frigid winters and hot, dry summers and to the region's poor soils – "poor cereal for poor people" (Magalhães 1993: 258). Sorghum or millet, another grain crop consid-ered of inferior quality, could be found in fields of the northwest, thanks to the temperate marine clime. It was also planted in Estremadura in the vicinity of Alcobaça, in a close second place behind wheat (Gonçalves 1989). As a spring crop, it was usually combined with wheat, rye, or barley. Among the various bread-making grains, barley was planted everywhere in the kingdom, especially in the Estremadura and Minho where it was part of the diet of the poorest, and was even more important as a feed grain for horses and mules (Marques 1978: 83, 227).

Two new cereal crops were introduced in early sixteenth-century Portugal, respectively rice and maize (*Zea maïs*), albeit with mixed results.

The former remained confined to a few wetlands, mostly in Estremadura, like Asseca, Ota, and Muge. The unhealthy conditions of marshy areas, which entailed added risks for contracting malaria, might have contributed to the grain's unpopularity (Magalhães 1993: 260–261). Maize, on the other hand, was well accepted. Originating in the Americas, maize was introduced to Andaluzia in the early 1500s, from where it spread to the rest of Europe. In Portugal it was first grown in the area of Coimbra, probably between 1515 and 1525. By the 1530s, maize was being successfully combined with other grain crops and livestock on the fields of Minho, in the northwest, where abundant water reserves provided suitable conditions (Almeida 1992). High yields and a rapid growth cycle (five months from sowing to harvest) explain its fast regional diffusion, so that by the 1600s it was the most popular crop in Minho, fueling the region's population growth throughout the early modern period. As successful as this grain was in the northwest, its influence remained regional throughout the sixteenth century. The country's wide spread of maize would occur only later in the 1600s and 1700s.

The other two staples of the Mediterranean husbandry – olives and grapes – were grown widely across Portugal since medieval times and were hardly a novelty for the early modern period. Although land reclamations were chiefly intended for grain crops, both olives and vineyards kept expanding. Natural conditions everywhere in the kingdom favored vine cultivation, allowing for abundant production with high levels of productivity (Marques 1987: 98). From the earliest days winemaking had been a commercial undertaking, targeting urban and overseas markets. Continuing with the expansionary efforts that began in the late Middle Ages, new vineyards were planted in Minho, as well as in Beira (between Aveiro, Viseu, and Coimbra) and in Alentejo (Alcácer do Sal). In the Algarve the wine continued to be exported to Spain and Flanders.[14] The trend was to be taken further in the last decades of the 1500s and throughout the 1600s when tradesmen made large-scale investments in vineyards (Magalhães 1993: 264). As for olive trees, urban as well as foreign demand for olive oil underpinned the dissemination of this culture to northern Portugal throughout the 1500s. Besides being an integral part of the Mediterranean diet, olive oil was used as fuel in illumination, and in the processing of industrial products, such as soap and wool. From Coimbra and Covilhã, the upper-north limit where it could be found in the fourteenth century, the olive tree spread to Trás-os-Montes and Minho.[15] The main production centers remained in Estremadura

---

[14] Oliveira 1990; Pereira 2003, vol. 1: 385.
[15] Magalhães 1993: 261–262; Ribeiro 1979.

(Coimbra, Tomar, and Lisbon), Alentejo (Montemor-o-Novo, Elvas, Évora, and Estremoz), and the Algarve. Although with a minor share in agricultural output, fruit trees played an important role in exports, at least at a regional level. Oranges from Estremadura were exported to London in considerable quantities, while in the Algarve figs contributed to integrate the region in the international trade, particularly with neighboring Spain (Godinho 1982–1984, vol. 3: 187). Besides their role in exports, figs were also an integral part of the local diet, replacing bread during times of famine (Magalhães 1970: 125–128).

As any agrarian economy of the *Ancién Régime*, the agricultural landscape included areas of uncultivated land, which played a crucial role in the rural economic system (Serrão 1993b: 74). Forests, natural grasslands, moorlands, and scrublands provided a wide range of raw materials and foodstuffs and were also used as pasture land for livestock (Rodrigues 1998: 165–167). Animal husbandry, as it happens, could increase the opportunity costs of these uncultivated, common lands in times of imbalance of resources and positive demographic trends. Going back to medieval times, livestock farming played an important role in all six provinces of the kingdom, but even more so in the Alentejo, Beira, and in the mountainous areas of the interior, where topography, poor soils, and adverse climate conditions discouraged land plowing (Trindade 1965: 113–114). Transhumant sheep grazed in a long belt running through the central mountainous areas, from the Serra da Estrela to the plains in the inner south (Campo de Ourique, Idanha). The large size of the herds, which comprised also animals from Spain, brought about tensions between the livestock owners and the municipalities, for the damages they caused to the arboreal vegetation (Devy-Vareta 1986: 16-17). Aristocratic families often mentioned cattle among their capital goods. A probate inventory of the largest of such aristocratic houses, the duchy of Bragança, dating from 1565, registers a herd of 3,000 heads (sheep and goats), a number on a par with the enormous herds in the *Mesta*.[16] The same prevalence of sheep was seen in Minho, although here oxen were raised in great numbers too – more so than anywhere else in the kingdom. In the hinterland of Braga (Minho), a contemporary observer in the mid-century assessed the number of oxen as high as 5,000, along with 12,800 sheep, goats, and pigs (Barros 1919: 127). In the north-central region of Lamego descriptions of the local economy in the mid sixteenth century estimate a total of 10,200 pigs and 5,100 sows in the town's

---

[16] Arquivo Histórico da Casa de Bragança, BDM II Res Ms 18 - Inventário dos bens do Duque de Bragança D. Teodósio I; Phillips and Phillips 1997: 103–105; Simpson 2004: 77.

surrounding countryside. Herds of 100, 120, and 150 head of cattle and bulls were common in the hills of Montemuro (Coelho 1986: 166). This portrait of agricultural production supports the belief that animal husbandry was undertaken on a par with the traditional triad of Mediterranean farming. In an estimate from the first decades of the 1500s, livestock stood out as the largest subsector, accounting for 43 percent of total agricultural output. Livestock was followed by cereal crops (38 percent), wine (16 percent), and for olive oil (3 percent) (Godinho 1978a: 17–18). The overall value is estimated at 1,634 million *réis*, the equivalent of 148 tons of silver, at a time when the average nominal daily earnings (unskilled labor) were 3.1 grams of silver.[17] There is no estimate for aggregate output for the end of the 1500s. However, the inventory of the duke of Bragança from the middle of the century quoted earlier sheds light on the structure of agricultural capital. Considering vines, olive trees, livestock, and grain livestock alone reached 34.7 percent (3 million *réis*). The value share of land allocated to grain crops amounted to 53 percent, the vineyards 10 percent, and olive trees just 1 percent.[18] How both structures (agricultural output and capital) evolved throughout the second half of the sixteenth century is an unresolved issue. It seems reasonable to assume that population pressure fostered the conversion of pasture, waste and woodland into land arable. Eventually this extensive growth might have upset the balance between cereal farming and livestock, as the outbreak of conflicts regarding the use of common lands in regional studies suggests. In fact, local disputes between crop farmers and livestock raisers became more and more common. They were triggered by the encroachment of agricultural use into land communally owned and mainly used as collective pasture.[19] Examples of these disputes can be taken from the attempts of crop farmers to plant broad beans (*favas*) and peas in plots of land lying fallow (*contrafolha*) as attested for some communities in central and southern Portugal.[20] Since it meant reducing resources to feed the livestock, needed for manure and draught power, those attempts were short-lived, as it happened in the Algarve. Like elsewhere in Europe, technical and institutional constraints were still challenging an efficient integration of crops and livestock.

As in medieval times, Portuguese peasants continued to exploit the land by resorting to the same crop rotations, i.e., the two- or three-field

---

[17] This value would pay 186,742 annual salaries. Assuming that the active population was one-third of the total population, this figure equals 51 percent of the salaries.
[18] Arquivo Histórico da Casa de Bragança, BDM II Res Ms 18 - Inventário dos bens do Duque de Bragança D. Teodósio I.
[19] Marques 1987: 104; Magalhães 1993: 274–275.
[20] Magalhães 1970: 45; Pereira 2003, vol. 1: 323.

system. Throughout the early modern period, the former was employed more extensively, since the Mediterranean climate conditions that affected a significant part of the territory did not encourage spring crops (Marques 1978: 91–92). Both, however, relied on fallow as natural fertilizer and involved a permanent division between arable and pasture lands. These technical limitations thus hindered productivity gains during the 1500s, regarding either land or labor.[21] Yield ratios remained low, as data for the early 1500s shows. Wheat yielded on average between 1:2 and 1:3.5 in Estremadura, although plots of land in more fertile areas allowed yields of 1:4 or 1:5, as has been noted for Central Portugal (Marques 1978: 49–50). These yields are far below those known for the Low Countries (1:7.4), and less so from those estimated for France, Spain, and Italy (1:6.3).[22] As a further comparison, it is worth considering the average yields of 1:4 and 1:6 noted for the Alentejo in the early nineteenth century (Silbert 1978, vol. 2: 483).

Looking beyond mainland Portugal and into the Atlantic islands, agriculture in the Azores provides a different story since the high soil fertility allowed for an intensive exploitation of land. Dating back to the beginning of the settlement in the 1440s and 1450s and continuing throughout the 1500s, wheat was cultivated in continuous crop rotation in both the most important islands of the archipelago, S. Miguel and Terceira, without resorting to fallow. The excellent soil and climate conditions gave rise to unusually high average yields of 1:15 (S. Miguel) and 1:10–12 (Terceira) (Gregório 2007: 329, 345). Soil depletion eventually occurred in most lands of S. Miguel in the 1530s, with yields dropping to 1:6–7, at a time when population was growing and demanding more food. These conditions forced the introduction of the two-field crop rotation and the cultivation of a fodder crop, sweet lupines, which enhanced the fertilization of the soil and gave way to a more efficient integration of cereal and livestock farming. Productivity rose again and by the 1570s S. Miguel became the main wheat producer of the archipelago, exporting regularly to Madeira, North African garrisons, and even to the mainland (Vieira 1985: 130–131, 137–138).

The exceptional gains of productivity in the Azores persisted, while the evolution of the agricultural output in mainland Portugal depended on the use of more land and labor, i.e., resting on extensive growth. The fall in real wages (skilled and unskilled labor) is consistent with the idea of declining output per capita, at least since the late sixteenth century. Therefore, farm output probably did not exceed population growth,

[21] Magalhães 1993: 244–246; Marques 1978: 89–99.
[22] Van Bath 1963; Malanima, 2009: 139.

as some recent estimates have sought to demonstrate (Palma e Reis 2016). Under these circumstances it has been stressed that allocation of capital to manufactures in rural areas signals the household search for a complementary source of income to countervail decreasing returns. How this trend shows up in data for industrial output during the sixteenth century is a topic discussed in the next section.

## Manufactures

From the third quarter of the fifteenth century onwards, industrial output improved across Europe led by rising demand in urban centers, and greater availability of labor, capital, and raw materials (Duplessis 1997: 88). New trade flows and maritime expansion also paved the way for the new role of certain industrial subsectors, such as shipbuilding and shipping, which would determine the capacity of northwestern powers to lead the European economic growth from the late sixteenth century onwards. Throughout most of the sixteenth century, Portugal rode this rising tide, although the share of labor strictly allocated to industry should not have increased radically. But like elsewhere in Europe, the spread of a new organizational system based on rural labor must have contributed to increase the sector's total output.

In transitioning to the Modern Age, indicators point to the spur of industrial work no longer exclusively allocated to self-consumption production. In fact, agrarian households started addressing the demands of urban and supra-regional markets due to the encroachment of urban agents, usually merchants. The emergence of these rural industries attests the relative advantages of the coordination of labor carried out by those agents, who had better information on distant markets. They ordered a given output to the home-based producers, often provided the raw materials, and incurred the risk of selling the finished goods at a regional or international level.

Market incentives explain the spread of this labor organization, changing the rationale of the peasant economy, for which the transformation of raw materials for the regional market had been a secondary use of labor. The involvement of peasant households in industry meant new forms of time use within the family, which in the sixteenth century must have been mainly propelled by decreasing returns from farming. Hence, population growth and abundant labor supply turned rural handicrafts into a complementary source of income and the extent of this labor organization signaled changes in the rural world, although their significance varied between the sixteenth and the seventeenth century. If the generalization of the system could derive from decreasing returns, it could also engender what has been called an "industrious revolution" allowing a "consuming revolution" later on. In other words, marketed industrial work in the countryside represented higher preferences for work against leisure, in order to raise returns that paid for the consumption of more diversified and sophisticated commodities (de Vries 2008).

Such organization of industrial labor in the countryside is known as *Verlagssystem* ("putting-out system"). Its inherently urban–rural complementarity was particularly adjustable to the demand and technical features of the textile sector. The scarcity of quantitative data makes it difficult to assess the contribution of the putting-out system for each sector or the structure of industrial labor. Even without figures that would confirm it, we may assume that the situation in Portugal was essentially the same as in the rest of Europe, where the textile sector was far and away the leader. As it addressed a basic need of the entire population, textile production – woolens, flax and linen, silks, and cotton fabrics – employed by far the greatest number of workers. Precisely because of the extraordinary dissemination of spinning wheels and looms in private homes, and the long tradition of making homespun cloth for family use, an estimate of its share in overall industry is particularly difficult. Nevertheless, there is evidence of a first stage of a regional specialization, which seems worthwhile to describe in detail because it would last well until the end of the *Ancién Régime*.

### Textiles

Linen production offers a textbook case for illustrating the domestic production and its complementarity to urban centers in a few areas of Portugal. Spinning and weaving of flax was a common practice throughout the country especially in areas with favorable conditions for the cultivation of the fiber (as in Minho, Beira, Estremadura, and to a lesser degree, the Algarve).[23] The success and the way that the industry was embraced by the population also stemmed from the widespread use of linen cloth, coarser or finer, for making shirts, undergarments, and most household "linens." This was without doubt the most popular industry, particularly in Minho, where the most intensive development of linen production occurred in the first decades of the 1500s. Using a raw material that for long had been a regular element of crop-rotation cycles, the Minho gathered all of the essential factors that spawned strong rural-based production, whose surpluses flowed to urban markets, for consumption there or for export (Garcia 1986: 332). An example of exported

[23] Garcia 1986: 331, 334; Magalhães 1970: 172, 173.

linen was sailcloth, finding its way to foreign markets via the port of Vila do Conde (Costa 1997: 360).

The making of linen cloth that characterized the northwestern region rested on a dispersed rural production that stood under the coordination of regional centers of manufacturing and consumption such as Braga and Guimarães. The latter was alone able to secure an annual production of over 100,000 *varas* (a variable unit of measure equal to *c*. 1 meter) (Costa 1993: 304). The success of the industry lies, among other reasons, in the high population density of the region, which provided sufficient labor supply. Linen production was rooted in an agrarian backdrop of very small plots of land, which did not provide enough revenue to meet the peasant household's needs. Besides the prevalence of insufficient income, increasing demand for sailcloth from the shipbuilding industry, as well as reasonable communications by sea and river also generated significant stimuli so that the industry would go on to flourish in the centuries ahead. Although the northwest was the core of the linen industry, other parts of the country, namely Beira, also developed the production of linen. In these cases, the link between linen weaving and low income is well documented. Spinning and weaving was always the labor of women, mostly widows and spinsters (Braga 1998: 186).

For similar reasons of century-old tradition, the manufacture of woolens was found across Portugal. Wherever it was possible to raise sheep, home weavers wove woolen fabrics for the production of a wide range of clothes, such as capes, overcoats, socks, and hats. This home production displayed high levels of concentration in some areas of the country as early as the fifteenth century. Unlike linen, which was located mostly in littoral zones, the major nodes of wool production were in the interior, in a strip stretching from northern Lower Beira to the Lower Alentejo (Garcia 1986: 333). In important production areas near the eastern border with Spain, such as Arronches, Portalegre, and Castelo de Vide, and in the perimeter of the Serra da Estrela free-range pasturing (and consequently sheep raising) ensured abundance of wool. Urban workshops in Covilhã and Portalegre supervised the rural-based production of woolens, indicating the boom that this regional industry would experience in the following century (Garcia 1986: 335–336).

Urban workshops and rural manufacturing were not competing organizational options. The latter delivered the preliminary-phase products (thread and bulk woven fabric), while the former specialized in the finishing stages, using more complex and capital-intensive techniques (dyeing and stamping, for instance). Through the influence of merchants and specialized artisans who coordinated the rural industrial units, the influence of the cities was extended out into the countryside. This dynamic tended to accelerate throughout the sixteenth century, as occurred for instance with linen for rope and cordage for naval use. The first phase of fiber production took place in the environs of Moncorvo and Santarém, for example, and the final line was turned out by the *cordoaria* (royal rope factory) in Lisbon (Costa 1993: 302–303).

As for the silk industry, it played a very minor role in Portugal's manufactures and demanded highly specialized labor concentrated in townships. Located in Trás-os-Montes since the thirteenth century, thanks to the planting of mulberry trees, this sector surged in the 1400s, when the factory belonging to the Duke of Bragança was granted a monopoly over production in 1475. The factory benefited from the labor of a high number of weavers concentrated in Bragança.[24] In fact, the settlement of Jewish weavers driven out of Castile in 1492 boosted the transformation of silk in this region (Garcia 1986: 337). Aside from Trás-os-Montes, it also came to be produced in the sixteenth century in Évora, Lamego, Lisbon, and Porto (Braga 1998: 186). After its first phase of transformation, the silk was sent off to urban centers. Porto attracted some of the production from Portugal's northeast, but most went to Lisbon and some was exported to Castile (Garcia 1986: 338).

In the second half of the sixteenth century, Portuguese industry branched out into a new textile segment, although it would not gain much traction until the mid 1700s. This was the spinning and weaving of cotton, activities that were entirely dependent on importing the raw material from Cape Verde and Brazil. Cotton working was centered in Lamego and Tomar, places with tradition rooted in linen cloth, where capital and labor were available. These two centers also had access to the Douro and Tagus Rivers, respectively, which was critical, as the cotton fiber arrived by sea and the finished products went to market by river transportation. Without this facility the whole industry would have faced unsurmountable opportunity costs (Garcia 1986: 339–340).

*Other sectors*

If we accept (along with all of the risks involved) retro-projecting the picture that we find in the last decades of the *Ancién Régime*, tanning industry, ceramics and pottery came next to textiles in the demand for labor (Pedreira 1994: 103). Leather working was extensive, far-reaching throughout the country and ancillary to a myriad of specialized work-shops in urban settings, which produced footwear, clothing, belts, bridles and other tack, furniture upholstery, etc. (Marques 1987: 121). Ceramics

---

[24] Garcia 1986: 337; Pedreira 1994: 92.

and pottery making were other extremely common undertakings, especially in regions where clays and appropriate minerals were plentiful. Construction materials such as roof tiles and bricks were turned out by numerous kiln operations in Lisbon and the Algarve. In addition to these factories, small local *ateliers* satisfied the demand in the countryside for ceramic household items (cooking pots and table wares).[25]

Technology determines the spread of the more sophisticated production of glass wares. The sector depended heavily on the use of equipment and specialized labor, and as a result, did not generally lend itself to small-scale workshops. Sources do record some artisan glass-blowers as early as the fifteenth century, working in Lisbon and Santarém, but the most important factories were in Coina (Aldeia Galega) and Oliveira de Azeméis (Côvo) (Braga 1998: 191). In any event, the quality of the glass was low, and a royal decree contributed to limit the industry's pace of growth on the grounds that the kilns consumed vast quantities of fuel in the form of oak and cork oak wood needed for ship construction (Costa 1997: 329).

Iron-working was the "poor relative of pre-industrial economies" (Braudel 1982–1984, vol. 1). Like elsewhere in Europe, the development of this sector in Portugal responded to technological constraints and depended on natural mineral deposits. There was very little metallurgical industry to speak of at any time in the early modern period, and this situation persisted well into the late eighteenth century (Pedreira 1994: 111). This is not to say, however, that metals were absent. The country was dotted with small ironmonger workshops (blacksmiths and horse-shoers) since medieval times, and there is also evidence on the importing of smelted iron (Duarte 1995: 99–100).

Other sectors of metallurgy, like mining, smelting, armor-making, as well as shipbuilding, demanded skills and capital not available on a small scale production. These were a set of industries which the putting-out system did not account for. Centralized manufacturing operations, with high investments in fixed capital, were rare and the few existing examples required the Crowns' funding. This is the case of the foundry and arms factory of Barcarena, which was in full operation in 1490, and the first to make use of hydraulic power (Duarte 1995: 105). Nevertheless, the output of arms-making was not enough to keep up with demand and artillery was regularly imported from Flanders and the German territories.

Shipbuilding, contrary to iron-making, responded favorably to growing demand and involved various shipyards around the country. In the royal

---

[25] Braga 1998: 191; Magalhães 1970: 181.

shipyard of *Ribeira das Naus* in Lisbon, the activity reached its greatest levels of complexity in what concerned the organization of labor, techniques, and inventory, since this was the shipyard where vessels to Asia were launched. Its Crown dependency afforded it with large financial resources and accounted for its large-scale organization, on a par with shipyards in other countries that also served the State's ambitions and needs, such as Venice (Lane 1973).

The royal shipyard in Lisbon built an average of 750 tons per year (between 300 and 400 tons per ship) (Costa 1997: 288). A comparison with an equally active shipyard in the northwestern region of the country draws a measure of the output level of the Lisbon shipyard. Aveiro built 405 tons per year, which means that Lisbon's output was twofold higher, although based on the launching of a reduced number of high-tonnage vessels. Admitting that this scale of output was related to the building of ships above 300–400 tons, which cost 6,000 *réis* per ton, and taking into account that outfitting costs increased 81 percent production costs, the works of *Ribeira das Naus* shipyard would represent gross capital formation hovering around 8.14 million *réis* per year. Funds transferred from the *Casa da Índia* financed between 75 and 92 percent of all expenses of the shipyard, representing on average 18 million *réis* (1521–1539) annually assigned to its inventory (Costa 1997: 298). The supply of raw materials and intermediate goods to the shipyard made the *Ribeira das Naus* a hub of domestic and foreign trade flows. The domestic market supplied woods for the ship's hull (stone pine and cork oak), some of the sailcloth, and caulking material, involving regions from Minho to the port of Vila do Conde. A different kind of linens, especially suited to produce large sails, was imported from Vitré and Pouldavid-sur-Mer in Brittany (Costa 1997: 361). For a few years in the 1530s, during the reign of King João III, when diplomatic relations with France were disrupted, the northern central region of Lamego responded to the Lisbon shipyard's orders, promoting a rural industry there. The restored diplomatic relations with France in the 1540s put an end to the royal shipyard's demand for Lamego fabrics, which testify the limited potentials of domestic production to substitute French imports in regard to large fabrics of linen cloth. The flax for hemp to be finished as rope had supply in further north, Torre de Moncorvo, which added to the Ribatejo's production, both regions providing intermediary goods to the royal rope factory in Lisbon.

The pine forests along the Leiria coast, presumed to have been planted in medieval times, were still important to Lisbon's shipyards, but the sources that mostly provisioned the *Ribeira das Naus'* were in

Table 2.5 *Structure of costs in shipbuilding, 1500–1550 (percent)*

| Hull | 68 |
|---|---|
| Masts | 9 |
| Rigging and related equipment | 17 |
| Sailcloth | 3 |
| Anchors | 3 |

*Source:* Costa 1997: 178.

Ribatejo and in the left bank of the Tagus River, in Charneca and Aldeia Galega (Costa 1997: 317–322). Masts were made from a single piece of Nordic pine, imported from the Baltic region, through the port of Riga. Only these timbers would serve for ships of ever greater size – *c.* 500–600 tons of freight by the mid 1500s. Other materials such as pitch, nails, and pig iron came regularly from Biscay, in southern France, to be worked by the blacksmiths of Lisbon allocated to the shipyard.

Imports and the domestic market supported this bulk industry in a maritime economy. Much of the production factors and raw materials had markets in Portugal and the financial significance of this self-sufficiency can be assessed through budgetary figures from the late sixteenth century, which inform us about the structure of costs (see Table 2.5). The hull (built almost entirely of domestically grown timber) accounted for 68 percent of the total. Additional parts of the construction and rigging needed linen, caulking, and rope, which were also made from national raw materials. Thus, it seems safe to say that shipbuilding was an industry supported by Portugal's own internal resources, pushing forward the output of a few ancillary industries, like linen fabrics.

In the broad view, in Portugal as everywhere else, shipbuilding was an industrial sector that stood out for being capital-intensive, geographically concentrated, and for using skilled labor. It was one of the industrial branches mostly incited by intercontinental trade, although its pace of growth depended on the capacity of each maritime economy to compete in the shipping sector. In Portugal, transportation was highly affected by the outbreak of the Dutch Revolt against Habsburg rule (1566), and this armed conflict therefore negatively impacted on shipbuilding. The next section takes the survey of the "long sixteenth century" a step further, by looking into maritime trade.

## International trade

Overseas expansion afforded Portugal a different role in intra-European economic relations. The mix of exports revealed a new pattern of specialization, in both the nature and the value of goods. In the Medieval "agrarian monarchy," a few primary products had stood out by reaching supra-regional markets, such as raisins and dried figs from the Algarve, some wines, and especially salt, with Setubal's leading position as an exporting port (Rau 1951b and 1984). Exploiting the resources of the empire added exotic commodities to this range of domestic primary goods. In fact, the economy did not cease to be based on agriculture. It continued as such, as did all of Europe. But some novelty came about in the "long sixteenth century" (1480–1620), when Portugal stood out for its middlemen role in the intercontinental trade. Therefore, rents reaped in the *entrepôt* trade meant that re-exports outstripped exports. This structure of foreign trade became a hallmark of any European colonial power, and Portugal was no exception in this regard. Moreover, this was also a consequence of the existing network of routes, polarized by a few ports where commodities were un-loaded and re-loaded, and whose function was determined either by strategic geographic location or by political constraints, thus becoming quite sensitive to the fortunes of wars.

The range of commodities with which Portugal participated in European trade networks widened and its structure changed according to the kingdom's overseas dynamics. Given the lack of trade balances or any reliable time series of foreign trade, in the next pages we can only shed some light on the volume and value of crucial commodities. The final intention is to assess the relative contribution of each part of the empire to Portuguese exports.

### *The Atlantic empire*

Long before its outstanding participation on pepper flows (1500–1530), Portugal participated in the making of a plantation system that characterized the Atlantic colonial pattern from the first half of the fifteenth century onwards (Godinho 1990: 478). Sugar was one of the pillars upon which the system stood, together with slaves and gold. In the islands of Madeira and São Tomé sugar plantation developed employing slave labor. Sixty years after the discovery of Madeira (1480), sugar exports were already so high that prices plummeted – even to the point that the economic viability of sugar mills was called into question. Market quotas imposed by the Duke of Viseu, who held the lordship of Madeira seemed a good policy to preserve the island's economy (Vieira 2002: 56). Despite the duke's

Table 2.6 *Sugar production in Madeira,*
*1455–1525* (arrobas) *

| 1455 | 1,600 |
| 1470 | 30,000 |
| 1494 | 105,000 |
| 1505 | 143,000 |
| 1515–1525 | 200,000 |

* 1 *arroba* = 32 lbs = 14.69 kg.
*Source:* Godinho 1982–1984, vol. 4: 75–78.

attempt to ration sugar supply, the inexorable and irreversible process of "consumption democratization" drove production over the ceilings initially imposed and the number of sugar mills multiplied rapidly. Eighty mills could be enrolled in the second half of the fifteenth century (Mauro 1983: 208) and the output of the island soared from 1,600 to 105,000 *arrobas* (1 *arroba* = 32 lbs, or 14.69 kg), peaking at 200,000 *arrobas* in 1515–1525 (Table 2.6). Marginal decreasing returns caused crops to fall in the succeeding decades until stabilizing around 40,000 *arrobas* in mid-century – a figure that is consistent with the data for the years 1581–1587 (Table 2.7) (Serrão 1951: 15).

The soaring growth of Madeira's sugar swept aside traditional Mediterranean producers such as Candia, Sicily, and Granada. The Italians, who were deeply involved in sugar trade, also sought to intervene in Portuguese colonies by investing in production (Vieira 2002: 65). Thus, the economic role of new producing areas and Portugal's potential to supply European markets crowded in foreign capital and skills, mostly Italian, joining Florentine and Genoese trading houses. But competition was not just a matter of highly productive lands jeopardizing prior European suppliers. Portuguese and foreign capital spread the crop to other areas of the Portuguese empire, which partially explains the cycles of growth and contraction of the economy of the colonies, which sketches a competition within the colonial regions as it happened between Madeira and Brazil. The island was unable to withstand Brazil's entry to the sugar market at the end of the sixteenth century, although it had coexisted well with the rise of São Tomé, as the quality of this island's sugar addressed different European staples. São Tomé thus participated in the sugar cycle without threatening the Madeiran economy.

Table 2.7 *Sugar production in the Portuguese colonial empire, 1515–1617* (arrobas)

|           | Madeira       | São Tomé | Brazil    |
|-----------|---------------|----------|-----------|
| 1515–1525 | 200,000       | 100,000  |           |
| 1527–1529 | 123,170       |          |           |
| 1535–1536 | 135,860       |          |           |
| 1550      | 40,000        | 150,000  |           |
| 1578      |               | 175,000  |           |
| 1581–1584 | 38,000–40,000 | 200,000  | 350,000   |
| 1610      |               |          | 735,000   |
| 1617      |               |          | 1,000,000 |

*Sources:* Godinho 1982–1984, vol. 4: 96; Mauro 1983: 209 and 298; Serrão 1951: 14–18.

The plantation system was introduced in São Tomé in the 1480s and despite the lower quality of sugar, the expansion of the crop was equally notable (Rau 1971). Within thirty or forty years output went beyond the 100,000 *arrobas* threshold, rising to 175,000–200,000 *arrobas* in the last quarter of the century (Godinho 1982–1984, vol. 4: 96). Slave revolts and cane blights discouraged the industry from 1610 to 1620 and onwards, at a time when production in Brazil was soaring. We do not know, however, how the sector evolved in Madeira in the mid-sixteenth century, but indications are that in the 1520s the two archipelagos together could account for 300,000 *arrobas* of exports per year, but Brazil's production alone surpassed this ceiling already in the 1580s (Table 2.7). International demand continued to favor high-quality sugar. In fact, Brazilian output first penetrated the market in the guise of Madeira's produce – a counterfeit arrangement which was a common business ploy. Its rise in the international market started, thus, by its ability to reproduce what consumers already acknowledged as a good product, sold at competitive prices. So, excellent natural conditions for sugar and easy access to slave labor in Brazil soon undermined the plantation system in the island of Madeira which gradually shifted to wine production.

An estimation of how much the sugar production in different areas of the empire added to Portuguese exports requires data on prices, but the information is missing for most of the sixteenth century. In the first half of the 1500s, taking into consideration a few benchmarks, prices fluctuated between 530 and 600 *réis* per *arroba* in the case of Madeira. They jumped to 2,400 *réis* in 1581–1587, well above the prices from São Tomé (660 *réis*) or Brazil (1600–1850 *réis*). The price ratios of the two producing islands for 1530 – as in 1580 – were between 3.2:1 and 3.6:1, with the advantage going to Madeira over São Tomé. It is plausible that the exports in 1515–1525 valued around 138.5 million *réis*. If we accept that the relative differences did not change and consider the entry of Brazil, the value of sugar would jump to 872 million *réis* in the years 1581–1584 at Lisbon prices. The peak in 1617 represented a value close to 1,000 million *réis*, supported by Brazilian output only. Hence, figures suggest that the first stage of the plantation system in the Atlantic history afforded substantial sums, whether in the early 1500s or in the last decades of the century, particularly when these numbers are compared to the value of cargos coming from other parts of the empire.

Gold and slaves were the second and third foundations underpinning the Atlantic economy of the Portuguese empire in the long sixteenth century. Slave labor on the plantations depended on the traffic organized in trading posts (*feitorias*) located on the Guinea coast (Map 2.3). Unlike what happened in seventeenth-century Brazil, in which the links to Angola were indispensable, the phase of sugar production on the islands stimulated the slaving voyages north of the Equator, making Cape Verde into a marketplace of redistribution of labor coming from Guinea. This also gave rise to the Cape Verdean cotton-cloth industry, producing goods to be bartered for slaves on the African coast. Based on a few sources available, an annual average of 1,400 slaves passed through Cape Verde in the first half of the sixteenth century – fetching prices that differed according to ethnicity, age, and supply-and-demand equilibria, varying between 3,500 and 7,000 *réis*.[26] Although the top prices rose from the year 1520 to 1530, the average price probably hovered around 5,000 *réis*, meaning that slaves accounted for *c*. 7 million *réis* per year.

Since the early stages of the Portuguese empire, slave trade involved a chain of permanent factories (*feitorias*) along the African coast and the islands of Cape Verde. Rents originated in this intermediation were not all directly diverted to the mother country; they were rather accumulated in the hands of colonists, settled in African posts or in Brazil, who played the overwhelming part in this business. In some trading posts, the transactions involved Portuguese and African middlemen in quite an original manner. Portuguese were the sellers and African the buyers of slaves, in exchange for gold. Thus, in certain nodes of the chain, European commodities paid for slaves who were resold further south in exchange for the second most demanded commodity in the area: gold. This trade was definitely institutionalized at the fortress-factory of São Jorge da Mina from the 1480s onwards.

---

[26] Klein 2010: 214; Torrão 1991: 275.

Map 2.3  The Portuguese empire in the Atlantic, sixteenth-seventeenth centuries

Information regarding the amount of gold obtained in Mina comes from official records, as the buying of gold in this factory was a royal monopoly. Estimates based on these records are shown in Figure 2.1. In two periods the shipments of gold almost reached 70 million *réis* (1496 and 1532, 649 and 681 kg, respectively). Legal private traffic did not exceed 20 percent of the value of the shipments belonging to the king.

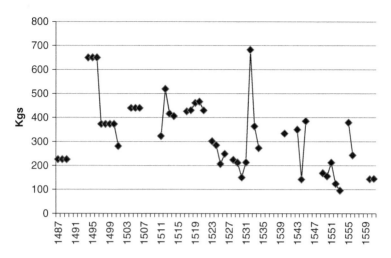

Figure 2.1  Imports of gold from the Guinea Coast, 1487–1559
Sources: Vogt 1979; Pereira J. C. 2003.

But, smoothing the peaks and troughs of gold flows, an annual average of 25 million *réis* (332 kg) stands out, an average value lower than that estimated for the exports of sugar in the first half of the sixteenth century.[27] The economic returns of this trading post gradually faded, but that was largely compensated by the rise of the pepper cycle, which had started with the first voyage to India in 1498.

*The Asian connections*

Vasco de Gama's first voyage around the Cape of Good Hope opened up a regular maritime route between the homeland and India. This route took Portugal to a singular staging area because prices fixed by the *Casa da Índia* in Lisbon reflected Portugal's ability to become a supplier to European markets, surpassing the Italian republics that had taken on this middlemen role since the "Commercial Revolution" of the thirteenth century (Lopez 1971). Our knowledge of the exact quantities of pepper unloaded onto Lisbon's docks going to the *Casa da Índia* is incomplete, but much of the picture is clear. In the first half of the 1500s, yearly averages of imports of pepper and other spices could amount to 35,000–40,000 *quintais* (1 *quintal* = 58.7 kg). The last quarter of the century witnessed a fall to 15,000 *quintais* per year, but volatility

[27] Vogt 1979: 218–219; Pereira J. C. 2003: 279.

Table 2.8  *Pepper unloaded at* Casa da Índia, *1501–1600 (million* réis*)*

| | Average | Number of observations |
|---|---|---|
| 1501–1510 | 97.9 | 6 |
| 1511–1520 | 258.7 | 4 |
| 1521–1530 | 125.9 | 3 |
| 1531–1540 | 166 | 1 |
| 1541–1550 | 265 | 2 |
| 1581–1590 | 234.1 | 5 |
| 1591–1600 | 136.9 | 9 |

*Sources:* Godinho 1978: 301–304; Godinho 1982–1984, vol. 3: 17, 21, 24; Boyajian 1993: appendix 2.

Table 2.9  *Prices and freigth in pepper trade, 1506–1607 (*cruzados *per* quintal*)*

| | Price at origin (Cochin) | Freight | Total cost (price at origin + freight) | Price at destination (*Casa da Índia*) | Markup (price at destination / price at origin) |
|---|---|---|---|---|---|
| 1506 | 3.0 | 1.0 | 4.0 | 22.0 | 7.3 |
| 1558 | 5.3 | 4.0 | 9.3 | 34.0 | 6.4 |
| 1607 | 7.1 | 8.0 | 15.2 | 32.0 | 4.5 |

1 *cruzado* = 390 *réis* (1506) = 400 (1558 and 1607).
*Source:* Godinho 1982–1984, vol. 3: 17, 21, 24.

increased due to the varying success of each individual fleet making the homeward voyage.[28]

The value of cargo and rates of return depended on price trends, both in Lisbon and in Asia. In fact, the fall of pepper imports occurred at the same time that prices went up in the second half of the sixteenth century in Europe. Spices and pepper were no exception, although their positive variation was less pronounced than that of other edible items like wheat or meat. Nevertheless, the decrease in quantities did not translate into a fall in the value of cargo unloaded in Lisbon. Shipments were still worth above 200 million *réis* in the 1580s (Table 2.8).[29] This coincided with markups decline and with the rise of Portuguese shipping costs between 1558 and 1607, which affected rates of return (see Table 2.9).

[28] Godinho 1978: 301–304; Boyajian 1993, appendix 2.
[29] Godinho 1982–1984, vol. 3: 17, 21, 24; Boyajian 1993, appendix.

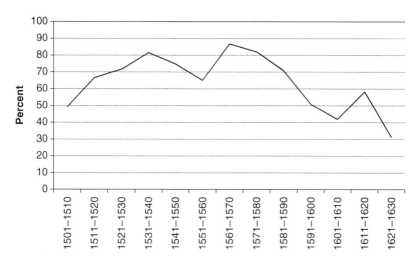

Figure 2.2  Cape Route shipping, 1501–1630 (tonnage returned as
percentage of tonnage departed)
Source: De Vries 2003.

Regarding the pepper trade, it seems that Portugal faced its "twilight"
in the first decade of the seventeenth century, prompting the gradual shift
toward the colonization of Brazil during the years of the Iberian Union
(Disney 1978). In fact, considering sugar produced in the Atlantic islands
and in Brazil, the value of this commodity largely outstripped the one
strictly based on pepper (872 million *réis* from sugar against 234 million
from pepper). Moreover, the challenge of maintaining the Cape Route
was exacerbated by shipwrecks, the probability of which can be measured
by comparing departures from Lisbon to safe returns, after discarding the
cases of ships that departed to Asia and were not meant to return.

From 1505 to 1520, the contribution of Portugal's shipyards to the
enlargement of the naval forces in Asia was crucial, when twenty-seven
ships were transferred to the Indian Ocean (Rodrigues 2004: 201–202).
As such, the comparison between departures and safe returns assesses the
probability of casualties only from the 1530s onwards (Figure 2.2).
Shipping improvements in this route were reflected in the downward
trend of vessels lost at sea. This trend saw a dramatic reversal after 1570
when the number of losses started to climb fairly steadily. There were thus
many signs that the entire shipping system had serious built-in flaws.

Technological, institutional, and economic factors challenged shipping
efficiency in this route (Costa 2013: 38–60). The contemporary

explanations for losses focused on overloaded vessels and on technological issues. Aiming to respond to the demand for more space on board, shipwrights added decks without any significant change in the framework of the hull, thereby reducing the vessel's stability. This represented the adaptation of technical skills to the Crown's policy to dispatch larger vessels, rather than to send a greater number of smaller ships, which were actually more seaworthy. Even though such a strategy implied economies of scale, ships over 600 tons of cargo, sailing too heavily laden, were much more prone to disaster.

The Iberian Union and the war against the Dutch created an entirely new institutional and political framework, which justified the king's strategy based on investments in the pepper trade. The intention was to wage an economic war with the prices of commodities. It was expected that imports of pepper in Portugal contributed to the fall of prices and markups in all European markets, which would squeeze the benefits that the Dutch secured when they conquered or threatened Portuguese strongholds in Asia. Pondering this new political framework, the Portuguese Cape Route had to be kept in motion, while this very strategy forced the king to finance shipping and shipbuilding. As for the cargo, each merchantman became ever more open to private capital invested in new commodities such as China silk and Indian cotton, apart from pepper that was still under royal monopoly. The Asian fabrics, albeit freely traded, ensured markups large enough to pay for freights and cover the higher risks in this route. Such a new range of commodities, which allowed exorbitant profits, not only made the whole route financially viable, but it also came to be a mechanism by which Asian manufactures gained entry into Europe. Hence, in the late sixteenth and early seventeenth centuries, before these goods reached similar importance in the VOC or in the EIC shipping, the Portuguese Cape Route was already a supply line of Asian textiles (see Figure 2.3). As it would happen later with those corporate companies, the growing Portuguese interest for cotton textiles resided in the slave trade. The demand schedule was being shifted forward because South American colonies (either Spanish or Portuguese) needed labor, whether for mining or for the sugar industry.

With this shift in the structure of cargos that came right at the end of the 1500s, the Cape Route involved trade flows at a global scale, and showed the advantages of Portugal having access both to Indian textiles and to protected markets of slaves in Angola and in the Gulf of Guinea. Despite the flop of the pepper trade (Table 2.10), the Cape Route continued to move the most valued merchandise in the empire as part of a global business. In other words, judging by the range of the geographical origins

Table 2.10 *Value of return cargos in the*
*Cape Route, 1586–1600 (million* réis*)*

| | |
|------|-------|
| 1586 | 1,883 |
| 1587 | 1,692 |
| 1588 | 3,106 |
| 1589 | 3,663 |
| 1590 | 2,553 |
| 1592 | 1,051 |
| 1593 | 1,668 |
| 1594 | 904   |
| 1595 | 2,717 |
| 1596 | 1,059 |
| 1597 | 3,631 |
| 1600 | 2,553 |

*Source:* Boyajian 1993, appendix 2.

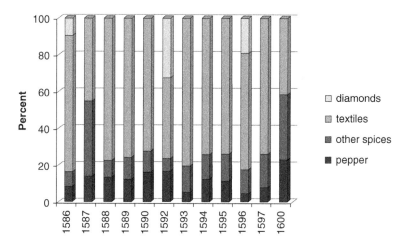

Figure 2.3 Structure of return cargos in the Cape Route, 1586–1600
Source: Boyajian 1993, appendix 2.

of merchandises and its effects on re-exports, the empire reached its maximum potential during the Iberian Union (1580–1640).

Presumably, a great deal of colonial goods paid for Portugal's imports from Europe. Indeed, the *entrepôt* trade proved to be indispensable in providing commodities used as means of trade overseas (Magalhães 1998a: 314). For instance, in São Jorge da Mina, since its founding in the late fifteenth century, gold remittances were the last step of a chain of transactions that involved various linens (many of them of French origin, such as Rouen cloth), assorted items of copper, tin (notably basins for various, specific purposes, all with different names), all sorts of trinkets from Flemish cities, especially Antwerp, and north African woolen fabrics (*alambéis*) (Pereira J. C. 2003: 278–292). With the few exceptions of woolen fabrics produced in the Alentejo in substitution for North African *alambéis*, the need to import these items illustrates that Portugal did not develop the industries that would meet the colonial demand and swap for gold on the African coast. In the same way, at the moment the ships set sail from Lisbon on their outbound voyage to India, they left with cargo and *cabedal* (money) needed to exchange or pay for pepper, based on imports to resell in Asia.

During the first half of the 1500s the main item traded for pepper was copper from Central Europe. Asian markets consumed few European manufactures, but the Italian scarlet cloths, velvets or damasks, the taffetas from Toledo, and the silks from Valencia had consumers in Asia. However, copper, more than European textiles, played a critical role in this trade. The Crown's agents located in the trading post (*feitoria*) at Antwerp were assigned to manage and negotiate the valued contracts with merchant houses that supplied the metal. The great German mercantile houses – Hochstetter, Welser, and Fugger – had two contracts of copper with *Casa da Índia* involving the sale of 6,000 *quintais* per year (first contract) and 12,000 *quintais* (second contract) in the years from 1514 to 1521. At an average price in Lisbon of 1,636 *réis* per *quintal*, imports in copper alone for the first contract amounted to 3.6 million *réis* per year, and twice that for the second contract (Goris 1925: 233).

Assuming that in the first half of the 1500s each ship set to sail to India carried cargo and money valuing 9.6 million *réis*, and that there were routinely five vessels leaving per year, 38 million *réis* worth of imports would have been necessary every year in order to operate this imperial business (Godinho 1978b: 303). Some examples drawn from official lading manifests illustrate the extent to which distance added value to this cargo. In 1520 three ships carried between them 3,355 *quintais* of copper that was worth 5.4 million *réis* in Lisbon. But on the Malabar Coast this same copper was worth 15.3 million *réis* in exchange for pepper (Godinho 1982–1984, vol. 3: 10). The same thing occurred on the return voyage. Bound for Lisbon, each ship carried spices (more than half of which was always pepper) worth between 66.4 million and 80 million *réis*, that is, about eight times the value of the cargo (9.6 million *réis*) upon departing Lisbon at the start of the journey (Godinho 1982–1984, vol. 3: 72). This level of rents was extraordinary as were capital and risks involved. Thus, royal records from 1534, while telling us that the India trade allowed gross revenues in the amount of 272 million *réis*, also confirm that the net surplus of 72 million *réis* pointed to rates of return around 40 percent.[30]

The changes in the structure of cargos after 1580 did not alter these earnings – only greater losses at sea would threaten the revenues and profits of the king inherent to the route. Copper gave way to silver – in the form of Castilian coin – and the greater share of non-monopolized cargos fostered this link to Asia under Habsburg rule. Spain extracted silver in the New World at competitive prices – partly through labor of native populations, and partly through slaves supplied by Portuguese ships coming from Portuguese trading posts in Western Africa. For the economic groups that embodied the globalization of capital flows, the economic integration of the two Iberian empires held out the promise of advantages in the union of the two kingdoms. Access to silver was one of the possible reasons for the peaceful acceptance of Philip II's right to the Portuguese throne in 1580 (Godinho 1978b: 393–395). The evidence thus points to an economic integration of the Portuguese and Spanish empires during the years of the Iberian Union that not only undermined the significance of the boundaries agreed in the Treaty of Tordesillas but also led to the arrival of silver at the Mint House of Lisbon (Mauro 1983: 606).

*Trade with Europe*

Portugal's trade relations with Europe were not exclusively determined by the colonial dimension of the Portuguese economy. Cereals, for instance, were critical to weave the domestic market to intra-European flows. As already happened in the Middle Ages, grain imports had a strong tie to the salt trade promoted by fishing industries in northwestern regions. It is certain that wheat from Azores made up for the shortfalls in the mother country, while also supplying the Portuguese strongholds in North Africa. Castile also contributed during crisis years. But all indications are that the cities and villages along Portugal's coast – Lisbon above all others – consumed cereals arriving by sea at an increasing rate. To guarantee the supply, royal dispositions time and again waived the levy of any customs duties on grain imports in Lisbon, a measure swiftly extended to other port cities such as Viana do Castelo and Porto

---

[30] *Coleção de São Lourenço*, vol. 1: 39.

(Magalhães 1993: 332). In the late sixteenth century and throughout the first half of the next, the cultivation of maize in Minho and Beira brought some relief to these serious grain shortages felt in the kingdom's littoral (Godinho 1982–1984, vol. 4: 38). Nevertheless, imports of cereal became one of the trading flows that mostly explain the number of north European vessels calling at Portugal's ports and returning with salt from Aveiro or Setúbal (Rau 1984: 150–151).

The lack of regular customs records or balances of trade makes it difficult to assess the value or quantities of commodities passing through Portuguese customhouses. Thus the share of cereals in the total of imports cannot be determined. An estimate for the years 1527–1533, however, allows for a few calculations. Over those six years, imported grain probably reached 100,000 *moios* (1 *moio* = 828 liters), thus *c.* 828,000 hectoliters (Godinho 1982–1984, vol. 4: 21). With an estimated population of 1,215.6 million, at an average annual consumption per capita estimated at 3 hectoliters per year, a yearly import of *c.* 138,000 hectoliters would cover roughly the consumption needs of 46,000 people (3.7 percent of the population). Considering that Lisbon alone had 56,000–60,000 inhabitants in the 1520s, the grain from the sea did not cover the needs of the coastal and urban populations, to which it was mostly destined.

As already mentioned, the lack of sources prevents us from addressing the issue of whether Portugal's imports of bulk commodities caused trade imbalance. But, information for some local markets, at least, supports a patchy work on the structure of foreign trade. It certifies that notwithstanding the demand for wheat, textiles were the leading commodity among Portuguese imports. In Vila do Conde, in 1504 and 1505, merchandise arrived with the total value of 4.3 million *réis*, 32.6 percent of which derived from trade relations with England, followed by France and Flanders with 26.6 and 26.1 percent, respectively. Finally, Ireland registered 14.7 percent of these imports. Within this geographic breakdown there is no notable difference in the mix of goods imported. Textiles accounted for 90.9 percent of their value. The remaining 9.1 percent was made up of a wide assortment of items, including paper, iron manufactures, household utensils, and nautical fittings (Pereira 1983: 104, 109). In the Algarve, in 1520, the customs house in Faro admitted textiles valued at 4.6 million *réis*, mainly from England, although most of these fabrics, in fact, were transshipments coming through Castile (Magalhães 1970: 195). The entry of English cloth into Portugal via Castile is noted in English sources and records from the customs house of Faro corroborate it (Shillington and Chapman 1907: 133).

Finally, ledgers of Portuguese merchants in Antwerp in 1552 show that textiles amounted to 98 percent of the value of all merchandise exported

Table 2.11 *Imports into Flanders, 1551*

| Region | Products | Value in *ducats* |
|---|---|---|
| Spain | Dried fruits, wines, olive oil, dyes, raw silk | 500,000 |
| Portugal | Spices, sugar | 500,000 |
| England | Tin, wool, textiles | 300,000 |
| France and Germany | Wines, metals | 800,000 |
| Italy | Velvets, silk fabrics | 1,000,000 |
| Ostend | Wood, linen, cereals | 250,000 |

*Source:* Goris 1925: 319.

to Portugal (Goris 1925: 314–315). Some intermediate goods and raw materials used by coopers, such as barrel hoops and casks, raw flax, caulking, iron, and pitch, were imported to meet the demand of industries newly developing in the sixteenth century, now including shipbuilding. This trade was mostly paid by re-exporting goods from the empire. Information delivered by Italian observers from the mid 1500s offers a glimpse of how Portugal's specialization was rooted in supplying exotic goods, within a Mediterranean sea that was still bordered by prosperous industrial centers in Italy (see Table 2.11).

Throughout the reign of King Manuel, the activity of the royal trading post at Antwerp confirms the importance of spices, mostly pepper, as well as other savory condiments, such as *malaguetas* (hot chili peppers) from Africa, widening the range of exports, that included dyes from the Azores and wine (unfortunately without any indication of origin). The values of the merchandise or the exchange rate employed are unrecorded in these ledgers. At the prices prevailing in Lisbon, the pepper traded by the royal officials in Antwerp between 1495 and 1521 would have been on the order of 76 million *réis* (Goris 1925: 239).

The accounts of the *feitoria* at Antwerp do not reflect the kingdom's structure of trade, since exports could also include a more significant share of domestic products that are not so well represented in the activity of the royal agency. The data is sparse, but since it is based on trade flows involving the core-city of the European world economy (Braudel 1982–1984, vol. 3) it must be somewhat representative. Privately carried trade and shipping from Portugal to Antwerp dated from 1535–1537 sheds light on the structure for the Portuguese exports, in which agricultural products accounted for 3 percent of the value of all exports and 36 percent

Table 2.12 *Portuguese exports to Antwerp, 1535–1537*

|  | Domestic foodstuffs | Merchandise from the empire | Total |
|---|---|---|---|
| Value in thousand *réis* | 8,200 | 250,100 | 258,300 |
| Volume in tons | 1,632 | 2,856 | 4,488 |

*Source:* ANTT, Feitoria de Antuérpia, Livro de Avarias, liv. 1.

of the volume (Table 2.12). Among the 8.2 million *réis* worth of agricultural exports, figs accounted for 7 percent, far below olive oil, with 88 percent.[31] The ledgers of a Portuguese merchant, named Francisco Ximenes, dating from 1552 allow the same interpretation, according to which olive oil was the main agricultural export (76 percent of the value of all the merchandise he traded on); as for sugar from São Tomé, it just represented 15 percent (Goris 1925: 314–315). The other items of this merchant's trade operations did not involve dealings with Portugal. The scattered data go only so far as to illustrate the fact that Portugal's exports to Antwerp comprised products from its domestic agricultural output. However, in terms of both volume and value the overwhelming share depended on the empire – 97 percent of the value in the three-year sample reported here. Portuguese exports to London in the years 1574–1576 show a very similar structure. Among 20,384 pounds sterling worth of exports to London, pepper amounted to 63 percent. Sugars, molasses, and *marmeladas* (candied fruits) accounted for 9.3 percent, and there were small quantities of cotton fabrics from India. Regarding goods originating in the Portuguese homeland, manufactured goods were represented only by a single item – soap – comprising less than 1 percent of the total value, while agricultural products – oranges and salt – accounted for 3.2 percent (Godinho 1982–1984, vol. 3: 187).

In the sixteenth century, foreign trade added to the Middle Ages pattern the re-export of exotic and high-valued products derived from the colonial dimension of the kingdom's economy. Domestic commodities were still largely rooted in the primary sector, comprising fruits, salt, wine, cork, and olive oil. Yet, the agricultural output reflected the effects of greater openness of the economy, particularly in the case of oil, whose foreign demand may explain the widening of the olive tree's growing area

[31] ANTT, Feitoria de Antuérpia, Livros de Avarias, liv. 1.

(see the section *The main crops*). As for imports, manufactures made up the greatest share.

Considering the sample based on Antwerp, the high weight of re-exports of exotic goods suggests trade balance surpluses, and to some extent the export of services accompanied this expansion of the foreign trade. However, in the middle of the sixteenth century the royal agency in Antwerp was shut down because capital flows annulled the trade surplus that might have been accumulated throughout 1500–1548. In fact, the *feitoria* at Antwerp amassed debts in the amount of 778 million *réis* in 1543 – c. three times the fiscal revenues forecast in the 1519 budget. The interest rates implied in bills of exchange attained 25 and 30 percent and must have been one of the reasons for the financial situation of the royal *feitoria*. Coinciding with the influx of gold from Mina, the royal treasury's short-term debt soared, going from 160 million *réis* in 1534 to 778 million *réis* in 1543 (Pedreira 2007: 61–62). The closure of the agency and subsequent conversion of the king's debts into consolidated debt by issuing perpetual bonds at 5 percent interest were the financial solutions to the problem, which illustrates the Crown's precocious recourse to long-term debt that required creditors' trust on the payment of interest backed up by fiscal revenues.

The shutdown of the agency at Antwerp forced the king to forfeit direct control over the flow of spices to Europe, and to admit a system of wholesale of pepper to international consortia of Germans and Italians at *Casa da Índia* prices. The fate of the *feitoria* at Antwerp does not necessarily describe difficulties involving the entire economy of the kingdom, since it just may reflect the vagaries of a business managed by royal officials. Above all, the fate of the *feitoria* should not ignore the fact that Portugal could countervail capital flows with the selling of shipping services. In fact, the Portuguese merchant marine was quite active, and had already deserved the royal attention.

Legislation of King Manuel made it mandatory in Portuguese ports to give freighting priority to Portuguese ships, resembling William Cromwell's Shipping Acts enacted 150 years later. As a stimulus for the shipbuilding industry, the king granted subsidies for the construction of ships larger than 120 tons (Costa 1997: 31–33). The measures were well received, and there are numerous instances recording the concession of the construction subsidy.

Meanwhile, the burgeoning fleet was threatened by pillage on the seas – from pirates and privateers, which around the middle of the sixteenth century were mainly French. Losses inflicted by corsairs affected the ships and capital of every port in Portugal, but such an order of magnitude was a function of a large freight capacity, an

Table 2.13  *Shipping capacity of England, Dutch Republic and Portugal, 1503–1607 (tons)*

|      | England | Dutch Republic | Portugal |
|------|---------|----------------|----------|
| 1503 |         | 38,000         |          |
| 1530 |         |                | 26,760   |
| 1552 |         |                | 62,305   |
| 1565 |         | 60,000         |          |
| 1572 | 50,000  |                |          |
| 1582 | 67,000  |                | 24,640   |
| 1607 |         | 300,000        | 33,340   |

*Sources:* For England: Davis 1962: 27; Dutch Republic: Van Tielhof and Van Zanden 2009 table I; Portugal: estimation based on Costa 1997, Ferreira 1995 and De Vries 2003.

intuition supported by the assumption that the likelihood of capture depended on a greater number of ships at sea. Indeed, the Portuguese shipping suffered the greatest losses – in terms of the number of victims, volume of lost cargos, and sum of lost capital – in the Flemish routes, which were the most demanding on shipping services. The ports of Minho and the Algarve shared the brunt of losses, with 35 and 27.2 percent of all shipping, respectively, assuring their prevailing involvement in shipping to Antwerp. The coastal strip south of the Mondego River incurred another 27 percent, with Lisbon accounting for most of that figure (Ferreira 1995: 276). As for tonnage shipped, estimates for Antwerp tell us that until 1547 the trend was for increasing volume, rising in ten years from 500 tons to a peak of 2,400 tons, which suggest that the first half of the sixteenth century Portugal's foreign trade boosted seaborne transportation and shipbuilding.

The closure of the *feitoria* at Antwerp must have affected the maritime sectors, since exports of pepper were no longer dealt by the royal agency. But the greatest shock occurred upon the outbreak of war in the Low Countries (1568), when Portugal seems to have lost shipping capacity from then on (Magalhães 1970: 204). Notwithstanding the critical issue of nautical metrology that makes any comparison slippery, numbers point to the loss of Portugal for both England and the United Provinces, whose fleet increased fivefold in half a century, while in 1550 both economies may have had a similar transportation capacity (Table 2.13). From 1570 onwards, registers regarding the port of Antwerp certify that Portuguese ships were excluded from the Flanders route, presumably because the risk

Table 2.14 *Shipbuilding costs according to tonnage, 1510–1604 (*réis *per ton)*

|  | 40–70 tons | 71–100 tons | 101–130 tons | 131–200 tons | 201–300 tons | 301–400 tons | 401–500 tons |
|---|---|---|---|---|---|---|---|
| 1510–1520 | 2,750 |  |  |  | 3,000 |  | 6,000 |
| 1520–1550 | 2,057 | 2,171 | 1,826 | 1,666 |  | 3,779 |  |
| 1580–1604 | 8,000 |  |  | 11,250 | 11,000 | 14,857 | 15,000 |

*Source:* Costa 1997: 176.

soared when hostilities began and Portuguese merchants lacked the scale of business or the international connections that enabled them to contract insurance. Thus, after the outbreak of the war in the Low Countries, French and Dutch flagged ships came to dominate the lanes connecting the kingdom to European ports until then controlled by Portuguese shippers.

The devastating competition in the shipping sector coincided with the rise of shipbuilding costs in Portugal, which suggests that the cost of capital added to the war in Flanders as a factor for the decline of Portuguese shipping in intra-European trade (see Table 2.14). In fact, prices rose for all of the materials and intermediary goods, more than for labor, reflecting the increased cost of every ton built. Moreover, this price hike was greater than that for final consumer goods, demonstrating that rising capital costs impaired the vitality of the sector – undeniably true from roughly 1500 to 1575 (Costa 1997: 184).

In a list dating to 1586, however, Portugal had a merchant marine fleet of considerable standing compared to that of Spain. As Spain's population was *c.* five times larger than Portugal's, the 304 vessels recorded for Portugal next to Spain's 650 discredits the notion that Portugal was a decadent maritime nation (Silva 1867, vol. 3: 529). The growing sugar production in Brazil provided another new stimulus to Portugal's merchant marine, and in 1605 Philip II's government reiterated the spirit of King Manuel's legislation, excluding foreign merchants and ships from direct trade with colonial offshoots in the South Atlantic (Silva 1854–1859, vol. 1: 103–104). In the first decades of the seventeenth century, Brazilian sugar production demanded around 12,000 tons of shipping (Costa 2002b, vol. 1: 203). In spite of the intervention of northwestern fleets in particular periods (Boxer 1957), the second stage of the Atlantic empire, based on Brazil's growth, was assisted by Portuguese merchants financing shipping and Portuguese shippers buying foreign ships. Trade barriers enforced by protectionist legislation thus led the Portuguese merchant marine to concentrate on colonial trade circuits, which simultaneously opened the routes between Portugal and Europe to the fleets with foreign flags. The intercontinental dimension of the Portuguese economy put pressure on the domestic demand for transportation while mitigating the exposure of the sector to the competition of European fleets. Such protectionism required the enforcement of the *entrepôt* trade, which had fiscal consequences since the Crown's financial resources relied heavily on customs duties. Hence, besides widening the range of goods and services Portugal exported, the empire shaped the fiscal history of the kingdom. This meant that the Crown attained new resources for furthering political centralization without defying the power assigned to other social bodies, namely the nobility, the Church, and the urban elites, represented in municipal councils.

## State building

The first decades of the sixteenth century witnessed a few changes in the financial administration and in the structure of the Crown's revenues. First of all, a set of reforms were put in place, which aimed to standardize the array of seigneurial dues collected across the kingdom rather than achieve political centralization. It ended up producing long-term effects that go beyond the short period examined in this brief section, lasting until the liberal revolutions of the nineteenth century (Ramos, Sousa, and Monteiro 2009: 227–228).

King Manuel completed a vast reform of the charters that had been granted to the municipalities (*cartas de foral* or *forais*), since the eleventh and twelfth century (see Chapter 1). Upon careful revision in the king's court, the statements of the specific rights and privileges regarding local government were cleared from all the charters. Those statements had become redundant since the codification of the Portuguese law in the so-called *Ordenações Afonsinas* in 1446. As a result, the revised charters were mainly an updated list of "royal rights," i.e., land rents and seigneurial dues owed, in recognition of lordship, to the Crown or to its grantees (*donatários*), whenever the king chose to devolve his jurisdictional rights. It is certain that the prevailing idea on the reformed *forais* (1497–1520) was one of diversity, reflected in the nature, typology of the rights covered, and in the fiscal burden gauged by its share on the gross agricultural output (Monteiro 2005a: 70). In any event, the reform had a long-lasting effect. Once defined, the "royal rights" stated in the reformed *forais* crystallized in the form and under the terms set out during the reign of Manuel I, inhibiting the grantees (members of the nobility or

Church institutions) from arbitrarily rising the burden of rents and seigneurial dues. Thus, this reform follows the track of the Crown's interventions to control and check the fiscal prerogatives of competing powers (Hespanha 1994: 141).

At the same time, the central institutions were given additional power to overview the local financial government. On the one hand, in 1516, the so-called *Regimento da Fazenda*, put in place a new set of procedures for the *almoxarifes* and *contadores*. On the other hand, the two governing bodies of the financial organization at the central level underwent successive reformulations, becoming more complex. First, the active administration of the Treasury by the earlier *vedor da Fazenda* was divided among three of these magistrates. Second, the general accounting office (*Casa dos Contos do Reino e Casa*) underwent wide-reaching reforms designed to strengthen its accounting techniques and redefine its place within the organizational framework. By 1514 this office controlled the thirteen fiscal districts into which the kingdom was divided (*contadorias*) and the human resources allocated to its service grew in number.[32] The king's intention was to achieve a greater degree of scrutiny over the fiscal organization that had grown since medieval times and had raised monitoring costs. Finally, in 1560, the *Casa dos Contos do Reino e Casa* absorbed the smaller body of the *Casa dos Contos de Lisboa* and became a full-fledged chamber of accounts.

During the Iberian Union, this functional structure was not called into question, even though some further alterations occurred. The most important one was the creation in 1591 of the *Conselho da Fazenda* (Treasury Council), which absorbed the three preexisting *vedores da fazenda*. Its main responsibilities were the coordination and supervision of the Treasury and to this end the *Conselho da Fazenda* was placed at the top of the financial organization, ranging from the local treasurers to the customs houses, the *Casa da Índia* and the *Casa da Moeda*.[33]

Despite these early attempts of centralization, the administrative system remained decentralized, a common feature of the financial government of the European monarchies throughout the early modern period. The local treasurers (*almoxarifes*) were key to this system considering that they collected taxes and made the necessary disbursements. This structure ultimately fragmented the Crown's overall income into multiple small local surpluses, which did not always flow to the central coffers. This decentralized model of organization was transferred to the empire. Whether in the Portuguese archipelagos, in Portuguese America, or in Portuguese Asia,

---

[32] Hespanha 1994: 213; Rau 1951a: 26–30.
[33] Hespanha 1994: 236–238; Subtil 1993: 171–172.

the administrative extensions set up for financial government were based on a network of local administrators.

In the case of Portuguese Asia, the political submission of a handful of fortresses and territories enabled the integration of the native taxation systems, resulting from the replacement of the previously existing Asian rulers by Portugal's rule. By the mid 1500s, the king of Portugal was able to use taxation as a source of revenue that allowed for the self-sustainability of the *Estado da Índia* (Miranda 2009: 3). Varied in nature, revenues derived from land rents in those cases where territories had been integrated into the empire (e.g., Island of Goa, Salcete, Bardez, Bassein, and Daman), but mainly from customs duties levied on intra-Asian trade. From 1581 to 1620, *c.* 60 percent of the total revenue of the *Estado da Índia* derived from customs duties, while landed income accounted for 16–25 percent (Miranda 2011: 111). The revenues were spent locally on maintaining the administrative, ecclesiastic, military, and naval organization that sustained Portuguese Asia. Thus, the fiscal resources collected in the *Estado da Índia* were not supposed to flow back to the mother country. Moreover, if capital was yearly transferred to the *Estado da Índia*, it was mainly intended for the acquisition of the cargos, which shows that the financial flows of the *Carreira da Índia* and the fiscal resources that sustained the *Estado* were administratively separated. A similar self-financing system was also implemented in the Atlantic Islands and in Brazil, although revenues derived from taxation were shared with other social and political bodies. Given the fact that those territories were uninhabited or sparsely populated, the king resorted to the medieval tradition of granting lordships (*senhorios*) to promote settlement. As such, the grantees received a large portion of royal jurisdiction over a given territory (*capitania*) and acted thereafter as captains and governors (*capitães-donatários*). In exchange for promoting the settlement, the captains were given the right to levy seigneurial dues, such as the right to license mills for grinding cane, which was in fact a banal right. Other resources of the captains included the *redízima*, a tenth of all royal revenues, which comprised custom duties, the monopoly of the dyewood trade and the tithe due to the Order of Christ, managed by the Portuguese Crown since 1495. Following the same practices prevailing in the mother country, the king's revenues thus raised in Brazil were earmarked to finance local expenditures.

The financial organization of the empire did not call for the routine transfer of tax revenues to central bodies, but it is certain that there were occasional exceptions to this rule. Cash transfers in the form of bills of exchange are recorded coming from Madeira in the years 1581–1586 (Miranda 1994: 181). It is equally true that the cost of sustaining the

Table 2.15 *Revenues of the Crown, 1506–1607 (million* réis*)*

| | 1506 | 1519 | 1527 | 1534 | 1557 | 1588 | 1607 |
|---|---|---|---|---|---|---|---|
| KINGDOM | 74.8 | 111.7 | 131.3 | 153.7 | 288.8 | 421.0 | 460.8 |
| *Almoxarifados* | 65.7 | 96.1 | 84.0 | | 190.5 | 198.2 | 198.3 |
| Customs-houses | | | 5.7 | | | 125.0 | 186.5 |
| Customs-houses (Lisbon) | 9.1 | 15.7 | 41.6 | | 98.3 | 97.8 | 76.0 |
| EMPIRE | 104.1 | 164.6 | na | 284.8 | na | 347.0 | 521.0 |
| Cape Route | 51.3 | 117.6 | na | 252.0 | na | 245.0 | 397.5 |
| Guiné, Cape Verde, Mina | 50.9 | 47.0 | na | 24.8 | na | 56.4 | 27.0 |
| Angola | | | na | | na | 11.0 | 21.0 |
| São Tomé | | | 6.0 | 8.0 | na | 7.8 | 9.5 |
| *Dyewood* | 1.9 | na | na | | na | 13.6 | 24.0 |
| TOTAL | 178.9 | 276.3 | na | 438.5 | na | 754.8 | 939.8 |

*Sources:* Pedreira 2007; *Coleção de São Lourenço*, vol. 1; Pereira J. C. 2003; *Gavetas da Torre do Tombo*, vol. I, 891–894; BNL, cód. 637, 17 v.° and 24; Falcão 1859.

empire did not rely entirely on local revenues. During the Iberian Union, as the military expenses increased with the Dutch and English military pressure on Portugal's possessions, the Crown resorted to forced loans and extraordinary taxes in the kingdom to pay for the defense of the *Estado da Índia* and Brazil (Pedreira 2007: 59–61).

The fiscal role of the empire was mainly based on its contribution to customs duties, which justified the reinforcement of the *entrepôt* trade. It also contributed to the royal treasury through the king's rights of monopoly over the distribution of certain goods, thereby creating property rights that could be traded with other social bodies by means of a contract. This is what happened with the gold from Mina, the pepper, the slave trade, and the *pau-brasil* (dyewood). In addition, the empire drove the opening of the economy by enlarging the range of goods Portugal exchanged with other European powers. In this regard, the Crown's revenues mirror the intensification of external exchanges and how they fostered both the domestic economy and a change in its fiscal structure (Table 2.15).

The empire supplied revenues encompassed under the category "Empire (total)." It gathers monopoly rights over slaves, gold, dyewood, and pepper, and taxes levied on private cargo collected at the *Casa da Índia* (Table 2.15). The category "kingdom" comprises the excise, land rents, and royal rights collected by the *almoxarifados*, and customs duties. These categories of revenues are assumed to reflect the evolution of the

Table 2.16 *Revenues of the Crown, 1506–1607 (growth rates, percent)*

|          | 1506–1519 | 1519–1534 | 1534–1557 | 1557–1588 | 1588–1607 |
|----------|-----------|-----------|-----------|-----------|-----------|
| Kingdom  | 3.1       | 2.2       | 5.0       | 1.9       | 0.5       |
| Empire   | 3.6       | 3.7       |           | 0.3       | 2.2       |
| Total    | 3.4       | 3.1       |           | 1.0       | 1.2       |

*Source:* Table 2.15.

domestic economy under the stimuli of the empire. A comparison of the growth rate of these two categories (kingdom and empire) is provided in Table 2.16, which completes the information in Table 2.15. Revenues varied above 3 percent per year in the first half of the sixteenth century mostly thanks to amounts derived from the empire. Although their pace slowed down, revenues kept increasing in the second half of the century, but data show a turning point during the decades 1534–1557 marked by an exceptional growth of domestic taxes. A sharp rise of customs collected in Lisbon (see Table 2.15) occurred in the first half of the sixteenth century, contributing heavily to the growth of the kingdom's overall revenues.

Even the regions less influenced by the upturn in seaborne activities were assisted by the rising weight of monies from the *almoxarifados*. In fact, a detailed observation of the contribution of each *almoxarifado* discloses that fiscal revenues in the regions of Trás-os-Montes and Beira grew faster than that of Minho. Data on the *comarca* of Estremadura display an average (non-accumulated) growth of 118 percent, followed closely by the Alentejo, with 107 percent (Pereira J. C. 2003: 148). It is probable that population growth and its repercussions on transactions, worked in tandem to drive the kingdom's tax collection to higher levels.

This vitality is harder to find after 1588, and from then until 1607 the data tell us a somewhat different story. Comparing the variations of revenues from the kingdom to those of the empire, we now find rates of 0.5 against 2.2 percent. More importantly, the contribution of the *almoxarifados* flattened out, and customs revenue from Lisbon fell. The 0.5 percent growth of domestic taxes derived from the relative stability of the amounts collected by the *almoxarifados*, in the aftermath of the institutional arrangements that altered the execution of the *sisa*. This arrangement brought about a new relationship between the Crown and the municipalities (Hespanha 1994: 123). The so-called *encabeçamento* (contracted lump-sum) that became common from the mid 1560s onwards shifted the accountability of the tax collection to the *concelhos* (municipalities). It stipulated the payment of a fixed sum (*cabeção*) to the Crown assigned to each *concelho*, with the exception of the city of Lisbon, where the collection of the *sisa* remained under the direct control of the king. With the *encabeçamento* in place, one of two things would occur. If the tax actually collected fell short of the fixed sum, the shortfall had to be made up through a surtax levied at the local level, usually on wealth, which occurred, for instance, in Coimbra in the early 1600s (Oliveira 1971–1972, vol. 1: 307); but, if the tax actually collected exceeded the predefined amount, the municipal council was free to keep the surplus. This system admitted a possible gap between real economic growth and the revenues raised through this tax. The rigidity of revenue implied in this new arrangement showed up already in the budgets for the years 1588 and 1607 and definitively shaped the structure of the State's emerging fiscal system, turning it increasingly sensitive to the economic dynamic of the empire.

Two factors stand out as causes for the strong growth of income depending on the empire between 1588 and 1607: the customs duties collected at *Casa da Índia* and the monopoly of the slave trade of Angola, whose contract was awarded to private merchants (Table 2.15). These two showed higher growth rates than those of the customs houses – excluding Lisbon's. Revenues from Angola almost doubled during the first forty years of the Iberian Union (i.e., 1580–1620) while the *Casa da Índia* retained its financial contribution, due to the change in the structure of cargos. If total nominal income grew between 1588 and 1607, it was undoubtedly due to the uptick in the overseas activities. The flattening of the domestic income compared with the variation of the revenues from the imperial monopolies supports the view commonly held by historians about the political and institutional consequences of the expansion overseas. It is supposed to have enforced the exploitation of royal property rights over a few traded goods, which ultimately strengthened the features of a "domain state" and postponed the transition to a "fiscal state." Moreover, it allowed the Crown to keep redistributing wealth among the nobility and to rule according to the principles of a gift economy. This capacity was even enlarged when King João III was granted perpetual control over the masterships of the three military orders – Christ, Avis, and Santiago in 1551. The ensuing incorporation of *c.* 600 commanderies (*comendas*), made up of tithes, land rents, and seigneurial dues afforded the Crown with additional resources to reward military and administrative services.[34] To sum up, a new balance of power involving the monarchy, the nobility, the Church, and the municipalities counted on the riches provided by the empire and on a fiscal system that

[34] Olival 2001 and 2004; Monteiro 2007b: 257.

transferred to the municipalities the accountability of tax collection in the kingdom. This fiscal balance prevailed during the first decades of the Iberian Union, but was challenged after the 1620s when military pressure demanded much higher levels of tax income.

## The Iberian Union

In 1581 Philip II of Spain was acclaimed as Philip I of Portugal, whereby the crisis of dynastic succession ended after three years of uncertainty caused by the death of the childless king Sebastião in Al-Ksar al-Kibir. For the next sixty years Portugal and the Spanish Habsburgs had intertwined successes. Notwithstanding the Spanish victory in the Battle of Alcântara, the new king did not proceed to incorporate Portugal into Castile by reason of conquest. Fully aware of anti-Castilian sentiments among the Portuguese, Philip II sought to achieve an integration based upon a political negotiation held at the *Cortes* of Tomar. The assembly of the three estates – nobility, clergy, and the people – met for this purpose in April 1581 and by virtue of the pact agreed upon there, the kingdom of Portugal retained its legal system and its administrative and institutional autonomy. At the same time the rights and privileges of the nobility and urban elites were recognized, and even strengthened.[35]

The conditions sworn at Tomar laid down a union of crowns. The offices of the royal administration in Portugal and its empire were to be reserved exclusively to the Portuguese and the political and administrative framework of the territories overseas was to be maintained in its current form. In other words, despite the union of the crowns nothing changed legally, which meant that the monopolies of trade and navigation with and within the colonial dominions were to be exploited exclusively by the Portuguese subjects.

As a result of the Iberian Union, however, Portugal was thrust into a new position in Europe. Prior to 1580 the kingdom had been able to keep to the sidelines in the northern and central European conflicts that came after the Protestant Reformation. Also, through adroit diplomacy the kingdom's overseas domains had been spared any serious threats. With the Habsburg rule, Portugal was eventually dragged into the multiple fronts of war in which the Spanish Habsburgs were embroiled. Inevitably, the war took its toll on Portugal in many ways. These included tax pressures and recruitment of soldiers sent to the battle fronts of Flanders, mostly after 1624 due to the Union of Arms enacted by the *valido* of King Philip IV, the count duke of Olivares.

[35] Bouza-Álvarez 2008; Schaub 2001.

But already in the first years of the 1600s, Dutch, English, and to a lesser degree French forces had targeted Portugal's possessions overseas. In light of these circumstances, history handbooks of the nineteenth and early twentieth centuries judged the sixty years of the Iberian Union as detrimental. Examples of "decadence" were taken from the *Carreira da Índia* and the *Estado da Índia*. Admittedly, the crisis was already unfolding as early as 1570, but it accelerated in the late 1580s with the arrival of Dutch and English warships in the Indian Ocean – ending Portugal's hegemony over the Cape route (Peres 1933).

Portugal's entanglement with Europe's politics and warfare brought on undeniable military hardships, but not even this involvement can be seen entirely in a negative light. The interpretation of the period of Iberian Union as a gloomy phase of Portugal's history is countered by scholarly work that has stressed many signs of economic vitality. In Brazil, the expanding Portuguese interests and territorial control reached as far as Pará to the north, and the colony was effectively defended from French threats in Maranhão (Magalhães 1998b). The South Atlantic economy developed further in the last quarter of the sixteenth century driven by the sugar industry.[36] Portugal's situation in Asia changed too. Examples include extending the influence beyond Ceylon (Sri Lanka) and the retreat of the Crown's direct exploitation of the intra-Asian trade routes in favor of private enterprise (Subrahmanyam 1993). At the same time, new means of exploiting the *Carreira da Índia* since the 1600s enhanced the role of non-monopolized cargos, such as cotton textiles, ensuring rewarding rates of return to capital invested for two more decades. Therefore, the notion of a general decay seems to be inappropriate, even if the kingdom had to bear the rising costs of defending its distant colonial offshoots.

Eventually, the changes in the balance of interests in Portugal within the Iberian Union would be linked to the international conflict that pitted the Spanish Habsburg kings against the rising maritime powers (primarily the United Provinces and England, and up to a certain point, France). By virtue of its aggregation to Spain, Portugal was drawn into struggles in Europe with repercussions on its possessions in Africa, Asia, and the New World. However, the economic integration of the two Iberian Crowns and their respective empires was also on Portugal's interests, so that the advantages of broadening the scope of businesses in American territories prevailed over the tensions that would arise after the 1620s, which prepared the conditions for the restoration of political autonomy (Godinho 1978b: 381–421).

---

[36] The notion of a colonial prosperity under the Iberian Union was first put forward by Cortesão 1940b.

At the onset of the Iberian Union, the empire's economic potential was rooted in the Asian trade and in customs duties deriving from the sugar industry that was just being set up in Portuguese America. The spread of sugar mills in the largest-producing captaincies (Pernambuco and Bahia) is mirrored in a fast expansion of production between 1570 and 1585. From 1600 to 1610 sugar mills churned out c. 735,000 arrobas per year. The output kept rising during the next decade and in 1625 stood at around 900,000 arrobas per year (Schwartz 1985: 145, 150). The Atlantic trade also comprised the traffic of slaves who would work the cane fields and operate the mills. When Portugal gained its foothold in Luanda (1575) the kingdom's presence on both sides of the South Atlantic was established, providing the basis for its trade networks woven by sugar and slave flows (Ferlini 1988). By the end of the sixteenth century, while the empire's center of gravity was still in Asia, a second phase of the Atlantic system was emerging, and it held out the promise of boosting the income of the king and private interests alike. The rising South Atlantic trade provided an additional source of fiscal revenues through custom duties from the 1580s onwards.

The rising revenues coming from custom duties demonstrate the limited impact of repeated embargos on trade between the United Provinces and the Iberian kingdoms, within a conflict that employed tactics of economic warfare. In this confrontation the States-General prohibited trade with Spain and Portugal in 1581 and 1582, to which the Spanish kings retaliated in 1585, 1595, 1598, and 1605.[37] Unquestionably, these embargos – always accompanied by threats of confiscation of ships – interrupted trade relations, but the effects were far from long lasting. One of the longest interruptions (1585–1588) was soon compensated for by a surge of commercial contacts in the 1590s, when the embargo was lifted by Philip II in response to a prolonged grain shortage.

As these trade links were mutually critical, the embargos had adverse effects for both economies caught up in the conflict. If the supply of grain was indispensable to the Portuguese coastal towns, the salt from Setúbal was equally vital to the Dutch herring industry and to the markets in the Baltic, the supply of which would need to be shipped by Dutch vessels. The coming and going of ships in the ports of Setúbal and Aveiro attests to this interdependence of salt and grain circuits that went into place in the sixteenth century. Ships left the Low Countries, called at ports in the Baltic, and then sailed on to Portugal with silver, and in ballast or with grain, to exchange for salt destined for the Dutch fisheries or for sale in the Baltic (Rau 1984: 150–151).

[37] Van Veen 2000: 129, contrary to Israel 1989.

Due to this interdependence, the embargos of 1595 and 1598 were only partially effective, and could not long disrupt the connection between Amsterdam and Setúbal (Antunes 2008). In the same way, the expulsion of Dutch merchants from Portuguese ports decreed in 1605 did not interrupt trade with the United Provinces. Even when, later on, the Dutch merchant community in Lisbon was dismantled, the vacuum in its wake was soon filled with Portuguese merchants' connections with the Jewish community in Amsterdam.[38] In fact, business was sufficiently attractive to the agents involved, whether Portuguese or Dutch, that the official prohibitions were routinely circumvented. The Dutch needed the intermediate role of Baltic goods in order to trade with the Mediterranean, and the Portuguese could not get by without the wheat imports. About 3,000 ships loaded with wheat arrived every year in Lisbon, according to a description dating to 1608.[39] The estimate is perhaps exaggerated, but it emphasizes the role of trade routes from north-central Europe tracing the crucial maritime lanes of early modern Europe. Salt, sugar, as well as pepper, were bartered for cereals from Poland shipped out of Danzig. These were essential products that were carried on these trade routes, which, at least until the early 1590s, also connected Portugal with the ports of Holland and Zeeland.

The Twelve Years' Truce (1609–1621) between Spain and the United Provinces breathed new life into these trade links, drawing in Portugal's three main ports for traffic to and from Brazil: Lisbon, the kingdom's largest port, followed by Porto and Viana do Castelo, other nodes of articulation between Brazil and Europe's marketplaces (Oliveira 1990: 68–69). Viana do Castelo enjoyed great prosperity in the Union's first forty years, thanks to direct connections to Brazil. It was served by a fleet of *c*. 70 ships from 1619 to 1629 and acted as a port in the network of merchants living in Lisbon.[40] The upsurge of sugar planting in Brazil and of slave traffic not only boosted Portugal's homeland port activity, but also promoted some specialization among the most active ports, primarily that of Vila do Conde, whose shipping was especially leveraged by the demand for the slaves in Spanish America, while other ports addressed the sugar shipping demand, as was the case with Viana do Castelo.[41] Any of these trades positively impacted on the United Provinces too. The Republic was able to acquire at least half of Brazil's sugar, and consequently refineries multiplied in Amsterdam. With three units operating in 1594, twenty-five years later there were twenty-five in production (De Vries and Woude 1997: 397).

[38] Van Veen 2000: 134; Ebert 2008: 61–84.    [39] *Do Sítio de Lisboa*: 207.
[40] Costa 2002a: 47; Moreira 1990.    [41] Moreira 1990; Polónia 2007.

Not even the slide in sugar prices, which began to dip in 1612, was enough to deter the trade with the United Provinces. The Brazilian sugar industry entered into hard times in that year, hitting the producers and the merchants with ever-shrinking markups. Prices fell in Europe, but not in the colony. The declining trend worsened in 1618, with the start of the Thirty Years' War and the resulting contraction of Central European markets.[42] Yet, the Dutch ships continued to call on Iberian ports, notably Lisbon, apparently undaunted by the deteriorating economic backdrop. It was only in 1621, with the renewal of hostilities between Spain and the United Provinces and another embargo on Dutch shipping (this time with more concerted efforts toward enforcement), that Portugal's inclusion in the European trade routes was genuinely threatened.

Portugal's economic integration in the trans-Atlantic trade was thus advanced as a result of the Iberian Union, a time that ushered in new opportunities for Portuguese merchants in business undertakings in Spanish America, and even in the Iberian Peninsula. Although the original spirit of the union called for the overseas domains to remain separate, their operation under a single monarch favored a temporary suspension of the boundaries between the Portuguese and Spanish spheres of influence established by the Treaty of Tordesillas (1494). If prior to the Iberian Union there were Portuguese merchants who encroached on the trade networks of Spain's kingdom and empire, after 1580 this encroachment became even more intense (Godinho 1978a: 264–265).

As a result of its dominant position as supplier of slaves from the Guinea coast and Angola, Portuguese merchants were able to step into the markets of Castile's West Indies. This was achieved by the establishment of contracts, the so-called *asientos*, between the Habsburg kings and a set of traders (*asientistas*), which granted them the exclusive right to supply slaves to the Spanish possessions in the New World. But Portugal's slaving activity was not limited to just the number of slaves sold. Portuguese vessels also dominated the shipping routes that carried them across the Atlantic. Capital that underwrote and lubricated the links between Lisbon, Seville, the slaving posts in Africa, and the ports in Spanish America was Portuguese too.[43] A clearly complementary relationship emerged in the economies of both Iberian kingdoms that involved slaves and silver, and that benefitted all of the stakeholders, i.e., private investors and the royal treasuries of both Castile and

---

[42] For this crisis, see Kindleberger 1991. For the sugar shipping and trade in Portugal, see Costa 2002b, vol. 1: 243–246.

[43] Costa 2002a: 50; Mauro 1983: 178–183.

Portugal. However, Portugal's meddling in the affairs of Spain's empire – which peaked in the 1620s – caused some discontent in the merchant community of Seville, revealing that in their eyes, Portugal's merchants were on the receiving end of too much American silver. Overall, from 1580 to 1620 the Iberian Union witnessed rewarding interactions with the Spanish empire in which there was, apparently, a greater amount of Portuguese encroachment into Castile's exclusive affairs than the other way around. Even the Canary Islands gained a spot on the trade route as a loading stop for wine on its way to Brazil. Madeira switched over to a new economic specialization in which sugar gave way to wine production, but the Canaries seem to have benefitted more than Madeira as suppliers of wine to the westbound Atlantic trade.[44]

The Iberian Union encouraged migration flows, principally to Castile, where both Seville and Madrid harbored large communities of Portuguese. This emigration was justified by the economic opportunities existing in those urban centers, but was also due in part to the persecutions of the Inquisition. The exodus of "new Christian" (Jewish) merchants from the Algarve certainly reflects the Church's repression in this regard (Magalhães 1988: 365). Once settled in Madrid, many of the approximately 2,000 Portuguese residing there were active in the Spanish *Carrera de Indias* trade, accounting for a fifth of its total business volume – not even counting the traffic in contraband and slaves (Boyajian 1983: 43–44). The second-place destination of emigrants was the Spanish dominions in the New World, continuing a trend that had begun earlier, but which accelerated during the Iberian Union. Coming from Seville and even from Bahia and Pernambuco, many Portuguese headed for places like Cuzco, Lima, Cartagena of the Indies, Acapulco, and Buenos Aires. Their residency and activity in these Spanish-held cities bolstered the economic fusion of the two Iberian Americas, and is reflected in the popularity of the *peruleiros*, merchants, and fortune seekers of Portuguese origins with business dealings in southern Peru. Here they sought the silver of Potosí, vital for sustaining the economic transactions in Portuguese America.

From the late sixteenth century on, despite the king's decrees, the illegal trade between Buenos Aires and Rio de Janeiro grew particularly intense. The contraband traffic included slaves and sugar, bartered for considerable quantities of silver, which displayed the economic connections between the Rio de la Plata basin and Rio de Janeiro.[45] In this case, the interactions with the Spanish empire ran against the interests of the

---

[44] Costa 2002b, vol.1: 276–285; Mauro 1983.
[45] Alencastro 2000; Canabrava 1984; Moutoukias 1988.

Habsburg kings, but other examples can be cited that reveal a convergence of interests regarding Brazil, which would work to the benefit of the Portuguese Crown. It is enough to recall the conquest of Paraíba in 1585, involving a joint Luso-Castilian armada, or even the expulsion of the French from Maranhão, where the local elites' interests were aligned with the imperial strategy of the Spanish Habsburgs (Marques 2002: 22–24).

Although the overall picture of the union of kingdoms points to Portugal's benefits, there were problems too, notably in the European war that played out in the Americas, which generated rising costs for Portugal protecting its empire. In the Atlantic, from 1598 on, the Dutch undertook a series of expeditions retaliating for the embargo. The isle of São Tomé was conquered in this year, but soon lost, while an armada caused panic in Salvador of Bahia, attacking and capturing Portuguese vessels. In 1604 a new Dutch fleet crossed the Atlantic with the same designs but still without the intention of replacing the Iberian trade routes (Emmer 2003: 8, 13). The outlet for Brazilian sugar thus remained essentially undisrupted, and the re-exports of this good remained in the hands of Lisbon merchants, in a forwarding network to Portuguese merchants in Amsterdam (Strum 2013). Dutch vessels (about twenty per year in the 1610s) regularly visited the west coast of Africa in search of gold and ivory, but Portugal lost none of its possessions there.[46]

In the Indian Ocean the Dutch incursions met with more success. There the Dutch East India Company (*Vereenigde Oost-Indische Compagnie* – VOC), established in 1602, served as the commercial weapon of the States-General in its fight against the Spanish monarchy. The seventy-six ships sailing from Holland to Asia between 1602 and 1610 grew to 117 over the next decade, a clear exhibition of the VOC's naval and military might in Asia (Veen 2000: 408). Around 1610, the Dutch company had already put an end to Portugal's pepper monopoly due to its rapid advances in Southeast Asia, which had proceeded despite the Twelve Years' Truce (Costa 2002a: 28). In 1605, the Portuguese lost Ambon to the VOC and, in the following years, attacks and sieges disrupted links with Malacca, Mozambique, and Goa.

Fierce competition from the Dutch took a toll both on the Portuguese monopoly of the Cape Route and on the *Estado da Índia*'s expenditures. Still, for the years before 1620, the effects of the Dutch offensive should not be overestimated. Losses on the Cape Route were actually driven by storms, forced port stops, and shipwreck rather than by Dutch privateering, per se (Murteira 2010: 496). The externalities of these losses are not to be

[46] De Vries and Woude 1997: 397; Emmer 2003: 7.

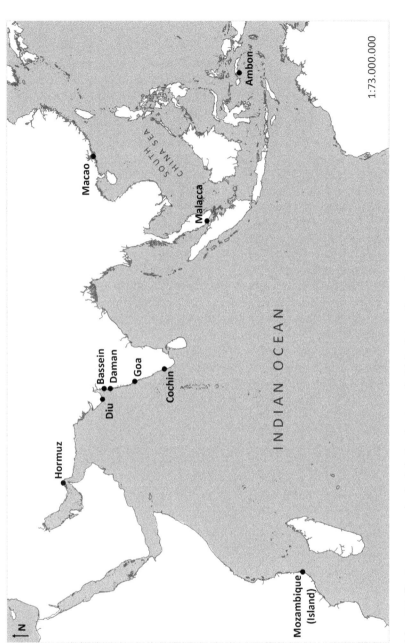

Map 2.4 Portuguese empire in Asia (main strongholds), sixteenth century

disregarded, of course, as the increasing risk underpinned the changes of the structure of cargos, as described earlier, and forced the strengthening of the military protection of the fleets. This, in turn, prompted the occasional search for extraordinary revenues, such as in 1614 when the king borrowed money from the *Câmara de Lisboa* (Lisbon city council) (Santos 2006: 84). As for the *Estado da Índia*, if the local military expenditures rose steeply as attacks on ships and trading posts increased, the Portuguese monopoly over intra-Asian sea routes was not seriously challenged before the 1620s. As such, indirect taxes, derived from custom duties collected at port cities such as Goa, Diu, Hormuz, and Malacca, continued to feed the coffers of the *Estado da Índia* (Map 2.4).

The most recent research on trade and shipping in the Atlantic front of the Portuguese empire has followed the rich and yet not fully explored insights of the classic Portuguese historiography. The work of Jaime Cortesão, dated back to the 1940s, acknowledged the Iberian Union as a period that embraced promising deeds until the 1620s. The resuming war of the Habsburg monarchy with the United Provinces and the outbreak of the Thirty Years' War offer a precise time benchmark to a European crisis, which also affected the Portuguese economic backdrop. The renewal of hostilities plunged international trade into recession, and soon thereafter, the costs of military power threatened the political union of the Iberian kingdoms. The new state of international affairs derailed Portugal's productive activities and the tax base's ability to pay for the rising fiscal demand. Therefore, the last two decades of the Union faced a number of tensions, and the fiscal situation was as good a pretext as any to call for the restoration of political autonomy.

# 3   War and recovery, 1620–1703

From 1620 onwards in the Iberian Peninsula, like elsewhere around the Mediterranean, the flattening out of the demographic trend indicates that the long sixteenth century of prosperity had come to an end (Parker and Smith 1978). Somewhat differently, in Europe's northwest the slowdown of population growth occurred only after 1650 and did not prevent this region from keeping its path toward financial, industrial, and commercial leadership.[1] The shift of the economic core from Mediterranean borders to the northwestern Atlantic shores occurred within two military benchmarks that challenged the Habsburgs' hegemony (Braudel 1966). The first refers to the Thirty Years' War (1618–1648), a series of conflicts that began as a religious war in the Holy Roman Empire, but gradually widened, involving several European states. This protracted hostility coincided with the struggle for independence in the northern Low Countries, and as it happened, with the outbreak of the revolution in Catalonia and the Portuguese Restoration, which revealed the multiple, internal and external, tensions the Spanish monarchy faced thereupon. The second conflict that also gained European scope was the War of the Spanish Succession (1702–1714), a dispute for the throne between the French Bourbons and the Austrian Habsburgs. Each of these wars established political alliances drawn in the treaties of Westphalia (1648) and of Utrecht (1715), framing an international order dependent on the military might of the northwestern European states.

The political motivations of various European powers fostered institutional changes inherent in the rise of military expenditure which became the main justification for raising funds, either by public borrowing or by increased taxation. Thus, military concerns exposed the financial constraints of the traditional "domain state," which drew income from royal property rights claimed over different types of assets and paved the way to the making of the fiscal state.[2] Besides fiscal innovations, this institutional

---

[1] Braudel 1982–1984, vol. 3; De Vries 2009: 156–157.
[2] Bonney 1995, 1999; Bonney and Ormrod 1999; Bordo and Cortés Conde 1993; Brewer 1989; 'T Hart 1993; Yun-Casalilla and O'Brien 2012.

watershed comprised import-substitution policies, and all sorts of economic policies directed to strengthen the national state usually denoted in
scholarship as the era of "mercantilism."

Portugal was an active player in this backdrop that ascribed a different
economic role to the state. The kingdom's political independence was
reaffirmed in 1640, though it required a twenty-eight-year war against
Spain (1640–1668) as well as an increasing tax burden that underpinned
noteworthy steps toward the making of a fiscal state. It was also the
Restoration War that steered Portugal's alliance with England through
treaties signed in 1654 and 1661, later reiterated by means of a new
agreement that comprised commercial clauses (the Methuen Treaty
(1703). The history of the Anglo-Portuguese alliance gives evidence of
Portugal's need of external military protection, particularly at sea, which
England was able to provide thereafter. However, the new ally was also
setting up an efficient exploitation of colonies in America thereby putting
Portugal's position in the market for selling sugar and tobacco under
fierce competition. The kingdom's trade deficits caught the attention of
policy makers at the court of King Pedro II (1683–1706), who recognized
the advantages of import-substitution policies, reproducing in Portugal
a few of Jean-Baptiste Colbert's reforms. For these reasons, the war of
independence should be considered a milestone of Portugal's economic
and political history.

Fiscal issues seem to have been a main cause of social unrest that led to
the recovery of political autonomy attained through a *coup d'état* in 1640,
whereas the war against Spain that lasted until 1668 must have hindered
output growth. Once the peace was signed, trends in population and
agricultural output showed signs of recovery, but international trade did
not undergo a similar tendency. Thus, by the end of the seventeenth
century, the state's financial resources came under pressure, which
encouraged the quest for precious metals in colonial Brazil.

### War, taxes, and rebellion

The end of the Twelve Years' Truce between Spain and the Dutch
Republic in 1621 was accompanied by a severe downturn in foreign
trade, plummeting prices of colonial commodities, and contracting markets associated with the outbreak of the Thirty Years' War.[3] The warfare
affected the Portuguese economy in several ways, first of all through its
maritime trade and shipping. The embargo on trade with the United
Provinces, decreed early in 1621, and the kingdom's port-controls over

[3] Kindleberger 1991; Romano 1962.

commodities from and to enemy territories were now effectively enforced, due to an entirely new administration (*Almirantado*) imposed by the count-duke of Olivares, the favorite minister of King Philip IV (Elliott 1991: 175). Dutch shipping to Portugal fell off dramatically, hitting Lisbon hardest of all, while Faro and Setúbal suffered considerable decline in the number of ships calling for these ports. In Viana do Castelo, the fall of sugar imports compounded the embargo's effect and caused a reduction of its commercial fleet.[4] Thus a crisis in the *entrepôt* trade of sugar constrained the activity of secondary ports, such as Viana do Castelo or Vila do Conde from 1620 on (Polónia 2007). Revenues from customs duties dropped with these developments.[5]

Adverse effects of the international scenario were not confined to the distribution of colonial products. Regarding the export of domestic commodities, the sale of salt traditionally exported to the United Provinces was hit hard, and shipping between the main ports, like Aveiro, Setúbal, and Amsterdam, fell into a recession that lasted until the Restoration (Antunes 2008: 166). The dwindling port activity coincided with rising costs of maintaining the empire on several fronts. The Dutch West India Company (WIC), chartered in 1621, challenged Portugal's position in the Atlantic. The Company began operations in 1624 and in that same year seized Salvador da Bahia, the seat of colonial government. The fall of Bahia received full attention of the Spanish king, who dispatched a Luso-Spanish armada in the following year that recaptured the city.[6] The success of this joint military expedition was not to be repeated when the Dutch subsequently seized Olinda (1630). A second Luso-Spanish fleet set sail from Lisbon in 1631, but did not dislodge the Dutch, who thereafter sought to strengthen their position in Brazil's northeast. The conquest of Paraíba, in 1634, granted them full control of the main sugar-producing region. In 1635 and 1639, two further Luso-Spanish attempts to wrest the Dutch from Brazil failed and contributed to an endemic state of war in the colony, with critical consequences on the Iberian Union. Since sugar was a pivotal commodity at the time, the struggle between the Habsburgs and the United Provinces raised the risk at sea and hampered the Portuguese merchants from reaping full benefits of this trade, while putting at stake the solvency of the royal treasury in Portugal (Boxer 1957; Mello 1998).

The warfare also attained critical levels in Asia. The *Estado da Índia* was fast coming under heavy strain, as the attacks on ships and strongholds from the Dutch and the English increased the military expenditures,

---

[4] Magalhães 1988; Moreira 1990; Oliveira 1990: 72–73.
[5] Costa 2002b: 63–65; Oliveira 1990: 73–74.    [6] Guedes 1990: 51–56; Schwartz 2003.

challenging the financial wealth Portuguese Asia had enjoyed. Difficulties had started earlier, following the confrontations with the English at the Bay of Surat in 1611 and 1614, but grew tenser thereafter. The conflict with the English and the shifting Portuguese relations with Safavid Persia came to a head in 1622 when Hormuz fell to an Anglo-Persian alliance, opening up a political crisis that would last until 1641. Although the financial strains of the *Estado da India* were not exactly new, they became worse in the 1620s and 1630s. The extraordinarily steep rise in military spending went hand in hand with the loss of customs duties collected on trade passing through the port of Hormuz, which had accounted for about 20 percent of the revenues collected in the *Estado da Índia* (Miranda 2011: 114–115). Hence, multiple fronts of war threatening the integrity of the empire demanded harsh fiscal measures that deserved little acquiescence from the subjects, particularly during Philip IV's reign in Portugal (1621–1640).

*The fiscal burden*

During the Iberian Union and prior to the reign of Philip IV, there had been occasions of fiscal pressure, accepted with little resistance. One such example is the tax to protect the shores, named *consulado*, of Spanish origin, voluntarily granted to Philip II by the Portuguese merchants to fund the upkeep of a coastal fleet (Hespanha 1993: 216–217). Another example is an extraordinary tax on salt exported by sea, first levied in 1601. Besides taxation, the issuing of public bonds (*padrões de juro*) had already been a well-experimented means of raising funds. Since the empire assured regular and large fiscal revenues, the payment of interest (6.25 percent) had been often backed up by revenue streams of *Casa da Índia*. Royal borrowing envisaged a wide variety of purposes, not the least of which was the provision of shipping to India. From 1600 to 1608 the outstanding debt must have reached 520 million *réis*, a sum that represented 8 percent of the monarch's total revenues for the year of 1607 (Boyajian 1993: 92–94). However, the issuing of bonds (*padrões de juro*) in the kingdom fell off over the next decade, generating only 371.2 million *réis*, which fostered the search for other sources of credit and income (Hespanha 1993: 224–225).

In order to address military threats in Asia, several extraordinary measures to raise money were implemented, all of them common among European monarchies. In the *Estado da Índia*, loans were increasingly granted by institutions, such as the charitable lay-brotherhoods (*Misericórdias*) and municipalities, as well as by wealthy noblemen and merchants. Moreover, between 1617 and 1623, new taxes, such as the *consulado* and the *colecta*, burdened the subjects of Portuguese Asia. The former consisted of a tax levied on imported commodities, while the latter bore on transactions of meat and wine. In order to raise additional funds, the Crown claimed monopoly rights over the retail sail of Brazilian tobacco in Portuguese Asia (Miranda 2011: 115–118).

The subjects residing in the kingdom were also asked to contribute directly to the defense of the empire in Asia, in the form of loans and compulsory contributions. The money thus raised was dispatched in cash subsidies (*socorros*) to Goa, in gold and silver. The fleets of 1622 and 1623, for example, carried 200 million *réis*, which represented about 62 percent of all the revenues of the *Estado da Índia* in each of those years, to pay for local military expenses (Santos 2006: 91). Notwithstanding these previous experiences of fundraising through diversified means, Philip IV's policy (1621–1640) was progressively more demanding. It touched on traditionally exempted social bodies, thereby disrupting the vested interests that had framed the constitutionality of the Iberian Union. From then on, the acquiescence of any tax rising in *Cortes* became a political issue for Portuguese subjects, since this was a prerogative negotiated in the *Cortes* in Tomar in 1581 that was being ignored. Problems, however, did not stem only from royal demands to defend the empire without convening the *Cortes*. The military policy of Philip IV clashed with Portugal's interests in what concerned the European fronts too. This comprised the establishment of a standing military force that was called *Unión de Armas* (Union of Arms). The proposal had been under consideration since 1615, but became effective only ten years later. It was the largest troop mobilization, involving all the kingdoms and territories under the Spanish Habsburg rule, for which Portugal was called upon to raise a reserve force of 16,000 infantrymen (Elliot 1991: 254).

In light of the drain on state funds, it comes as no surprise that the requests for funding – quite frequent in the 1620s and 1630s – touched upon social groups traditionally exempt of taxation, such as the nobility and the clergy. "Loans" were also extorted from Lisbon's so-called "new Christian" business community (i.e., Jewish converts to Catholicism) in return for general "pardons" (*perdão geral*) or immunity to persecution by the Inquisition, which meant that they were forced purchases of protection.[7] Lisbon's municipal council, too, was instructed to make up for the shortfalls in ordinary revenues. A sum of 80 million *réis* was raised in 1623 from Lisbon's contribution and from the issuing of municipal securities involving the city's new-Christian merchants as coerced

---

[7] Azevedo 1921; Bethencourt 1994.

lenders. This, together with the lump sum of 80 million *réis* demanded of the Church, brought about 160 million *réis* of extraordinary funds raised from 1621 to 1630.[8] The fall of Olinda (Brazil) to the WIC (1630) and the subsequent loss of customs revenues caused a new round of impositions that included a tax levied on the income of royal offices, on pensions and on grants from the Crown (*meias-anatas*) (1631) and a rent derived from the monopoly of salt exports (*estanco do sal*) (Hespanha 1989: 64).

The last five years of the Habsburgs' rule witnessed desperate measures to raise an amount of 200 million *réis* (Oliveira 2002: 423). Among them was the 25 percent increase in the *cabeção da sisa*. This decision met with widespread resistance on the grounds that it lacked the *Cortes*'s approval. Moreover, in the very same year, Philip IV extended the *real-d'água* (a municipal excise on the retail sale of meat and wine collected in the major urban centers) to the whole country, with no exemptions. It is not easy to estimate the amount involved at a national scale, but in Lisbon, alone, the *real-d'agua* took in about 35 million *réis* (Costa L. F. 2009: 10).

Maintaining the Habsburg empire unified, while under threat both in its colonial offshoots and in its European territories, called for sacrifices from all the king's subjects, whether residing in the homeland or overseas. But according to the Portuguese constitutional order, any of the measures mentioned earlier should have had the formal consent of the subjects convened at *Cortes*. No such assembly was ever convened for the purpose. The disregard of this constitutional principle prompted social disorder on an extraordinary scale and led some factions of the aristocracy to conspiracy.

### The 1640 coup d'état

In response to the pressures of Olivares' taxation, protests arose everywhere in the country, culminating in the protests of 1637–1638, which broke out in Évora and spread quickly to the rest of the Alentejo and to the Algarve. Mostly urban, and orchestrated by the municipal authorities, the uprisings pushed back against the burden of taxes that the common people were now called upon to bear. Against the backdrop of food shortages, the insurrections strained to the breaking point the political and economic limits of taxation in Portugal (Oliveira 2002). The unrest played into the hands of separatist factions among the nation's nobility and Church. A successful *coup d'état* on the 1st of December 1640, hatched by aristocrats in the circle of the duke of Bragança, brought political autonomy back to Portugal. The duke was elevated to the throne as King João IV in

---

[8] Costa 2009: 10; Mauro 1983: 468–469; Santos 2006: 91.

a coronation ceremony on the 15th of December.[9] Propaganda endorsing the *coup* accused the Habsburg of having usurped the throne and the Castilian rule of misappropriating Portugal's resources, through both recruitment of troops and extraordinary impositions to support a war machine. Introducing new taxes without assembling the *Cortes* was an opportune argument for casting off foreign subjugation, and one that made restored independence a ready solution to "Castilian tyranny."

Those who carried out the *coup* were well aware that the event would be followed by war, thus financial stress was expected to remain an issue. However, the new political agents also acknowledged that taxes could not be perceived as extortion, rather as a voluntary participation, in a collective effort to salvage the *status quo* prior to 1580. For this reason, raising funds was accompanied by an effective propaganda operation, which aimed to assure that the higher ranks of the Portuguese society were not only accountable for the conspiracy but also for the success of the political undertaking. A flood of pamphlets extolling the rights of King João IV and narrating heroic deeds in the struggle against Spain were printed. They intended to ascertain Portugal's right to regain independence in order to distinguish the *coup d'état* from a rebellion. Divine signs that supposedly sanctified the events from December 1, 1640 were preached enthusiastically from the pulpits of the churches throughout the realm. Three threads – print, diplomacy, and preaching – wove together all social bodies and reinforced their commitment to a "native" king (Costa and Cunha 2006: 151–168). The swelling tide of support gained even further impetus as the *Cortes* convened regularly from then on, providing a forum where the people's complaints and requests could be heard (Cardim 1998).

In accordance with the constitution of the Portuguese monarchy, the succession to the throne of the eldest son of João IV, Prince Teodósio, was recognized at the *Cortes* assembled on January 28, 1641, i.e., immediately after the revolt. At these *Cortes*, the clergy, the nobility, and the commoners (the third estate) adhered to the king's extraordinary "petition" for subsidizing the expenditures of war with new taxes. The earlier fiscal measures, notably the *real-d'água*, were revoked on the ground of their illegitimate features. But what the king offered with one hand, he took back with the other. The people were promptly informed in the same assembly (January 1641) that the impending war against Spain would demand further financing as well as recruitment of men to fill the ranks.

Thus, in the midst of popular anger with Philip IV's (alleged) overstepping the constitutional limits of taxation, and with war looming large,

---

[9] Costa and Cunha 2006, Chapter 1. For an assessment of the wealth and power of the House of Bragança, see Cunha 1990.

the *coup d'état* was more than a simple exchange of royal crowns to pacify a population bled dry from the Habsburg rule. It was a step further to state building, begging an altogether new approach to the social distribution of taxation, thus requiring a new tax base (Costa and Cunha 2006).

## The economy of war

Equipping and fielding an army to fight for the success of the new dynasty was calculated to amount to 720 million *réis* per year – approximately one year of the state's revenues, not including the monopoly rents from the empire. The forecast was soon recognized to be too low and was revised upward to 860 million *réis*. The expenditure was to be financed by a new tax approved in 1641.[10] The new duty, which got the acquiescence of the people as a "temporary donation," was called the *décima*, an entirely new income tax that would remain part of the fiscal system in Portugal until the nineteenth century.

### Fiscal innovations: an income tax

The tax that would pay for the war took its name from the Church's *dízimo* (tithe/tenth), revealing the intent to replicate the ecclesiastical practice of taxing a proportion of the agricultural produce. But unlike its clerical predecessor, the *décima* was levied on the taxpayer's net income. The legislation was clear about what was implied, differentiating this fiscal transformation from any other that had prevailed in earlier extraordinary levies. In the case of the *décima*, it involved wages and salaries, profits, revenues from rental fees, and interest payments. At the same time, the state was now invading the rights of the clergy and nobility, groups that had hitherto been exempt from taxation, as the *Cortes* of 1641 consented to the principle of the universality of the fiscal contribution, and reaffirmed it again in 1645. Yielding to popular pressure, which was adamant in its demands to end any exemptions from paying taxes destined for warfare, the Church was to pay a 10 percent tax on the income of religious orders and bishoprics. In the 1650s the nobility was forced to pay an additional tax of 20 percent on income derived from the Crown's grants (land rents and seigneurial dues). All of this was accompanied by a reduction on the rate levied on wages of unskilled labor to 2 percent.

The implementation of this fiscal innovation demanded an entirely new administrative structure, at both a central and local level, to address operational issues. In Lisbon a board called *Junta dos Três Estados* (Board of

[10] Biblioteca da Ajuda, cód. 51-VI-19, fls. 359–364.

Three Social Bodies), similar to any other royal court, was created. It was vested with jurisdiction to oversee the collection of the *décima* and to control the spending of this tax stream. Considering that the cash thus raised was earmarked for war, the *junta* was given complete autonomy from the treasury council (*Conselho da Fazenda*). The allocation of the *décima's* revenue was thus kept separate from the other state's revenues that remained under direct control of the *Conselho da Fazenda*. At the local level, the municipalities became involved with the fiscal reformation, which might have granted the levels of success it reached (Romero 2004: 162–163). Municipal councils collaborated with a body of officials appointed by the central administration, namely for assessment procedures and recording tax data in the so-called *cadernos de lançamento* (assessment ledgers). The administrative apparatus was gradually calibrated through regulations, the last of which, in 1656, established procedures and tax rates, namely the one benefiting unskilled labor.[11] Once the war ended, the state kept collecting the tax, although at a 4.5 percent rate, which assures that its legitimacy was not effectively challenged further at *Cortes*. From 1641 onwards, Portugal's fiscal constitution comprised an income tax that was still funding public expenditure in the nineteenth century.

In spite of this precocious intrusion of taxation into private income, the *décima* faced serious costs of information and compliance, indicating the downsides of such originality in early modern public finance. The state's lack of information, more than operational costs, might have constrained the levels of efficacy reached by such an institutional innovation. Forward-looking revenues were founded on taxpayers' declaration of income and the state could do little to screen its sources. In the agrarian sector, information could be obtained from the tithe records that the Church provided. But in many other productive activities there must have been a large margin of error between the information on which the state's budgets were based and the amounts actually collected. Even so, the documentation available today regarding the *décima* provides a fairly good impression of its implementation – challenged, as it was, by the dominant social ranks (Hespanha 2004). The collection records of the *Junta dos Três Estados* show considerable year-on-year fluctuations, especially during the 1640s, which is probably a reliable indication that the agricultural sector was contributing a great deal. For example, harvests in 1652 were poor, and this is reflected in a lower tax collection (47 percent of the assessment). Aside from this critical year, compliance ranged from 72 to 81 percent of amounts assessed (see Table 3.1).

[11] For the legislation on the *décima*, see www.iuslusitaneae.fcsh.unl.pt.

Table 3.1 *Revenue from the* décima, *1650–1653 (million* réis)

| | Assessment | Collection | Rate of compliance |
|---|---|---|---|
| 1650 | 628.2 | 502.7 | 80% |
| 1651 | 632.7 | 454.7 | 72% |
| 1652 | 635.9 | 296.6 | 47% |
| 1653 | 642.2 | 523.3 | 81% |

*Source:* Hespanha 2004: 182.

The level of compliance attests that the royal administration somehow overcame information costs, while operational costs still represented the inherent challenges of the new tax. Although exhibiting significant levels of efficacy, data also show that the social rank of taxpayers probably affected the financial outcome, because figures organized by social bodies tell us that some taxpayers paid less willingly than others. This is seen in the case of the Church, where the contemporary breakdown into "clergy," "religious orders," and "bishoprics" discloses shortfalls that ranged from 58 to 74 percent between assessment and amounts collected (Hespanha 2004: 182). We should recall that the early estimates about the revenue-raising potential of the new tax were based on the tithe's records, thanks to which the contribution of the Church had been assessed at approximately 640 million *réis* in 1641. In other words, the best information available at the time with regard to economic output was in possession of the Church. Hence the shortfalls derived from this particular category of taxpayers are to be ascribed to non-compliance rather than to critical errors of assessment. The military orders, too, were non-compliers – their contribution hovering around 52 percent of what was assessed. By contrast, at the level of regional *comarcas*, the compliance with the tax obligation is clear. This category may be assumed as describing the levy on income of middling social ranks, which overall met 87 percent of their expected contributions.

Considering the taxpayer's behavior as an indicator of his will to cope with tax reforms, it is a fact that the nobility and the clergy provided less financial support than the rest of the society (Costa 2009). Nevertheless, the support of the political cause cut across all social strata somehow. The aristocracy did contribute with services in the form of military command postings at senior and junior levels, as decision-makers in the political realm, and as ambassadors. In some cases, such as that of the marquis of Nisa, ambassador in Paris in the 1640s, the appointees spent their own wealth in order to serve their office. His is not the only instance known, and the possession of personal wealth was often the criterion that determined the selection of ambassadors. The clergy participated actively by promulgating propaganda from the pulpit and by furnishing the church interiors with ornate altarpieces and other accoutrements in the Portuguese Baroque style – a special pictorial expression of a proto-nationalistic sentiment (Marques 1989).

Despite all the energy involved in giving support to the Restoration, as early as 1643, budgetary shortfalls could have endangered the military success. The amounts of funds transferred to headquarters at the regional level (*governos de armas*) were far below the necessary mark. In some cases, funds just covered 73.9 percent of the costs of the infantry (as it happened in Trás-os-Montes). In the Alentejo, only 63.6 percent of the expenses for cavalry troops reached the headquarters. The causes of such shortfalls went beyond the weaknesses of any income tax in the early modern period. The decentralized administration of expenditures added new factors for errors. Besides, the state outsourced the military provisioning by awarding contracts to merchants, to whom the amounts of tax revenue were assigned (Freitas 2007).

Thus, the logistics of the conflict implied that the taxable income was directly diverted to moneyed classes, who were called upon to back up the troops. Other impacts of the war reinforced the position of merchants, namely the growth of the state's debt due to budget deficits. The scarcity of funds actually transferred to regional military units and the difference between assessments and the amounts of tax collected drove up public debt and justified the debasement of coinage, causing inflation at unprecedented levels. All in all, budgetary deficits and monetary policies may have impacted on the redistribution of wealth.

### State's debt and debasements

To make up for the lack of funds, the state resorted to the usual means of extraordinary financing, which were, however, not sufficient to prevent routine deficits. First of all, the new king João IV contributed personally to the war effort with revenues derived from the patrimony of the House of Bragança. The estates of the duke had not been integrated in the Royal House, enabling the king to manage them as his personal patrimony (Costa and Cunha 2006: 247). The donations of the House of Bragança to the *Junta dos Três Estados* worked as an example that the financial burden was actually universal, not even exempting the king, and thus used as a means to legitimize additional taxes. Thanks to the king's personal involvement in the war effort, a decade after the *coup d'état* it was now possible to reinstate some of the earlier measures of the Habsburg's rule without any major social disruptions. The *real-d'água* was reinstated, along with a new tax levied on sugar from Brazil.[12]

Regardless of the funds raised, regular deficits led to an increase of public debt. One of the short-term solutions consisted simply of postponing the soldiers' payday, or supplying military headquarters with incomplete or irregular installments. Field officers' reports are rife with complaints and warnings about the consequences of unpaid and unmotivated soldiery. Desertions were routine and soldiers had to survive on informal credit from local shop owners for their food and footwear, thus dragging several elements of the social fabric into a burgeoning credit trap.[13]

Further up the social pyramid, the budget deficits justified the Treasury's ever greater indebtedness to major lenders, individuals who bid for the concession of short-term lending, the payment of which (both principal and interest) was assigned to revenue streams. These financial contracts were called *assentos*, following the traditional terminology of the Habsburgs. A financial report of 1652 shows that the first ten years of war had forced the Crown into two *assentos* in which the signatory lender actually represented a syndicate of investors. The first contract was for a credit of 533 million *réis*, at 2.5 percent interest. The second, for a sum of 200 million *réis*, was auctioned off to a leading businessman, a catholic, of untarnished reputation, who later on became *assentista* of military supplies. Often the portion of tax revenues assigned to the payment of the principal proved to be insufficient, as the interest payments needed revision (Smith 1975). Turning to these types of contracts became a routine measure in the Treasury Council as a way to guarantee provisions to the armed forces along with meeting all of the associated expenses.

The amounts of money involved and the underwriters of the *assentos* give evidence of the encroachment of merchants (both Catholics and new Christians) in public finance, contracting with the state loans that reached four billion *réis*, approximately four times the amount scheduled in an annual budget. These lenders also drew other social groups into play, because they acted as bankers, investing deposits of the aristocracy in public loans. In this way, the public debt became a mechanism for cementing the social elite into a pact that pivoted on the victorious outcome of the struggle for autonomy. It also demanded the solvency of the state.

The other device to manage public financing was debasement. The monetary policy targeted silver shortages, which underpinned

---

[12] Biblioteca da Ajuda, cód. 51-VI-19, fls. 359–364.
[13] Costa 2004b: 73; Freitas 2007: 206.

debasements of the unit of account (*real*) from 1640 to 1688. Prior to 1640 the mark of silver (*marco de prata*) was worth 2,800 *réis*. In 1643, the *real* saw its first large devaluation, and the silver mark was fixed at 4,000 *réis*. In 1663 a new devaluation established the mark at 5,000 *réis*. This monetary policy did not end once the peace was signed. In 1680, a new devaluation determined the value of the mark at 5,300 *réis*. Finally, the face value of coins was cut by 20 percent and the *marco de prata* was revalued at 6,000 *réis* in 1688 (Sousa 2006: 86 and appendix 2.1). In roughly forty years the *real* had depreciated by almost 100 percent. Accompanying these measures there were alterations of the legal gold-to-silver ratio, which was set in 1668 at 16.5:1, and redefined in 1688 as 15.5:1, in an effort to encourage individuals to bring their silver to the Royal Mint (*Casa da Moeda*), to be struck into coin.

As for other economic consequences of warfare, the state could actually do very little to help the situation. In fact, the efficacy of the fiscal innovation was correlated with the overall risk of the economy, not to mention the effects of conscription of troops, all in all hampering the growth of taxable income. Hence, gauging the costs of the war is not straightforward in light of the poor data available. However, the evolution of land rents, insurance premiums, or interest rates charged on maritime credit deliver data to evaluate the risk affecting the economy. The risk must have increased both in land, where the troops were stationed, and at sea, where other opponents undermined the prosperity of colonial trade.

*Risk on land and at sea*

Beginning with disturbances on land, price volatility of cereals could not always be blamed on the fortunes of war, but certainly the hostilities did not favor rural production, especially not in the years when the Spanish armies swarmed over the Portuguese countryside. Fear and uncertainty plunged the land market into stark crisis. The Alentejo suffered from raids and looting, as well as poor harvests. Records from the archbishopric of Évora provide us the best information on how the war impacted the agricultural output and which institutional arrangements managed the landowners' risk, including the relentless turnover of tenants, many fleeing their obligations (Santos 2003: 325–334).

Land tenure contracts dealt with the probability of poor harvests or of war damage to the properties. The foresight of such situations determined that many contracts began to specify the tenants' right (or not) to a remission of the terms or outright annulment of the contract – that is, a freedom from obligation, in part or in whole, without penalty or interest on the unfulfilled part of their commitment. Lack of reliable tenants, contractual agreements that favored the leaseholders, land rents that were often substantially lower than previously agreed to – all these risks negatively affected the landlord's income and agricultural output, illustrating the state of affairs that prevailed in the agrarian sector. The disruption in the landowners' income translated into the failure of the *décima* to perform as it was designed to. Thus, whether as a result of the detrimental nature (for the landlord) of the lease contracts or the high turnover of tenants, the 1640s and 1660s were decades of pure trauma in the agricultural sector. An increasing discrepancy between the nominal (contracted) rent and the income actually collected allows assessing the risk incurred by landlords, which reached a rate close to 8 percent (Santos 2006: 302).

The other significant portion of the kingdom's income – the size of which is difficult to ascertain – derived from maritime sectors. Here, the threat did not come from Spain, but rather from the Dutch, the inherited adversaries from the times of the Iberian Union, who also contributed to raise the overall risk of Portugal's economy throughout the mid-seventeenth century. The links between Portugal and Brazil had been time and again endangered by the military strength of the WIC. The company briefly occupied Salvador (1624–1625) and in the early 1630s went on to conquer the shores of Brazil's northeast. After the *coup d'état*, Portuguese political circles considered the Dutch presence in Brazil an issue inherited from the Spanish rule, thus diplomatic attempts were carried out to solve the problem. The new King João IV entered eagerly into ceasefire negotiations. But between the proposal of a treaty and its ratification by both parties, the WIC wrested Luanda from Portuguese control and gradually extended the Dutch possessions in Brazil to Rio Real (Sergipe) on the south and São Luís do Maranhão on the north.

Seeking to take back the lost colonial territories, Portugal met with resistance in its negotiations in The Hague. The talks opened with the suggestion that Portugal would purchase the northeastern territories occupied by the WIC. Several mechanisms for this were pondered, including Portugal's purchase of shares in the Dutch company (Mello 2002: 54–71). The Hague saw no great advantage in this, given the superior position it had in negotiations, especially after 1644, when the price of sugar began to soar in Europe. However, the Dutch favored the payment of 800 million *réis* for "selling" their property rights over Brazil's northeast. According to the Portuguese proposal, the amount would be raised through a tax on sugar production that would be collected and paid over a number of decades.

In June 1645, while the negotiations were still in deadlock, events in the colony altered the terms that diplomacy had observed until then. The Luso-Brazilian population living in northeastern Brazil rebelled against the Dutch, rallying to the cry that they were "faithful subjects of the king of Portugal." War in the colony soon followed while the conflict also extended to South Atlantic waters. These hostilities were yet another drain on capital, now bleeding the economic affairs between Portugal and Brazil. Capital depended on maritime activities, and trade was exposed to privateers. The Portuguese ships, which were mostly lightly armed caravels, were no match for the heavily gunned Dutch ships of the line, and there was usually little to do other than surrender the cargo (Boxer 1957).

The Dutch piracy on the seas was to Portugal's maritime lifeblood what the Spanish troop incursions and raiding were to the country's agriculture: an economic warfare of attrition. But where the cross-border raids and sorties were tactics used by both sides, the maritime contest was no equal match (Costa 2004b: 77–78). Portugal lacked the ability, or at least the strategy, for retaliation. Apparently the agents involved were unwilling to arm their merchant vessels with sufficient firepower to fight the Dutch privateers either for defensive purposes or for turning the tables on them offensively. Nor was the state providing support in the form of naval escorts for convoys, saving instead its scarce resources to wage war on land. Even so, in 1648 the Treasury Council (*Conselho da Fazenda*) appraised the state of affairs and admitted that reduced private profits would mean decreasing customs duties in the future. The Council sought out the records of insurance underwritings and realized that in 1647 and 1648 from a total of 259 ships sailing back and forth from Brazil, 35 had been captured in 1647 and 73 in 1648 (108 in total). The loss of capital in circulation thus stood at 30 percent in 1647 and 51 percent in the following year.[14]

Some of these casualties were covered by loans, the terms of which were rather like gambling. The interest rates on these instruments were exorbitant at first glance (*c.* 100 percent during the Restoration war), but this included the lenders' opportunity costs (estimated by markups on goods) and the insurance premium. Known as bottomry loans, under their terms the lender would reclaim the principal and the interest only in the event of the undertaking's good fortune. If not, the borrower was exempt from any debt or obligation. Naturally, in time of war, interest rates skyrocketed (see Figure 3.1). Investments in this business, even if the lenders faced a strong possibility of sustaining considerable loss, seem to represent

[14] Recalculated after Boxer 1957, annex 3.

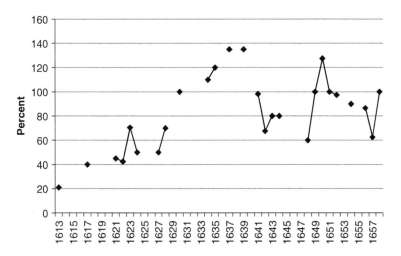

Figure 3.1  Interest rates on bottomry loans from round trip voyages to
Brazil, 1613–1658
Source: Costa 2006.

good opportunities, partly because there were ways to spread the risk.
Lenders, thus, took satisfactory returns from the steep interest rate charged.

Underwriting lent capital was a well-known practice, and one that was
not rare in the cities of Europe, especially those with higher exposure to
the risks of maritime shipping, such as Amsterdam and Middelburg.
In 1625, the Treasury Council in Portugal was already aware of the
internationalization of insurances, including those of bottomry loans,
and debated its pros and cons in correspondence with the central government in Madrid. Officials cleverly understood the drawbacks of the
insurance business developing in Amsterdam or Middelburg, the same
cities that outfitted ships to attack Iberian fleets. They synthesized the
matter by claiming that insurers were also those who pushed the maritime
risk up, turning the insurance premium into a sort of a tribute, instead of
a charge for an honest trade (Costa 2002b: 227–235; 2006). It is not
certain whether the restoration of the political autonomy cut off the
international connections of the Portuguese merchants who kept dealing
with Brazil's shipping and trade. Still, sources from 1649 mention the
prevailing insurance premiums on maritime policies as being 15 percent,
a premium quite close to the one charged in Amsterdam for the Antilles
(14 percent).[15] This is the best yardstick by which to measure the effect

[15] Silva 1854–1859: 31–40; Spooner 1983.

on the Portuguese economy of the Dutch-Portuguese war in the Southern Atlantic. The 15 percent rate was undoubtedly higher than that estimated for the primary sector.

Even though the colonial business was experiencing high risk, the state did not come to its aid with protection. There is no record of any funds raised through the *décima* being assigned to maritime defense. We should note, however, that when stacked up alongside the expenses of maintaining the armies and the expected profits, naval expenses were enormously greater. Escorting convoys of private vessels would have required 18 warships, and this would have cost about 286 million *réis* per year, i.e., about one-third of the estimated yield of the *décima* (Hespanha 2004: 186). The size of this price tag encouraged putting matters off as long as possible. In other words, this would leave the merchants and private ship owners to fend for themselves as best they could. Still, this political choice was taking its toll in the form of dwindling customs revenues.

In 1648 the loss of half of the fleet forced Portugal back to the bargaining table with the Dutch. There seemed to be no option but to give up Pernambuco. However, the terms of the negotiation scandalized the kingdom. The conditions enraged those who profited most from increased aggregate risk, i.e., the interest group who took on contracts to supply munitions to the army, lent short-term credits to the state and kept outfitting ships to Brazil. The closed circle of advisers of João IV foresaw a trade-off with this powerful group of capitalists, by informing them that conditions of the peace negotiated in The Hague would be ignored as long as they themselves would provide for the defense of the Atlantic fleets. Their investment would be backed up with monopoly rights over the principal exports to the colonies (olive oil, wine, wheat flour, and codfish), assuming that the costs of defense would be covered with additional fees on imported cargo and freight charges (Costa 2002b, vol.1: 508–515).

To these ends several merchants formed the *Companhia Geral do Comércio do Brasil* (Brazilian Commerce Company), chartered on March 11, 1649. This arrangement provided for a system of armed fleet escorts, which although offering safety, also slowed the turnover, and the cargos moved across the Atlantic at a slower pace than they had at any time before. The rhythm of shipments did not coincide well with market dynamics on either side of the ocean, which increased the markups. These Atlantic convoys continued until the middle of the eighteenth century, even after the Brazilian Commerce Company went out of operation in 1663, following the withdrawal of the monopoly rights in 1656 (Freitas 1951). After the peace with Spain in 1668, the state reassumed the mantle of providing defense by incurring the costs of escorting the ships and collecting the fees over cargo and freight charges. The whole organization of *escoltas* was assigned to a *Junta do Comércio* (Board of Trade), equal in its authority to a royal council.

The consequences of this new arrangement for the nation's port system became apparent early in the 1650s. As the organization of the fleets was now centralized in Lisbon, there were advantages to be had in locating business offices and agencies in the capital, which grew into a hub of movement for colonial merchandise. Lisbon thereby took on a character as the prime clearing house in Atlantic colonial relations that it had not had in the sixteenth century. The transfer of the defense to a company went along with the protest of the *terceiro estado* (commoners) at the *Cortes* where it was claimed that centralizing shipping in Lisbon diverted foreign trade from local ports. The rising overall risk and the political solution to privatize defense at sea gave reasons for contest at the *Cortes*. But what mostly affected the common people were the implications of the war on households' labor. In fact, the enlistment of male sons, together with the new income tax, was perceived as a double cost of the war. Thus, conscription became another major cause of economic disturbance.

*Crowding out labor force*

By the time the *Cortes* convened in 1641, estimates for the war effort were that 25,000 soldiers would suffice, along with 6,000 cavalry. This mobilization was considerably greater than the one called for in the Union of Arms that Olivares had planned. Financial costs of such a level of mobilization are known from documents of 1653. They indicate that 55 percent of all expenditures went toward the infantry. The remainder amounts were used to maintain the cavalry (20 percent), pay for artillery (10 percent) and for works on fortifications (5 percent), and 10 percent on other matters (Hespanha 2004: 182). The percentage attributed to the costs of each soldier, 1,500 *réis* per month, seems extraordinarily low, since it corresponded to half the monthly wage of unskilled labor in a city like Lisbon. Besides, 55 percent of the war budget assigned to infantry included neither feeding the soldiers nor any of their personal expenses at all, as they were expected to afford for these items out of their normal pay (Freitas 2007: 198–199, 348–349). Cavalry troops received a substantial bonus in food allowance – to cover their horses – so the payment was four times that of a soldier, reaching 6,000 *réis*. Accepting these figures, Table 3.2 gathers information on the number of men enlisted to assess a minimum level of costs for mobilizing troops.

The valuation of the impacts of conscription may go further and include the fiscal effects of greater mobilization in the 1660s, since

Table 3.2 *The Portuguese army, 1643–1666*

|  | Infantry | | Cavalry | | |
|  | Number of soldiers | Annual cost (million *réis*) | Number of soldiers | Annual Cost (million *réis*) | Total annual cost |
|---|---|---|---|---|---|
| 1643 | 14,996 | 269.9 | 4,044 | 291.0 | 560.9 |
| 1652 | 15,671 | 282.0 | 3,099 | 223.1 | 505.1 |
| 1666 | 30,000 | 540.0 | 7,800 | 561.6 | 1,101.6 |

*Source:* Freitas 2007: 348–349.

the number of those assigned to military tasks did not earn a taxable wage. The nominal wage of a farmhand was close to that of an unskilled urban laborer – about 100 *réis* per day. A work year varied between 250 and 270 days (Sá 2005: 114). Admittedly, in 1643 there was a shortfall of 514 million *réis* of taxable income, and 1,026 million in 1666. The state was thus incurring two costs, i.e., paying the troops (or would-be farm laborers), and shrinking the tax base as a result of falling income. As for the king's subjects, there were ways of escaping conscription. The terms of enlistment might include the payment of a fee for discharge. Social status and privilege exempted some from military service, shielding a few. Still, the conscription observed the principle that households with only one son should be exempted of military service, providing us a testimony that conscription was perceived as having effects on household income and the state's interest to spare those families (Costa 2004a: 78–83).

The new level of threat that marked the final phase of the war came after the peace between Spain and France (1659), which freed the Spanish army to invade Portugal, thus justifying the urgency for recruitment to bolster the front lines (see Table 3.2). These last years of conflict witnessed violence surpassing anything known earlier. Hence the war caused mortality changes in Portuguese demography, at least in the 1660s. The pace of recovery in the aftermath of the war is the subject of the next section.

#### Population and agriculture

The struggle for political autonomy (1640–1668) must have hindered population growth, but it was not the only cause of a lasting demographic stagnation. In fact, the acclamation of João IV came about during a period of population downturn, both in Portugal and elsewhere in Europe. From 1600 to 1650 the number of European inhabitants fell by *c.* 9 percent above

Table 3.3 *Population growth in Europe,*
*1650–1700 (annual average, percent)*

| | |
|---|---|
| United Provinces | 0,00 |
| Germany | 0,68 |
| France | 0,14 |
| England | −0,11 |
| Spain | 0,11 |
| Italy | 0,33 |
| Portugal | 0,31 |
| Northwest | 0,12 |
| Mediterranean | 0,30 |

*Sources:* De Vries 1994b: 13; Pfister and Fertig
2010: 5 (Germany); Palma and Reis 2016
(Portugal).

all because Spain, Italy, as well as Germany, were particularly struck by demographic holdups. However, growth resumed during the second half of the century, thus in 1700 Europe's population numbers were 5 percent above the level of the beginning of the seventeenth century (Nash 2001: 13–14). Generally speaking, Portugal accompanied this European trend.

It is not certain if the lowest point in Portugal's trends of the seventeenth century, which historians date from the 1660s, represented a retreat to the numbers of 1527–1532 (*c.* 1,200,000). Some authors have put forward this possibility.[16] Contemporary sources describe cyclical downturns in births in several of the country's northern, central, and southern parishes (*freguesias*), supporting this thesis.[17] For the Alentejo, however, interpolating the data for 1527 and 1720, the hypothesis seems quite implausible (Santos 2005: 335). Thus, different interpretations have rejected the notion of a protracted slump, and argued that Portuguese population experienced stagnation, rather than a recession, from the 1620s–1630s and the 1660s (Palma and Reis 2016; Serrão 1993a: 65). Growth resumed after the peace with Spain (1668). Recent scholarly work has estimated a yearly rate of 0.31 percent from 1650 to 1700, indicating that Portugal's demographic recovery was swifter when compared with northwest Europe but in line with the Mediterranean basin (Table 3.3).[18]

Any explanation of these trends calls for mortality changes. The war with Spain accounted for the rising of the death rates, but data for actual combat casualties are approximate at best. The chronicle of the Restoration

[16] Oliveira 1990: 54; Magalhães 1988: 23.
[17] For Alentejo, see Santos 2005: 355; for Beira, see Oliveira 1971–1972.
[18] Magalhães 1988: 23–28; Serrão 1993: 51.

of Portugal written between 1679 and 1698 by the count of Ericeira offers some valuable clues, as the author provides numbers for those who fell in battle. Overall data suggest that a total of 19,217 Portuguese troops were killed in action over the 28-year span of conflict (Ericeira 1945 [1679]). Considering that the major engagements occurred during the 1660s, the number of war victims must have been concentrated in this decade.

In the regions most affected by war, civilian population endured subsistence crises and epidemic diseases spread by the troops.[19] However, the particularly high mortality levels in the 1650s and 1660s do not dismiss Malthusian explanations, since harvest failures may stem from an imbalance between resources and population growth. Data for the archbishopric of Évora ensure that during crises of subsistence baptisms plummeted. The combination of higher death rates and lower birth rates in the 1660s spells nothing less than the worst crisis in the whole period from 1590 to 1815 in this region of the country (Santos 2003: 203).

As mortality is sensitive to many factors, external shocks such as outbreaks of epidemic disease, which ravaged the Mediterranean basin from 1620 on, should also be recalled (Nash 2001: 14–15). Diphtheria, influenza, and smallpox caused sudden spikes in mortality rates, in areas as widely distant as the Minho, Coimbra, Viseu, and Évora, which often worked in tandem with harvest failure.[20] As a few scholars have argued, death rates together with poor agricultural performance could have been the result of a Little Ice Age, thus climate might have played a part in the demographic downturn of the middle of the seventeenth century.[21] Even if the effects of a Little Ice Age are still a matter for debate, there is agreement among scholars about the second half of the seventeenth century witnessing a significant modification in the nature of the mortality crises. They became more frequent but caused fewer victims, thereby affecting the demographic trend less than did the outbreaks of bubonic plague that devastated Europe in the fifteenth and sixteenth centuries. Throughout the last thirty years of the 1600s mortality crises certainly took their toll on the net population evolution (i.e., the difference between the births and deaths), but did not curb growth over the long run. From the 1670s the number of inhabitants recovered everywhere, despite regional differences. Table 3.4 shows that Minho and Alentejo were the provinces with the strongest growth, altering their weights in the overall national perspective.

---

[19] Magalhães 1988: 20; Santos 2003: 192–194; Oliveira 1979: 498–502.
[20] Oliveira 1989: 143; for a chronology of the major causes of death, see Rodrigues 2008: 231–232.
[21] Campbell 2010; Parker 2013: 112.

Table 3.4 *Regional distribution of population, 1527–1700 (percent)*

|  | 1527 | 1700 |
|---|---|---|
| Minho | 19.5 | 23.4 |
| Trás-os-Montes | 12.6 | 9.6 |
| Beira | 23.9 | 21.6 |
| Estremadura | 23.2 | 23.8 |
| Alentejo | 17.3 | 18.7 |
| Algarve | 3.5 | 2.9 |

*Source:* Rodrigues 2008: 177–178.

Table 3.5 *Urbanization in Portugal, 1527–1700 (percent of total population)*

|  | Urban population | | | |
|---|---|---|---|---|
|  | >5000 hab. | | >10 000 hab. | |
|  | 1527 | 1700 | 1527 | 1700 |
| Minho | 16.0 | 10.1 | 5.5 | 8.6 |
| Trás-os-Montes | 0.0 | 3.0 | 0.0 | 0.0 |
| Beira | 0.0 | 9.2 | 0.0 | 3.8 |
| Estremadura | 41.0 | 31.4 | 19.9 | 23.6 |
| Alentejo | 62.4 | 34.1 | 5.8 | 15.6 |
| Algarve | 64.3 | 41.4 | 0.0 | 0.0 |
| Portugal | 12.8 | 18.1 | 6.7 | 10.3 |

*Source:* Rodrigues 2008: 193.

Beira, the province with the greatest number of hearths in the sixteenth century, lost its leading position to Estremadura and Minho, as the population north of the Tagus slowly shifted toward the coastal regions. In the Algarve, population growth went hand-in-hand with a structural transformation of the regional economy in which the slowdown of urban and maritime activities was partly compensated by progress in the primary sector. Until 1672 the number of urban dwellers shrank, and if population in the Algarve increased afterwards, the urban rates did not (Magalhães 1988: 120 and appendix 3). The case of the Algarve illustrates well that demographic recovery in the late seventeenth century was not necessarily accompanied by higher rates of urbanization.

Elsewhere in the kingdom, the number of large cities climbed (Table 3.5). Considering 10,000 inhabitants as the minimum threshold, the rate of urbanization throughout Portugal reached 10.3 percent in 1700. This population shift occurred mostly in the Alentejo, Minho, and Beira, and less so in the Estremadura, where Lisbon (with *c.* 150,000 residents), hampered the development of other great centers in the region. When compared to European countries, though, the picture needs to be toned down. From 1650 to 1700 Portugal's urbanization was progressing slower, even if population grew faster than that of the sea-power economies in northeastern Europe. In the United Provinces and England urbanization stood at 33.6 and 13.3 percent, respectively, in 1700, while these two countries had witnessed lower rates of population growth than Portugal over the preceding fifty years (Vries 1994b). This difference reveals that economic activities in Portugal did not encourage rural labor reallocation in urban centers in the same way as it happened in the Northern economies. Thus, rural activities must have kept labor in strong demand.

*Agriculture and income*

Land rents reached a peak in the early 1600s. This positive trend stopped around 1620, when the rental value of lands held by Church institutions and brotherhoods (*Misericórdias*) across the kingdom displayed an overall downward trend. The incomes of the Chapter of the *Sé de Coimbra* (Coimbra See) and the *Misericórdia de Évora*, for example, began to wane.[22] The tithes, too, of the Chapter of the *Sé de Faro* (Algarve) suffered a like decline for 1618–1646 (Magalhães 1988: 187–188). However, it should be stressed that until the mid-seventeenth century land rents were highly volatile in the short term, with years of acute falls followed by recovery and growth. From the 1670s onwards several regional studies point to a recovery in agricultural activities together with a steadier rise in rents. Among the better-studied institutions is the Benedictine religious order, in the northwest. Yearly fees from land use (*foros*) and seigneurial dues in the form of wheat or mixed grains (rye and maize) climbed steadily from 1662 until 1674–1677. After that, revenues remained at a high stable level until the end of the century (Oliveira 1980). In the same province, and for the same monastic order, the collection of tithes of a monastery on the south bank of the Douro River (Grijó), records an upward trend, although cut by some crisis years between 1689 and 1694, during which real revenues fell back to levels typical of the war years. Only by the end of the 1690s did the values regain the lost ground and move further ahead. This bleak showing for the early

---

[22] Santos 2005: 370–371; Oliveira 1990: 64.

1690s is in stark contrast to the prosperity enjoyed throughout the 1680s (Amorim 1997b).

For all effects, records of different Benedictine monasteries in this region give evidence of expanded production in 1670 and 1680, due to a succession of good yield ratios, as occurred in the Bustelo Monastery (1:7.3) (Maia 1991: 226). The monastery of Ganfei (Minho) provides another example that real output was increasing (Minho). Here, land rents had hit rock bottom in 1638, when the *foros* amounted to 62,289 *réis*, but from 1665 this value was surpassed and never dipped below that figure from then on (Silva 1993: 208).

Only a single institution departs from this pattern that prevails throughout the northwest. The nominal income of the collegiate church of Guimarães clearly increases, but the tax farming contracts of the tithe progress at a rate below that of cereal prices, pointing to falling real income (Oliveira 1981). In fact, these are early signs of problems that are specific to this institution. As no equivalent difficulty is detected in any of the other religious orders in the region, the interference of rent- and tithe-collectors might have cut into the institution's revenues. A social group, foreign to land ownership and exploitation, i.e., merchants acting as rent farmers, became increasingly involved in the collection of land rents and seigneurial dues. Whenever landowners resorted to this solution, their income would inevitably be constrained by the profit share of these intermediaries.

For the interior of the kingdom (Beira), the bishopric of Viseu speaks of the overall satisfactory results of maize cultivation in the late seventeenth century. The volume of cereal production was almost always greater in the 1660s and 1670s than in the early years of the century. However, in those years rye, coupled with wheat, still had the major share in grain output. The preference for rye waned from 1680 onwards. Maize together with wheat spurred output to levels of production above the highest peak in 1605 (Oliveira J. N. 1990).

The production ceilings of the war years were surpassed from 1680 onwards, and it is widely held that this was driven by the diffusion of maize, which became popular among poor people. Not all regions met with the same success in maize cultivation, though. As mentioned in the preceding chapter, the crop had been introduced to Portugal in the 1500s, but it was only in the second half of the 1600s that it spread out from the northwest to the littoral of Beira, and in some areas of the interior, including Guarda and Viseu (Almeida 1992). Maize was particularly well-suited to irrigated and intensive farming carried out in small landholdings in Portugal's northern littoral. Nevertheless, the revenues of certain ecclesiastic institutions, such as the collegiate church of

Guimarães, albeit falling within the maize-growing area, failed to stay abreast of those of the Bishopric of Viseu.

Neither the Alentejo nor the Inner Beira lent itself to the maize cultivation, but there is no doubt that the population pressure here also prompted a growth in agricultural production, adding more land and labor. The *Misericórdia de Évora*'s rental land values showed a strong and steady upward trend from 1670 to 1700, free from any significant agricultural hardship, allowing for output recovery in the 1680s and 1690s (Santos 2003: 350). This positive trend was interrupted early in the eighteenth century with Portugal's participation in the War of the Spanish Succession.

As for the Algarve, agriculture attracted investments, which ended up affecting institutional arrangements that regulated rural resources. Members of the local elites endeavored to obtain long-term leases on common lands administered by municipal councils, something that raised a cry of protest from raisers of livestock, as it deprived them of grazing lands. Though competing with livestock, cereal production witnessed significant progress in the 1660s and 1670s, even without any apparent improvement in productivity since gains in total production were achieved by putting new land under cultivation (Magalhães 1988: 147). Besides the increase in grain production, the last quarter of the seventeenth century in the Algarve attests a diversification of agricultural output, with livestock and vines playing a significant role. Indeed, in the southern region of Portugal, vines expanded – some into previously uncultivated terrains, but some also encroaching into common lands (Magalhães 1988: 165–180).

In light of the positive demographic trend and considering the rise of real rents that are documented for both northern and southern areas of the country, the primary sector of the economy likely improved in the last thirty years of the 1600s, at least achieving the same level as the early 1600s. How this improvement is reflected in living standards is a question that needs an other sort of data, namely trends in prices. The levels of inflation and the volatility of prices of the war period vanished after 1668, when peace was signed. However, prices display a sustained upward trend from 1670 onwards (Figure 3.2). Demographic pressure must have caused supply–demand imbalances, but inflation had also a monetary cause. Hence, in the second half of the century, real and monetary factors caused the price index to rise in Portugal, while, for instance, in the western part of the Netherlands prices displayed a stationary trend between *c.* 1650 and 1750 (Van Zanden 2005: 183).

As for rural nominal wages, data for Minho display a flattened trend (Oliveira 1980), which implied a fall of real income. This affected a large

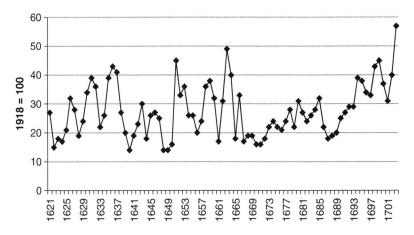

Figure 3.2  Price index, 1621–1703 (1918 =100)
Source: Valério 1997.

range of the population, even in areas of the country where land productivity could have increased due to the spread of maize. Assuming that
urban wages of unskilled labor showed a similar pattern to rural wages
over time, data from this variable with regard to Lisbon provide us with an
adequate long-term series to draw some conclusions (Figure 3.3). After
the political restoration there was no improvement in real wages. Since
real rents varied positively and wages declined, inflation in the second half
of the seventeenth century penalized labor, while those who relied on land
rents fared considerably better (Palma e Reis 2016). Thus, considering
the redistributive effects of inflation, it is not safe to assume that the
recovery of agricultural output after the war allowed Portugal to surpass
in aggregate terms the levels of income already attained at some point in
the past, namely those estimated for the first half of the sixteenth century.

There is no trustworthy information on how profits evolved, although
the elite of businessmen might have also fared well, considering their
involvement in the state's finances during the war, through military
provisioning and tax farming. Moreover, as rent-collectors, taking on
the collection of land rents under long-term contracts, they might have
benefited from the inflation too. In fact, the increased encroachment of
new *rentiers* shows that their undertakings were profitable.

Portugal's downturn of real wages is unlike what is known for northwestern regions of Europe whose economies started to diverge from those
along the Mediterranean borders. Recent studies have attested a long-run
stability in real wages from 1570 to 1750 in the western parts of the

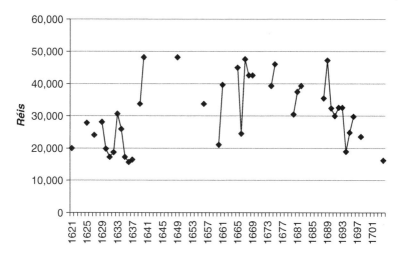

Figure 3.3 Yearly wages in Lisbon (skilled labor), 1621–1703 (1620 prices)
Source: Prices wages and rents in Portugal 1300–1910, directed by Jaime Reis, http://pwr-portugal.ics.ul.pt/

United Provinces. Even in Spain, after a pronounced decline from the mid-fifteenth to mid-seventeenth century, stability also characterizes the evolution of real wages.[23] Hence, in relative terms, if Portugal displays a divergent path this was due to a fall of real wages in the second half of the seventeenth century, rather than a relative rise of wages elsewhere in Europe. The particular trend in Portugal seems to be closely connected to the aftermath of the war of Restoration, which forced currency devaluations that fueled the rise of the consumer price index.

Debasement was the only device used by the state to overcome the shortage of silver that affected the economy after the severing of political ties to Spain. It is also true that the state's concerns about the economy were visible in other policies beyond its tampering with the currency, notably in boosting manufacturing output. Even so, these were pragmatic solutions for solving liquidity issues. The policy of promoting import-substitution sectors intended to stop the drainage of means of payment. Thus several incentives were introduced toward the end of the 1670s by the minister of King Pedro II, count of Ericeira. In the next section we describe this government intervention. Although its actual influence on industry is impossible to estimate, historians have deemed it a remarkable attempt to develop an economic specialization according to the

---

[23] Álvarez Nogal and Prado de La Escosura 2013: 7; Van Zanden 2005: 184.

mercantilist principles of the time, which put Portuguese policy in line with that of the most powerful monarchies of the time.

## Industry

Since medieval times, a few manufactures had relied on royal support in the form of capital and management. The cases of the royal shipyard (*Ribeira das Naus*), ironworking (foundries), and rope making in Lisbon are good examples of "public enterprising" in select industries, as early as the sixteenth century. Though silks were included in the stimulus package, affecting enterprises in Trás-os-Montes and Minho[24], what was different at the end of the seventeenth century was the government's new interest in bulky and final consumer goods.

Taking into consideration its economic results, the endeavor that deserves special attention refers to the setting up of woolen manufactures. These industrial units received public support to ensure the fabrication of several varieties of woven wool, notably baize (*baetas*) and serge (*sarjas*), the demand for which had been met largely by English fabrics. The adoption of this manufacturing policy followed the advices included in a report of the former ambassador to the French court, Duarte Ribeiro de Macedo (1618–1680), dated from 1675 where he described the success of economic policies implemented in other European countries, namely France. In fact, the economic reforms of the Treasury minister Jean-Baptiste Colbert were discussed in Macedo's report entitled "On the Introduction of the Arts in Portugal" (Amzalak 1928). Macedo's assessment was actually a response to a message sent by the Portuguese secretary of state, lamenting the "pitiful state" of Portugal's commerce and the resulting drain on the nation's money stock. The royal court was sensitive to this issue, which drew the attention of the overseer of the treasury, the count of Ericeira, Luís de Meneses.

Although the control of imports was perceived as a necessity to promote the industry, the main problem was indeed the scarcity of silver. As such, a policy focused on bullion would eventually condemn to failure any other oriented by import-substitution strategies. This was particularly the case when southern areas of Brazil gave access to Spanish silver, through an illegal trade which benefited Portuguese businesses. Eventually, import-substitution policies and the search for new sources of precious metals became contradicting policies.

---

[24] Hanson 1986: 151–152, 186–187; Macedo 1982b: 37.

*Import-substitution policies*

Regardless of the differences that split political circles, trade deficits were a common concern. A plan for the best way to address the problem was not endorsed unanimously. For one faction, the simple solution was to ban the import of "superfluous" (i.e., luxury) goods, whose only purpose was to meet the conspicuous consumption of the nobility. The merchants, on the other hand, claimed that the problem resided in heavy taxes on re-exports of Brazilian commodities, at a time when other colonial powers supplied the international economy with the very same products. As a result, prices of sugar, tobacco, and other tropical products sold by Portugal were not competitive for fiscal reasons. The solution should reside on a revision of tariffs, since the loss of market share undercut the potential of re-exports to surpass imports, causing trade balance deficits.

Ribeiro de Macedo, the Portuguese ambassador to the French court of Paris, once aware of this discussion in the kingdom, acknowledged both arguments in his long technical report. He claimed they were not mutually exclusive, although neither one attacked the problem at its fundamental cause. The politicians' vision largely ignored the fact that many of the imported goods were no longer luxuries, since they had already become items of mainstream consumption. Woolen fabrics such as serge (*sarja*), baize (*baeta*), woolen and silk stockings were in high demand in the urban centers and were the main items causing trade deficits. Serge, "the wrap of women," actually made up the lion's share of textile imports. In Paris, London, Geneva, Venice, and Holland – all places that Macedo knew well – he could safely say that when the consumption of a luxury good gained widespread demand, to the point that imports skyrocketed, the state developed the respective "art" domestically at any cost, favoring those who could do the work best, and blocking any further imports. If raw materials were lacking, he continued, their import was facilitated, while if they were in abundance, exporting them had to be strictly prohibited.

What was actually happening with the case of woolens illustrates well Portugal's deeply engrained economic problems. The raw material – wool – was plentiful in Portugal, but supplied England, and then re-imported in the form of cloth – awarding the value-added to foreign economies, and further exacerbating the trade deficit. Hence, the woolen textiles were among those sectors that drew the attention of politicians. Regarding the factors of production and the relative simplicity of production processes, the fine woolens usually imported from England were considered of "easy transformation," in contrast to silk, brocades, and paper, technically more demanding. Portugal would benefit from import-substitution policies if the target were English baizes and serge, since these commodities were of "easier" manufacturing processes and one of the principal causes of the drain of Portugal's currency (Amzalak 1928: 18). In his diplomatic correspondence, Ribeiro de Macedo went into considerable detail about the policies common elsewhere in Europe. Encouraging manufacturing in other countries followed a two-pronged approach. On the one hand, it took the form of high customs duties levied on substitutable goods, or a consumption ban (which was not the same thing as an import ban, and allowed transshipment). On the other hand, it consisted of subsidizing the enterprises that produced the substitute goods (Rau 1968).

Public intervention in the economy did not need a great deal of state financing or meddling in industry. The count of Ericeira, the minister who welcomed Ribeira de Macedo's report, adopted a policy of industrial stimulus that targeted several subsectors – woolen textiles, silks, glass working, and iron-working– but made no effort to increase the number of units working under state supervision. According to him, capital should come from the private sector, and the state should limit its encouragement by granting operating permits. These licenses afforded the status of "royal factories" (*reais fábricas*) to private investments, which meant that they enjoyed monopoly rights granted by the state.

All of the subsectors mentioned earlier saw the creation of sponsored manufacturing units that did not eliminate non-sponsored facilities across the kingdom. With regard to ironworking, just one foundry, in Figueiró dos Vinhos, was under direct state administration – furnishing the arsenals and shipyards of Lisbon, while another, in Prado de Tomar, supplying the same market destinations, was run by private contractors and had the statute of royal factory. Its more efficient production was acknowledged by contemporary testimonies (Macedo 1982: 39–40).

In the textile sector, at least, neither availability nor lack of public funds determined the success or failure of these enterprises. Their success stemmed rather from their actual producing capacity to meet the demand that had earlier been satisfied with imports. As would occur later, during the rule of the marquis of Pombal, the policies were not enacted with the intention to create industry, but rather to reorganize it, at least in part according to models that required concentration in manufacturing, or benefited from monopolistic protectionism (Macedo 1982b: 31). Hence, manufacturing stimulus at the end of the seventeenth century impacted on a number of activities whose supply was already regionalized. Not surprisingly, the textile industry was one of the subsectors that were very receptive to these policies. It was a widely disseminated industry across the kingdom, mostly in rural areas where a putting-out system was already rooted. From the sixteenth century onwards, as stated in the previous chapter, dispersed producers, mostly rural households, were called upon to supply urban and supra-regional markets. This translated into less allocation of resources to self-consumption and moving forward to a market-oriented economy (Vries 1994a).

Recognized throughout Europe in the seventeenth century, the spread of the putting-out system paved the way for the emergence of rural industrial "districts" thus giving meaning to the concept of proto-industrialization, as "the first phase of the industrialization process."[25] The spread of the putting-out system reveals that market incentives favored the persistence of rural industries, as low farming revenues pushed households to find additional sources of income. The persistence of this system carries ambivalent interpretations. It can be seen as a means of raising the living standards of rural populations and allowing opportunities for growing consumption. But rural industries postponed migration to urban centers, retarded work specialization, and specialization is deemed an engine of productivity growth. In that sense, the putting-out system may signal economic hindrances and the social benefits of the policy that tended to reinforce this organization may not be equal to the costs in the long run.

Despite the criticisms that challenged the applicability of the concept of *proto-industrialization* to denote a stage that preceded an industrialized economy, it is still pertinent when pointing to the presence of manufacturing "districts." In Portugal, just as elsewhere in Europe, proto-industrialization emerged in areas that combined raw materials with abundant labor supply. This could happen either in pastoral areas, where labor-extensive animal husbandry often meant underemployment, or in predominantly arable areas, since villagers could take up industrial work during slack periods in agricultural cycle. The production of woolen fabrics in Inner Beira, and in Alentejo provides a good example of a successful rural industry. The seasonal herding of sheep ran side-by-side with the tradition of manufacturing woolens, both of which needed running water. As these areas were also suitable for growing olive trees, olive oil was used in processing the fiber (Pedreira 1994: 82).

---

[25] Franklin Mendels (1972) is the leading author on the concept of proto-industrialization, although there have been later reinterpretations by both economic historians and demographic historians. For a survey, see Ogilvie and Cerman 1996.

*The royal factories*

Between 1675 and 1690, the government's policy was directed to some of these "rural industrial districts" to improve the production of baize and serge. If this was feasible with the kingdom's resources, it is no surprise that the response came from the regions where the production of woolens had long been rooted in dispersed household units. Three "new Christian" weavers in Covilhã (Beira) signed a contract with the state in 1677 for the production of woolen cloth (*baetas* and *sarjas*). The arrangement involved certain innovations on technical matters alone. Only in a second stage did the organization of production undergo significant investments in order to concentrate all phases of manufacturing in one single plant. To get the businesses underway, English experts were enlisted to transmit skills and provide training for the workforce.

The state's involvement included three essential elements (none of which placed much of a financial burden): providing the means to monitor the contract; assistance of the diplomatic network in London for recruiting technicians (paying their travel and lodging expenses, and their wages, for the first month of their contract); enforcing a customs policy that protected this endeavor from English competition.[26] This called for ignoring what had been established by the treaty of 1654 with England, in which a secret clause assured the admittance of English woolens at a tax rate of 23 percent, lower than the one usually applied to other imported woolen textiles. These customs measures were later reinforced with the prohibition of the *use* of English-imported cloth in the kingdom.[27]

The outcome of this unprecedented initiative was summed up by the superintendent of this enterprise, Gonçalo da Cunha Vilas Boas, the institutional linkage between the state's sponsorship and the contractors, and the person who would be held accountable should any circumstance threaten the outcome of this policy. Vilas Boas' report sheds light into the technical and business practice features of the Covilhã initiative. Rural household units carried out the carding and spinning activities, while the more capital-intensive stage of dyeing, which required separate facilities, stood under control of yet another contractor (Dias 1954: 69).

The quality of the first batches was rejected by Lisbon's tailors, forcing the entrepreneurs to try another tactic (Dias 1954: 8). They erected a large building on the bank of a water stream. The plant housed various production stages including carders and fullers, and called in additional technicians for the more specialized and costly tasks, such as dyeing.

---

[26] For details on royal manufacturing processes in Covilhã, see Dias 1954.
[27] For all issues raised by the Anglo-Portuguese treaties, see Shaw 1998.

Spinning, however, was still performed by rural households. In time, the investment increased. Three years into the scheme there were seventeen looms, each one employing twenty-three people (Macedo 1982b: 34). Aside from the fabric workers, the industry employed shop owners in Lisbon, overseers for each step of the transformation process and machine operators (printers and fullers). All these occupations accounted for another thirty-four employees. In 1680 the enterprise had 415 people on the payroll. The scale and quality of its production encouraged the contractors to branch out to a neighboring town, Manteigas, and to push the state to help find new entrepreneurs to replicate the undertaking in Estremoz (Alentejo).

In the economic struggle waged against English manufactures all indications are that Portugal's productive capacity responded well. In 1680 the seventeen looms in Covilhã accounted for 3,000 bolts of cloth, which represented about half the consumption of *baetas* and *sarjas* in the country (Dias 1954: 58). Each bolt was 33 meters long, on average, meaning that the total consumption was on the order of 198,000 meters. The installed capacity of the facilities was insufficient, but it was expected that the installation of four new looms in the township of Manteigas would help to satisfy the plan to meet domestic demand with the country's own resources very soon.

Considering the difference in the size of the linen market to the woolens market, the manufacturing innovations at Covilhã revealed higher productivity for *baetas* and *sarjas*. Each loom operated by twenty-three persons produced four bolts of cloth (i.e., 132 meters) per week, making a rate of 5.7 meters per worker; while estimates for linen production are for 4.2 meters per worker (Pedreira 1994: 80). It cost about 15,000 *réis* to produce each bolt of cloth in Covilhã, excluding the factory's fixed costs, as the amount refers only to raw materials and labor, and does not comprise administrative expenses. In Lisbon, each bolt of cloth was worth 21,000 and 22,000 *réis*. As for English cloth, the price was 27,000 *réis* in Lisbon, including the costs of shipping and taxes (Dias 1954: 60). Under these circumstances, and in spite of the comparatively higher productivity of the workers of the woolen industry, the entrepreneurs operated within the framework of a very narrow margin of profit, since the difference of 4,500 *réis* between production costs and sale price (in Lisbon) did not include fixed costs of the factory. Entrepreneurs needed both monopoly rights in the domestic market and protective measures to override the admittance of English woolens at a custom-duty rate of 23 percent, which must have regularly occurred, judging by the constant tensions between the English merchants residing in Lisbon and the Portuguese customs officials (Shaw 1998: 19).

The comparison of domestic prices with imports, at a port town like Lisbon, indicates the fragile sustainability of the state's policy for several reasons, mainly for its sensitivity to political circumstances that loosened the barriers to imports and eroded markups or required heightening Portugal's productivity. This factor, however, was technically constrained by scarce know-how, which was embodied in skilled, immigrant labor that operated in certain segments of the production chain. The small margin of profit for domestic producers was further challenged by the fact that imports of English cloth did not halt. In fact the protective barriers to the entry of the foreign commodity just prohibited *consumption* (of English cloth in the kingdom), but did not impose any restriction on *importing* it. No wonder, then, that on the eve of a new trade agreement with Britain in 1703, no less than 11 percent of the cloth exported from England was loaded onto ships bound for Portugal, part of which was re-exported to Brazil (Macedo 1982b: 49). Hence, Portugal's output was short for domestic and Brazilian markets together. Thus, to protect national production regarding the supply of domestic markets, customs houses officials may have been instructed not to comply with the English advantages based on the 23 percent rate of duties determined by the 1654 treaty. On balance, from the economic upshot of the policy we may deduce the significance of any alteration in customs-duty rates.[28]

In the end, Ericeira's program was detrimental to the British community in Portugal, but added arguments to a faction of the Court that considered customs duties as the sinew of the state's finances, which were not performing as expected due to the import-substitution policy. The program had technical and market fragilities besides being threatened by political decisions and other sorts of adverse factors. Local opposition to the royal contract came from individuals left out from the monopoly arrangements but with interests in the woolens industry. These ultimately clashed with the three businessmen of Covilhã and Manteigas. Charges were made that the scale of manufacturing was crowding out cottage spinners, a claim that the supervisor strove to contend, arguing that there were a sufficient number of spinners to keep up with the growing demand for thread. His argument does not hold, since boosting production beyond the level of 6,000 bolts of cloth would raise labor costs in the region. Second, as would often be the case later on, some parties affected by the monopoly granted to the entrepreneurs of the fabric called for the intervention of the Inquisition. Therefore, the persecution of merchants and workers of the cloth industry destabilized the woolens textile production throughout the region

---

[28] Hanson 1986: 295; Shaw 1998: Chapter 1.

and not just the one allocated to contractors of the factories of Covilhã and Manteigas (Dias 1954: 59–60).

A cost–benefit analysis of Ericeira's policy was done at the royal court (Macedo 1982b: 36–41). The complaints spoke of its failure to guarantee the competitiveness of Covilhã's woolens in the urban markets of the littoral and to overcome the problem raised by trade balance deficits. The program seemed inappropriate to deal with the issue on which the Court was actually focused – the scarcity of precious metals and its consequences on money supply. While Lisbon witnessed Ericeira's rise and demise, which led him to commit suicide (Hanson 1986: 293), colonial authorities in Portuguese America were putting in place an inconspicuous expansion to the mouth of the Rio de la Plata to gain access to silver. Choosing an import-substitution policy was an autarchic way out for a financial crisis. But politicians and historians as well, claimed that the causes of the crisis resided elsewhere, on Portugal's declining market share of colonial goods. Thus, a comprehensive interpretation of the outcome of Ericeira's program asks for an overall view of the foreign trade and the empire's role.

## Trade and diplomacy

In the last quarter of the seventeenth century, the precious metals' shortage led royal cronies to debate its causes and the best policies to solve the problem. One of the identified reasons for the outflows of silver was Portugal's shrinking market-share of tropical goods as a result of colonial achievements of other European powers in Barbados, the Caribbean, and the Chesapeake. The issue drew the attention of the king's ministers, and later on, of Portuguese historians alike. The dominant intuition among historians is that Portugal's foreign relations determined the odds of the *entrepôt* trade ensuring trade surpluses. The sixteenth century is thought of as bearing such positive features, which represented a benefit of the empire that vanished in the last decades of the seventeenth century (Godinho 1978b). In fact, the downturn in exports became a topic of discussion in the court of King Pedro II and the debate left documental proof that the problem was perceived as a new concern. Notwithstanding the evidence provided by political documental sources, the question seldom posed in scholarly analyses is whether the concern of political circles about the deficits derived from the fact that screening information on foreign trade became a common practice of governance just then. So, the new issue may be political in itself. In other words, deficits of the balance of trade could have already been a fact in the

Table 3.6 *Lisbon's imports in 1685 (million* réis*)*

|  | Value | Percent |
|---|---|---|
| Manufactures | 1,251 | 79.7 |
| Foodstuffs, of which | 273 | 17.3 |
| *Cereals* | *187* | *11.9* |
| *Dairy products* | *45* | *2.9* |
| *Cod* | *41* | *2.6* |
| Raw materials and intermediate goods | 46 | 2.9 |
| Total | 1570 | 100 |

*Source:* Rau 1954: 257.

past, albeit they were not a topic for political debate due to the lack of an aggregate view on foreign trade accounts.

The accepted notion that external deficits display the novel features of the late seventeenth century lacks confirmation based on long-term series, although it may be consistent with some changes in the structure of imports and exports that the scarce data available allow us to identify. The unique report providing figures of a balance of trade dates from May 11, 1685. It is an unreplaceable source to begin the discussion of the contemporary perception of a commercial downturn, which was thought to cause financial and monetary distress (Rau 1954). In fact, the larger share of exports of primary goods relative to re-exports may point to Portugal losing markets for its colonial goods.

*Trade in foodstuffs*

The aforementioned report from 1685 estimates a 782 million *réis* deficit since imports achieved 2,092 million *réis* and exports (also comprising re-exports) did not surpass 1,310 million *réis*. These calculations made use of customs records of all seaports, but excluded duties collected on the land-border which would much better mirror the trade with Spain. The volume of trade varied distinctly among the seaports. The traffic into Lisbon was the most diversified of all. The capital city was the hub of foreign relations and the seat of the royal court, thus 77 percent of all imports (1,570 million *réis*) and 75 percent of exports (969 million *réis*) passed through its wharf facilities (Rau 1954: 256–257).

A fair amount of European imports were manufactured goods. In Lisbon, they count for 79.7 percent (Table 3.6). Such preponderance does not challenge the prevailing idea among historians that cereals were a main article in the Portuguese trade balance and its import should be seen as a consequence of an ineffective primary sector. Foodstuffs did contribute to the integration of Portugal in the international economy of the time. Cereals, however, should not have been the main cause of balance of trade deficits. From 1679 to 1684, 619,957 hectoliters (74,874 *moios*) of cereal came from European shores to Lisbon's docks, of which 180,115 hectoliters were wheat (Rau 1954: 257). Data points to an annual average of 36,022 hectoliters. At an estimated annual consumption of three hectoliters *per capita* (similar to the one of the sixteenth century) and with a roughly estimated population of 2 million people, grain imports via Lisbon covered 0.5 percent of the country's annual needs.[29] Considering that the city handled three-quarters of Portugal's foreign trade, the volume of cereals in this port is deemed representative of levels of imports. However, the figures also suggest that in the late seventeenth century Portugal was consuming fewer European cereals than had been the case in the sixteenth century. Population trends (growth in the 1500s and stagnation for a great part of the seventeenth century) and the diffusion of maize in the north of the Tagus River probably account for the declining imports of this bulky commodity.

Together with less reliance on foreign cereals, the second half of the seventeenth century was noticeable for the rise of imports of cod, which kept the English fleet busy serving Portugal's growing consumption since mid-century.[30] This trend common to the rest of the Iberian Peninsula may rest on the substitution of sources of protein, so that the price elasticity of cod points to its becoming a staple good. Indeed, representative cases of monastic consumption, whose preferences for fish are homogeneous for religious reasons, showed that the share of cod varied negatively with the religious orders' wealth. Although the increased consumption of cod is still a matter for further scrutiny, it has been suggested that it gained importance where living standards were not significantly improving, as it happened in the Mediterranean regions from the seventeenth century onwards (Grafe 2012: 69–79).

Portuguese data from 1689 about cod imports do not provide information on quantities, while it tells us that it summed up 280 million *réis*. Accepting this figure as consistent with the evolution of cod trade, roughly 13 percent of all Portuguese imports were assigned to this single item, both to domestic consumption and to re-export to Brazil, where it was part of the slaves' diet. Under the regime of monopoly granted to the

---

[29] For the daily food allotments already considered in Chapter 2, see Godinho 1982–1984, IV: 21.
[30] Hanson 1986: 224; Shillington and Chapman 1907: 212.

*Companhia Geral do Comércio do Brasil* (Brazilian Commerce Company) (1649), the supply of cod was assigned to English fleets, suggesting that the members of the board of the company had connections to English traders (Costa 2002b, vol. I: 568).

As for exports there is no safe means to assess the value of domestic products sent to European markets. Some references about olive oil and wine together point to 914 million *réis* bound for northern Europe, in 1690. If the value of exports did not change critically since 1685 (1,310 million *réis*), these two primary products accounted for 70 percent of exports. The largest part (10,000 pipas, i.e., barrels) referred to olive oil shipped in Lisbon, against 5,000 in Porto. Portugal's largest European market for wine (England) received just 2,230 barrels (1 ton equal to 2 barrels) (Hanson 1986: 216). Therefore, among Portugal's primary production, olive oil made up a portion of exports that has been underestimated. Economic studies have been focused on wine flows, which no doubt picked up after 1703. The expansion of olive cultivation throughout the sixteenth and seventeenth centuries deserves consideration in order to better understand its place in the country's agricultural output, as well as the contribution of the primary sector to the integration of the Portuguese economy in international markets.

Despite the fact that the aforementioned figures are based on sparse data, it is reasonable to assume that importation of foodstuffs was balanced with the same kind of exports, not to mention intense salt flows. In the last quarter of the seventeenth century, the annual Lisbon salt exports were worth 27.5 million *réis* (Rau 1954). But Setúbal, not Lisbon, was the leading port in this trade. From 1680 to 1703 an annual average of 95,270 *moios* (moio = 828 lt) of the product left the docks of Setúbal, for which the going price was 1,500 *réis* per *moio* (Hanson 1986: 212). Setúbal's salt may have reached 143 million *réis*, thereby significantly contributing to the nation's foreign trade balance. Considering that 1,310 million *réis* represented all exports in 1685, Lisbon and Setúbal together, just considering salt flows, accounted for 13 percent.

After the Restoration, salt became a milestone in diplomatic arrangements. The terms of the peace signed in 1669 that settled, once and for all, the issue of restoring the Brazilian northeast to Portuguese control made the Dutch the leading buyers of Portuguese salt. Through the Treaty of The Hague (1669) Portugal paid an indemnity of 1 billion *réis*, funded by the revenues from a tax levied on Setúbal's salt which, in turn, supplied the Dutch fisheries. The treaty had foreseen twenty years to pay off the full amount but throughout the 1690s the Dutch consul was still overseeing the collection of the tax, which reached then the sum of 270 million *réis* (Antunes 2004: 170). Although the flow of the merchandise was less than anticipated, thus prolonging the term of the agreement, what should be stressed is the sort of arrangement to fulfill the service of an external debt that Portugal acknowledged in diplomatic terms. In fact, Portugal paid to regain its sovereignty over the sugar-producing regions by affording the Dutch access to a strategic commodity in fisheries, which in turn, was an industry determining the development of maritime sectors and the control of the Baltic trade. The negotiation between Portugal and the Dutch did not go unnoticed by England, which had an expansionist agenda as well and eventually collided with the Dutch supremacy in the Baltic (Mello 2002: 268–269).

### Colonial trade

Diplomatic arrangements with the United Provinces (1661, 1669) ensured that Portugal regained control over Brazil's northeast, the main sugar-producing area. The crop, however, no longer found heavy demand in the northwestern European markets. As a consequence of the shrinking market share of Portugal's sugar in Amsterdam or in English ports, the sales were progressively redirected to Hamburg or to Italian ports, like Livorno. Therefore, the final demand for Portugal's colonial commodities depended on the evolution of regions that were not assisted by improvements in living standards, which could have impacted the aggregate decline of re-exports and respective effects on trade deficits. Still, the peace with the Dutch gave the colony a new chance for recovery and for diversifying agricultural output, which enabled Portugal to participate in economic streams involving new goods, such as tobacco.

Unfortunately, long-term series are missing to assess the significance of the Brazilian economic diversification, as records from Lisbon's customs house were destroyed by the 1755 earthquake. The city centralized the colonial traffic since the Brazilian Commerce Company was founded. The extinction of the Company in 1663 did not alter the navigation scheme which remained regulated by the convoy system, affecting negatively the activity of other Portuguese port towns. Thus Lisbon would be the best case to study the revitalization of the Brazilian economy and to discuss how much the scale of its tobacco boom differed from that of the North American regions.

Since data for Lisbon is missing, customs duties collected in Porto shed some light on the relative variation of the two main crops, tobacco and sugar, in the early stages of growing plantation of tobacco (Table 3.7). Some decades earlier, when WIC's privateering affected the Brazilian fleets in the decade from 1625 to 1634, the loots on tobacco relative

Table 3.7 *Imports of sugar and tobacco in Porto, 1640–1679 (1,000 of lbs)*

|  | Number of observations | Sugar | Tobacco | Tobacco/Sugar |
|---|---|---|---|---|
| 1640–1644 | 2 | 1,137 | – | – |
| 1645–1649 | 2 | 1,679 | 49 | 0,03 |
| 1650–1654 | 3 | 464 | 13 | 0,03 |
| 1655–1659 | 3 | 1,569 | 127 | 0,08 |
| 1660–1664 | 2 | 3,944 | 250 | 0,06 |
| 1668–1679 | 3 | 2,843 | 187 | 0,07 |

*Source:* Arquivo Distrital do Porto, Arcebispado da Sé, Livros de Portagem e Redízima.

to those on sugar were just 0.4 percent of the volume and 0.7 percent of the value (174 chests of tobacco against 39,255 chests of sugar) (Laet 1925 II: 621–636). Forty years later, the volume of tobacco passing through Porto customs increased threefold and achieved 7 percent of the volume of the sugar shipping. Thus, as it happened in Chesapeake, the mid-seventeenth century appears as a turning point in trade of Brazilian tobacco.

The rampant cargo of tobacco on board Portuguese fleets was taxed according to a fixed value (50 *réis*) per unity of weight (1 *arrátel* = 1 pound). In case prices went down, this system of taxation actually represented a raise of tariffs. Even so, the rapid increase of the volume of imports is reflected on the need to alter the weight unity in 1659 for tax purposes, changing from *arrátel* (= 1 pound) to *arroba* (32 pounds), paying 1,600 *réis*. The upward trend of the business went together with changes in the social features of agents. Before attracting wholesalers, tobacco trade was carried out by shippers and members of the crew, which is consistent with missing information on freight charges on tobacco and traces a picture similar to that found in North Atlantic. Also here, tobacco started as a subsidiary trade (Price and Clemens 1987: 15).

Notwithstanding the similarities stressed so far, the development of the business in both American hemispheres traces divergent paths. Any comparison of tobacco shipped to Europe shows critical differences between Brazil and the Chesapeake from the last years of the seventeenth century onwards, partly because of the scale of plantations, partly because the regions involved in transactions determined the volume of Brazilian tobacco that reached European ports. In the Portuguese case, Brazilian smoke was diverted to the African coast to barter for slaves. Thus, the crop outlined maritime routes directly linking colonial spots, spearing the intervention of capital or know-how of merchants residing in the mother country (Verger 1976). Information dating from 1726 ensures that half the production of the colony was sent to the West African coast (Schwartz 1984: 458). The same partition of the production between both markets is attested for in documental sources from the 1780s, which ensures us that the pattern of trade established in the middle of the seventeenth century persisted until the late eighteenth century (Verger 1976: 16).

Brazilian tobacco was produced and transformed primarily to meet the taste of the African consumer. The selection of the quality concerned the habit of smoking (instead of chewing). Leaves were twisted into ropes processed with molasses. A regular trade connecting Bahia to Africa (Angola and Guinea Coast) was already in motion in the 1680s when it called upon five ships sailing annually in this route. Ten years later there were twenty vessels, providing almost the same shipping capacity as the Portugal–Brazil route in that decade, which occupied about 25–29 vessels of 250 tons.

The supply of Brazilian tobacco to the West African coast affected quantities that would reach Portugal, thus international comparisons based on amounts of cargo shipped to European ports do not allow an accurate assessment of each colony's production. It tells us, however, how the different direction of flows affected the hierarchy of markets in Europe. A comparison of amounts arrived at Porto (a secondary port) with those arriving at Liverpool (a secondary port as well) indicates the possibility of the latter outstripping the former after the 1680s. While in the 1660s there is no information on the commodity in Liverpool, in the 1670s 200,000 pounds were shipped. By that time, in Porto quantities were not critically lower, reaching 180,000 pounds. However, by 1679 divergence began and Liverpool was importing double the quantity Porto was importing (680,000 pounds against 348,000) (Clemens 1976: 212). For the decade of the 1680 onwards, estimations point to the Portuguese imports hovering around 5.3 million pounds (Schwartz 1984: 459). Other sources suggest that this figure should be 6.6 million, which indicates that Portugal was then dealing with quantities that represented around 26 percent of the tobacco passing through English ports.[31] In the following years, divergence between the Atlantic traders turned out even clearer. Data for both countries indicate that in the early 1700s England could import almost four times as much as Portugal (34.6 million pounds against 9 million, respectively).[32] By that

---

[31] English quantities in Steensgaard 1990, table 3.19; Portuguese figures Nardi 1996: 366, converting *arroba* to pound on the base of 1 *arroba* = 32 pound.

[32] Price and Clemens 1987: 5. Portuguese imports in Nardi 1996: 366 taking the year of 1708, as the highest level of the first decade of the 1700s. Philips 1993: 67, table 2.3, points to 524,800 pounds based on Pinto 1979: 202.

time, quantities of sugar might not have surpassed 42.4 million pounds, which suggests a significant change in the relative importance of each Brazilian crop in the last quarter of the seventeenth century. The sugar cycle achieved its lowest point in the 1680s to start recovering only in the second half of the eighteenth century (Schwartz 2008: 431, 452). The diversion of Brazilian tobacco to Africa had two other effects besides putting Portuguese ports in the lowest ranks among the European staples that could deal with this commodity at an international level. One was the dependence of European powers on the Brazilian product if they intended to engage in slave trade. Thus, an intense contraband developed in Dutch African trading posts, which undermined the enforcement of national monopolies inherent in colonial systems in the mercantilist era. The second consequence dwells upon the state fiscal interest in these flows. Since Brazilian tobacco was not consumed in northwestern Europe, re-exports offered the slightest base of taxation, enhancing the role of the domestic consumption for fiscal purposes. Established around 1634, the tobacco monopoly afforded the Crown with a new source of revenue that was already significant in 1674 (Hanson 1982: 153). The yields of the monopoly kept rising in the following decades providing one of the most rampant state receipts of the early modern era.

The colonial economy underwent remarkable changes in the second half of the seventeenth century, which assigned a new role to tobacco. This transformation did not alter the need for a wide range of goods that Portugal had to buy in European staples, actually in the very regions where Portuguese re-exports were facing recession. Identifying the precise origins of the cargo sent to the colony is not possible, although references to England are the most common. Diplomatic correspondence of the 1690s reveals that each ship bound for Brazil carried a vast range of merchandises, half of which was of English origin (Prestage 1935: 28). In 1700 the same correspondence reports that the fleet sailing to Brazil had 70 percent of the cargo mostly made up with English cloth in a clear demonstration that English textiles had competitive prices in the colony (Morineau 1985: 169). Thus, the growth of the colonial market, boosted by continuous immigration, did not lead the exports of domestic sectors. It pushed instead the demand for foreign manufactures, which would end up by checking the efficacy of Ericeira's policy (Dias 1954: 69).

Declining enthusiasm among European markets for Portugal's re-exports of New World goods went together with the ever-noticed intrusion of European fleets in Portuguese ports. The ships that served the Portuguese foreign trade sailed under the flags of other nations, a feature

Table 3.8 *European shipping in the Lisbon trade, 1641–1688*

| Origin of the flag | Number of ships | % |
|---|---|---|
| Dutch | 477 | 42.8 |
| English | 398 | 35.7 |
| Hanseatic | 145 | 13.0 |
| Danish | 22 | 2.0 |
| French | 20 | 1.8 |
| Swedish and Norwegian | 31 | 2.8 |
| Polish | 2 | 0.2 |
| Portuguese | 1 | 0.1 |
| Non Identified | 19 | 1.7 |
| Total | 1115 | 100.0 |

*Source:* Rau 1954: 241. Note: Lisbon concentrated 3/4 of shipping arrivals.

of the economy going back to the days of the Iberian Union. Not only did this arrangement persist, but it actually turned more acute, attracting especially the merchant marines of England, United Provinces, France, and the Hanseatic League. From 1641 to 1688, with a gap in the series from 1649 to 1677, 1,115 vessels entered the Lisbon harbor revealing the overwhelming interest of the fleets of northern Europe in carrying Portuguese cargos (Table 3.8).

Shipping into and out of Lisbon and Faro – the two ports for which there is better information – allows us to say that the kingdom's foreign trade was "in foreign hands." In other words, there was a regular outflow of invisibles, and a reinforcement of the Portuguese fleet allocation to routes within the empire. The Portuguese shipping depended on barriers to entry imposed on foreign flags in imperial waters since 1605 and the Restoration left this norm untouched. It just confirmed the low capacity of the Portuguese fleets to operate under a competitive market (Rau 1954). Such a situation added to the downturn of re-export trade, another factor for current-account deficits and the drain of means of payment. In light of the similarity of this situation to others that recurred in later times, Portuguese historians have identified swings in re-exports of colonial goods as a check on Portugal's domestic production, which is an issue that elaborates on costs and benefits of colonial empires in early modern economies.

*The economic policy of the empire*

For several decades, Portuguese historians have argued that the role of the empire in supplying goods for resale boosted the imports of greater value-added merchandise, thereby hampering the development of domestic manufactures. Furthermore, studies have been focused on counter-cyclical policies, assuming that the state's particular ability to diagnose economic crises derived from its financial dependency on customs duties. Therefore, policies reflecting the state's perception of a macroeconomic scenario were supposed to denote an actual economic constraint.[33] Although the linkage of public finance to economic troubles does not clearly show up in data from the second half of the seventeenth century, since demography and agricultural output recovered the levels reached before the war, there is no doubt that the international order revealed Portugal's vulnerable position. This was carefully weighed by the count of Ericeira, whose policy was focused on trade deficits and faced the opposition of a different political wing that better echoed the interests of settlers in the southern borders of Brazil. This line of thought at the royal court foresaw some advantages of interloping the Spanish trade in America, moving the border further to the Rio de la Plata. In fact, the territorial expansion that had occurred in the last decades of the century pushed the demand for manufactures in the colony, which required a level of industrial output that the domestic infrastructure had not achieved yet. Hence, the success of Ericeira's policy was not just contingent to struggles among royal cronies. It was also depending on the course of the events that were attracting more settlers to the southern areas of Brazil.

In 1680, the Portuguese established a colony in Sacramento, at the mouth of the Rio de la Plata aiming to engage in illicit trade with Spanish America, which would grant them access to silver. More important, perhaps, for the future course of events was the local surge in demand for woolen cloth, which exposed the incapacity of the manufactures in Covilhã, Manteigas, or Estremoz to grow at a pace that could meet the Brazilian demand. Besides, if customs duties on the English fabrics were reduced, which would occur upon the signing of the commercial treaty with England in 1703, the colony could be supplied with the English product at highly competitive prices (Macedo 1982b: 58). Hence, the prosperous though illicit trade, at the borders of the Iberian empires in South America, would soon challenge the policy that had promoted the production of manufactures in Portugal. Meanwhile, this southward shift of the Brazilian colony, almost entirely due to the enterprise of the

---

[33] Macedo 1982a and Godinho 1955, and the discussion in Pedreira 1994.

colonists themselves, was taken by political circles in Lisbon as an opportunity to incite the private prospection of mines. New settlements gradually sprang up from Curitiba (1668) to the isle of Santa Catarina (1677), while the Pope authorized the creation of the Rio de Janeiro's diocese (1676) with the Rio de la Plata as its southern boundary.

The founding of an enclave at the mouth of the Rio de la Plata fulfilled an ancient Portuguese aspiration for using the river as the border between the two Iberian empires, foreseeing its potential for illicit access to Peruvian silver. Acting on instructions from the royal court, a colonizing expedition organized by the government of Rio de Janeiro set foot on the northern bank of the Rio de la Plata in 1680. The governor erected a fortification and founded the colony of Sacramento, right in front of the city of Buenos Aires. Recognizing the danger of the Portuguese approach, the Spanish garrison immediately attacked the new Portuguese fortress (Map 3.1).

The hostilities might have led to much graver consequences, but they were mollified by a provisional treaty in 1681 that tolerated the Portuguese presence until the rights of both parties could be determined through further negotiations. Portugal's claim was not entirely clear due to problems in accurately determining the line of demarcation settled in the Treaty of Tordesillas (1494). The standstill afforded enough time for the military outpost to grow into a populous village having its own governor. The new leader of this settlement took care to promote the colonization of the surrounding region and to circumvent the Spanish efforts to suppress the smuggling and illegal trade.[34] In 1692 the colony of Sacramento reached the 1,000-inhabitants mark and proved to be a satellite of the merchant community in Rio de Janeiro, informing Lisbon about the exceptional profit margins earned in doing business with the Spanish American territories (Possamai 2006). These profits were secured by selling Brazilian cow hides, the crucial raw material for many transformed goods that had recently come into high demand, paid with Spanish silver.

While Portugal's discreet expansion in the last quarter of the seventeenth century targeted the furthest reaches of the Brazilian colony, on the other side of the world, the connections to Asia were visibly and forcefully maintained by sending two or three warships along with each of the annual merchant convoys. After decades of capitulation to the military inroads of European trading companies, the remains of the *Estado da Índia* were ever more depending on the exploitation of commercial connections within the Asian regions, including Batavia, and mostly through Macao, the Portuguese

---

[34] For all events in Sacramento, see Almeida 1973.

Map 3.1  Portuguese America, seventeenth-eighteenth centuries

conclave in China.[35] These markets became important outlets for
Brazilian tobacco, while the port of Salvador (Bahia), on the return
route from India, welcomed the privately funded transshipments of
Asian cotton textiles that were carried on board the king's armed
vessels.[36] When international conflict broke out in the War of the

[35] Souza 1986, 2014.    [36] Lapa 1968; Hanson 1986: 265.

Spanish Succession, the numerous regions of the Portuguese empire were more integrated within Portugal's economic space than they had ever been before.

## The Atlantic alliance

At the outbreak of the War of the Spanish Succession (1702), the royal court was well informed about the role that the Sacramento enclave played in attracting Peruvian silver. Thus, the unresolved issue of the border between the two Iberian empires must have played in favor of Portugal's alignment with the Atlantic powers. As with many earlier and later international conflicts, the war had a dynastic groundwork and the central actors were split into two distinct blocs. The armed conflict pitted England, the Dutch Republic, and the Holy Roman Empire against Spain and France and pivoted on the succession of the childless king Charles II, the last of the Spanish Habsburg kings. In his will, dated from 1700, Charles designated a Bourbon, the duke of Anjou, as his successor, under the condition that the duke (a grandson of Louis XIV) renounce his right to the throne of France. The other claimant to the Spanish throne, through his lineage to the Austrian Habsburgs, was the archduke Charles, second son of the Emperor Leopold, who gained the support of the northern maritime powers.

Upon the death of Charles II, the duke of Anjou took the throne as Philip V, thus triggering the fear in Europe that Spain and France could be united under one monarch. Considering that the inheritance of the Spanish Crown included not only Spain but also territories in Italy, the Low Countries and colonies in the Americas, a French hegemony was perceived as a threat to the European balance of power. The war, in truth, put France and England against each other. These were the two nations that most disputed European geopolitics in the eighteenth century. Considering this balance of powers, the ambassadors in The Hague, Paris, and London advised for Portugal's neutrality, but there were factions in the Court that thought supporting the duke of Anjou was the best choice for Portugal's interests (Cluny 2003). In 1701, Portugal formally adhered to the cause of Philip V, signing two treaties respectively with Spain and France. In the same year England, the Dutch Republic, and the Holy Roman Empire formed the Grand Alliance (also known as the League of Augsburg), to back the claim of the archduke Charles.

In a turnabout of diplomatic maneuvering, Portugal joined the Grand Alliance in 1703 and was thrust into a war in the Iberian Peninsula. This required the signing of three treaties: two of a military nature, making defensive and offensive commitments (dated May 16, 1703, with

England, the Dutch Republic, and the Holy Roman Empire); the other of an economic nature (signed on December 27th with England). According to the terms of the latter, named after the English special envoy to Portugal John Methuen, Portugal was to tax English cloth in accordance with the secret clause in the 1654 treaty, which stipulated preferential rates (23 percent) for English textiles. In return, England agreed to reduce the import duties on Portuguese wine, which would be one-third less than the import duties on French wines. In short, the item actually new in the Methuen Treaty referred to Portugal's exports of wine. As for textiles, the treaty seems more like a new attempt of the English diplomacy to enforce a clause of a contract signed fifty years earlier.

Portugal's switch in diplomatic commitments can be interpreted in many ways. It may reflect the bargaining skills of its chief author, John Methuen; but some historians have emphasized evidence of bribery; and still others point to the private interests of some noblemen who participated in the negotiation, notably those who were owners of vineyards.[37] Yet, Portugal's diplomatic alignment may point to other underlying causes. On the one hand, maritime powers encouraged Portugal's decision by promising moratoria on debt raised in the wake of the Restoration, from both England and the United Provinces, which Portugal was paying off with customs revenues. The 1654 peace treaty with England contained several terms that allowed English enterprising in Brazil and that forced Portugal to hand over an indemnity for having detained English ships in Lisbon in 1650. The secret clause prescribing preferential rates for imports of English manufactures was then established, albeit roughly obeyed by royal officials at the customs houses, according to complaints of English merchants. In January of the same year (1654) the last Dutch stronghold in Recife surrendered to the armed fleet of the *Companhia Geral do Comércio do Brasil*, but in order to secure the transfer of sovereignty the Portuguese paid the Dutch a compensation in the amount of 1 billion *réis*, payable in salt from 1669 on, according to a treaty signed in the same year.[38] This liability, carried over from the Restoration, must have driven Portugal's swing to the Grand Alliance.

On the other hand, having two powerful seafaring nations as adversaries spelled dire consequences, in view of the fact that crucial food items, such as codfish and cereals, were caught by their fishing fleets and shipped on their vessels. Moreover, relations with the empire also played their part, since piracy and privateering had been detrimental in the 1640s, so that in this new context of war there was no intention to let the national fleet incur such a risk again.

---

[37] Monteiro 2001; Francis 1966.    [38] Costa 2003; Mello 2002.

The treaty signed in December 1703 comprised economic articles that enhanced the economic specialization that each ally had already exhibited since 1690, when the hostilities between England and France opened the English market to Portuguese wines. Gaining access to a growing market was no small matter and would eventually ensure the rise of Portuguese exports which in the 1690s had just wavered in accordance with the economic war England carried out against French wines. Thus, the advantages Portugal gained by adhering to the Grand Alliance are easy to see, but it remains to know what England expected to gain with Portugal's non-neutrality.

An assessment of England's expected benefits from Portugal's realignment should take into account the Dutch Republic, which came out as the defrauded partner – deceived by Britain's diplomatic maneuvering (Israel 1989: 361–365). In the wake of the Methuen treaty the Dutch lost control over the Portuguese salt, the advantages of which were well-known to the British. Salt was one of the key-factors needed for breaking into the fishing industry in the Baltic, and even for enjoying a degree of hegemony in that region, where Dutch competition was fierce. In fact, during the second half of the seventeenth century, the Baltic had become a crucial area for military and naval powers. The region supplied raw materials (timber, iron, copper, flax, and hemp) and partially finished items that were strategically important in shipbuilding and artillery making. Aside from importing a wide range of colonial products, fish, manufactures, and transportation services, the Baltic had trade surpluses with England, draining the kingdom's means of payment derived from trade balances with other nations, which were in Britain's favor (Ormrod 2003: 61–65). Any maritime power that envisaged increasing its market share of the fishing industry needed the Baltic markets, indeed, but also needed access to salt produced in southern Europe. Thus, in the English perspective, obtaining it under the same conditions as other fishing nations was a means of weakening the Dutch Republic's position, which would happen if Portugal joined the Grand Alliance. The maneuver was spurred on by England, who foresaw the cancellation of Portugal's debt toward the United Provinces linked to the restoration of Pernambuco, paid in salt.

In Portuguese economic history, the War of the Spanish Succession is relevant due to the Methuen Treaty. It is worth bearing in mind that the United Provinces signed an identical agreement with Portugal in 1705 (Antunes 2004). But, in the long run, it was England that took advantage of the favorable treaty conditions, as the Dutch proved unable to export similar amounts of textiles, most likely because of problems in its own industry. As for Portugal, the close of the seventeenth century held out the prospect of new horizons for wine exports along with a brighter and burgeoning Brazilian market.

A new international order changed Portugal's role in the European trade network. On the domestic front, twenty eight years of war against the Spanish Habsburgs, together with the kingdom's involvement in the War of the Spanish Succession forty years later raised significant challenges to the state's budgets. In the next section we discuss whether wars and trade imbalances paved the way for new stages in the making of the fiscal state, as it happened elsewhere in Europe.

### The fiscal state

The discourse intending to legitimize the Restoration argued against the fiscal burden imposed by the Spanish kings. However, it was the military campaigning in the aftermath of the 1st of December *coup* that prompted the most pronounced tax rise in the seventeenth century. The very concept of a taxable income (*décima*) and respective yields compared to other sources of public revenue display the state's ability to extract a higher share of domestic product in the context of the war. An examination of this issue needs a few time benchmarks for which there is information on state budgets, in order to adequately weigh out any change of the structure of sources of revenue. In a first approach, the focus will be strictly on the tax base within the kingdom (including Madeira and the Azores), which ignores the contribution of the empire (Table 3.9).

Table 3.9 *Revenue of the State in mainland Portugal, 1619–1680 (million* réis*)*

| | |
|------|-------|
| 1619 | 760 |
| 1632 | 823 |
| 1641 | 1,612 |
| 1660 | 1,650 |
| 1680 | 1,256 |

\* Revenues from the empire not included.
*Sources:* Godinho 1978; Hespanha 1994: 114, 156 e 158; Dias 1985; Biblioteca da Ajuda, cód. 51-VI-19, fls. 127 and 359–365.

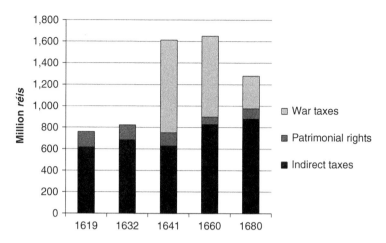

Figure 3.4 Tax revenues, 1619–1680
Sources: see table 3.9.

According to this criterion, the fiscal burden after the Restoration stands out in the variation of receipts from 822.5 million to 1,612 million *réis* between 1632 and 1641 (Hespanha 2004: 183). King João IV managed to negotiate a doubling of the fiscal burden immediately in the *Cortes* assembled in 1641. This confirms that the popular uprisings during the final days of the Habsburg rule were indeed sparked more by constitutional issues than by an excessive fiscal burden. State budgets contradict recurrent remarks preached from churches' pulpits condemning the Spanish monarch, while they confirm that regaining political autonomy allowed for a deepening of the state's capacity to extract an economic surplus.

A breakdown of the budgetary data in three main categories enhances the role of the new income tax and the restructuring of sources of income thus achieved (Figure 3.4). The category "domain revenue" encompasses rents collected both in the kingdom and the Atlantic islands (the Azores and Madeira), which comprised levies on agricultural production as well as royal monopolies on soap, playing cards, and mercury chloride. These latter yields stemmed from the authority of the king to enforce monopoly rights thereby denoting royal property rights. This same category also covers rents from confiscated assets (which reveal how coercive extraction was regarding subjects condemned for treason, namely the branches of the Portuguese aristocratic houses that sided with the Habsburg king).

"Indirect taxes" mainly refer to customs duties and the *sisa* (the sales tax collected by the municipalities – see Chapter 2). The third category, "revenues to pay for the war," comprises yields of the income tax (*décima*), as well as small amounts provided by an extraordinary levy on sugar and on a new tax payable by the holders of the main Crown grants (titles, seigneuries, and commanderies). Each of these new taxes was accepted at *Cortes* to pay for the war.

Not surprisingly, the structure of receipts changed during the war years. The income tax (*décima*) accounted approximately for 40–50 percent of the budgets in 1641 and 1660, but the momentum for change fell off twelve years after the peace treaty was signed (1668). In 1680, the revenues previously assigned to the fight for political autonomy stood at only 16 percent of the total budget. The decreasing share of the *décima* was due to the lowering of its rate to 4.5 percent since 1668, whereby indirect taxes outweighed that of the income tax. However, it seems clear that this fiscal innovation turned out to be a constitutional tax also in times of peace and it would prove useful in future events. The War of the Spanish Succession (1702–1713) provided a good reason to adjust again the rate of the tax to 10 percent and to double the lump sums of the *sisa* assigned to municipalities. But now tax hikes were restrained from even greater increases because allies promised to come forward with vast amounts of cash and troops (Costa 2003: 73–75). The legitimacy of raising the *décima* rate was beyond reproach in forthcoming circumstances. Under the rule of the marquis of Pombal, when international struggles were once again evoked as a justification, the *décima* at a 10 percent rate became a permanent part of the Portuguese fiscal system. The budgets for the 1760s show that the measures enacted to secure autonomy between 1640 and 1668 opened the opportunity for the state's encroachment into the income of royal subjects once and for all (see Chapter 4).

Therefore, the *décima*'s longevity allows us to describe the Restoration as the birth of a fiscal innovation in much the same way as the wars with Castile in the fourteenth century led to the conversion of the *sisa* into the first tax collected at a national level (see Chapter 1). Thus two long-lasting taxes of the Portuguese fiscal constitution had their origins in the struggle against Spain's efforts to politically unify the Iberian Peninsula.

Notwithstanding institutional innovations, the 1680s budget displays a structure similar to previous centuries, where the major share of indirect taxes (Figure 3.5), namely through customs duties, was still characterizing state revenue. Such fiscal dependence on foreign trade was used as an argument against the program of the count of Ericeira by his opponents. In fact, the import substitution policy was expected to impact negatively

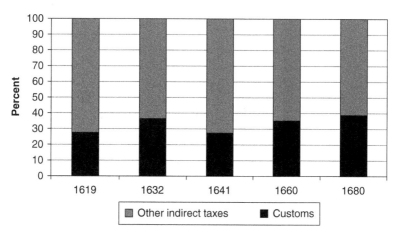

Figure 3.5 Customs and other indirect taxes, 1619–1680
Sources: See table 3.9.

on fiscal yields. State's budgets from the last decade of the seventeenth century would provide an informed assessment of the treasury's dependence on customs revenue and of the efficacy of Ericeira's program. However, since these are missing, the information available pertains to the single year of 1716, by which time revenues of a patrimonial sort, such as the fifth on gold production in Brazil and the tobacco monopoly, had introduced changes to the structure of financial resources. The former demonstrated its potentials through the transfer of a fifth of mining production to the kingdom. The domestic indirect taxes register a 2 percent increase between 1680 and 1716, which comprised the *sisa*, varying 0.5 percent, and the Lisbon customs houses 1.5 percent, also because they polarized 40 percent of the domestic flows. Besides, the 2 percent variation in domestic indirect taxes was just 0.7 points lower than that verified in customs of the kingdom in a whole, which suggests that between 1680 and 1716 domestic transactions underwent some improvements.[39] The aforementioned figures converted into grams of silver reveal that twenty years after the peace with Spain, the budget's total barely surpassed the one from 1619 (Table 3.10). Thus, both the structure of receipts and the real amounts collected were similar to those of a stage of "stateness" (Tilly 1975: 42) already attained at the beginning of the century.

[39] For the 1716 budget, see Macedo 1982b: 209.

Table 3.10 *Revenue of the State in mainland Portugal, 1619–1680 (marks of silver)*

| | |
|---|---|
| 1619 | 271,388 |
| 1632 | 269,597 |
| 1641 | 403,010 |
| 1660 | 388,031 |
| 1680 | 291,744 |

*Sources:* See table 3.9 and text.

Lacking estimates for the variation of the gross domestic product, but accepting that the increase of population was accompanied by aggregate output growth, the most probable scenario is that the Portuguese state mislaid its ability to increasingly extract economic surpluses in real terms. This being the case, Portugal followed a path unlike that of England, which in the 1680s steadily improved fiscal revenue through the extension of indirect taxation as well as by building up a professional civil service that allowed to abandon the tax-farming system. As such, a comparison of the evolution of fiscal income in both national cases gives a relative measure of the Portuguese lack of administrative progresses (O'Brien and Hunt 1999: 73). Considering real exchange rates, and converting the nominal values to a common currency (*réis*), we learn that in the second half of the seventeenth century (1660–1716 benchmarks) the total income of the Portuguese state (monopolies over the colonial empire ignored) varied 0.1 percent less than in the English case.[40] Bearing in mind that the population grew faster in Portugal in this period, we may say that the tax burden was becoming much heavier in England.[41]

Although the Portuguese tax system resembled that already prevailing a hundred years earlier, there was a fundamental difference regarding the place of Lisbon in the hierarchy of the kingdom's customs houses in the late seventeenth century. In 1632 Lisbon accounted for 34 percent of total customs income, whereas it accounted for 42 percent in 1680 and 77 percent in 1716. The fiscal significance of the capital mirrors immigrant inflows and also points to the effects of the convoy system that turned Lisbon into the single port city of trade with Portuguese America, thereby enhancing the city's role as a transshipment port. Nevertheless, Portugal's greater integration in the Atlantic system throughout the

[40] We are grateful to Rita Martins de Sousa for providing data on real exchange rates.
[41] English data in O'Brien 1988.

seventeenth century did not immediately translate into an increase of the empire's contribution to the state budget, which indeed displays a decline from 1619 to 1680 (25 percent in 1680 against 33 percent in 1619; Pedreira 2007). Fiscal sources are consistent with the general view of the second half of the century as one of relative stagnation of the colonial impact on the economy. Before the gold mining altered this trend, the monopoly over the transformation and distribution of tobacco, although not yet the fiscal mainstay that it would become in the next century, was already showing its financial potential. The tobacco rent almost doubled between 1680 and 1716, at which point the monopoly was routinely exploited by private consortiums.

Financial history is beyond the state's ability to extract revenues through fiscal mechanisms. It is worth noting Portugal's capability to impose universal taxes to the whole territory since medieval times as it happened with the *sisa*. But what should be stressed as significantly original in the Portuguese case is the persistence of an income tax, integrated in the fiscal system since 1641, even if the aggregate fiscal burden might have been lighter than in other dynastic states in the last quarter of the seventeenth century. Besides, the amount of taxes or the efficacy of a tax system seem to have not affected the state's proficiency to interfere in economic matters, such as regulating trade flows through the enforcement of customs policy, or by subsidizing private enterprising in order to influence the allocation of productive factors. In these respects, Portugal's path toward institutional modernization shows a pattern closer to that of Colbert's France. Institutional divergence relative to England, however, did not prevent Portugal's ally to exert the greatest influence on diplomatic affairs and in economic relations, particularly after the Methuen Treaty of 1703, as will be discussed in Chapter 4 (Hanson 1986: 292).

# 4    The Atlantic economy, 1703–1807

Throughout the eighteenth century, the Western world experienced remarkable changes. The usually labeled "Malthusian regime," defining technological constraints to per capita production growth and tracing a flat long-term trend for most of the European economies, came to a halt for the first time in England. The new economic era brought about gains in total factor productivity, together with population growth. Living standards increased and implied a dynamic change in aggregate demand.[1] These features of the modern economic growth that began in the final decades of the 1700s made headway through the modest and restricted spread of technology. They reached northwestern countries after the first steps had been given in England, while Mediterranean and Scandinavian regions fell behind. Different potentials to follow the English path in the nineteenth century led scholars to look back to previous centuries, particularly to the eighteenth century, to find both the roots of structural changes and causes of its pace of diffusion (Van Zanden 2009).

The present chapter focuses on this period that raised conditions for a greater divergence among European countries' economic growth. It covers the time span that starts with the Peace of Utrecht (1715) and ends with the first Napoleonic invasion, when the Portuguese royal court fled to Brazil (1808). Portugal's economy is here described taking into account the fact that this was one case among other Mediterranean countries that fell behind. A set of constraints were still impending over macroeconomic variables, which show a downward trend clearly from 1780 on, like urbanization rates and real wages. Nevertheless, a higher integration of the primary sector in international markets occurred and the empire increasingly played in favor of the kingdom's economic performance. The former contributed to the rise of agricultural output and led to some productivity improvements and the latter contributed to the rise of gold money stock and justified protectionist policies that made Brazil the outlet of Portuguese manufactures.

---

[1] Galor 2005: 171–293; Clark 2007.

164

In spite of the fact that these positive trends derived from the greater openness of the economy, the country suffered two exogenous shocks. The earthquake of 1755 caused a dramatic destruction of fixed capital in many regions. Recovery was a lengthy affair but also an opportunity for the institutional innovation carried out by the marquis of Pombal (Pereira 2009). The Napoleonic wars represented a second shock, involving Portugal in the turmoil of the European conflict at a time when the economy displayed signs of a recession which scholars have linked to the decline of gold mining. Other macroeconomic indicators translated in to falling living standards reinforcing the view of a critical juncture on the eve of the General Junot's invasion. Hence, in the beginning of the nineteenth century Portugal's economic position was grim. The departure of the royal court and the settlement of the government in Rio de Janeiro is the event that symbolizes the end of the *Ancién Régime*, which closes this chapter.

## Demographic trends

Portugal appears to fit with the European secular trend of steady demographic growth in the eighteenth century. Accepting the uncertainty of the figures (derived, as for earlier periods, from sources that do not always match), the estimates point to a total of 2.3 million inhabitants in 1700, and 2.9 million in 1801 (Moreira 2009: 253; Palma and Reis 2016) (Table 4.1). However, the variation was somewhat lower than in other European countries, i.e., 0.3 percent annual rate against 0.5 percent in the north and northwest, or 0.4 percent in Spain.[2]

Like elsewhere in Europe, this population trend occurred in the framework of a premodern demographic regime, marked by high birth and death rates. Considering that economic and sanitary progress remained poor in Europe, scholars have suggested that changes in the pattern of epidemics may be important in explaining this phase of demographic expansion.[3] Such an interpretation would sit well with the Portuguese case too. Rather than the bubonic plague, in the eighteenth century diseases such as typhus, cholera, and yellow fever struck the population from time to time, and the mortality crises tended to be less severe.[4] Portugal's population growth was uneven throughout the entire century (Table 4.2) and bore the particularity of showing periods of negative variation. Between 1700 and 1730, the number of hearths in Portugal fell at a rate of 0.2 percent per year in

---

[2] De Vries 1994b: 13; Álvarez Nogal and Prados de la Escosura 2007: 330 (data for 1700 and 1787).
[3] Dupâquier 1997: 255; Livi-Bacci 1999: 139.
[4] Moreira and Veiga 2005: 52; Moreira 2008: 267–276.

Table 4.1 *Population of selected European countries, 1700–1800 (thousand inhabitants)*

|  | 1700 | 1800 |
|---|---|---|
| Germany | 11,100–11,700 | 19,000 |
| Austria-Bohemia | 4,600 | 7,900 |
| Scandinavia | 2,900 | 5,000 |
| Spain | 7,500 | 11,000 |
| France | 22,000 | 27,300 |
| British Isles | 8,400 | 15,300 |
| Italy | 13,300 | 17,800 |
| Northern Low Countries | 1,900 | 2,100 |
| Southern Low Countries | 1,900 | 2,900 |
| Portugal | 2,336 | 2,941 |
| Switzerland | 1,200 | 1,700 |

*Sources:* De Vries 1994b: 13; Rodrigues 2009: 177; Álvarez Nogal and Prados de la Escosura 2007: 330; Palma and Reis 2016; Pfister and Fertig 2010: 5.

Table 4.2 *Population change, 1700–1801 (annual growth, percent)*

| | |
|---|---|
| *c.* 1700/1732 | −0.20 |
| 1732/1758 | 0.64 |
| 1758/1801 | 0.31 |

*Source:* Moreira 2008: 256.

response to external factors. On the one hand, emigration to Brazil during the gold-mining cycle acted as a brake on population growth, particularly in the first decades of the 1700s. The emigration flows are difficult to gauge accurately and estimates vary between a minimum of 3,000–4,000 and a maximum of 8,000–10,000 per year.[5] On the other hand, Portugal's involvement in the War of the Spanish Succession and the cumulative effect of mortality crises also explain the downward trend during the first three decades of the 1700s. After 1732, recovery ensued and Portugal's population participated in the general European positive trend. By 1760, however, the Portuguese pace was remarkably slower, and contrasting regional trends, counted for such global effect.

[5] Godinho 1978a: 9. For a synthesis, see Livi-Bacci 2002: 144–147.

Table 4.3 *Regional distribution of population, 1706–1800 (percent)*

|  | 1706 | 1800 |
|---|---|---|
| Minho | 22.3 | 25.1 |
| Trás-os-Montes | 8.7 | 8.9 |
| Beira | 30.5 | 30.1 |
| Estremadura | 20.7 | 21.7 |
| Alentejo | 14.9 | 10.7 |
| Algarve | 2.8 | 3.5 |

*Source:* Serrão 1993a: 54.

In fact, regional differences in population distribution even deepened throughout the eighteenth century (Table 4.3). Due to persistent demographic vitality, the northwest (Minho) became more densely populated, accounting for a quarter of the total population. In contrast, the Alentejo, already scarcely populated in 1700, experienced population loss (Santos 2003). Therefore, the long-standing north–south contrast became more acute throughout the century. In 1801, 86 percent of the population was located in the four provinces lying to the north of the Tagus River, where the density was 12 hearths per km$^2$, compared to 3.5 per km$^2$ to the south (Serrão 1996: 70). Such dissimilarities derived from different agrarian practices and social customs (Rowland 1984).

The diffusion of maize, for instance, which dates back to the 1530s, was in the case of the northwest, a determinant of the higher rates of population growth there. This crop allowed increased food energy per unit of land. By the eighteenth century, the improvement in the food intake combined with lower exposure to diseases, provided by a disperse settlement pattern, accounted for lower death rates and for a rise in life expectancy at birth (Amorim 1999: 13–21). Fertility levels, on the other hand, remained unchanged. A relatively high average age of marriage for women (age 24–27), and high incidence of women's celibacy restricted the number of births among rural families. Hence, changes in mortality prompted the extraordinary growth recorded in the region, which the steady emigration flows to other parts of the kingdom and to the empire did not bring to a halt. This demographic pattern that characterized the Minho region derived from a rural economy largely based on small landholdings, exploited by peasant families. In accordance with mitigated property rights implied in emphyteutic contracts, the transmission of landholdings was limited to a single heir (Durães 2004b). The principle of primogeniture together with the population vitality explains high levels of emigration of second-born sons, deprived of inheritance. Hence, in a densely settled area, primogeniture inheritance and emigration were key to the social reproduction of peasant families (Rowland 2009: 400–401).

The demographic pattern in the south of the Tagus was considerably different. In the case of the Alentejo, higher fertility levels, by virtue of a lower average age of marriage (21) were counteracted by high mortality rates that affected the region between 1760 and 1780 due to the combined effects of military activity, poor harvests, and outbreaks of disease. Aside from these contingent problems, the intensity of mortality crises throughout the century was driven by other factors which seemed more acute in this region. Both the concentrated pattern of settlement and the high proportion of poor, landless rural workers tell us why the Alentejo became particularly vulnerable to famines and epidemics.[6]

### Urbanization

From 1706 to 1801 the share of Portugal's urban population hardly changed – which stands in stark contrast to the surge of the 1500s and early 1600s. The percentage of urban dwellers in relation to the total population went from 6.7 percent in the early 1500s to 10.3 percent in 1706, and then retreated slightly to 9.8 percent in 1801 (Table 4.4). In the long run, urbanization was far from even – a common feature throughout Europe, where the sixteenth century's intense advance gave way to stagnation from 1650 to 1750.[7] A spurt in the second half of the eighteenth century, however, drove the urbanization rate upward once again, in both Western and Mediterranean Europe – but not in Portugal, where the rate remained below the European average (Moreira and Veiga 2005: 44). By the end of the century the percentage of Portuguese inhabitants living in cities above 10,000 was lower than the average in both Western Europe (14.9 percent) and Mediterranean Europe (12.9 percent) (Livi-Bacci 1999: 56–57). The number of cities fell from ten to seven by 1801.

The loss of vitality in Portuguese urbanization throughout the eighteenth century was more severe in some regions than in others. The decrease in the relative percentage of urban dwellers in the regions of Alentejo, Beira, and Minho encompasses a few cases of deurbanization (Portalegre and Beja in the Alentejo, Viseu in Beira, and Guimarães in Minho (Table 4.5) (Serrão 1996: 75). The exception of Estremadura derives from the growth of Setúbal, the other port city besides Lisbon, in the south of Tagus.

[6] Sá 2005: 100–103; Santos 2003: 33.    [7] Livi-Bacci 1999: 60; Clark 2009: 119–123.

Table 4.4 *Urbanization in Europe, 1700–1800 (percentage of population living in cities of 10,000 or more inhabitants)*

|                        | 1700 | 1800 |
|------------------------|------|------|
| Germany                | 4.8  | 5.5  |
| Spain                  | 9.0  | 11.1 |
| France                 | 9.2  | 8.8  |
| Holland                | 33.6 | 28.0 |
| England and Wales      | 13.3 | 20.3 |
| Central Italy          | 14.3 | 13.6 |
| Southern Italy         | 12.2 | 15.3 |
| Northern Italy         | 13.6 | 14.3 |
| Southern Low Countries | 23.9 | 18.9 |
| Scandinavia            | 4.0  | 4.6  |
| Portugal               | 10.3 | 9.8  |
| Switzerland            | 3.3  | 3.7  |
| Western Europe         | 13.1 | 14.9 |
| Southern Europe        | 11.7 | 12.9 |

*Sources:* De Vries 1984: 58; Serrão 1996: 75.

Table 4.5 *Urbanization in Portugal, 1706–1801 (cities with 10,000 or more inhabitants)*

|                | 1706 | | 1801 | |
|----------------|------|------|------|------|
|                | Number of cities | % of total population | Number of cities | % of total population |
| Minho          | 3  | 8.6  | 2 | 8.1  |
| Trás-os-Montes | –  | –    | – | –    |
| Beira          | 2  | 3.8  | 1 | 1.8  |
| Estremadura    | 1  | 23.6 | 2 | 29.0 |
| Alentejo       | 4  | 15.6 | 2 | 8.0  |
| Algarve        | –  | –    | – | –    |
| Portugal       | 10 | 10.3 | 7 | 9.8  |

*Source:* Serrão 1996: 75.

The notable exceptions were Lisbon and Porto which grew significantly, respectively by 56 and 148 percent, from 1700 to 1800 (Serrão 1996: 75). In the case of the capital, the positive variation occurred in spite of the 1755 earthquake, whose devastating effects lasted until the late 1700s, when the city finally caught up with the levels prior to 1755 (Moreira and Veiga 2005: 44). Lisbon was by far the largest city in 1800 with roughly 165,000 residents (6 percent of the country's population). Porto trailed in second place, failing to reach the 45,000 mark by 1800, even though it underwent a significant growth from the late 1600s on. Of the other five cities with more than 10,000 dwellers (Braga, Coimbra, Setúbal, Évora, and Elvas), none reached 20,000. The urban network comprised another twelve cities of more than 5,000.[8] It seems clear that by the early nineteenth century Portugal's urban structure was marked by strong polarization, with Lisbon being the leading center and Porto emerging as a secondary one. These two cities prospered within the sparse network of small and medium-sized cities and shaped the domestic market, which evolved fragmented into two, non-complementary regions: Porto to the north, and the capital (Lisbon) to the south. Porto acted as regional trade center, distributing Minho's manufactured goods as well as the wines produced in the Alto Douro region. As for Lisbon, in addition to being served by the country's largest seaport, it was also the seat of the royal court and capital of the kingdom and the empire, which explains its ability to concentrate most of the revenues derived from the international and overseas trade. It was also the place where leading aristocratic houses spent large sums of their wealth rebuilding palaces after the earthquake.

Lisbon had an economic role which was, nonetheless, somewhat different from that of other capital cities that were also their countries' leading seaports. Such other cities expanded rapidly and had considerable impact on their respective national economies, as in the case of London. But unlike what unfolded in England, the lack of investment in transportation and communications kept domestic transaction costs very high. In fact, Portugal did not witness anything similar to what scholars have identified for England or even Spain, where the speed of inland transportation increased remarkably in the eighteenth century, which contributed to higher integration of urban markets and price convergence at the national level (Grafe 2012:109). Portugal missed those sorts of improvements, which explains Lisbon's heavy dependence on imported food, particularly wheat, whose price could compete with that of the grain produced in inland Portugal (Serrão 2004).

Despite its inability to drag the integration of the domestic market, Lisbon still attracted many immigrants from the countryside, and as such the number of its inhabitants increased steadily, particularly in the second half of the eighteenth century. The constant influx of immigrants may have hindered the rise of wages, while it represented greater pressure on the demand for essential goods, both trends undermining the

[8] Silva 1997: 783–786; Rodrigues 2008: 350.

standards of living in the city. Indeed, there is evidence that real wages fell in the second half of the eighteenth century, so that in 1800, living standards in Lisbon, measured by real wages of skilled labor, were 60 percent of those in London. (Costa, Palma, and Reis 2015). Notwithstanding Lisbon and Porto's exceptional growth, the eighteenth-century Portuguese demography depicts a stagnant urbanization rate while the total population of the kingdom was varying at 0.3 percent. This allows the assumption that non-urban activities were allocating a higher share of labor, following a trend dating back to the last quarter of the seventeenth century.

## New landscapes and old techniques

By the eighteenth century the so-called "little divergence" within Europe regarding the GDP per capita variation deepened even further, as economic growth concentrated mainly in England. Several factors contributed to this divergence, and among those most studied is the increase in agricultural productivity. The slow but steady diffusion of new crop rotations and convertible husbandry boosted the productivity of English farmers considerably beyond the level prior to 1700 (Allen 2001). However, there is no consensus among historians about the conditions for these improvements in regard to the structure and size of landholdings that would have best suited the introduction and spread of those innovative practices.[9]

With the exception of England, in most European countries farming techniques as well as the institutional settings changed very little throughout the eighteenth century. The seigneurial system and the common exploitation of land still dominated most of the rural economy well into the 1800s, even though output and productivity varied widely (Ogilvie 2000: 94). Portugal was among the countries characterized by the lack of any breakthrough in agricultural techniques in the 1700s and as such provides a good case study of growth and diversification of output occurring within the framework of traditional institutions. The examination undertaken here begins with a look at social property relations and their possible impact – either positive or negative – on the evolution of the sector's output. Whether there was sustained growth of *per capita* agricultural produce is still a matter for debate, but it is certain that between 1700 and 1808 there was crop diversification and greater integration of the primary sector in the market.

[9] Allen 1999; Simpson 2004.

*Land ownership and tenure*

Landed property was still detained by the traditional *Ancién Régime* landlords, i.e., the Crown, Nobility, the Church, and to a lesser degree by municipal institutions and commoners. The apportionment between these social bodies is not known for the whole country, but taking the example of the region of Évora, we learn that 50 percent of the land was held by the aristocracy, 36 percent by religious institutions and lay-brotherhoods, and the remaining 14 percent were in the hands of commoners (Santos 2003: 33). Overall, this social distribution of land-ownership did not differ greatly from what we know about other European contexts.[10] However, a closer look over the agrarian structures reveals some specific features. In fact, as in the rest of Iberia, plural property rights over land and rents were still the norm, while in other parts of Western Europe property rights tended to become exclusive (Monteiro 2005a: 77–78). In the Portuguese case, the persistence of fragmented property rights has been usually viewed as an obstacle to land market and agricultural investment. Forms of "imperfect" property, stemming from the widespread use of emphyteutical contracts, constrained market transactions of full property rights over land. Moreover, so the argument goes, entailed estates (*morgadios* and *capelas*) and land held in mortmain by the Church kept a large bulk of landed property out of the market, since the legal framework of these institutions prohibited transfers of the eminent domain. The *capelas* consisted of entailed assets, whose income was allocated to a pious duty. Both the enjoyment and disposition of the *capelas* were ruled by restrictive norms similar to those applied to *morgadios*.[11]

This property rights system became the target of the enlightened government of the marquis of Pombal (1750–1777). Under the pressure of a growing land demand, due to the demographic growth and to increased financial wealth related to the influx of Brazilian gold, the government enacted legislation to boost the land market. Pombal imposed restrictions on property transfers to the Church, suppressed entailments with a low level of annual income and introduced stricter rules for new lay entails.[12] According to contemporary observers, the results were significant (Serrão and Santos 2013). Close to 15,000 low-value entailments across the country were abolished, a clear indicator of the pervasiveness of the entailments in Portuguese society. Previously entailed estates were released into the market, although it is impossible to gauge the scale it attained.

---

[10] O'Brien 2005; Ogilvie 2000: 94–96.
[11] On the practice of entailing estates, see Chapter 1.
[12] Monteiro 2005a: 87–89; Serrão 1993: 87.

However, the effects of this policy in promoting the liquidity of the land market should not be overestimated for two reasons. First, larger entailments of aristocratic houses were untouched by this reform. Second, recent investigations have shown that the regime of entailments allowed the mobility of this factor of production more often than it is usually believed (Serrão 2000: 560). One of the devices that allowed for circumventing the legal restrictions was subrogation, by which entailed land could be transferred to new owners, provided the estates were exchanged by other sorts of assets, such as buildings or royal debt bonds. (Monteiro 2005a: 75). Furthermore, land tenure contracts also allowed for transactions of the useful domain (Monteiro 2003: 223, 379–380). Any assessment of the influence of the juridical framework on Portuguese agriculture must, therefore, consider the role played by agrarian contracts in setting up a secondary market of property rights over land.[13]

Lease and emphyteutic contracts were common across the country, but their use differed markedly between the north and the south. To the north of the Tagus, the emphyteusis was the most widespread contractual arrangement and the Atlantic northwest region provides a good example of how it worked and coped with demographic changes. Here the secular occupation of the region and population pressure resulted in the fragmentation of landed property and in the proliferation of small plots of land. Subject to ecclesiastic and lay lords, the land was tilled by peasant households, mainly through emphyteutic agreements for lives.[14] The Alentejo and especially the area around the city of Évora offers a different picture. On the one hand, the low population density went together with a concentrated pattern of settlement in larger towns and on the other, the region's ecosystem – hot and dry – favored large-sized landholdings with hundreds of hectares, called *herdades*. Clearly market-orientated and resorting to wage workers, these *herdades* were let to farmers through short-term leases (Santos 2005). Emphyteutic contracts were, however, not unknown and not even limited to small tracts of land. In Beja and also in the aforementioned case of Évora, for example, *herdades* could be farmed under emphyteusis as well (Silbert 1978, vol. II: 756–757). Still, the global view on the juridical system ruling the access to land defined the south of the Tagus as a region where large plots of land were more often exploited by short-term leases than it was the case in the northwestern side of the country.

Apart from these two contrasting systems, the central-west region (Estremadura) deserves special mention due to the complexity and variety of its agrarian features. Emphyteusis and short-term leases were both

[13] Santos 2003; Santos and Serrão 2013.   [14] Durães 2004b; Rau 1961.

widely used in this region where medium- or large-sized landholdings coexisted with small-scale units intended to provide the subsistence of peasant families.[15] In the rural hinterland of Lisbon, an average of 45 percent of real estate was held in emphyteusis.[16] Likewise, the marshy bottomlands along the Tagus held by ecclesiastic institutions were mostly exploited under the same sort of contracts (Monteiro 2003: 300–302). By contrast, lay landlords resorted to short-term leases of wealthier farms, as seen in the areas of Muge, Golegã, and Valada.[17]

From these examples across the country, it seems clear that the emphyteutic lease was widely used for different types of landholdings. It was considered a powerful device to bring investment to the land and to provide the producer, especially small farmers, with more stable conditions to till the land. By the eighteenth century, the situation had changed. Given its large diffusion in the past, a dynamic market of useful domains was in place and emphyteutic leases assisted transactions of land already under cultivation, thus providing an entitlement to collect a rent derived from the value added between the ground-rent due to the landlord and the rent paid by the direct producer (Serrão and Santos 2013). As several studies have proved, this use of the emphyteusis as *rentier* investment, was particularly widespread in Portuguese society; local and urban elites, businessmen, and even aristocratic houses participated in the transaction of rights over a land revenue.[18]

Against the backdrop of a growing population and increased financial wealth, the market for the useful domain of land was also a means to concentrate landholdings that would broaden the scale of exploitation and not just a *rentier* investment. Again, the region of the Alentejo (south of Tagus) is a good example of this tendency. During the second half of the eighteenth century, wealthy farmers managed to take advantage of subrogations and emphyteusis and began concentrating landholdings, which eventually paved the way to full ownership through the enactment of other institutional reforms by the liberal state of the nineteenth century. [19] Although on a smaller scale, in the Douro region farms also "grew in size," by transactions in the emphyteutic market (Monteiro 2005a: 84).

Finally, the growing pressure for land contributed to changes in the agrarian landscape by challenging communitarian traditions. While collective use of land was not uniformly distributed across the country (more

---

[15] Salvado 2009: 269–273; Serrão 1993b: 75.
[16] Serrão 2000: 479; Serrão and Santos 2013.
[17] Rau 1961: 24; Salvado 2009: 271–272; Serrão 2000: 324, 394.
[18] Serrão 2000: 324, 495; Monteiro 2005a: 82–83; for specific examples, see Maia 1991: 127–129; Mota 2000: 462; Neto 1997: 305.
[19] Fonseca 1990: 118–138; Santos 2003: 33–34; Serrão e Santos 2011.

common in the north than in the south), it was still widespread in the early 1700s.[20] The system imposed a collective discipline on cultivation and livestock grazing that, among other things, needed common lands for use as free pasture and as a source of firewood. Despite its role in providing welfare to peasantry, strong and coherent collectivism tended to exacerbate agrarian immobility and to impede experimentation with new farming techniques. Collectivism also aggravated tensions and discouraged individual attempts to alter cultivation practices in response to market incentives. Nevertheless, private appropriation of village commons, which has been called "farming individualism," expanded, usually by means of emphyteutic contracts. This occurred everywhere in the country.[21] The Royal Academy of Sciences also contributed to this trend, supporting the opinion that collective ownership was an obstacle to agrarian development.[22] The features of the sector described earlier had roots in the medieval period. It still comprised forms of imperfect property, social partition of land rents, and the entailment regime, which altogether display its mostly unchanged backdrop. But, overall, this seemingly unaltered framework of property rights did not stand in the way of crop diversification, since the sector coped with population pressure and heavier demand for some particular produce as was the case with wine.

*The diversification of crops*

The upturn in population coming after 1732 translated into a greater supply of labor and a growing demand for food. The domestic market was further fueled by the growth of Lisbon and Porto, at rates that stood above the national average. The capital had a polarizing effect in this regard. Not only because it accounted for *c.* 6 percent of the kingdom's population, but also because a substantial portion of Portugal's wealthiest families, whether aristocratic or mercantile, resided there, thus pressing demand. Unsurprisingly, Lisbon's agrarian hinterland served as one of the preferred locations for the leading merchants to invest their wealth accumulated through trading activities (Serrão 2000). Another key factor of change in the agrarian sector lay in favorable market conditions. In fact, the eighteenth century in Portugal witnessed simultaneous growth of the domestic, overseas, and European markets. The overseas market flourished mainly as a result of the gold rush. As for the European market, demand picked up largely through favorable diplomatic relations with

---

[20] Magalhães 1988; Monteiro 1996b: 134–135. Note, however, that in the south, agrarian collectivism was strong in the area of livestock breeding. See Silbert 1978, vol. 2: 847.

[21] Durães 2004b: 6; Magalhães 1988: 147–148; Neto 1984; Silbert 1978: 1059.

[22] Cardoso 1990; Santos 2003.

Britain that resulted from the War of the Spanish Succession. By virtue of the Methuen Commercial Treaty of 1703, Portuguese wine was able to compete with French wine. This favorable context was to last for the remainder of the century and the commercial wine sector expanded steadily. Thanks to the combination of these stimuli, agriculture underwent several changes.

Although there is no statistical data to gauge the advances, indirect evidence points to an enlargement of the area under cultivation. Across the country, arable land was claimed by clearings, drainage of swamps, and private appropriation of pastures and common lands in a constant and piecemeal way rather than by large and costly undertakings. As regional studies suggest, cultivation was extended to marginal soils, of poorer quality, particularly in Minho, Alentejo, and the Algarve.[23] In response to the population pressure, the land thus converted from pastoral to arable husbandry was probably used mostly for traditional grain cultivation. In addition to a rising output, a second change lies in the diversification of the crops, fostered by favorable market conditions for agricultural produce. In Minho, the Algarve, the Alentejo, and along the Douro River, farmers extended market-oriented crops, such as olive trees, vine, and orchard trees. Innumerable reports in the hinterlands of the main urban centers, especially those served by seaports and some infrastructure of communication (by river and overland transportation), such as Lisbon and Porto, testify to upturns in these crops. Within this framework, viticulture and winemaking developed remarkably during the eighteenth century.

Favorable conditions for an increase in wine production go back to the 1690s. Portuguese wines proved to be a welcoming alternative for the English markets whenever international issues raised barriers to the imports of French wines. In fact, during the Nine Years' War (1688–1697), the importation of French produce was banned from English markets, opening up an opportunity for Portugal's exports. This advantage was later reinforced by the Methuen Commercial Treaty of 1703, which taxed Portuguese wines at one-third less than the import duty imposed on French wines, in exchange for 23 percent *ad valorem* on English woolens imported into Portugal. In the five years from 1695 to 1699, Portuguese wines accounted for 37 percent of English consumption, and in the 1740s this figure rose to 80 percent (Martins 1998: 33). This dominance of the English wine market continued (at this level) until the end of the century, while, at the same time, Portugal was branching out into new export markets.

---

[23] Magalhães 1988: 175; Silbert 1978, vol. 2: 445–457; Serrão 2005: 151.

This growing specialization as a wine producer and exporter became tightly regulated through the institution of the *Companhia das Vinhas do Alto Douro* (Upper Douro Wine Company) in 1756, one of the most effective economic measures introduced by Sebastião José de Carvalho e Melo (1699–1782), first marquis of Pombal. King José I's minister sought to regulate the pricing and improve the quality of the wine produced along the river Douro and exported through the city of Porto. In order to enhance the reputation of the commodity, he counteracted the uncontrolled vineyard expansion of previous decades and the ensuing deterioration of the wine quality, which had dragged the prices down. He promoted the foundation of the corporate company, whose statutes granted it an immense power to regulate production and distribution by carefully selecting the output destined for export.

Among other resources, the *Companhia* was funded by the revenues of the monopoly exerted over the wholesale of wine to the retailers in Porto and the shipments bound for Brazil. Soon after its founding, it was granted a further monopoly over the distilling of *aguardente* (grape-based spirits), an essential ingredient in the aging and fortification of the type of wine that would become known as *vinho do Porto* (port wine). The far-reaching impact of the *Companhia das Vinhas* regarding production supervision, production techniques, transportation, and marketing of the grapes and wine led to the establishment of the world's first exclusive demarcated zone (*região demarcada*) in the history of wine-making. Subject to several adjustments introduced during the time of Pombal and during the reign of Queen Maria I (1777–1816), the demarcated zone of port wine production extended to areas of Beira, Trás-os-Montes, and Minho, to include sixty-seven civil parishes (Map 4.1). Rather than small-scale operations, wine-making in the demarcated region was carried out mostly by medium- to large-sized farms (Martins 1998: 210). The increasing role of port wine did not discourage production outside of the demarcated zone, despite the fact that legal directives from 1765 and 1766 ordered the destruction of vines on the pretext that land could be put to better use by cropping cereals. The banks and plains along the Tagus, Vouga, and Mondego Rivers and areas of Estremadura, notably around Torres Vedras, were the regions targeted by these ordinances.

Notwithstanding these efforts to limit the area of viticulture, output grew at an estimated 1.2 percent per year rate (Martins 1998: 217). By the end of the 1700s, wine production had almost doubled over where it had stood one hundred years earlier, but the Douro valley accounted for only 13 percent of this variation. By the end of the 1780s, the growing of vines had spread to the entire country, from Minho, to Alentejo, Algarve, Coastal

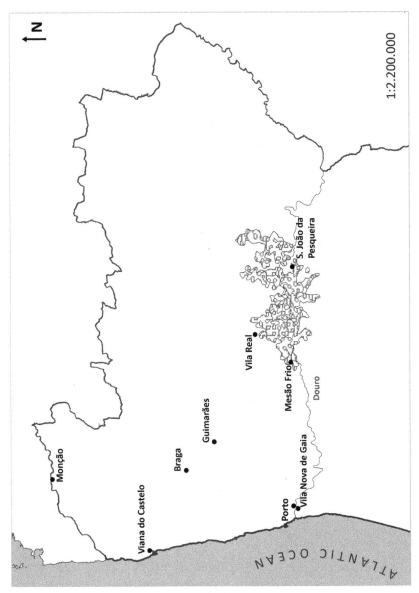

Map 4.1 The Douro wine region, 1761

Table 4.6 *Domestic production of wine, distilled spirits, and vinegar, 1782–1783 (casks)*

|  | Average | Percentage |
|---|---|---|
| Viana, Guimarães, and Porto | 42,263 | 21.1 |
| Miranda, Moncorvo | 9,020 | 4.5 |
| Lamego, Viseu* | 20,028 | 10.0 |
| Demarcated region (Douro River) | 30,250 | 15.1 |
| Guarda, Castelo Branco | 11,005 | 5.5 |
| Aveiro, Coimbra | 12,131 | 6.0 |
| Leiria, Torres Vedras | 25,161 | 12.5 |
| Tomar, Santarém | 18,089 | 9.0 |
| Lisbon, Setúbal* | 10,999 | 5.5 |
| Alentejo | 14,935 | 7.4 |
| Algarve | 6,668 | 3.3 |
| Total | 200,549 | 100 |

* Incomplete data.
*Source:* Martins 1998: 216.

Beira, and Estremadura.[24] For the years 1782–1783, figures regarding production at the national level, although incomplete but otherwise reliable for understanding the geography of winemaking, point to a considerable volume of output outside of the Douro region. Of a total of 200,551 casks (*pipas*) of wine, which accounted for 74.9 percent of the country's total production during those years, the demarcated region supplied 15.1 percent, even less than the Viana do Castelo / Guimarães / Porto area, which contributed 21.1 percent (see Table 4.6). Trade records for 1783 indicate that 28,180 casks (*c.* 14 percent of the year's production) were exported to all foreign markets excluding Brazil, while 70.1 percent of the port wine alone was exported to England, altogether revealing the strong impact of foreign demand on the performance of the sector (Martins 1990: 219).

If winemaking underwent an unparalleled expansion in the eighteenth century, other crops also benefitted from market incentives. As local and regional studies have shown, olive trees kept spreading across the country in response to the growth of Brazilian demand.[25] By the end of the 1700s olive orchards were an omnipresent feature of the Portuguese countryside from the Minho to the Algarve (Ribeiro 1979). The same is to be said of fruit growing. Groves sprang up on the outskirts of urban centers, serving

---

[24] Magalhães 1988: 167–168; Martins 2003: 122; Meneses 2001: 248.
[25] Amorim 1997: 213–289–290; Magalhães 1988: 163–174; Oliveira 2002: 216; Serrão 2009.

both urban and foreign markets. Particularly successful was the production of citrus fruit in the Algarve and in Lisbon's hinterland that aimed to meet the rising demand of northern Europe (Serrão 1993b and 2009). The deeper integration of the primary sector in the market is also reflected in the southern province of Alentejo (after 1710–1712), where rising prices for meat prompted farmers to partly replace cereal crops with pig, sheep, and goat breeding mostly to satisfy Lisbon consumers.[26] In the Algarve, animal husbandry also proved successful. The existing intra-regional complementarity between mountainous areas and seacoast deepened even further by means of a fruitful combination of livestock farming with cereal cultivation and orchards. By 1722, livestock production in the southernmost province of Portugal was efficient enough to meet regional as well as supra-regional demand. An overwhelming percentage of its oxen (93 percent) and sheep (75 percent) were made available for sale (Magalhães 1988: 158).

Within the changes that took place in eighteenth-century agriculture, the evolution of grain production deserves special attention, in an attempt to assess the effects of output diversification and the extension of livestock farming over the most important item within the consumption basket. Regarding maize, and following its successful introduction in northwest Portugal in the sixteenth century, it continued its wide diffusion, spreading into Upper Beira and Estremadura. By the early nineteenth century it was not only cultivated everywhere in the country, but was also the main grain crop north of the Tagus river.[27] Rice was also sown but on a much smaller scale and its share in total grain output must have been small. However, its consumption must have gained a more widespread basis, which encouraged its planting in northern Brazil to export to Portugal by the end of the 1700s (Silbert 1978 vol. II: 511–513).

Despite these improvements in relative terms within grain production, it is hard to speak of a steady growth of grain productivity. In the northwest, the yield ratio of wheat and rye did not exceed 1:4, a figure that could rise to 1:6 or 1:7 on lands where maize was also cultivated (Oliveira 1980: 15). With such yields, after paying land fees, taxes, and the overhead expenses, the remaining balance for small farming operations could not have been above 30 or 35 percent, which was not enough to offset harvest fluctuations. In small and family-run agrarian units, the narrow margin of surplus meant that farmers were still facing famines in case of a bad harvest.[28] In the Alentejo (Montemor-o-Novo) grain ratios were

[26] Justino 1988: 66; Santos 2003: 388.
[27] Magalhães 1988: 183–184; Serrão 2005: 149.
[28] Durães 2004a: 248–249; Neto 1997: 79–80; Oliveira 1980: 16–18; Silva 1993: 93–95.

somewhat higher. Between 1721 and 1723 the wheat yield ratio stood at 1:6 and 1:7, a level that was still considered fairly high in the early 1800s, as the average ranged from 1:4 to 1:6.[29] Only in the Low Countries and England were yield ratios significantly higher, hovering around 10 and 11 by 1800. Portugal's average yield ratios were in line with the Mediterranean area (Ogilvie 2000: 97). However, an examination of the wheat prices in Portugal reveals a few problems affecting the sector's output.

Indexing the prices of 100 kg of wheat to the years 1601–1650, in grams of silver, we find a downward trend throughout the eighteenth century and the first half of the nineteenth, in France, Spain, England, and also in Portugal. This trend changes sooner for England, from 1760 on, followed by Portugal and Spain (in 1790), or France in the 1810s. Still, Portugal's curve differs somewhat from the other cases, and notably from that of Spain, which depicts five decades of prices 60 percent lower than the benchmark (1601–1650). Portugal's prices never dipped below that level thus becoming the economy in which one of the most important consumer goods – wheat – had prices that most negatively affected the standard of living.[30]

It could hence be argued that changes in the composition of the agrarian output reduced grain production, which would back the criticism expressed in sources of the late eighteenth century regarding the country's grain deficit. According to the political and economic discourse of the time, cereal shortages were a direct result of the conversion of grain fields into vineyards and pastureland. The lack of data on cereal production makes it hard to verify this notion. Local studies point to the decline of traditional crops, such as cereals, following the farmer's investment in products that had better markets and fetched relatively higher prices, such as wine, olive oil, and meat (Santos 2003). Indeed, a comparison between cereal prices (maize and wheat) with wine prices suggests that the latter, despite its greater volatility, had on average a higher variation than those of cereals (13 percent for wine against 3.4 percent for maize and wheat). Winemaking could be meeting conditions to attract factors of production, namely capital, just like extensive animal husbandry was doing in some areas south of the Tagus River. In both cases, it is reasonable to assume that the changes in land use called more for reallocating capital rather than labor. In fact, the wage variations of the eighteenth century do not reflect higher demand for labor as real wages were lower in 1800 than in

---

[29] Fonseca 1995: 139; Silbert 1978, vol. 2: 483–484.

[30] For all countries referred to (except Portugal), see Simpson 2004; for Portugal, data from project on prices, wages, and rents in Portugal 1300–1910, directed by Jaime Reis, http://pwr-portugal.ics.ul.pt/

1750 (Costa, Palma, and Reis 2015). Moreover, the expansion of the vineyards often came at the cost of encroaching onto land unsuited to cereal crops, whether wasteland or the slopes of the hills overlooking the Douro terraced for that purpose. Sometimes, the expansion took the form of more intensive cultivation, such as in the case of "hanging vine" (*vinha em enforcado*) cultivation.[31] With the exception of the Douro region and certain small areas in Estremadura, where vines were grown almost in monoculture, the spread of vineyards occurred without critically disrupting cereal production. Still, planting vines demanded investment that was beyond the reach of most farmers. This is why ownership of the large farms and terraced vineyards of the Douro (in the mid 1700s) was dominated by local nobility, career military officers, religious orders, and wealthy city dwellers, as well as English capitalists (Martins 2003: 124).

It seems, thus, that the sector became more capital intensive. But the investment in livestock apparently did not have an overall impact on productivity, contrary to what was happening in England where the spread of a better integration of corn and livestock (mixed husbandry) allowed for productivity improvements (Allen 2008). In the case of the Alentejo, the potential benefits of the conversion of grain fields to pasture was still countered by the planting of cereals elsewhere, in poor soils, at least during the first half of the eighteenth century (Santos 2003: 388). One estimate points to an annual decline of total factor productivity of 0.44 percent during 1750–1800 (Fonseca and Reis 2011: 179, 189). Long-lasting habits of rural consumers and a growing demand for food can explain the insistent choice for grain cultivation. Thus, the expansion of arable land also boosted cereal production, even in poor and marginal soils where opportunity costs were higher, as it occurred in the Algarve, for example, with the cultivation of rye (Magalhães 1988: 175–176). Therefore, the country kept importing grain and this dependence on foreign supply was perceived as an economic fragility and a subject of intense debate.

In the last quarter of the century, the Royal Academy of Sciences expressed harsh criticism on the country's agriculture. As historians of economic thought have shown, the discourse of the Royal Academics is not to be taken as an impartial source regarding the agrarian problems. On the one hand, they were ready to incorporate ideas from abroad, a circumstance that explains the influence of Spanish agrarianism and its critiques toward animal husbandry in their discourse (Santos 2003: 51).

---

[31] This was a combination of orchard and vineyard, in which the vines climbed into the trees' branches, using these for their support instead of trellises.

On the other hand, we should keep in mind that the intellectual elite represented in the Royal Academy of Sciences sought political recognition through the production of testimonies following the tradition of the *arbitristas* of the previous century (Cardoso 1989).

Seeking to depict the economic situation in the Alentejo on the eve of the liberal revolution, historical researches freed their inquiries from the discourse propelled by the Royal Academy of Sciences. They have come up with two contrasting views: the first one considers the agrarian crisis of the last decades of the 1700s as an indicator that production had reached its limits following decades of pressure on resources from an increasing population (Justino 1981); the second one sees the grain shortages as the outcome of changes in the landscape and in the composition of agrarian output following an adaptation to market incentives. According to the latter view, the expectation of returns determined land uses within an economic rationale that also accounted for labor costs and low yields of the lands less appropriate for grain crops (Santos 2003). Even the arguments on the extent of the country's grain shortage have been downplayed by estimates on data for cereal imports into Lisbon (Silbert 1978). The evidence shows that throughout the 1700s, Lisbon's grain market was becoming more dependent on maritime imports, as domestic cereal production was accounting for a diminishing share of the supply. In 1729, 45 percent of the grain supply derived from domestic production while the remaining 55 percent came from imports. From 1778 to 1787, the share stood at 28 and 72 percent, respectively.

Data seem to corroborate the notion of a mounting dependence on imports to feed Lisbon toward the end of the century. However, these figures are to be checked taking the kingdom's overall population in to consideration and a mean *per capita* annual consumption estimated at 350 liters (Serrão 2005: 171). Assuming that between 1776 and 1795 the population grew at rate of 0.24 percent per year, the share of grain imports varied between 5.5 and 7 percent of the annual consumption needs of the whole kingdom (Table 4.7). This grain dependence was, however, more pronounced in the cities of the littoral, where foreign cereal was more competitive than its domestic counterparts, just as it was already documented for the sixteenth century. Nevertheless, it should be stressed that the weight of grain imports within the aggregate consumption of the kingdom might have been somewhat larger in comparison with economies undergoing significant transformations in their transition to modern economic growth. In fact, in this respect, Portugal was different from Great Britain, which regularly imported approximately just 3 percent of the wheat it consumed (Mathias 1993: 308–321).

Table 4.7 *Consumption and imports of cereals in Portugal, 1776–1795*

|  | Population | Consumption (hectoliters) | Imports (hectoliters) | Imports (as a % of per capita consumption) | Imports per capita |
|---|---|---|---|---|---|
| 1776–1777 | 2,274,351 | 9,602,296 | 532,263 | 5.5 | 152,075 |
| 1778–1787 | 2,779,383 | 9,727,841 | 683,946 | 7 | 195,413 |
| 1788–1795 | 2,833,187 | 9,916,155 | 686,416 | 6.9 | 196,119 |

*Source:* Serrão 2005: 171.

Generally speaking, throughout the 1700s Portuguese agriculture went through some improvements but it still faced Malthusian checks, which seem to be critical from the 1760s onwards. Whatever the transformations it carried out, agricultural output grew with no radical changes in farming techniques – certainly nothing on a par with the changes underway in Great Britain (Crouzet 1990: 12–44). In Portugal gains in productivity are uncertain, since the structural changes that go together with productivity increases, including higher urbanization rates and a constant pressure on the demand for labor driven by growing specialization, are not entirely recognizable. In fact, it was the high demand for labor that made England and the Dutch Republic the textbook cases of high-wage economies in the *Ancién Régime*. For Portugal's agricultural performance, the institutional framework might have been of little importance, although to some extent the emphyteusis and subrogation responded to rent-seeking choices, rather than to an investment expecting returns from improvements in agricultural output. But more relevant than this, inadequate inland transportation together with internal customs barriers must have impacted on the overall performance of the primary sector, since the retarded integration of regional markets favored imports of grain from the sea to feed the leading port cities, while also protecting inefficient producers of cereals in regions of the country distant from maritime routes (Macedo 1982b: 141).

Therefore, the diversification of crops as a result of market incentives is the clearest transformation the Portuguese agriculture underwent in the eighteenth century and we should presume that this positively affected the living standards well until the 1760s (Palma e Reis, 2016). Responding to the domestic and foreign demand, farmers turned to winemaking, maize, and livestock. The rise of woolens that contributed greatly to boosting industrial output during the eighteenth century is another example of the success and the limits of the market integration of the primary sector.

## Industrial organization

In most European countries, the eighteenth century witnessed an industrial advance through a more intensive use of the existing techniques and forms of industrial organization. The technological breakthrough that would increase total productivity occurred after the 1760s and 1770s in Great Britain, but the widespread adoption of new forms of energy and engines would have to wait a few more decades, a time lag that illustrates the complex interaction between the rise of the stock of knowledge and the social, economic, and institutional contexts receptive to new technology and its diffusion (Mokyr 1994, 2009).

Portugal's industrial evolution followed the general European pattern, which displays changes in labor organization but little technical innovation. Manufacturing needs continued to depend mostly on local crafts and domestic industry. However, in the eighteenth century there was room for the implementation of several large factories following an ambitious policy of industrial development pursued by the government. In fact, state incentives played a leading role in promoting new forms of organizing labor with good results in exports of manufactures to colonial markets. Government intervention, effective as it was in what regards the textile sector, proved to be compatible with old and traditional forms of production and was mainly directed at regions where labor and skills were relatively abundant, due to the rural industries' contribution.

The demand for non-agricultural goods was still largely determined by the predominance of a rural population of low income whose patterns of consumption were marginally diversified, and whose regular consumption of clothing, footwear, furniture, and farming tools was satisfied by domestic handicrafts, just as it had been in medieval times (Pedreira 2005: 178–180). Nevertheless, rural households demanded other kinds of goods, the supply of which was not fulfilled within the domestic organization of labor. This was the case with certain exotic foodstuffs and building tools, particularly those that were increasingly made of metals, as well as with finer clothing items. Exceeding the capacities and skills of the rural families, these commodities called for specialized craftsmen and justified the widespread existence of artisan workshops in urban and rural centers.

The share of skilled craftsmen within the labor force is, however, difficult to assess. According to local studies, the percentage of those employed in non-rural activities could vary between 15 and 25 percent of the total population.[32] The distribution of craftsmanship by skill is also impossible

[32] For Cascais, see Macedo 1982b: 118 and for Oeiras, see Silva 1987: 536. For the whole country at different times, see Sá 2005.

Table 4.8 *Industrial labor in Trás-os-Montes, 1796*

| Crafts | Number | Crafts | Number | Crafts | Number |
|---|---|---|---|---|---|
| Textile (total) | 1238 | Leather work (total) | 327 | Wax work (total) | 18 |
| Carder | 273 | Leather workers | 301 | Candle makers | 18 |
| Hat maker | 40 | Tanner | 2 | Bone work (total) | 11 |
| Silk maker | 498 | Saddle maker | 24 | Comb maker | 11 |
| Wool worker | 335 | Pottery (total) | 125 | | |
| Dyer | 27 | Potter | 125 | | |
| Silk twister | 65 | Woodwork (total) | 52 | | |
| Metal work (total) | 575 | Cooper | 17 | | |
| Blacksmiths | 575 | Clogger | 35 | | |

*Source:* Macedo 1982a: 111.

to gauge but it is certain that these were diverse and varied in eighteenth-century Portugal, as shown in the snapshot for a single region – Trás-os-Montes – for the year 1796. Considering that this region harbored 265,852 inhabitants in 1801, 28 percent were employed in non-rural activities.[33] Craftsmen comprised 21 percent of this number – a percentage that is underestimated, as the source does not account for cobblers and tailors (Table 4.8).

Undoubtedly these figures show the tight links between artisanship and agriculture, given the high number of blacksmith/ironworking in a region such as Trás-os-Montes where large cities were nonexistent. The number of workers attached to the silk industry is also noteworthy, displaying a long-term regional specialization which went back to medieval times when local production already supplied supra-regional demand. After having survived a serious crisis in the years after 1760, due to Lisbon's development of the silk industry, the 563 silk makers and twisters counted in 1796 in Trás-os-Montes point to a partial recovery of the regional output (Pedreira 1994: 288–289). These and other data for craft trades across the country point to an industrial organization that relied on rural

[33] Sá 2005: 106 (assuming that 30 percent of 265,852 inhabitants were employed).

industries or proto-industries, common in Portugal since the sixteenth century as stated in a previous chapter. The production, mostly of textiles, was carried out by peasant households under the coordination of a merchant-employer, who subsequently organized the sale of the finished goods in urban and supra-regional markets. As in other European countries, the expansion of both demand and labor supply (due to low agricultural productivity) deepened the diffusion of rural industries in Portugal.

An overview of the geographical distribution of the textile sector in the 1700s illustrates the combination of the three main forms of labor organization we have described: household production, rural industries (putting-out system), and crafts. The production of linen cloth in the northwest, for instance, exemplifies the success of a home-based industry organized in a putting-out system. By the end of the eighteenth century and early nineteenth century, there is ample evidence of the high levels of output serving markets in Portugal, Brazil, and Galicia (Pedreira 1994: 71). Burgeoning exports even demanded the import of additional raw material from the Baltic, as it happened in the last quarter of the 1700s because the local production of flax could not keep up with the demand. The weight of this industry, which surely justified its resilience under an entirely new technological backdrop in the nineteenth century, can be seen in the fact that there were 6,158 looms in the district of Viana do Castelo and 2,453 in Porto in the mid 1800s (Pedreira 1994: 75–76). In Beira, production also reached significant concentrations. In Lamego (Coimbra district), 1,208 looms were still recorded in the middle of the nineteenth century (Pedreira 1994: 77). Some fifty years earlier, at the end of the eighteenth century, the country had an estimated 120,000–200,000 active looms, located mostly in these two regions. Assuming that each loom produced 60 cm of cloth per day, this would translate into 18 million meters of cloth per year, for a total population of around 3 million (Pedreira 1994: 79–80). Further rural linen industries could be found in Estremadura, in the interior north – Trás-os-Montes – and in the Alentejo, although none of these areas surpassed the level attained in the northwest or Beira.

As it was with linen, the production of woolen cloth combined factors of production typical of a pre-industrial economy, meeting the accessibility of labor and raw materials. It was located for the most part in the interior, following a tradition going back to the 1400s. The most important centers of wool production were in Beira and Alentejo. In Beira, spinning and weaving took place in the countryside, with the city of Covilhã serving as a hub to collect the local output and manage the final phases of production, which involved more specialized tasks such as dyeing. As for the Alentejo, urban workshops in Portalegre and Redondo organized a putting-out network that employed about a third of the rural population (Pedreira 1994: 86).

The diffusion of these textile industries responded to the demand coming from the larger urban centers, especially from Lisbon, which in the early 1700s obtained manufactured articles produced across the country, such as woolen fabrics, silks, and linens (Macedo 1982b: 61–62). Being the seat of the royal family and aristocracy, Lisbon concentrated unusual levels of wealth, which favored the consumption of manufactures, even if transaction costs raised by the inefficient transportation network that linked the city to the regional production centers translated into relatively higher prices. Furthermore, within the industrial organization of the country, Lisbon had an exceptional position. In the 1760s nearly 10,000 craftsmen were distributed among 200 trades, depicting the impact on industrial labor of a more diversified and demanding pattern of consumption than the one prevailing out in the countryside.[34] This slow growth of the industrial capacity during the eighteenth century occurred within the framework of traditional forms of industrial organization. This same continuity with earlier times can also be seen in the industrial geography. Thus, the new feature of the 1700s refers to the State becoming a prominent stakeholder due to policies that aimed to promote the output and substitute importations.

*State intervention*

The state's role in the industry has been thought of by historians as correlated with the spurts and halts of the colonial trade, as was the case in the late 1600s with the program of the count of Ericeira (see Chapters 3 and 5). Hence, state's incentives to increase the industrial output in the eighteenth century were not entirely new, but would reach an unprecedented scale in the mid eighteenth century thanks to the impressive program designed by the marquis of Pombal. Yet his program followed up measures implemented in the 1720s and 1730s, which sought to nurture the creation of factories that were relatively scarce within the scope of the Portuguese industry. Among the industrial enterprises founded were a paper factory in Lousã and the leatherworking factories in Alenquer and Lisbon. Glassware and silks destined to satisfy finer tastes also received government backing. The former was supported through the establishment of a glassworks in Coina in the south margin of the river Tagus, which employed forty-four workers, and the latter by

---

[34] Macedo 1982b: 90–92; Pedreira 2005: 190–191.

way of the so-called royal silk factory (*real fábrica das sedas*), set up in Lisbon in the mid 1730s – perhaps the most emblematic of the industrial enterprising of King João V's reign (1707–1750) (Macedo 1982b: 69–72). In all of these instances, the initiative and investment of both foreign technicians and Portuguese businessmen relied on the State's support in the form of tax exemptions and monopoly rights.

The upshot of the program during King João V's reign is unclear, however. The policy did not seem to be directed at specific sectors, and the results they brought about were very limited (Madureira and Matos 2005: 128–129). The same cannot be said about the more comprehensive policy of the count of Oeiras, the future marquis of Pombal, who put into place a set of institutional reforms affecting the regulation of industry to propel an import-substitution program. Pombal's intervention aimed at creating new factories – some directly administered by the state, others by private concessionaires, but with state sponsorship (the so-called royal factories). The sector grew according to this model that called for a special legal statute granted by the state, which encompassed licenses for the setting up of new factories, tax exemptions, monopolies, and other privileges (Macedo 1982b: 149–179). This policy, which was discretionary to a certain extent, by making use of license refusals, not only resulted in the substitution of imports, but also called for the introduction of innovative techniques often dominated by foreign investors.

An example of Pombal's strong support in the form of subsidies and privileges can be found in the setting up of the royal glass factory in Marinha Grande, following the shutdown of the glasswork in Coina. The business was managed by an Englishman, William Stephens, and became the largest manufacturing unit in the kingdom. In yet another example of the marquis' manufacturing initiatives, the re-establishment of the royal woolens factories in Portalegre and Covilhã, also called for the contribution of foreigners, in this case of French technicians. Among the forms of state assistance, the concession of manufacturing monopolies gave rise to price cap measures and to the creation of an agency to supervise the enforcement of the policy – the Board of Trade (*Junta do Comércio*, see later) (Madureira 1997: 38–45, 113). This central institution licensed new industrial enterprises and, in due time, managed the sale or transfer of exploitation rights to private investors as was the case with the royal factory of Covilhã.

The diffusion of these more complex and large-scale enterprises coexisted with private investments in small workshops, which still persisted as a favored option. Besides, at least partly, these traditional forms of organizing the industry showed important complementarities with the larger factories, even with those that had benefited from state sponsorship

(Pedreira 1994: 89). The Royal Factory of Covilhã, working with the fine and high-quality wool from Elvas and other sheep-grazing regions from the Alentejo to Guarda and Viseu, illustrates the significance of that complementarity as far as we can learn from records of 1781–1782. During that year, the output of the royal factory depended on a putting-out network which delivered about 135,933 meters of cloth. One hundred years earlier, the looms of the industrial enterprises of the count of Ericeira in Covilhã and Manteigas produced 198,000 meters of cloth, an amount quite close to that provided by peasant households to the new royal factory at the end of the eighteenth century.

There is no estimate for the total output of the factory for that fiscal year (1781–1782), but looking at the annual average of the preceding decade, the 19,267 meters produced by the looms in its facilities suggest that the largest portion of the factory output was based on outsourcing to the cottage industry (Madureira 1997: 405). By the same token, the royal factory of Portalegre took advantage of the existing spinning and weaving tradition in the region: of the 1,348 persons working for the factory, 979 were spinners and weavers working at their homes or in small workshops widely scattered over the countryside (Macedo 1982b: 149–152).

As in the case of woolens, the royal silk factory in Lisbon was reorganized during the government of Pombal, and became the hub of a network of small workshops scattered in a parish of Lisbon, named Rato, where the enterprise was located. If Lisbon was the leading center of silk transformation, we cannot disregard the contribution of the Trás-os-Montes region, where the surge of activity in the 1700s and the abundance of raw silk spurred the establishment of several industrial units. Among the biggest producing areas of raw materials, Moncorvo was able to supply manufacturing enterprises in Chacim and in Freixo de Espada à Cinta, both in Trás-os-Montes. The first of these villages had no fewer than five manufactures, which in 1793–1794 employed 479 men and women, approximately 75 percent of the local work force. Enjoying royal support, the production was managed by the Italian Arnaud of Piemonte, which denotes an attempt to introduce innovative methods of working with silk. In Bragança too, the local economy depended on the silk works, which encompassed a large production unit. In 1794, the enterprise employed 915 persons (407 men and 508 women), which is to say, about 18 percent of the city's entire population. Velvets, taffetas, and satins left these factories for every corner of the kingdom, and were exported to Spain and Brazil (Sousa 1978: 69–72).

The silk industrial surge was threatened by the war with Spain in 1801. Several entrepreneurs fled the city of Bragança, looms were abandoned and the technological potential fell into underutilization. Recovery attempts spearheaded by a group of investors from Porto and Lisbon joined Arnaud in founding a company for silk spinning, which received a royal charter in 1802. The royal silk company (*real companhia das sedas*) sought to modernize the industry by adopting the Piedmontese methods in silk spinning. Other incentives included the plantation of mulberry trees and the granting of prizes to those who could find new and more successful ways to raise silk worms and spin their threads. The French invasions cut these hopes short. The industry did not disappear altogether, however, and there were some efforts to catch up after 1810, but the boom times that prevailed prior to 1797 never returned.

The state's intervention in the industrial structure meant that "royal factories" were above all facilities working as organizers and managers of production and labor already installed either in rural or in urban context. There is little in this model that differs from the one advanced by the count of Ericeira a century earlier. It is reasonable to admit that the industrial policy of the marquis of Pombal gave a small contribution to changes in the business structure. According to a report for the year 1777, even among the 200 manufactures created or reformed under this program, the workshops and small units outnumbered the large factories (Macedo 1982b: 155–160). Hence, considering that the organization model based on the concentration of all phases of production in factories remained an exception, the fragmentation in small, local units seems to account for the slowness with which Portuguese industry adopted new equipment and steam-powered machinery in the early nineteenth century.

The reasons for choosing small units over large ones are manifold, and even though the high upfront investments would not have been the only discouraging factor, it was surely a leading one. From what can be seen in isolated cases at the end of the 1700s, the factories needed high investments in facilities. In Portugal we find examples of partnerships that raised capital ranging from 71 million to 96 million *réis*, substantial sums, to be sure (Pedreira 1994: 375). This is unlike what we know about many cases in England, in which pioneering units in mechanized industry did not require huge installation costs, but instead often converted storehouses into industrial plants (Mathias 1979).

In Portugal, the few large investments in facilities were made under a regime of state protectionism, which lasted without interruption until the end of the century. Protectionist laws and import bans typified the policies that followed Pombal's administration, even though the state relinquished the royal factories to private managers and withdrew its financial support. Indeed, in the last quarter of the century, the concession of new business licenses was partially liberalized, often

Table 4.9 *Number of factories founded, 1769–1788*

| Manufactures | Before 1769 | 1770–1777 | 1777–1788 |
|---|---|---|---|
| Sugar refinery | 2 | 2 | 2 |
| Ceramics | 1 | 2 | 11 |
| Hat making | 1 | 4 | 15 |
| Tanning | 1 | 3 | 24 |
| Distillery | | | 3 |
| Metallurgy | | 4 | 20 |
| Cutlery | | 2 | 5 |
| Assorted metal items | | 3 | 18 |
| Furniture (wood & stone) | | | 1 |
| Paper products | 2 | 2 | 2 |
| Chemicals, gypsum, gunpowder | | | 4 |
| Textiles (total) | 4 | 26 | 84 |
| Cotton | 1 | 5 | 4 |
| Fabric printing | | 1 | 18 |
| Woolens | 1 | 4 | 6 |
| Linen | 1 | | 5 |
| Silk | | | 6 |
| Dyeing | | | 13 |
| Silk stockings | | 16 | 28 |
| Thread and cloth of gold and silver | 1 | | 4 |
| Glass | 1 | 1 | |
| Trinkets / combs | 1 | 4 | 41 |
| Other | 2 | 2 | 5 |
| Total | 15 | 55 | 235 |

*Source:* Pedreira 1994: 59.

contemplating small-scale undertakings as can be seen in the great number of start-ups (Table 4.9). The city of Porto provides a good example of this profusion of new licenses. From 1766 to 1788 forty-one new factories were established and three transfers of existing licenses were granted to new entrepreneurs (Madureira 1997: 354). Of these, twenty-seven were chartered between 1778 and 1788. The openness of the sector to foreign knowledge and methods was notable. From 1757 to 1832, of the 180 applications submitted, 114 (63 percent) came from foreigners (Pedreira 1994: 209).

From 1770 to 1777, 47 percent of the licenses went to textile operations, but in the next period that figure fell to 37 percent, notwithstanding the impressive rise in fabric printing and the making of silk stockings. While the textile industry remained the dominant sector, the advances in tanning, hat making, and comb making were noteworthy as a percentage of total production. A great deal of the increasing number of production units benefitted from protectionist measures in the Brazilian market. From the 1770s on, the government sought to suppress local manufacturers in Brazil. The enforcement of this policy, which bolstered the colonial system, came with the decree of January 5, 1785, in which the manufacturing activity in the colony was prohibited, including the refining of sugar.

As it turned out, in the final phase of the Portuguese *Ancién Régime* economic agents came to recognize the Brazilian market as the main outlet of the homeland's industrial output, which is visible in the upturn of manufactures in exports. In 1703 domestic goods (foodstuffs together with manufactures) represented 30 percent of the total value of exports to Brazil, the remaining 70 percent being performed by re-exports of European commodities. By 1800 Portuguese manufactures, alone, accounted for 35 percent of the whole cargo sent to the colony.[35] Due to the upsurge of colonial demand, it seems clear that industrial output rose. Although a larger number of factory units must have played a part in this surge, it must be recalled that the linen industry – the quintessentially small, household-based, and decentralized production – also was driven by Brazilian demand. To sum up, the colonial system turned out to be an engine of industrial prosperity, which became one of the main novelties of the 1700s in Portugal's economy. If it became a significant variable of the economic performance of the kingdom, it was but one among other variables affecting the performance of Portugal's foreign trade. This economic sector also underwent significant alterations in the final decades of the *Ancién Régime*, after being deeply molded by the Methuen Treaty during the first half of the century.

## The Empire and the foreign sector

Despite armed conflicts, mercantilist policies, and bilateral trade agreements, the 1700s witnessed a boom in international trade (Findlay and O'Rourke 2007: 238–244). Portugal backed this upsurge of intercontinental economic relations by enlarging settlements in Brazil. The South American offshoot confirmed its overwhelming role in the economic performance of the mother country, from the days when the contribution of the colony was mainly for the production of gold, to a later phase in which agricultural production came to include cotton, thereby broadening Portugal's supply of strategic goods to the rest of Europe.

[35] Morineau 1985: 169; Pedreira 1994: 272.

The impact of the empire will be first examined by taking into consideration bilateral economic relations, namely with Great Britain, which will shed light on the importance of gold as an exceptional resource in Portugal's foreign relations. Gold was a commodity with transaction costs lower than any other merchandise the colonial system had ever granted the kingdom before. It could be converted into coin or bullion bars, a means of payment accepted anywhere, a store of value, thus making it one of the most liquid assets of the time. The colonial system assured Portugal's privileged access to this resource, promoting a national rent that was leveraged by new settlements in mining regions facing scarcity of consuming goods. The local abundance of gold pushed prices up and raised markups in all exchanges, which were entrusted to the mother country's middlemen. Thereby, gold flooded Portugal's economy not only because of the royal fifth on gold extracted, but also, and mainly, because mining activities were carried out by private agents, many of them recent immigrants, who shipped considerable amounts of gold to the homeland. In the eighteenth century, the colonial system seems to positively affect the evolution of the domestic product. It may have contributed to raise wages in Portugal by 20 percent (Costa, Palma, and Reis 2015). Nevertheless, historians have also asserted that the access to gold reinforced the long-lasting structure of Portugal's foreign trade, which may have borne negative impact on the country's economic specialization as a supplier of primary products to the international market.

*Structure and trends in foreign trade*

The structure of foreign trade underwent no significant changes in the first half of the eighteenth century, in spite of the financial wealth the domestic economy achieved due to the colonial mining sector. Manufactured goods continued to dominate imports, some bound for re-export to the colonies (Africa, Asia, and especially Brazil) and some for consumption in the homeland itself. This persistence of a trade structure inherited from the past suggests that domestic production was little affected by the liquidity granted by the colonial system. Therefore, the rise in income gauged by real wages must have impacted on the demand for imports of European final consuming goods (Madureira 1997: 297). Into this essentially unchanged structure, where Portuguese manufactures had an insignificant share among exports, some modifications occurred, though. As a consequence of the diplomatic alliances arising from the War of Spanish Succession, and especially from the Methuen Treaty (December 1703), Portuguese wines were widely exported to the

British market and came to account for two-thirds of all wine exports already in 1715 (Schneider 1980: 48, n. 11) (see this chapter's section on agriculture).

Diplomacy thus became a necessary means to reinforce the country's specialization within the international division of labor and it eventually paved the way for Britain's leading part in bilateral trade. However, other factors came together to open Portugal further to British woolens, not just the wine exports. The discovery of gold in Brazil and the growth of the colonial market greatly contributed to making Portugal a significant trade partner. Most of the English cloth was re-exported to Portuguese America, partly through the enterprising of English agents who cut off the intermediary role of national ports. The English interlopers, as the marquis of Pombal would call the English investors in the Portuguese colonial monopoly, dated back to 1654 when diplomatic agreements allowed English shipping and commercial agencies to encroach on the Brazilian fleets (Boxer 1951).

Both contemporary historians and observers looked upon this over-whelming position of Britain in Portugal's foreign relations as a cause of serious trade imbalances. Already in the first decades of the eighteenth century the Portuguese deficit was considerably worse than it had been in 1680. Our data for this decade (Chapter 3) point to 782 million *réis* of deficit, originating from 1,310 million *réis* in exports and 2,092 million *réis* in imports.[36] A report from 1729, ascribed to a successful English businessman living in Portugal, referred to a deficit around 2,964 million *réis*. We must note that the deterioration of the Portuguese situation did not prevent exports from growing and surpassing the level of the seventeenth century. Still, this value varied only 474.5 million *réis*, while imports reached 2,357 million *réis*, totaling 4,449 million *réis* in the year 1729 (Costa 2005: 268). If Portugal's trade deficit reached 2,964 million *réis* in 1729, as the English report claimed, Britain accounted for 67 percent of this shortfall while France represented only 23 percent (670 million *réis*).[37] The re-export of gold coin or bullion was a necessity to finance the kingdom's deficit. Thus Portugal's trade with the two European powers, whose armed conflicts framed the political and military history of eighteenth-century Europe, justified 90 percent of the re-export of the gold shipped from Brazil.

For analytical purposes, the overwhelming weight of these two trade partners allows them to be taken as representative of the full scope of Portugal's foreign relations and make up a time series that substitutes the

[36] See Chapter 3.
[37] For series on England, see Fisher 1971; for France, see Labourdette 1988.

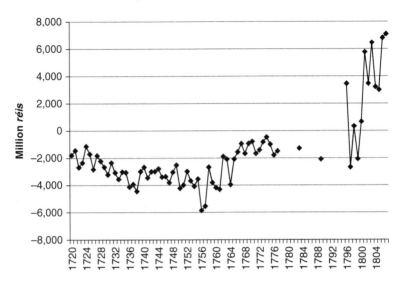

Figure 4.1 Balance of trade, 1720–1807
Sources: Fisher 1971: 206–208; Labourdette 1988. For the years 1776, 1777, 1783, 1789, 1796–1807, Balanças Gerais do Comércio, AHMOP, Fundo Superintendência Geral dos Contrabandos.

missing commercial balances with all partners until 1776. Afterwards, official trade balances offer a more complete picture, so they will be considered to characterize the last quarter of the century. Up to the 1750s the figures are well into the negative. The pronounced trade short-falls together with a stability of exports (Figure 4.1 and 4.2) coincide with Great Britain's leadership of Portugal's foreign trade. The period of Pombal's government (1750–1777) marked the end of pronounced shortfalls although the earthquake (1755) and the Seven Years' War (1756–1763) prompted a few critical years. In 1756 and 1757, for exam-ple, the trade balance account plunged to 6 million *réis*. Imports also showed peaks in 1760 and 1761; thereby deficits being 4,180.6 and 4,316 million *réis*, respectively. The figures point to a critical phase driven by the post-earthquake imports of raw materials and intermediary goods needed for the rebuilding of the destroyed capital, followed by a growing demand for war munitions. The conditions improved afterwards and a remarkable relief came by the end of the century. Then trade surplus occurred, even with Great Britain.

The improvement that started in 1776 altered the structure of foreign trade, which is best described as a steady fall of imports, since exports

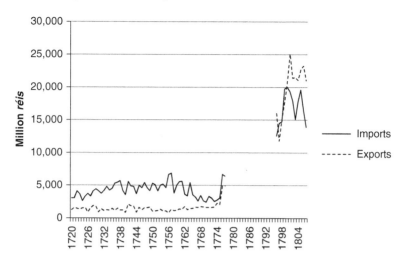

Figure 4.2  Foreign trade, 1720–1807
Sources: Fisher 1971: 206–208; Labourdette 1988. For the years 1776,
1777, 1783, 1789, 1796–1807, Balanças Gerais do Comércio,
AHMOP, Fundo Superintendência Geral dos Contrabandos.

overtook imports only after 1790. The turnaround in the trade balance at
the end of the century coincided with a sharp rise in the face value of
imports and exports, in part because the inflation of the 1790s hit all of
Europe – not just Portugal. Trade surpluses combined with inflation tell
us that the final decade of the eighteenth century bore specific features
(Costa, Palma, and Reis 2015).

The account equilibrium in trade balance occurred when real domestic
income (gauged by real wages) was declining, which suggests that lower
revenue reduced domestic consumption. However, the trends just
described coincided with the diversification of imports which included
a greater share of raw materials, ferrous and non-ferrous metals, signaling
that import-substitution policies altered the aggregate demand as well as
the scope of trade partners. For instance, the Scandinavian regions and
Imperial Russia – suppliers of semi-transformed goods with applications
in various industries – show a sudden and unprecedented jump in
Portugal's trade records toward the end of the 1700s (Carvalho 1979).
The new trading partners of the Baltic Sea diluted Britain's overwhelming
share that had characterized Portugal's foreign relations throughout the
first half of the eighteenth century. The causes of the alteration ask for

a more detailed view on the Anglo-Portuguese trade throughout the eighteenth century, while a few comparisons with the French relations will help to single out the specific aspects of the former.

### Portugal, Great Britain, and the Methuen Treaty

A glance at the trade with Great Britain and France reveals that between 1703/1716 and 1775 exports oscillated between 1 and 2 billion *réis*, while imports varied within a range of 3 billion *réis*. The Anglo-Portuguese economic relations were based more on the domestic resources of each economy than on their role as distributors of colonial goods. This means that re-exports performed only a minor role in this bilateral trade. Around 80 percent of exports bound for England consisted of wines, while Portugal's trade with France involved about 50 percent of re-exports of colonial goods (notably Brazilian hides).

As for Portugal's position, it represented 19.1 percent of all Britain's foreign trade from 1736 to 1740 (Sideri 1978: 332). Disaggregating the figures by merchandise, we see that textiles bound for Portugal accounted for 50 percent of that sector's total exports. Numbers point to the relative dependence of the English industry on Portugal's demand but they also explain the drainage of gold, since the kingdom's pronounced deficit had its main cause in this trade. We do not know the significance of imports from England within the range of trade partners as a whole during the first half of the century, but the idea of the rising share of Great Britain is corroborated by patchy data for maritime traffic. Newspapers from 1718, for example, report that between January and April 125 ships set sail from Lisbon, 65 percent of which were British, and 23 percent were French. Similar figures are provided by the French Ambassador who asserted that Portugal's trade with France was only about 35 percent of that with Britain. This trend continued in the next decades. In 1720 English ships amounted to 40 percent of Lisbon's traffic; 54.5 percent in 1725; and achieved 74.8 percent in 1732 (Godinho 1955: 323).

Such preeminence of the English trade was not sought by advisors of King João V, who took it as evidence of Portugal incurring unintended consequences of both economies' specialization. At the height of mercantilist policies, policy makers understood that the Methuen Treaty, which threw Portugal's doors open to English textiles, endangered the industrial program that had been implemented at the end of the 1600s (see Chapter 3) (Pedreira 2003: 131 and 134). The political discourse of the time elaborated on the problems raised by the abundance of a strategic resource (gold), and its relationship to the lower competitiveness of Portugal's industry. The topic of American precious metals causing the "deindustrialization" of Iberian economies in the *Ancién Régime* has motivated renowned studies in economic history, since the earliest works of Earl Hamilton on prices and wages (Hamilton 1934). The most recent approaches transpose what economics designates as a "Dutch disease" to the effects of precious metals' inflows in the Spanish economy during the early modern period. The abundance of a natural resource increased domestic revenues, putting an upward pressure on real exchange rates and affecting the competitiveness of tradable sectors, thus having detrimental consequences on current account balance (Drelichman 2005). The situation bears some common aspects with eighteenth-century Portugal due to gold inflows, but investment in wine production, which was a tradable sector, is a noteworthy difference, albeit the advantage of the Portuguese product derived from diplomatic arrangements.

Scholarly literature on the subject has stressed different sides of the problem at a time. For some historians, the negative course of events resided in rents extracted from the empire, which allowed increasing imports and caused the interruption of the industrial program inherited from the last quarter of the seventeenth century (Godinho 1955). Another prevailing view emphasizes the short-term benefits of an extraordinary natural resource against long-term costs of a certain specialization in the international economy.[38] Therefore, the Methuen Treaty and the gold inflows have caught the scholars' attention, since the country's pronounced trade imbalance is thought of as a "Dutch disease" effect and thus a cause for the economy falling behind thereafter. Still, according to another contending perspective, there are reasons to downplay the impact of both the Methuen Treaty and the gold inflows in a possible "deindustrialization." It has been claimed that the concept of "deindustrialization" is misleading when applied to pre-modern economies, because, for all of the unfavorable effects to come to pass, we would have to assume that there was an efficient employment of factors of production (Pedreira 1994: 41). Finally, a focus on geostrategic issues appraises the military aspects of the treaty. Diplomacy served the kingdom's strategic interests in Brazil, which had been threatened since the 1640 Restoration; therefore the cost–benefit assessments of the diplomatic agreement of 1703 should reckon the kingdom's financial inability to arm a naval and military force. The treaty endorsed the defense to an allied power implying some costs, namely the country's losses in the industrial sector. Eventually, this cost paid returns at a political level, granting Portugal its sovereignty after the French Revolution, when Napoleon subjected

---

[38] Sideri 1978; Valério 1980.

Europe to a global war and the royal family's departure to Brazil in 1807 left the realm to the British army's protection (Macedo 1989: 77).

Despite the historians' diversified interpretations of the commercial treaty, diplomacy ensured the rise of Portuguese wines in the international markets and brought about more capital-intensive agriculture. Besides, we cannot ignore that Portuguese industry was ill equipped to compete with English woolens, so that the Treaty of 1703 could have just anticipated the interruption of the program to promote industrial output that had started twenty years earlier (Chapter 3). Not surprisingly, the diplomatic arrangement contributed to reinforce both economies' relative advantages in specializing in one or the other product, so that the structures of both countries' exports at the end of the 1700s exposed the long-term consequences of this event dating from 1703 and discussed in the classic works of Adam Smith, David Ricardo, and Friedrich List. During the 1790s, 87.2 percent of England's exports were manufactures, while 78 percent of Portugal's were food items of one sort or another.[39] However, the notion that the Treaty of Methuen confined Portugal's foreign trade to a bilateral relation in which Britain had the lion's share is not consistent with the verified changes in the structure of the Portuguese foreign trade after 1770. They occurred, despite the Treaty being still in force. From 1770, Portugal reduced its trade deficits and in the 1790s attained surpluses. Above all there was a shift in the mix of Portugal's imports from England. As a result, we infer that Portugal's trade balance account and the structure of commerce were not dictated exclusively by either the terms of the Methuen Treaty or Portugal's ability to enforce its privileged access to a means of payment supported on colonial rents. A complete discussion of this issue should encompass Britain's own interests in the verified changes and as such calls for an examination of the consequences of the Seven Years' War.

### The Seven Years' War

Until the 1760s, when the value of Portuguese imports started a downward trend, 70–84 percent of England's exports to Portugal consisted of different types of textiles, with the greatest growth being in baizes. In 1706–1710 (before the Methuen Treaty came into effect) imports of baizes stood at an annual average of around 572.4 million *réis* (159,000 pounds sterling). From 1736 to 1740 this figure shot up to 1,566 million *réis*, and then to 1,594.8 million *réis* in 1756–1760. The perpetuanas and serges, woolen socks, or felt hats amounted to

---

[39] Engerman 1995: 189. Portuguese trade balance, 1796.

nothing even close to this figure. Serges, for example, in 1736–1740 accounted for 619.2 million *réis*, while combed-wool socks and hats amounted to about 288 million *réis*.[40] These categories of manufactured goods fell sharply from 1762 onwards, when imports of wheat and flour from Britain's American colonies surged in the prolonged aftermath of the 1755 earthquake. At the same time, imports of metals such as iron and copper grew annually by 5.4 percent from 1761 to 1775 (Macedo 1982b: 202). Metals destined for the production of capital goods (iron and copper) and heavy industry (shipbuilding), as well as foodstuffs (wheat from Sicily and Turkey, codfish, rice, and American flour) handled by British middlemen established in Portugal, continued to attract English ships to Portuguese ports. Thus, imports of manufactures fell while there was a rise in foodstuffs of American origin and raw materials – merchandises with lower bulk value than textiles. At this same time there was a slight increase in Portuguese exports to England.

The structure of the bilateral trade thus changed, which does not support the belief in a single explanatory cause for the reduction of the Portuguese trade balance deficits. Historians' analysis has been mostly guided by the dwindling of Brazilian gold and the financial crisis that spread to the business sector after 1760. From there, so the argument goes, the crisis affected the country's productive sectors, including agriculture, and became an issue addressed by Pombal. His policy sought to stimulate industry and was patterned after the policies dating from the last quarter of the 1600s, when a similar scarcity of means of payment brought on the need for import substitution.[41] But contrary to what occurred in the late seventeenth century, the import substitution policy of Pombal enabled the alteration of trade balance accounts eventually (Pedreira 1994).

As described earlier, the manufacturing policies enacted during Pombal's government did not have enough time to fully mature by the 1760s, when the structure of Portugal's imports from Great Britain underwent some significant transformations. Besides, the notion of less cash inflowing the country at that time lacks evidence, according to data compiled in a recent research on gold flows (Costa, Rocha, and Sousa 2013). Even if this had been demonstrated, it would not defy any explanation based on changes at the international level that came about with the Seven Years' War. To grasp the factors for Portugal's foreign trade performance in the second half of the eighteenth century, we should start by focusing on the international order and then switch to a more

---

[40] Fisher 1971: 187 (1 pound sterling = 3,600 *réis*).
[41] Macedo 1989: 85–99; Godinho 1955: 255; Pedreira 1994.

detailed description of gold trends, not as determinants of the structure of Portugal's exports, but rather as part of the imperial dimension of the economy.

The war had a significant impact on English and French colonial systems. It involved a struggle for resources in North America. When the war ended, most of French Canada and the four Caribbean islands under French sovereignty went over to British sway. This boosted English exports to the American colonies thereafter, providing greater profits than those obtained from trade in European markets, including Portugal. In fact, the Seven Years' War reshaped Britain's place in international trade. From the 1770s on, English exports dominated trade goods bound for the New World, Asia, and Africa. Britain's exports to its colonies and other sovereign powers climbed from 5,461 million pounds sterling to 19,787 million pounds between 1772/1775 and 1797/1812. British exports to Europe also display a positive trend, although much less spectacular, jumping from 6,068 million to 11,306 million pounds during the same period. The current account balances with each of these areas attest that the English advantages resided in its extra-European economic relations, which soared from 2,085 million to 7,793 million pounds, while with Europe it dropped from 4,157 million pounds to 336 million (Cuenca Esteban 2004: Table 2.5). This shift of Britain's economic interests, which was far greater than what occurred with any of the other colonial powers, came about after the Seven Years' War.

Regarding the activities of English businessmen established in Portugal, a case study of a merchant trading house reveals the new opportunities that arose after the 1760s when the woolens' share in Portugal's imports shows a downward trend. The fact is that the firm stopped importing textiles by switching over to discounting bills of exchange in Portugal and exporting gold (Sutherland 1933). Importing manufactures into Portugal was, thus, returning less of a premium, which prompted the British merchant community residing in Portugal to seek new opportunities, including the supply of shipping services on an international scope, connecting, for instance, Portugal to the Mediterranean ports, notwithstanding the cargo belonging to other business communities.[42] Hence, English interests in Portugal became less driven by profits earned in trading textiles and more by the supply of services and gold arbitrage, which were items neglected at that time in the assessment of external accounts and so this alteration prevents us from gauging how much it affected the Portuguese current account balance. But we know that the English colonial system that came about after the Seven Years'

---

[42] On bilateral trade, see Fisher 1981.

War altered the choices of English firms in Portugal and led Portugal's trade balance to improve, at the point of displaying surpluses in the last decade of the eighteenth century. Thus, we can say that trends in gold flows from Brazil played a minor role in all this, at best.

### Brazilian trade

Mining in Brazil extracted 856.5 metric tons (*toneladas*) of gold during the 1700s, which may represent about 53–61 percent of the total world production.[43] As a result of the prominent position of a Portuguese colony, on the one hand, European powers saw an obvious advantage in trading with Portugal, the country that was at the fore in supplying one of the commodities that underpinned the world's monetary system. On the other hand, the gold rush pushed the colonial frontier southward and inland and paved the way to an impressive rise of the slave trade. The most recent literature on the subject keeps revising the figures. Present estimates point to a threefold growth of the number of African slaves disembarked in Brazilian ports, from 297,000 in 1676–1700 to 670,000 in 1776–1800.[44] The business was managed directly by residents in Portuguese America, meaning that the middlemen role of the kingdom in this trade was occasional. This prompted outflows of gold together with tobacco to African trading posts to pay for slaves. Therefore, both the growth of the slave traffic and the new settlements in mining areas challenged the state's ability to control these far distant territories and levy taxes on gold production.

It comes as no surprise that the decades of the gold rush were marked by the State's constant struggle with contraband. The royal intention to assess the amounts of metal extracted was impelled by perceptions of fiscal non-compliance in mining regions, which was thought of as a cost of the colonial system that should be mitigated through fiscal innovations rather than armed force (Cortesão 1984). But settlers empowered by local networks led riots against fiscal charges, reflecting the political and social consequences of upsurges of immigrants before a loosely administrative framework provided by the mother country.[45]

---

[43] Not including the production from Bahia, see Pinto 1979: 114. For estimates of world gold production, see Barrett 1990: 228–229.

[44] Transatlantic slave trade database, http://www.slavevoyages.org/tast/index.faces; Klein 1999.

[45] Literature on political and administrative history of Brazilian colony is extensive. For the particular topics of the impact of fiscal issues and the building of the administrative network, see Bicalho, Furtado, and Souza 2009; Carrara and Sánchez Santiró, 2012; Magalhães 2012; Souza 2006 as representative examples.

Notwithstanding such precarious control of the state on mining regions, historians' evaluations of mining output point to 80 percent of the gold extracted reaching European ports, of which 70 percent was re-exported by Portugal. It has been a foregone conclusion – lacking proper demonstration – that most of this gold simply passed through Portugal's ports on its way to foreign markets, notably to London – and that a paltry remainder was applied to ostentatious consumer goods. The topic needs further discussion based on new data on gold remittances. Let us first consider the inflow, which varied from time to time and as a function of the two principal recipients: the State, to which in principle a fifth of all production was due (by means of the so-called *quinto* – the fifth – tax); and private parties who owned the other four-fifths. Private remittances of gold included payments from emigrants, capital transfers, and revenues from businessmen and parties contracted to collect and handle public funds.

Data from a fiscal source pertaining to the payment of the 1 percent transportation tax on gold shipments reveal a total of 271 billion *réis* unloaded between 1720 and 1807 (557 tons), of which 211 billion *réis* belonged to private parties and 59.9 billion *réis* to the State (Costa, Rocha, and Sousa 2013). These two types of remittances (public and private) fluctuated according to factors that were not just related to the actual mining. For instance, throughout the government of the marquis of Pombal, although the public transfers achieved their peak in the 1760s, they were also quite volatile, due to fiscal reforms and to the allocation of local tax revenue to pay the rising administrative and military expenditure in the colony.[46] As for private remittances, they peaked in the 1740s. A fall begins in the 1750s, accentuates in 1760, and hits very low levels only after 1780 (Table 4.10). Thus, the best years for the State's remittances coincided with Pombal's government, which were also the years when English imports started to dip. Historians have repeatedly attributed these falling imports to a supposed financial crisis with consequences on import-substitution policies.[47] But this assumption is not borne out by the data gathered from the most reliable fiscal source recording the 1 percent tax levied on these flows of gold (Table 4.10).

A great deal of the amounts unloaded in Lisbon through private businesses was indeed re-exported. Despite the long-standing legal prohibitions on exporting the precious metal, private interests were able to

---

[46] For the reformations in Brazil during and after Pombal's government, see the still updated work of Alden 1968.

[47] Macedo 1982a; Maxwell 1995.

Table 4.10 *Remittances of gold from Brazil, 1720–1807 (million* réis*)*

|  | Private | | State | |
| --- | --- | --- | --- | --- |
|  | Value | Annual change | Value | Annual change |
| 1720–1724 | 13,290 |  | 2,118 |  |
| 1725–1729 | 18,807 | 0.42 | 6,403 | 2.02 |
| 1730–1734 | 14,257 | −0.24 | 6,764 | 0.06 |
| 1735–1739 | 15,948 | 0.12 | 3,456 | −0.49 |
| 1740–1744 | 23,621 | 0.48 | 5,835 | 0.69 |
| 1745–1749 | 23,766 | 0.01 | 2,397 | −0.59 |
| 1750–1754 | 21,331 | −0.10 | 4,912 | 1.05 |
| 1755–1759 | 16,356 | −0.23 | 4,880 | −0.01 |
| 1760–1764 | 12,212 | −0.25 | 6,192 | 0.27 |
| 1765–1769 | 13,306 | 0.09 | 6,406 | 0.03 |
| 1770–1774 | 12,443 | −0.06 | 3,015 | −0.53 |
| 1775–1779 | 9,427 | −0.24 | 1,285 | −0.57 |
| 1780–1784 | 4,688 | −0.50 | 2,313 | 0.80 |
| 1785–1789 | 873 | −0.81 | 780 | −0.66 |
| 1790–1794 | 791 | −0.09 | 519 | −0.92 |
| 1795–1799 | 3,661 | 3.60 | 1,321 | 1.54 |
| 1800–1807 | 6,303 | 0.72 | 1,369 | 0.04 |

*Source:* Costa, Rocha and Sousa 2013.

circumvent the law. Throughout the eighteenth century the connections between Portugal and Great Britain justified the arrival of regular paquebots from Plymouth bearing the official stamp of approval for trade of information between the two States (Boxer 1962: 157). Diplomatic immunity made these ships the ideal carriers for outgoing gold and cash, destined to offset Portugal's deficits. Besides, the value of practically all of the gold coined in England parallels Portugal's trade deficit figures, and this does reveal a genuine dependence of the London mint house on the supply of Portuguese gold.[48] But the drain of cash did not prevent the accumulation of stock in Portugal. Looking at inflows next to the trade and capital balances leads us to reconsider the contribution of the empire regarding the rise of the money stock. It is unquestionable that considerable quantities were shipped abroad, but still, the value of remittances exceeded the trade deficits in many years, which allowed the gold stock to grow in the homeland (Figure 4.3).

[48] Godinho 1955: 231; Sousa 2006: 165–168.

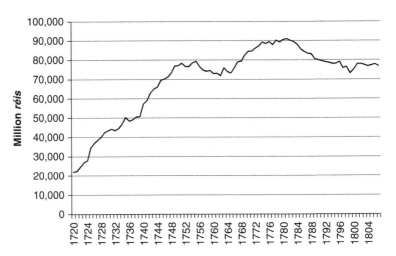

Figure 4.3 Gold stock, 1720–1807
Source: Costa, Rocha and Sousa 2013.

The stock of gold shows a notable progression, and more than 80 percent of it was in the form of coin.[49] Part of the remaining 20 percent was used to produce luxury goods that were also a store of value (table wares, decorative home accessories, jewelry, and other items that gave the golden glow to the Portuguese baroque). Considering the whole time span, the years 1755–1765 stand out, not because of any critical contraction, but rather because of a short-lived halt in the accumulation process. Moreover, in the years when remittances hit low levels, the positive trade balance held off the erosion of the country's gold stock. This new approach on stocks' trends allows us to claim that fluctuations in money supply do not add to the explanations of the contraction of imports of English textiles from the 1760s on. So, the search for more reasons, this time based on Portugal's economic dynamics, should be focused on the kingdom's eventual ability to substitute the British manufactures that were usually re-exported to Brazil. This bolstering of colonial systems as a means of guaranteeing protected markets for homeland manufactures was a common issue among European colonial powers. Portugal's political enlightened circles became aware of that and promoted conditions for an import substitution policy that altered the structure of Portugal's exports to the colony too.

Since the early 1700s Brazil was Portugal's leading overseas market, during and following the mining heyday. It absorbed 80–90 percent of the

[49] Costa, Rocha and Sousa 2013; Sousa 2006.

homeland's colonial trade. The pattern of trade in the first half of the century was based on exporting domestic linens and foodstuffs (olive oil, wine, and flour) and re-expediting European goods, mostly textiles, decorative items, clothing, and metals. As for codfish, it followed another trade circuit, since Portugal's fishing fleet was largely incapable of sailing all the way to the New World, and for this reason the supply of cod to those markets relied on the intermediation of English shipping (Serrão 1993b). Tentative estimates for the share of foreign commodities shipped to the colony hover around 70 percent. On the return voyage the merchant marine carried leather and hides in ever-growing quantities, sugar, and tobacco. Gold remained as the leading merchandise in terms of cargo value, climbing at an annual 1.5 percent rate from 1703 to 1750.[50]

By the middle of the century, the cargos coming from Brazil started to include new items, some dealt within the monopoly granted to colonial chartered companies, one for the region of Grão-Pará and Maranhão (1755–1778), other for Pernambuco and Paraíba.[51] These companies played a role in the growth of the Brazilian economy in the years of declining gold mining. The sugar production operations in Pernambuco and Paraíba boosted the economy considerably with exports, especially to Hamburg. Exploiting credit mechanisms, the Company of Grão-Pará and Maranhão promoted the cultivation of native plants such as cacao, and introduced rice and coffee – all products that were enjoying growing demand in Europe. Aside from these new products that added to sugar and tobacco, the other remarkable event of this era was Brazil's new place in the market for cotton, a crucial raw material with emergent demand in England. Records of the Company of Grão-Pará and Maranhão Company for 1758–1778 reveal that cotton accounted for 18 percent of the value of transactions, against 15 percent for hides and leather and 34 percent for cacao (Carreira 1988, vol. 2).

The growing contribution of the Brazilian primary sector to the Portuguese economy made up for the falling value of gold flows to the homeland (Figure 4.4). These other exports, which had remained flat during the best years of gold production, climbed sharply from 1770 on.[52] This expansion and diversification in Brazilian output became a new engine of growth for the kingdom's manufacturing exports. The changes that were underway reinforced the colonial system, not without the mother country enacting legislation to hinder the colony

---

[50] Morineau 1985; Pinto 1979.

[51] For the business history of these companies, see Carreira 1983a, 1983b, and 1988. For their legal framework, see Marcos 1997.

[52] For the diversification of the colony's primary sector during and after the gold rush, see Carrara 2007; Osório 2007.

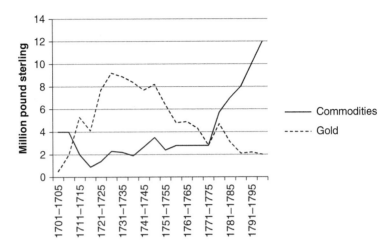

Figure 4.4 Exports from Brazil, 1701–1800
Source: Morineau 1985: 484 (4,5 piastras=1 pound sterling, according to conversion given on p. 307, n.186).

from developing manufactures or any form of adding value to primary products, including the refining of sugar (Arruda 1980).

The features of this restructuring of the colonial system are seen in the homeland's exports to Brazil, with manufactures varying from 34.9 to 43.1 percent. At the end of the century new factories sprang up throughout the country while Brazil became the dominant consumer of a few of them. In the case of hats, for instance, 8 percent of the domestic production had market in the colony. Further contribution of the empire to the Portuguese industrial growth is illustrated by tanning, which found demand not only in the colony, but elsewhere in Europe, as well, mostly in Italy. These leather goods and clothing accessories exemplify Brazil's new role in Portugal's industrial advance by providing an essential raw material. On the other hand, the development of colonial agriculture, with particular consequences on cotton output, leveraged the value of the homeland's re-exports to Europe, contributing to improve trade balances at the end of the century. It is well known that Brazil was only one among a number of raw cotton suppliers to Britain's industry, but it delivered a respectable 11 percent of the whole.[53] Furthermore, the cotton industry became another instance of the Anglo-Portuguese complementarity. By 1796, 20.3 percent of the cotton fabric that was printed in Portugal

[53] Godinho 1955: 262; Macedo 1982b: 199.

came from Asian markets. However, already in 1812 English-origin cotton fabrics represented 14 percent of Portugal's imports (Madureira 1997:
317). A modernized complementarity was woven between Brazil's exports
and intra-European trade flows reflecting anew the colonial dimension of
Portugal's economy. However, by the same time, the short-term rising
share of domestic production in the country's exports to the colony turned
downward once again in 1790, re-exports surpassing 70 percent.[54]

The Napoleonic wars impacted on the terms of trade with Europe,
giving a new advantage to Portuguese colonial re-exports (Madureira
1997). Therefore, the elimination of Portugal's trade deficits at the
end of the eighteenth century was an achievement that once again
derived from the reinforcement of the colonial pact and from the
colonial dimension of the Portuguese economy. Politics of the era
added some new thinking to the whole colonial system by acknowl-
edging its similarities to an international division of labor. Brazil was
a region integrated into the economic space of Portugal, by selling to
the homeland a wide range of raw materials and foodstuffs and purchasing manufactured goods produced in the mother country
(Cardoso 2001: 84–85).

Notwithstanding the discourse about the advantages of the colonial
system for the rising role of manufactured goods produced in the homeland, by the end of the century the structure of Portugal's foreign trade
was still characterized by the overwhelming share of primary products.
Therefore, even though Portugal was a grain-importing country, its
balance of trade of primary goods was positive. In 1796, 3,054 million
*réis* worth of wine, oil, and fruits surpassed 2,189 million *réis* of imports
of cereals and wheat flour. Regarding wine in particular, despite Brazil's
growing share in the market, England remained the leading purchaser,
absorbing 90 percent of exports. Thus the downturn in this bilateral
arrangement, which came around in the mid-century, did not affect
wine exports as much as it did the Portuguese imports of English
woolens.

The halt on the bilateral features of the Portuguese foreign trade
occurred because of England's international role after the Seven Years'
War. But it is also true that the institutional reforms carried out by the
marquis of Pombal must have played a part in the increasing share of
domestic manufactures exported to the protected Brazilian colony.
The new institutional framework underpinning the growth of the industrial sector was, nevertheless, entangled with the effects of the calamitous
earthquake in 1755, which gave the lead of the government to the

---

[54] Macedo 1982b: 202; Pedreira 1994: 53.

count of Oeiras, the former Portuguese diplomat in London, and future marquis of Pombal.[55]

## Institutional reforms

Two facts stand out as inextricably linked during the eighteenth century: the arrival on the political scene of one of the ministers of King José I, Sebastião José de Carvalho e Melo (1699–1782), and one of the greatest natural disasters ever to strike Europe, the earthquake of November 1, 1755. The magnitude of the quake is thought to have reached 8.5–9 on the Richter scale. A tsunami subsequently hit the coast and fires then broke out in the zone of destruction, devastating whatever was still standing in several civil parishes. The tremor was felt throughout the country, and as far away as Spain and North Africa, but nowhere was the damage as tragic as in Lisbon. Estimates at the time placed the number of dead at approximately 80,000, but historians suspect that this number is excessive. Nevertheless, casualties in Lisbon were certainly high – on the order of 16,000–18,000 – about 12 percent of the local population, which would not recover to its pre-quake size until twenty-five years later.[56]

Beyond the loss of life, the medium-term costs were enormous. Damage to buildings added to the loss of equipment and stocks. Among the State's infrastructures alone, losses included the capital's public facilities: the grain warehouse (*Terreiro de Trigo*), the customs house (*Alfândega Grande*), the tobacco customs house (*Alfândega do Tabaco*), and other administration facilities such as *Casa dos Cinco* and the *Paço da Madeira*. Somehow spared was the Royal Mint (*Casa da Moeda*), where the imported gold belonging to the king and private parties was held pending the payment of the 1 percent transportation tax. As for private damages, calculations indicate that 70 percent of the Church's buildings were destroyed. The royal palace (*Paço da Ribeira*), the impressive patriarchal church (*Sé Patriarcal*), and the recently built Opera House were all completely ruined (Serrão 2007: 145–146).

Aside from dozens of aristocratic palaces, more than 12,000 homes were destroyed, and most of the urban area was reduced to rubble. The loss of storehouses, presses, mills, and workshops, all of which provided the industrial fabric of the city, can scarcely be calculated in a meaningful way beyond simply recognizing that the loss of physical

---

[55] Maxwell 1995 gives a good survey of the man and the politician; Monteiro 2008; Subtil 2007.

[56] Pereira 2009; Serrão 2007: 151.

capital was overwhelming. It is plausible that 20 percent was wiped out, which is assumed to have affected 75 percent of the gross domestic product (GDP) (Cardoso 2007: 168). This level of havoc meant that in the following years investment in construction, to replace destroyed residential capital, may have diverted financial means. The one bright side was that employment (and wages) in civil construction was secure for a few years. Equilibrium was restored to Lisbon in time, during which the city became the destination for considerable numbers of manual laborers from other parts of the kingdom (Pereira 2009).

This natural disaster and the outbreak of the Seven Years' War (1756–1763) are most likely the causes of the economic distresses mentioned in the diplomatic correspondence of 1764 (Macedo 1982a: 93). Many foreign businessmen abandoned Lisbon as a consequence of these events, concluding that their loss of capital stemming from lost merchandise and unpaid debts precluded their continued presence in the city, and perhaps even in the country itself. Regarding the English mercantile community and despite the huge damages, the Consul informed London that, in his opinion the community was not financially under stress (Serrão 2007: 152).

The speed of recovery, which occurred alongside a number of state initiatives, supports the belief that new opportunities for private investment arose and a great deal of the gold stocked, 80 percent of which was in the form of coin, financed the reconstruction. We recognize in the 1755 earthquake – as we also do in wars – the effect of an external shock, whose unforeseen circumstances often require responses that introduce considerable change(s) to the structure of the economic system. The marquis of Pombal stood out as the agent of such changes (Pereira 2009). Some of his economic measures have already been mentioned with regard to agriculture, industry, and trade with Brazil. We shall now describe the main features of the institutional framework he created and examine the importance of his legacy. Some of the effects were longer lasting than others, but it is undeniable that the eighteenth century is divided clearly between the pre- and post-Pombal government.

Carvalho e Melo began his career as a diplomat, first in London, then in Vienna. As did many other Portuguese diplomats, he thought about Portugal largely through a foreign insight. He produced influential writings that denounced his mercantilist slant in which Portugal played a subservient role to Britain's hegemony. His rise to power came about through royal intervention. In the aftermath of the 1755 earthquake, Carvalho e Melo was promoted from secretary of state for foreign affairs and war to the central post of secretary for internal affairs, which attests the confidence vested in him by the king. The latter office took precedence over all the other cabinet posts of the government, including the secretaries for the navy and overseas possessions, and foreign affairs and war (Subtil 1993: 176–177).

As the head of a central office in the state bureaucracy, with a say in every area of government, all correspondence directed to the king passed over his desk. Pombal took it upon himself, as part of his mandate, to enact legislative and executive measures. Coming into power amidst the destruction of the earthquake, he took the lead in implementing policies and reforms that lasted until 1777, the year of his political fall, immediately after King José I had passed away. The minister's measures were extended to social, cultural, and economic areas, as well as to the relations of the State with the Church and the Inquisition. Pombal's policy also addressed human capital through basic education and setting up an emergent school system, financed by the so-called literary tax (*subsídio literário*) levied on wine and brandy. The formalized teaching of noble and mercantile elites led to the creation of new and specialized institutions, such as the School of Commerce (*Aula do Comércio*) and the Royal College for Nobles (*Real Colégio dos Nobres*). New statutes were drawn up for the University of Coimbra as well (Monteiro 2008).

From among the complex package of reforms, many pragmatic measures emerged, and not necessarily in a well-defined way. Some approached economic issues, others the management of public finances. All in all, the institutional reforms tackled four major areas: the influence of Britain in Portugal's foreign affairs; the defense of national monopolies; the making of prominent financial groups; and the reformation of the accounting system in public finances together with fiscal alterations (Maxwell 1995). Reducing English dominance on Portugal's foreign trade – a policy that crossed with, but should not be identified with the institution of national monopolies – caused tensions with the English Factories of Porto and Lisbon (English business communities), whose wealth was reckoned even by England's own diplomats. Ambassador Lord Tyrawley wrote in a letter dated 1752 that, "a great body of his Majesty's subjects reside at Lisbon, rich, opulent and every day increasing their fortunes and enlarging their dealings" (Lodge 1933: 225). Twenty years earlier there had been 2,000 Englishmen in the capital, a city that counted about 160,000 inhabitants.[57] Registered in the English Factory, and enjoying considerable prerogatives of membership, were 155 businessmen at the time of the earthquake – a significant number next to the 450–500 Portuguese businessmen residing in Lisbon.[58]

---

[57] Boxer 1969: 465; Moreira 2008: 263.     [58] Shaw 1998: 54; Pedreira 1995: 127.

Pombal's policies confronted some of the operations of the English Factories notably in their positions in producing and distributing wines, seen as the main cause of the debased quality and reputation of the product. The Upper Douro Wine Company founded in 1756 was instrumental in mitigating the English mismanagement of the industry that was depreciating the exports' prices. The enterprise gathered the interests of the large vineyard owners in the Upper Douro, mostly wealthy aristocrats, but there were other stockholders too, some of whom were leading middlemen in Porto. As with other large monopolist companies, the Upper Douro quickly found itself at odds with various opposition groups, which the marquis of Pombal judged to be manipulated by the English Factory in Porto (Schneider 1980).

The wine company was one of the ticklish points between Pombal and the English community, but other monopolist companies, this time involving colonial trade, also caused tensions. Corporate business was considered a means to protect Portugal's economic affairs with its empire and a necessary condition to develop some economic sectors, such as distribution and transportation (Maxwell 1995). Sebastião José de Carvalho e Melo recognized the advantages of this enterprise model when he was ambassador in London from 1739 to 1742. He had argued in its correspondence that the advantages of the English economy in international trade were rooted in a large volume of trade in low-value goods (i.e., bulk trade), which demanded a powerful merchant marine fleet. He regarded the laws that had been enacted in the Navigation Acts (in the days of Cromwell) as the key to Britain's prosperity.[59] Seeing the difficulties Portuguese merchants faced in London convinced Sebastião José de Carvalho e Melo that there was a subaltern relationship in Portugal's trade vis-à-vis Britain, which had nothing to do with the Methuen Treaty. Hence, once a minister, he made use of what he had learned in London, and never questioned the diplomatic alliance, as he thought it promoted the nation's specialization and had proven economic potentials.

Although Pombal did not allow his anxiety with British domination of trade to threaten any of the Methuen treaty elements, he did pay attention to its possible effects their current account balance considering "invisible flows," freight, insurance, and credit, areas in which the British had advantages that were obstructing the growth of Portugal's healthier trade. With all of this in mind, the minister judged that the correct way forward was to defend the exclusivity of Portugal's merchant marine by

---

[59] For a summary of Pombal's idea of the Anglo-Portuguese trade, see the introduction in Barreto 1986.

sponsoring the foundation of corporate enterprise and fostering the economic relations with the empire. This policy would call for certain import substitutes, whether of English goods or goods traded by the English business community living in Portugal. Above all, it asked for a number of paths toward the rise of a new capitalist elite in the kingdom.

### Corporations and a new merchant elite

One of these paths consisted in raising a merchant's human capital and turning trade into a specialized occupation. To this end he founded the *Aula do Comércio*. At the same time, the poorly qualified itinerant traders (*comissários volantes*) who, in the eyes of Pombal, were the epitome of mediocrity of the national tradesmen – were banned from engaging in colonial trade, on the grounds that they were serving England's interest (Maxwell 1991; Pedreira 1995). However, research on merchant networks tones down the notion that these itinerant traders were pawns in the service of English capital, employed to interlope the protected colonial markets. In fact, some renowned financiers of Pombal's government had been itinerant traders before becoming part of the business elite in Lisbon and Porto (Madureira 1997). Nevertheless, these forms of agency do, it must be said, point to the poor social capital in which the colonial economy developed during the euphoric boom years of gold mining (Costa, Rocha, and Araujo 2011). In summary, constraints on certain forms of agency and formal education to boost occupational specialization were part of the package of Pombal's initiatives seeking to strengthen a group of merchants who could engage in a correlated program involving corporate business for colonial trade.

Elsewhere in Europe, large companies were usually granted rents of monopoly, on the grounds of remunerating the inherent risks (which occasionally called for the opening up of all new markets and often for funding military operations) and with the aim of rewarding those who had lent large sums of money – all of which established principles of reciprocity between the public authorities and interest groups.[60] Such a close relationship, in turn, offered an additional guarantee to investors. Examples drawn from the English and Dutch empires supported the argumentation of decision-makers and public opinion that chartered companies were effective instruments for international competition, seen as a zero-sum game.

However, in the various national cases, these companies were also prone to raise contenders. In the words of a Portuguese diplomat, "the

---

[60] Carlos and Nicholas 1988; Blussé and Gaastra 1981.

companies are nothing more than monopolies defended by law: as they deprive the people of the freedom to do certain business; and for this there is no lack of proof in England and Holland. But the princes and the republics allow it when they see that although it prejudices their vassals in other ways they seek greater utility" (Cardoso 2005: 352). Firmly following these principles of political economy of the time, Pombal advanced the constitution of monopolistic companies in Portugal. Through acts of pure despotism he eliminated the opposition to such enterprises, via new institutional reforms that asked for further organizations to regulate the economy, favoring an interest group whose networks interlocked the boards of these very organizations. The founding of the Company of Grão Pará and Maranhão was, for all intents and purposes, the first step in the making of this institutional matrix that ruled Portugal's commerce and industry.

The "greater utility" expected from this company in Brazil would derive from enjoying monopoly rights in the northern regions of the colony, where the issue of enslaving the Indians caused tensions between the Portuguese settlers, the local governor, and the missionary religious orders (i.e., the Jesuits). The governor of Maranhão, Mendonça Furtado, was one of the supporters of the foundation of a company that was expected to promote agrarian production in the region and supply African-slave labor to work the fields. He also was Pombal's brother and reported favorably the initiative of some locals who were gathering capital to found a company. The information that the central government was giving support to a corporate company which was granted the monopoly on slave traffic and on the distribution of new colonial foodstuffs, drew protests from some Lisbon businessmen collectively represented in the brotherhood called the *Mesa do Bem Comum dos Homens de Negócio* (Board of the Common Good of Merchants). This brotherhood congregated wholesalers and retailers, without any formal distinction. Pombal was displeased with their protests, seeing in them the seeds of insurrection. He therefore decreed the dissolution of the brotherhood, exiled the leaders of the movement, and reinstated a new business agency, called the Board of Trade (*Junta do Comércio*).[61]

The new *Junta do Comércio* put wholesalers in leadership positions. A decree of December 6, 1755 laying down the rules of the association turned it into a political device at the service of the merchants who, from the beginning, had interests aligned with those of Pombal's program. Hence, the *Junta do Comércio* was vested with expanded fiscal and economic competencies. It oversaw various areas of retail business and

[61] Azevedo 1990; Carreira 1988: 56.

imposed mandatory registration with the association. Aside from this establishment of an internal hierarchy within the mercantile class, the board had powers to regulate economic activities, including the industry, by being charged with supervising the management of the royal factories. It was also vested with the authority to grant or reject licenses for the setting up of private manufacturing units, even for those already in operation. It had the power to authorize the entry of raw materials for the kingdom's factories, and to refuse the naturalization of foreigners. Hence, the evolution of the industrial output described earlier actually occurred under the administration of this board, which also supervised port activities and the unloading of gold going to the mint (*Casa da Moeda*).[62] The *Junta do Comércio* was not equal to the Spanish *consulado*, the merchants' guild of Seville, nor was it anything even approaching a trade corporation, as the *Mesa do Bem Comum* had been. It was an arm of the State – a cadre of the businessmen's faction that went along with the monopolist model working in the empire.

The immense authority of the *Junta do Comércio* drew the battle lines between the majority of its members and an inner clique that spread its control from the association out into the colonial companies and the administrations of the royal factories. In turn, colonial companies, because they often were governed by members who had had posts in *Junta do Comércio*, became more of an instrument of social dissention among the domestic mercantile group than an effective means to counter English operations in Portuguese foreign trade. Still, the innovative side of this package of institutional reforms was its assembling conditions for the making of a strong and wealthy interest group, with just a few ties to land.[63] The economic clique the minister helped to form did not disappear along with his fall. In that sense a small and coherent moneyed elite seems to have been one of the most enduring legacies of his government (Pedreira 1995).

The wealthy merchants undertook the most capital-intensive ventures and provided financing in a system that still knew neither banks nor other specialized credit organizations.[64] Financial intermediation continued to be an activity that was well spread among all social classes, but capitalists during and after Pombal's government stood out in financial intermediations, partly due to lending to aristocratic families, but mainly due to their involvement in state finances (Monteiro 2003). The tobacco monopoly was one of these activities that involved another rent derived from

---

[62] For examples of the licensing process, see Macedo 1982a, document appendix. For the Business Association, see Madureira 1997; Pedreira 1995.
[63] Pedreira 1995, Serrão 2000.    [64] Rocha 1996, 1998.

the empire, which is deemed the cadre of the wealthiest businessmen of the second half of the eighteenth century (Pedreira 1995).

In fact, the Crown's monopoly over the transformation and distribution of tobacco in the domestic market was routinely farmed out to Lisbon's leading businessmen in the final quarter of the 1700s. In return, the royal treasury received an annual rent that reached 884 million *réis* during the years of Pombal's government leveling off there. This was not due to lower demand or less opportunities for business. The flattening trend in the value of contracts was mainly a consequence of the political and economic influence attained by the elite of businessmen. In fact, acting in cohesion when bidding for the contract these businessmen eroded the State's bargaining leverage. Besides, the possibility of extending the term of the contract gave the concessionaires an obvious advantage during periods of inflation, which is exactly what happened toward the end of the century. Despite the fact that the tobacco monopoly was a rent captured by private interest, which could have negatively affected public revenues, the government of King José I displays unequivocal signs of the state's modernization at the level of information management by implementing important reforms in the area of accounting.

## State finances toward the end of the *Ancién Régime*

The Seven Years' War demanded increased public spending and called attention to the need for more effective information flow in the central governing bodies. In 1761, the military backdrop led to the creation of the royal treasury (*Erário Régio*), an institution designed to exclusively handle the state's revenue and expenditure. With this central treasury, Pombal intended to improve the control over the royal finances and put an end to the decentralized system, that went back to the Middle Ages, based on the specific treasuries and local *almoxarifados*. In the new framework, the chamber of accounts (*Casa dos Contos*) was dissolved and replaced by the *Erário Régio*, which included four regional sub-treasuries: one for the Estremadura; one for all of the other homeland provinces; another for Western Africa, Maranhão, and Bahia; and one more for Rio de Janeiro, Asia, and Eastern Africa. Contrary to the former *Casa dos Contos*, where single entry bookkeeping was the norm, the *Erário* followed double-entry bookkeeping, a technique considered key in the modernization of the State, emulating what was being done in the so-called "advanced nations" of the era. According to the words of the legal acts instituting the Royal Treasury, double-entry was "the briefest and clearest method for managing large sums" (Tomaz 1988: 356–357).

This administrative reform became another stronghold of Pombal's policy, and it soon took on an organic structure of its own, with a president/general inspector – a post occupied by the marquis, himself. In the hierarchy, he was followed by a general treasurer and four general accountants who were responsible for each of the four regional sub-Treasuries. At the time of its creation the Royal Treasury had twenty-six employees, but its bureaucratic ranks soon swelled. In 1823 it had grown to 276 officials, even though 60 percent of these had no function to perform other than "learning," suggesting the increasing specialization that the public finances needed (Subtil 1993: 173). Sent out early in the reign of Queen Maria I, the all-powerful minister of King José I could claim to leave behind balanced books for the public accounts. But this was not one of his most praised legacies, since it was short-lived. The backdrop marked by the state of war in Europe from the 1790s onwards, pushed public spending up in all economies and Portugal was no exception. The times when the marquis of Pombal could claim he had balanced public financing were over.

*Revenue*

King José I's minister was rightly proud of having achieved balanced public accounts during his tenure in office. A unique time series available on public budgets, which covers the period from 1762 to 1776, gives evidence of regular surpluses. The annual average of revenues was 5,596 million *réis*.[65] This amount is quite above the number pointed out in the single budget known for the reign of King João V, dated 1716, which refers to 3,828 million *réis*.[66] Although documental sources for the first half of the eighteenth century are scanty, it is plausible to assume a rise of the states' revenues at a 0.8–1 percent rate, derived from both new sources of income and improvements in the collection of the income tax (*décima*).

In what regards the sources of revenue, the role of the colonial system stands out. First, the *fifth* on gold production represented a new and consistent inflow to public coffers. The budget for 1716 records 345 million *réis* (9 percent of the state's income of that year), while in the 1760s, the annual average of the *fifth* reached 615 million reis, representing 11 percent. Hence, the percentage of income based on gold flows was greater during Pombal's era than in 1716. Second, this percentage (11 percent) equaled that of the income tax called *décima*, whose rate of levy was raised anew to its maximum 10 percent. Since the origins of the

[65] For the evolution of public finances during Pombal's government, see Tomaz 1988.
[66] 1716 budgetary figures in Macedo 1982b: 209.

Table 4.11 *Composition of State's revenue, 1762–1804*

|  | 1762–1777 annual average in million *réis* | as a % of total | 1804 in million *réis* | as a % of total |
|---|---|---|---|---|
| *Décima* | 623 | 11.1 | 1,221 | 11.1 |
| *Sisa* | 350 | 6.3 | 381 | 3.4 |
| Customs* | 1,611 | 28.8 | 4,631 | 41.9 |
| Tobacco | 887 | 15.8 | 1,129 | 10.2 |
| *Pau-brasil* | 122 | 2.2 | 162 | 1.5 |
| Fifth of gold | 615 | 11.0 | 29 | 0.3 |
| Diamonds | 259 | 4.6 | 0 | 0.0 |
| Royal Mint | 118 | 2.1 | 50 | 0.5 |
| Other | 1,013 | 18.1 | 3,442 | 31.2 |
| Total | 5,598 | 100 | 11,045 | 100 |

* Includes *Casas de Arrecadação* in 1762–1777.
*Sources:* Tomaz 1988; Macedo 1982b: 209.

income tax had been the War of Restoration in 1641, the Seven Years' War gave the marquis of Pombal the opportunity of reforming the collection system and determining a rate identical to the one imposed in times of external threat. Therefore, the royal right of a fifth of the gold extracted in Brazil bore a financial effect equivalent to the income tax levied in the kingdom. Finally, the tobacco monopoly in the domestic market proved to be another significant contribution of the colonial empire to public financing. It achieved an effect greater than that of gold, by accounting for 16 percent on average. Only the customs duties funded more than this – with 29 percent. In short, considering the fifth of the gold, the tobacco monopoly, *pau-brasil* (both farmed out to syndicates of businessmen), and customs duties, we see the state's finances depending mostly on outward relations and links to the empire (62 percent).

Between Pombal's administration and the end of the *Ancién Régime,* these sources underwent some changes. Indeed, state budgets from the last decades of the century mirror the resumption of the Portuguese *entrepôt* trade (Table 4.11) meaning that revenues extracted from *ad valorem* duties seemed to be the far-reaching way for the state to increase its budget. An overview on totals shows a 2.5 percent rate of growth at current values, customs duties being in 1804 a more substantial source than they had been in the 1760s and 1770s. The weight of this fiscal income increased from 29 to 42 percent.

Aside from customs, the Portuguese fiscal system included the *décima* that could also become a significant source of state income as it happened in periods of war, when the rate of levy was raised to 10 percent and so remained after the Seven Years' War. However, among the budgetary entries specified in Table 4.11 we note the stability of the share ensured by the *décima* – steady at 11 percent. A detailed description of the income that provided this level of financial effect is not available, but we know that 60 percent was derived from rural and urban rents, while salaries, wages, and interests amounted to only 14 percent. The share of manufacturing activity, both workshop and home-based, stood at 25 percent during Pombal's administration, but in 1804 it was not itemized separately. In nominal terms, during Pombal's term in office the tax on income was 258 *réis* per capita, and in 1804, 419 *réis*. Both 258 *réis* in 1766–1777 and 419 *réis* in 1804 would buy the same 0.53 *alqueires* (approximately 13 liters) of wheat in Lisbon in either of these periods. This stable rate of taxation in terms of purchasing power was the result of an extended tax base. Therefore, the 1804 budget expresses one of the fiscal novelties triggered by the military backdrop started in the 1790s – that of including the ecclesiastic community as a taxable social group and the rise to 25 percent of the rate levied on the Crown's donations bestowed on the nobility.

The increasing encroachment of the state in private income points out one of the paths toward the making of a fiscal state, as it happened throughout Europe. However, on the eve of the French Invasions, despite rising public revenue and greater fiscal efficiency on the collection of an income tax, the Portuguese state did not hold the monopoly over taxation. Within the plurality of powers that marked the political organization of the Portuguese *Ancién Régime*, the nobility and the Church also had the power to collect tributes. Dating back to medieval times, the rights of taxation assigned to these groups were of a diverse nature, as already stated in previous chapters. First, the Church kept collecting the tithe (*dízimo*), even if after several transformations, by the end of the eighteenth century this tribute was also controlled by other institutions and social groups such as the Crown and the aristocracy. Second, noble houses and ecclesiastical institutions were entitled to collect "royal rights" (*direitos de foral*), following donations bestowed on them by the Crown to reward services. Enshrined in the municipal charters (*cartas de foral*), these rights encompassed land rents, seigneurial dues, and tributes which were not actual taxes.[67] But they were similar in nature, considering that they were compulsory payments. Unsurprisingly, as late as 1807, a significant part of domestic taxation was not controlled by the state.

[67] See Chapter 2.

The tithe and the *direitos de foral* represented a higher exaction than the domestic taxes collected by the Crown in several circumstances. In the case of Trás-os-Montes, a region where the *direitos de foral* represented a fixed amount and were less demanding on the population, the partition of the tax collection, still in 1792, reveals the state's lowest share. The public coffers amassed 130.3 million *réis* (of which only 30 million came from the *décima*), while the commanderies from the military orders, in the hands of the aristocracy were worth 148.7 million *réis*. The tithes (*dízimos*) appropriated by the Church reached 403.7 million *réis*. Thus, of 682.7 million *réis* in total taxable revenues, the State received 19 percent – and only 4.3 percent in the form of the income tax (Monteiro 2005a: 72). Since the state did not hold a fiscal monopoly, it is not surprising that Portugal's public taxation was not among the highest comparing to other European countries (Macedo, Silva, and Sousa 2001). However, fiscal efficiency, weighted by the variation of public revenues over the variation of domestic product, increased. In real values, between Pombal's government and 1804, public revenues rose 20 percent – a rate higher than any estimation of GDP growth, which actually must have decreased in the last quarter of the century (Palma and Reis 2014). Even so, the path toward a modern fiscal state is clearer on the side of expenditures which comprised military and administrative spending.

*Expenditure*

Despite the state's inability to monopolize fiscal receipts, it sought to monopolize the defense, one irrefutable feature of the development of political institutions (Costa F. D. 2010). From 1763 to 1777 an annual average of 2.5 billion *réis* (49.2 percent of the total expenditure) was assigned to navy and army, a disbursement that exceeded everything else. This percentage was considerably greater than that known from previous budgets dated from 1681 (Hespanha 1993: 233). The militarization of the state's expenditures made Portugal no different from the other states in Enlightened Europe. However, that 49.2 percent points to a financing effort higher than that showed in France's public accounts at the end of the *Ancién Régime* (25 percent) but far less than that of Great Britain in the eighteenth century, where military spending reached 71 percent of total expenditures from 1756 to 1763, and never dipped below 61 percent throughout the century. England's involvement in most of the European conflicts west of the Ural Mountains (spanning 80 years of the century) demanded men to fill the ranks of foot soldiers and crew the ships, with some units reaching strengths of 300,000. The effect of this on the British economy, and notably on the labor supply in the civil sector, is still to be determined, but surely needs to be included among the many factors that made England a high-wage economy (Brewer 1989: 40–42).

The military expenditures went hand in hand with the expansion of administrative staff, although this trend did not have great repercussions on public spending in the Portuguese case. There were 600 officials in the central administration during the reign of King Pedro II (1683–1704), which swelled to 2,869, according to estimates for 1820, an epoch that can be seen as a corollary in the consolidation of the state apparatus that took place during the second half of the 1700s (Subtil 1993). Budgets dating from the 1760s tell us how demanding this path toward greater bureaucracy was and enable a comparison with the financial effort needed to monopolize defense. The salaries of public officials justified an average expense of 894.7 million *réis* (17.2 percent), which were indeed considerably less than the 2.5 billion *réis* allocated to military spending (Tomaz 1988).

Regarding the service of public debt as the third major item among expenditures, the amounts assigned to pay interests provide evidence on the public financial wealth claimed by the marquis of Pombal. By that time, the payment of interests represented 6.45 percent of total spending, a burden much lower than the 227 million *réis* (25 percent) found in budgets from 1681, still shaped by financial setbacks in the aftermath of the War of Restoration (1640–1668).[68] The apparent success in public debt management in the eighteenth century is another issue pointing to colonial empire externalities. It is worth recalling that the remission of bonds paying 5 percent interest (*padrões de dívida*) and the following issue at a 4.5 percent interest in the reign of King João V were guaranteed by liquidity provided by public gold remittances. This public credit operation put in circulation 5 billion *réis* accumulated in royal coffers.[69] Debt amortization reduced the outstanding debt, and the issuing of bonds at 3.5 percent interest rates in the 1770 attests to the creditworthiness of the Portuguese state, although it was built on different grounds from those of the English state.[70]

The high levels of liquidity in the Portuguese economy underpinned a similar trend in interest rates on public debt, although this happened in the institutional framework of an absolutist regime. The Portuguese case recalls that monetary variables besides political constitutions should be called upon in further approaches on the causes of public interest rates' downturn that characterized the first three quarters of eighteenth-century Europe (Costa, Rocha, Brito, 2014).

[68] Hespanha 1993: 233; Tomaz 1988: 367.    [69] Azevedo 1973: 375. Gomes 1883: 80.
[70] See North and Weingast's 1989 article that has started a field of research on the political constitution of Great Britain as a precondition for public interest rates' to decrease. See also Coffman *et al.* 2013.

*The Napoleonic wars*

The positive trend in public finances, in Portugal as elsewhere in Europe vanished with the Napoleonic wars. The incursion of Junot's troops in 1807 was the culmination of the diplomatic "siege" brought against Portugal since 1790 – an international scenario in which Great Britain was seen as a bastion of resistance to revolutionary France's foreign policy. Portugal participated along with Spain in a military expedition against France – the so-called Roussillon Campaign (1793–1795). The rout of the Iberian forces dictated the options going forward for both countries. Spain signed a peace treaty with France shortly thereafter, passing into the sphere of French influence, whereas Portugal was able to obtain a position of neutrality through diplomatic maneuvering.[71]

Similar political contentions had taken place in 1703, following the outbreak of the War of Spanish Succession. Whereas at that time King Pedro II's turnaround of opinion and alignment with England had been swift, ninety years later the indecision of the regent, Prince João, left the country under the constant threat of Spanish invasion at the urging of the French, which finally came about in 1801. In the War of the Oranges Portugal lost part of its territory to the west of the Guadiana River, leaving Olivença to Spain. This military action was swift, but the threat of further incursion did not disappear, as Portugal resisted the Continental blockade declared against Britain. In accordance with the expansionist mindset of Napoleonic imperialism, a full assault by French troops followed, in 1807. As a result, between the years of the Roussillon Campaign (1793–1795) and the first of the French Invasions (1807), the Portuguese State was forced to spend enormous sums on maintaining a standing army. It is certain that the international environment and the neutrality that Portugal was able to secure in the 1790s were beneficial to the kingdom's maritime trade, especially with Asia. But even the favorable impact of foreign trade on the State's finances through customs proved insufficient to stave off the troubles that came with rising expenditure. Deficits reached unprecedented levels (Table 4.12), forcing the state to seek financing through credit. The novelty now was that bonds were used as fiat money, prompting the country's first-ever issue of paper money.

The first issue of these public debt bonds (the so-called "first loan") was in the amount of 6,367 million *réis*, but the amortization and interest payments required additional issues. By 1807 the total figure reached 17,176 million *réis* (Silveira 1987: 521). The population was required to use the bonds alongside cash, applying them as fiat money, first to pay

---

[71] Costa and Pedreira 2005; Alexandre 1993.

Table 4.12 *Public budget, 1800–1802 (million* réis*)*

|                                     | 1800              | 1801              | 1802              |
| ----------------------------------- | ----------------- | ----------------- | ----------------- |
| Revenue                             | 10,627            | 9,859             | 9,511             |
| Expenditure                         | 11,967            | 13,011            | 10,082            |
| *Of which Defense*                  | *6,880*           | *9,117*           | *6,025*           |
| *(percent of total)*                | *(57.4%)*         | *(70.0%)*         | *(59.8%)*         |
| Deficit                             | −1,340            | −3,152            | −571              |

*Source:* Silveira 1987.

taxes and, after that, for current transactions. At the same time, the instruments were not convertible into metallic coin, meaning that the bimetallic monetary regime was being challenged by new experiments on paper money without the state instilling confidence in the new means of payment. Naturally, this impinged a risk which exacerbated a discount rate charged on the use of paper money. Starting at 4 percent in 1798, the discount rose to 18–20 percent in the space of only two years, and in 1801 the paper was accepted only in Lisbon and at 30 percent less than its face value (Madureira 1997: 291–292). The emission of non-convertible paper money would become a feature common to all governments during the war. But in Portugal the state did not offer guarantees to its creditors, and the persistence of the deficits eroded confidence even further, as there was no bank contracted with the state. In 1812 the public debt was 4.3 times greater than the state's annual budget (Cardoso and Lains 2010: 255).

A swiftly increasing money supply and public deficits created the predictable inflationary pressures. The price index in Portugal climbed at a 3.7 percent rate from 1797 to 1810 (Figure 4.5). The price inflation in Portugal was driven by domestic factors in addition to higher prices paid for imports. The state of war in Europe had similar effects on prices in all of the countries that Portugal had economic relations with. Among the food items imported, such as codfish, no prices rose as dramatically as did those of wheat, the principal edible item in consuming baskets.

The price rise had redistributive effects, with impressive social impact. Wages, for instance, were the worst hit. Skilled labor (stone-masons and carpenters) were penalized by a loss of 50 percent, and unskilled labor, 66 percent (Figure 4.6). Thus the end of the *Ancién Régime* witnessed a downturn in the population's real wages, although this trend did not clearly show up in state revenues because the tax base for the *décima* was distended to embrace privileged social bodies

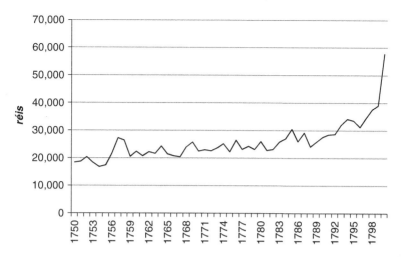

Figure 4.5 Price of a basket of goods in Lisbon, 1750–1800
Source: Prices, wages, and rents in Portugal 1300–1910, directed by
Jaime Reis, http://pwr-portugal.ics.ul.pt/

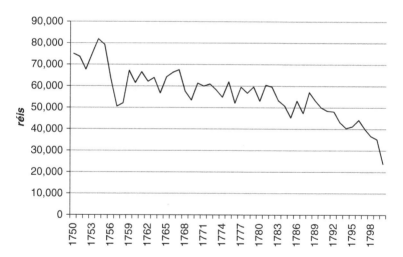

Figure 4.6 Real yearly wages in Lisbon, 1750–1808
Source: Prices, wages, and rents in Portugal 1300–1910, directed by
Jaime Reis, http://pwr-portugal.ics.ul.pt/

such as the Church. Besides, the international environment again favored the role of re-exporting, boosting customs revenues. Therefore, the income collected by the state was more protected from depreciation during the final decades of the *Ancién Régime* than that of other institutions and households. This might have signified an actual increase of the tax burden.

However, traditionally privileged groups, religious institutions and nobility alike, were also affected by the inflation (Monteiro 2003: 260–261). In fact, the financial impact of the Napoleonic war did not spare the aristocracy. Its income also plunged. Among the most important noble houses, rents fell by 21–35 percent. Even more pronounced was the case of the house of the counts of Resende, whose fortunes plummeted even further, by 50 percent between 1770 and 1810 (Monteiro 2003: 321–322).

### Tax farming

When the *Ancién Régime* came to a close, not only did the business community surge ahead in its lending capacity, but it also stood out for its capacity to farm out rents, either those controlled by the aristocracy or by public revenues. Thus, periods of inflation could be bad for those who had the right to collect land rents and tributes, but favorable to those who performed the financial intermediation in the collection of these very tributes. These rent collectors (*rendeiros*), who had capital applied in other business ventures, dealt with the rents of the aristocracy according to practices already employed successfully vis-à-vis the state. In fact significant shares of the state's revenues we have seen earlier were raised through the farming out of the fiscal collection.

In the public sphere, short-term contracts (of three years) were the most common, which mitigated the negative impact of inflation on the system. In any case, the resilience of this institutional device delayed the making of a specialized fiscal administration. Despite the three-year contract rule, exceptions touched upon important revenue sources, such as the concession for tobacco and soap, negotiated for contracts with a nine-year term. The staff allocated to the administration of these monopolies became a complementary structure of the state's bureaucracy itself and were appointed by the consortia of businessmen-contractors. The concessionaires of the tobacco contract became the most visible face of opulence that this system granted to a few financiers. These operators developed a network that paralleled the state, with regional superintendents. The only reason it was not openly accused of being a competitor of the state was because it was expected to offer services – no less necessary – as a para-banking lender to the State (Madureira 1997: 102–104).

Thus, among the political and economic reformations demanded by the most prominent members of the Academy of Sciences of Lisbon in the late 1700s, was the abolition of these forms of transfer of sovereignty, because of the exorbitant profits earned by tax farmers. Some estimates of the tobacco concession's return hover around 20 percent – a profit margin similar to that of arbitrage on colonial merchandise. Either investment, in fact, was reserved to the clique of wealthy businessmen that rose under the policies of the marquis of Pombal and could remain in business after the minister's political fall. Still, taking part in contracts to collect public income demanded fabulously high funds. Returning to the example of tobacco, sums such as 1,383 million *réis* could have been necessary to manage the contract – an amount comparable to the total income of all the aristocratic houses put together (Madureira 1997: 106). The fact that there are no records of any divestitures on the part of those involved in financing the state suggests that profits reaped in tax farming were not severely checked by the misfortunes of the last decade of the eighteenth century and the outbreak of the Napoleonic wars. The activities most exposed to recession due to lower wages and contraction of domestic demand might have been the industrial ventures. But exactly because of recession of domestic demand there would have been a greater advantage regarding the application of capital in the auctions for tax-farm contracts.

With French troops invading the homeland, the royal family decamped for Brazil, in a previously unknown reversal of roles in a colonial system. In so doing, Prince Regent João (future King João VI) accepted the advice of all those who assured him that moving the seat of government was the only way to guarantee Portugal's sovereignty, justifying the alignment with the "old ally" – now the world's greatest naval power. In truth, the royal court was leaving a kingdom with more than 900 km of coastline, which had in the sea not an economic resource, or a reason for owing a powerful navy and mercantile fleet, but a highway to overseas resources, with costs and benefits that differed as a function of the various empires that had four centuries of history behind them. Whether or not it impeded the modernization of the state, the Luso-Brazilian Empire of mercantile prosperity came to a close shortly after the royal family set sail for Rio de Janeiro, as will be discussed in the next chapter.

# 5    The rise of liberalism, 1807–1914

By the end of 1807, a French army led by General Junot entered Portugal at the northern border with Spain, to take Lisbon, the capital of the empire and main center of the commercial activity of the country, the city that was being used by the British despite the Continental Blockade Napoleon had decreed a year earlier. Prince Regent João, who had agreed on the French embargo to avoid war, fled from the French troops and embarked to Brazil, ending up in Rio de Janeiro by the beginning of 1808. The French invaded Portugal on two other occasions, in 1808 and 1811, and were finally expelled with the help of the British on the later date. Yet these events were to put an end to the old regime and leave the door open to the implementation of a parliamentary regime, much like those that would be introduced elsewhere in Europe. In 1820, a liberal revolution took place followed by the election of a Constitutional Assembly and adoption of a new constitution in 1822. This was only the beginning. The transition from the *Ancién Régime* to the new liberal order, however, took the best part of the first half of the nineteenth century and was punctuated by military coups, civil wars, and uninterrupted political unrest. The extent of the long institutional transformation was closely related to Portugal's level of economic, political, and social backwardness, which clearly made more difficult the needed consensus for change. To a certain extent, the implementation of the new political framework and the liberal economy emerging from it had to wait for another military coup, in 1851, the *Regeneração*, which ultimately led to the pacification of Portuguese society, at least for some decades, until other sources of distress emerged with the advent of the Republican forces.[1]

The British Industrial Revolution and the spread of industrialization that ensued throughout the nineteenth century widened the gap in levels

[1] The best account of Portugal's nineteenth-century political history is Ramos, Sousa, and Monteiro 2009. For the first half of the century, see also Valente 1997. For the economic impact of the Liberal revolution, see also Amaral 2012.

of income per capita within Europe, clearly distinguishing a core of industrializing countries and an outer periphery, to the south and the east, where the prevalence of backward agriculture lasted for several decades up to the twentieth century.[2] It still is a point of lively discussion in the literature to define when that "little divergence" commenced in the European continent, whether it is a heritage from the *Ancién Régime* or a feature of the century of industrialization. Regarding Portugal, for example, it has been argued that backwardness has to be mostly explained by events that occurred either in the revolutionary years of the first half of the nineteenth century, or in the decades of relative political pacification that followed.[3] Whatever the origins of backwardness in time, the fact was that the poorer peripheral European countries experienced economic growth and some degree of structural change across the nineteenth century.[4] In this chapter we start by identifying the economic consequences stemming from the French invasions, the end of the Brazilian Empire, and the civil and military strife that ensued from the fall of the *Ancién Régime*. Then, the chapter deals with the analysis of the trends in industrial and agricultural output growth, as well as changes in productivity and the structure of the economy. In this respect, the study of the first half of the century is different from that of the second half because there is more quantitative evidence on the main macroeconomic variables for the latter period. The chapter will also deal with other issues concerning the economy at large, of which the financial constraints of growth will receive due attention.

## The end of an empire

During the last decades of the eighteenth century, Portugal's foreign trade experienced quite a favorable period, which was largely due to imperial preference for Brazilian ports, as well as to the neutrality the country managed to keep among the warring nations in Europe, particularly Great Britain, France, and the Low Countries. The Continental Blockade, which was imposed by Napoleon to Portugal in 1806, led to an end of that prosperity, not in any direct manner, but because it led to the retreat

[2] Berend and Ránki 1982; Broadberry and O'Rourke 2010, vol. 2; Pollard 1994, Chapter 5.
[3] For the first half of the century, see Alexandre 1993 and Pedreira 1993; for the second half, see Pereira 1983, Reis 1993: Chapter 1, and Tortella 1994. Macedo 1982b provides probably the first account on how the eighteenth-century Portuguese economy was unable to follow British industrialization closely.
[4] See Lains and Silva, eds. 2005 and Lains 2012. For Spain, see Prados de la Escosura 1988 and 2003. See also Landes 1998 for a somehow opposing perspective, where peripheral countries' backwardness is seen as equivalent to lack of growth or industrialization.

of the Lisbon court to Brazil and ultimately to the end of the Portuguese Brazilian empire, in the following decade. The wars between Britain, France, and Spain, in the seas and on the European continent, had direct impact on Portugal ending the relatively peaceful situation which the country knew during the second half of the eighteenth century. In 1793, Portugal sent troops to fight on the Spanish side against the French at the Battle of Toulon, but two years later Portugal was put aside in the peace treaty signed between Spain and France at San Ildefonso. In 1801, Spain defeated Portugal at the War of the Oranges and Portugal had to accede to French demands to renounce its old alliance with Great Britain. Yet Portugal was for some time able to maintain a position of neutrality, which allowed it to continue its privileged economic relationship with its traditional ally. In 1806, Napoleon imposed the Continental Blockade on the entry of British ships into Europe, and reinforced his demand that Portugal also close its ports, threatening Portugal with a military intervention. Faced with this threat, Prince Regent João submitted to French pressure and, in October 1807, ordered all British ships to leave Portuguese ports. This brought Portuguese neutrality to an end, but it was insufficient since it did not satisfy two other demands: the arrest of all British citizens residing in Portugal and the confiscation of their property.[5] The blockade of British commerce in Portuguese ports was ineffective, as the data on the entry and exit of ships show (see Table 5.1). The entry of ships of all nationalities declined between 1801 and 1803, and stabilized in the following years, and in 1808, the first year of effective blockade, the number of ships in Portuguese ports was practically equal to that of 1803. On the other hand, the number of vessels that left the port of Lisbon increased between 1808 and 1811. Thus, the most important consequence of the French blockade was a brief contraction of British ships entering the Tagus, in the year 1808, immediately followed by a recovery. In fact, between 1801 and 1807, around three-quarters of the ships that entered Portuguese ports were British, a proportion that declined to less than one-half in 1808 before increasing again to higher values. As for British ships leaving Lisbon, there was a slight decline after 1808, followed by a strong recovery. At the city of Porto, the reduction in the number of British ships was larger, with arrivals falling by 27 percent and departures by 7 percent in 1808, but the recovery that followed was quite remarkable. Indeed, in 1812 the tonnage carried by British ships increased above the levels of the beginning of the century. The largest

---

[5] Macedo 1990; Pedreira 2000; Ramos, Sousa, and Monteiro 2009. The Continental blockade was, however, overcome in many ways, including by increasing imports from the United States. See Moreira and Eloranta 2011.

Table 5.1 *Ships in Portuguese ports, 1801–1814 (number of vessels)*
A. All ports *

|  | Inbound | | | | Outbound | | | |
|  | Total | British | Other | British/ total (%) | Total | British | Other | British/ total (%) |
|---|---|---|---|---|---|---|---|---|
| 1801 | 508 | 395 | 113 | 77.8 | 363 | 182 | 181 | 50.1 |
| 1802 | 415 | 373 | 42 | 89.9 | 353 | 246 | 107 | 69.7 |
| 1803 | 364 | 282 | 82 | 77.5 | 280 | 220 | 60 | 78.6 |
| 1804 | 372 | 241 | 131 | 64.8 | 314 | 197 | 117 | 62.7 |
| 1805 | 401 | 274 | 127 | 68.3 | 307 | 204 | 103 | 66.4 |
| 1806 | 468 | 354 | 114 | 75.6 | 332 | 210 | 122 | 63.3 |
| 1807 | 390 | 305 | 85 | 78.2 | 398 | 216 | 182 | 54.3 |
| 1808 | 358 | 165 | 193 | 46.1 | 390 | 231 | 159 | 59.2 |
| 1809 | 540 | 474 | 66 | 87.8 | 576 | 444 | 132 | 77.1 |
| 1810 | 627 | 536 | 91 | 85.5 | 642 | 466 | 176 | 72.6 |
| 1811 | 433 | 385 | 48 | 88.9 | 651 | 537 | 114 | 82.5 |
| 1814 | 551 | 428 | 123 | 77.7 | 436 | 296 | 140 | 67.9 |

B. Porto

|  | Inbound | | | | Outbound | | | |
|  | Total | British | Other | British/ total (%) | Total | British | Other | British/ total (%) |
|---|---|---|---|---|---|---|---|---|
| 1801 | 357 | 142 | 215 | 39.8 | 430 | 102 | 328 | 23.7 |
| 1806 | 327 | 150 | 177 | 45.9 | 251 | 74 | 177 | 29.5 |
| 1807 | 337 | 149 | 188 | 44.2 | 347 | 95 | 252 | 27.4 |
| 1808 | 263 | 72 | 191 | 27.4 | 258 | 17 | 241 | 6.6 |
| 1809 | 295 | 212 | 83 | 71.9 | 262 | 44 | 218 | 16.8 |
| 1810 | 233 | 154 | 79 | 66.1 | 230 | 35 | 195 | 15.2 |
| 1811 | 472 | 258 | 214 | 54.7 | 310 | 172 | 138 | 55.5 |
| 1812 | 391 | 197 | 194 | 50.4 | 349 | 228 | 121 | 65.3 |

* Portuguese ships not included
*Source:* Macedo 1990: 73–74.

portion of Portuguese foreign trade was conducted through Lisbon and it increased throughout the decade of the Napoleonic Wars, to the extent that "the increase in British influence was the truly important element of the continental blockade" (Macedo 1990: 102).

As a direct consequence of the failure to impose the blockade on British ships, in late 1807, French troops under Junot's command invaded Portugal, following the route of the river Tagus and taking about six weeks to arrive in Lisbon. The goal was to seize the ships and take control of the port of Lisbon (Macedo 1990: 46–47). Just before the French troops entered the capital, Queen Maria I, the Prince Regent João, the royal family, the Court, and a thousand more people left for Brazil under the escort of the British Royal Navy. The French troops were expelled in September 1808 with the aid of around 10,000 British troops under the command of General Wellesley, the future duke of Wellington. A second French invasion occurred soon after, in February 1809, and lasted until May, when they were again defeated by Anglo-Portuguese forces, under the command of Lord Beresford. A third and last attempt by Napoleon to occupy Portugal took place in July 1810 involving a much larger army of 80,000 men, but they were unable to go beyond the line of Torres Vedras, 50 kilometers to the north of Lisbon, which had been built under British command, and the French finally withdrew in March 1811 (Map 5.1).

Although they were territorially limited, the French invasions had some direct impact on the Portuguese economy, as they involved the raising of an army, death, the occupation of agricultural land, the confiscation of working animals and foodstuff, looting, and a generalized climate of unrest and instability. But the exact extent of such consequences have not yet been measured by economic historians. However, the fact is that the Portuguese economy overall was probably affected to a larger degree by the opening up of Brazilian ports to shipping from all nations, in 1808, and the Anglo-Portuguese Treaty of 1810, which conceded the most-favored-nation status for British imports and special privileges for British commercial agents. These two measures spelled the end of Portugal's exclusive colonial trade with Brazil, which remains to this day a hotly debated topic among Portuguese historians. The "oldest alliance" with Great Britain rescued Portugal's independence, but proved very costly too, very nearly shutting the country out of international trade altogether from 1808 to 1813 (Pedreira 1993). In the aftermath of the changes in trade relations with the rest of the world, in 1815, Prince Regent João declared the United Kingdom of Portugal and Brazil, and Rio de Janeiro, instead of Lisbon, became its capital. Queen Maria I died in the following year, and João VI was proclaimed king. But the new king had to face revolt back in Portugal, as the conditions there were worsening in political terms. This was a period in which the absolutist regimes were challenged across Europe, including Portugal.

The first revolt against the absent monarch and British rule under General Beresford took place in 1817 in Porto. In 1818 a group of discontents from the second city of Porto, in the north of the country and away from the court formed the first liberal political movement in the country, the *Sinédrio*, which on August 24, 1820, taking advantage of Beresford's absence on a trip to João in Brazil, made a *coup* together with

Map 5.1  The French invasions, 1807–1811

factions of the military.[6] The coup was followed by the election of a constitutional parliament (the *Cortes*) in December 1820, which demanded the return of the monarch, and João VI arrived in Lisbon in August 1821, having left his son Pedro as regent in Brazil. An unintended consequence of this occurred in September of the following year, when the government of Brazil declared the country's independence and appointed Pedro as emperor, and in that same year the *Cortes* in Lisbon approved a new constitution. In 1823 and 1824 two successive Absolutist coups took place but D. Miguel was defeated and ultimately fled to exile in Austria. The political and military instability continued nevertheless and culminated in an open civil war that lasted from 1832 to 1834, ending in a victory for the liberal forces, ensuring the gradual return to stability in the following decades.

### *The economic consequences of Brazilian independence*

The opening of the Brazilian ports to international trade and the substantial lowering of tariffs by the trade treaty with Great Britain, respectively, in 1808 and 1810, ended Portugal's trade monopoly in what was then its most important colony. This imposed a crucial change in the international context for the Portuguese economy and the study of the consequences is clearly one of the most debated topics of Portuguese historiography. It should be noted that the end of the Brazilian empire coincided with the advent of the industrialization of most of the European continent, a phenomenon from which Portugal was largely absent for a long time, at least in a way that can be compared to what happened in the pioneer nations or regions that followed closely the British leadership.[7] Yet it is quite difficult to establish a measure for the economic consequences of the end of colonial monopoly across the Atlantic as we need to build a complex counter-factual scenario. Moreover, that alternative scenario is particularly difficult to construct in the context of the first decades of the nineteenth century which were particularly unstable. Nevertheless, we may reach some conclusions regarding the impact of the end of Brazil's trade monopoly by looking at the development of the Portuguese economy in the period and, particularly, that of the industrial sector, and at international comparisons.

According to some scholars, the opening of Brazilian ports, the treaty with Great Britain, and the independence of Brazil were severe blows for the Portuguese economy because of the contraction of the exports of manufactures, which in turn resulted in a reduction in Portugal's industrial

---

[6] Valente 1997; Ramos, Sousa, and Monteiro 2010.
[7] Alexandre 1993; Haber and Klein 1997; Lains 1991 and 2005; Macedo 1982; Pedreira 1993 and 2000; Costa *et al.* 2014. See also O'Brien 1982 and O'Rourke 2006.

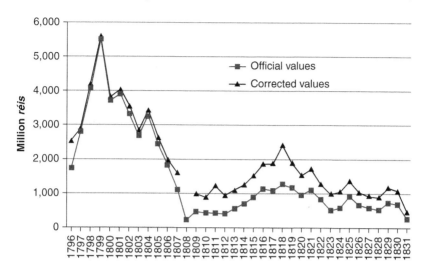

Figure 5.1 Exports of manufactures to Brazil, 1796–1831
Source: Lains 1991.

production.[8] This interpretation is based on the unproven assumption that exports to Brazil represented an important part of the total output of Portuguese industry and on a misinterpretation of export data. Yet the decline in the value of industrial exports began in 1799, well before Brazilian ports were opened to countries other than Portugal, and a recovery in the value of manufacturing exports can also be seen from 1808 until 1818, before Brazil's independence (see Figure 5.1). Manufactures exports from Portugal to Brazil were mainly affected by the convulsions of the French wars, and not as much by the loss of trade privileges. During the decade of 1796–1806, manufactures represented 35.6 percent of all Portuguese exports, and more than 90 percent of these exports, including cotton and linen cloth, printing presses, hats, and iron-work, were sent to Brazil. In the years 1825–1831 manufactures had declined and amounted to 16.8 percent of Portuguese exports, a decline that continued slowly until the 1850s, when it fell to 4 percent.[9] The Brazilian market was also important for Portuguese food exports, including wine and flour. Lisbon was furthermore the compulsory entry port for Brazilian cotton and sugar exports to Europe, an obligation that was profitable for the Portuguese merchants involved in this trade, for the

[8] Pedreira 1994; Sideri 1978.    [9] Pedreira 1993, Tables 2 and 12; 1998: 218.

Table 5.2  *The cost of Brazil in 1830 (1830 prices)*

| | |
|---|---|
| 1. Portuguese industrial exports to Brazil, 1796–1805 | 2,625 million *réis* |
| 2. Portuguese industrial exports to Brazil, 1806–1831 | 1,070 million *réis* |
| 3. Loss of Brazilian market for Portuguese industry | 1,555 million *réis* |
| 4. Minimum value of Portuguese GNP in 1830 | 66,900 million *réis* |
| 5. Maximum value of Portuguese GNP in 1830 | 155,400 million *réis* |
| 6. Loss of Brazilian market as percentage of GNP (minimum GNP) | 2.30% |
| 7. Loss of Brazilian market as percentage of GNP (maximum GNP) | 1.00% |

*Source:* Lains 1991: 156–158.

Portuguese state through the customs revenues and for the national economy.

Exports of manufactured goods to Brazil, however, only represented a small part of Portugal's manufacturing activity and thus the loss of that market can only account for a small part of demand. Let us first establish how much was lost in export values and for that we compare average annual total exports for the period from 1806 to 1831, with that of the golden period from 1796 to 1805. This periodization avoids any discussion of the dates at which there was an inflection of exports of manufactured goods. In order to compare real values, an index price based on linen exports was used as reference. Accordingly, exports of manufactured goods fell by 1,555 million *réis*, at 1830 prices (see Table 5.2). If we assume that the loss of exports to the Brazilian market was not replaced by an increase in sales in the domestic market, we can take the above value as the total industrial sector lost. Next, we need to convert that loss as a share of total industrial output or GDP. Yet Portugal's industrial output value for 1830 is unknown, as is the value of national output. However, controlled estimates can provide an idea of the importance relative to the value of the manufactured goods that stopped being sold in Brazil (Lains 1991). Table 5.2 also shows estimates of the value of per capita GNP in 1850 and some hypotheses about growth between 1830 and 1850. Based on these values, it is possible to conclude that the 1,555 million *réis* that were lost with the opening of Brazil's ports represented between 1 and 2.3 percent of Portugal's GNP in 1830. Brazilian independence was not accompanied only by a decline in manufactured exports. Portuguese traders also exported foodstuffs to Brazil and re-exported tropical products from there through Lisbon to ports in northern Europe, as well as imported manufactured goods from Europe, activities that earned considerable incomes. The state also benefited from the duties charged on all of this trade. According to one estimate, taking into account the whole commercial activity related to Brazil would increase the annual loss of income from the end of the empire to about 6,000 million *réis* between the period 1796–1806 and the period 1816–1822, or between 3.4 and 6.7 percent of Portugal's GNP in 1830. This is probably a maximum figure for the loss of the empire and it should be noted that it assumes that all trade with Brazil was not diverted elsewhere which is rather implausible.[10]

The production of manufactured goods for export markets is probably an activity that involves additional dynamism and innovation, in comparison to activities catering for local markets, and the fact that linen or iron apparel factories in Northwest Portugal sent their products across the Atlantic is certainly evidence of some degree of industrial dynamism which may also be gauged from other sources regarding the sector.[11] Moreover, Europe's early industrialized regions began in a similar fashion by taking advantage of demand from other regions or from overseas.[12] Additionally, the manufacture of goods for sale in protected markets could lead to the development of a sufficiently competitive manufacturing sector no longer requiring protected markets, as the argument of infant industry would stress. Thus, the notion that exports of manufactured goods to Brazil could have been relevant for Portuguese earlier industrialization would be at least partially valid. But this is not an argument about quality but, necessarily, about the dimension of the external market for industrial output. It should also be noted that European economic history clearly shows that industrial exports had but a marginal role in the early stages of industrialization of the more advanced economies.[13] Summing up, although the loss of the Brazilian market certainly had some sort of negative impact on Portugal's industrialization, albeit small, the deep causes of the country's persistent degree of economic backwardness have to be sought elsewhere.

---

[10] Pedreira 1993. The author points to a loss of 8 percent of GDP. See also Costa, Palma, and Reis 2015, who estimate a higher value for the share of Brazilian intercontinental trade in GDP, of about 20 percent in 1800, but they do not establish a counterfactual value for the loss of trade.
[11] Alexandre 1993; Pedreira 1994; Madureira 1997.
[12] Pollard 1994; Van Zanden 2009.
[13] Allen 2009; Crafts 1985; Crafts and Harley 2000.

## Growth and backwardness in agriculture

By the beginning of the nineteenth century, agriculture was by far the largest sector of economic activity in Portugal, employing between two-thirds and three-quarters of the labor force, and it was to a large extent trapped in a globally unfavorable environment of institutional and overall economic backwardness. Large stretches of land with productive capacity were unoccupied which implied that additional demand from population growth, from urbanization, or from the increase in income levels could be met by extending output into new areas and not through an increase in land or labor productivity. Agricultural workers had very low standards of living and were poorly educated, and employed little capital in terms of traction animals, tools, buildings, irrigation systems, and other infrastructures. The average productivities of land and labor were among the lowest in Western Europe (Lains 2003b, 2009). In order to study the development of agriculture in the century that followed, we need to take into account the constraints that it had to face and remember that absence of rapid change was both a consequence and a cause of that backward environment.[14] Portugal was by then more backward than most European countries, including Spain, and had to be compared to the most peripheral regions in Southern Iberia, Southern Italy, or the Balkan Peninsula. There was no relevant industrial region in this country, such as Catalonia or Lombardy, and it had a level of development closer to Spanish Andalusia in the south or Galicia in the north.[15] The dimension of the agricultural sector meant that the fluctuations in the total economy depended to a large extent on the changes in agricultural labor, rates of investment, factor productivity, and in the conditions of domestic and foreign markets. Without modernizing the agricultural sector, any major change in the overall economy was a daunting challenge. Thus, Portuguese agriculture had to deal with the persistent use of backward techniques, the scarcity of traction animals and natural fertilizers, and the excessive amount of labor per unit of land under acreage.

The structure of land ownership also contributed to the difficulties facing the sector. The relative abundance of water in the north allowed for more intensive agriculture, which, coupled with irregularities in the quality of the soil, led to the sub-division of properties into smaller plots. This, in turn, hindered the adoption of crop–fallow rotations, which were in use in the north of Europe, since at least the eighteenth century. In the south, land ownership followed a different pattern and was predominantly

[14] Lains 2009; Martins 2005.
[15] See Lains 2012 and, for regional income later in the century, Felice 2011 and Tirado and Badia-Miró 2014.

characterized by vast tracts of land concentrated in the hands of a small number of owners, many of whom were absentee landlords probably more interested in boosting income through cash crops than in the welfare of the land or of those who worked it. The type of land ownership in the Alentejo region is often blamed for the country's slow agricultural development, and in particular for limited investment and innovation, but that view has been challenged by a closer look at the management of a few large estates. In fact, lower levels of capital investment in the south were more closely related to the structure of supply and relative prices, as capital was relatively dearer compared to labor, than to the structure of land ownership.[16] As such, the idea that landlords in the south lacked sufficient business skills to run their operations has been put into question. In fact, mechanization and the use of chemical fertilizers, two of the most important steps in the modernization of agriculture and associated with the second "agricultural revolution," made their first appearance in Portugal precisely in the large estates of southern Alentejo from the 1890s onwards.

The use of machinery and chemical fertilizers spread more quickly in the southern region as larger estates allowed for economies of scale and the higher ability of landowners to raise the needed capital to invest.[17] Technological transformation of the agricultural sector is not limited to mechanization and chemical fertilization. It involves the development of new crops, the use of plants that provide nitrogen to the soil in the crop rotation system, as well as the intensification of animal husbandry. These were the changes brought by the "first farming revolution," with the intensification of the cultivation of maize that boosted yields more than three-fold over those of earlier grain crops, and the introduction of cattle breeding in the second half of the nineteenth century. But the achievements in Portugal were not impressive and average yields of grains, potatoes, or other products remained much below those of elsewhere in Europe during the same period (Lains 2009). Important for the fertilization of the land as well as traction, animal husbandry accounted for the greatest share of capital investment in the farming sector, and was crucial in both regards. Here again, the size of the farm and the number of animals on it certainly goes a long way toward explaining the differences in productivity seen between the north and the south. The small-plot farmers in the country's northwest faced great challenges in obtaining and effectively breeding cattle, as the limited size of the land they worked often did not justify the expenses of keeping traction animals, and sometimes

---

[16] Fonseca 2005; Fonseca and Reis 2011; Justino 1988–1989; Lains 2003 and 2009; Martins 2005; Pereira 1983; Reis 1992.
[17] Reis 1993. See also Bairoch 1989.

were too small to provide sufficient grazing for their subsistence. The situation worsened in the second half of the nineteenth century, when much of the common-access, free-ranging pastures were reclaimed for cultivation.

Not all of the north–south disparity of productivity can be attributed to the form of land ownership and use, namely the small-holdings in the northwest and large estates in the Alentejo. However, given the social and institutional environments of the period, the large-estate operation enjoyed certain advantages over the smaller, family-worked plots. Perhaps the disadvantages of working on smaller holdings could have been surpassed at these earlier stages by more advanced general or technical training for farmers, who would probably engage in the creation of cooperatives for production or distribution. Similarly, the creation of banks providing farm loans would have helped to secure the financial resources for investment at any scale of production. Indeed, in other parts of the European continent institutional arrangements such as cooperatives or farm banks allowed smaller holdings to invest in mechanization. Yet that occurred in more developed economies such as Denmark or Holland (Henriksen 2009). Despite the differences prevailing in Portugal's farming sector, the productivity of either labor or land did not vary considerably from region to region, as productivities were also dependent on the product mix. In fact, maize had higher yields per hectare than wheat across the country, and the use of husbandry also increased crop yields due to the use of manure. But certain areas enjoyed particularly high yields, for Portugal's standards, like the regions on the outskirts of Lisbon. On the other hand, the distant regions of the extreme northeast (Trás-os-Montes) had much lower productivity levels. The greater use of traction animals and chemical fertilizers in the south probably did little more than offset the disadvantage of poor soils in that region.

### The engines of agricultural growth

The evolution of Portugal's agriculture is known for the second half of the nineteenth century, thanks to an annual index for output, which shows four main cycles of output, between comparable years of maximum production (Lains 2003c). After a period of decline that lasted from 1848 to 1865, agricultural output increased at 0.76 percent per year until 1882 and at a relatively fast rate of 1.97 percent during the following decades up to 1902, and the rate declined to just 0.35 percent in the period to the next peak year in 1927 (see Table 5.3). The growth of Portuguese agriculture in the last three decades of the nineteenth century,

Table 5.3 *Growth of agricultural output,*
*1848–1927 (annual peak to peak growth*
*rates, percent)*

| 1848–1865 | −0.56 |
|-----------|-------|
| 1865–1882 | 0.76  |
| 1882–1902 | 1.97  |
| 1902–1927 | 0.35  |

*Source:* Lains 2009.

taken as a whole, was quite high when compared to that of other European countries, which is remarkable taking into account the fact that Portugal remained nevertheless a very backward country by the end of the century, but we need to take into account that the expansion of agricultural output came from very low levels of factor productivity and was not accompanied by relevant changes in the use of technology, capital, and also the structure of output.[18] In fact, any comparison of land productivity levels in grains and other crops, of shares of output from animal husbandry, use of technology, or the land–labor ratio puts Portugal at the bottom of the league, even by the turn of the century. In the following decade, agricultural output reached a limit and ceased to expand, due to the many growth constraints that had not been overcome. The increase in agricultural output was largely due to the expansion of farming into previously uncultivated lands, and the use of additional labor, and not to changes in the levels of factor productivity or increase in investment. In fact, land under cultivation expanded by about 35 percent between 1867 and 1902, contributing between 16 and 22 percent of overall growth of agricultural output (Lains 2003b). This is a fairly high number compared to Great Britain, where it stood at 6.5 percent from 1760 to 1831. Although growing more slowly than the area under cultivation, labor accounted for roughly the same amount of increase in agricultural output, that is, between 14 and 17 percent, and this was due to the fact that labor represents a greater share of input costs. The contribution of capital was considerably lower, somewhere between 4 and 8 percent. And, again, the contrast with Britain is revealing, as there capital accounted for 27.5 percent of growth between 1760 and 1831, and land expansion accounted for 10.5 percent, against 33 and 34 percent

[18] For international comparisons, see Federico 2008 and Lains 2009.

Table 5.4 *Growth of output, labor force, and labor productivity, 1850–1930 (annual growth rates, percent)*

|  | Agriculture | Industry | Services | Total |
|---|---|---|---|---|
| Output |  |  |  |  |
| 1850–1870 | −0.50 | 2.17 | 0.63 | 0.34 |
| 1870–1900 | 1.62 | 2.57 | 0.74 | 1.47 |
| 1900–1930 | 0.82 | 2.16 | 2.03 | 1.60 |
| Labor force |  |  |  |  |
| 1850–1870 | 0.70 | 0.95 | 0.59 | 0.72 |
| 1870–1900 | 0.72 | 1.19 | 0.18 | 0.71 |
| 1900–1930 | 0.59 | 1.13 | 1.55 | 0.85 |
| Labor productivity[1] |  |  |  |  |
| 1850–1870 | −1.20 | 1.22 | 0.04 | −0.38 |
| 1870–1900 | 0.90 | 1.39 | 0.57 | 0.76 |
| 1900–1930 | 0.23 | 1.03 | 0.48 | 0.75 |

(1) Growth of output minus growth of labor force.
*Source:* Lains 2009.

in Portugal, respectively.[19] Britain's use of new land was only 4 percent in the period 1760–1831, whereas in Portugal the same figure was 20 percent between 1867 and 1902. This means that Portugal's growth of agricultural labor productivity depended to a greater extent on expanding cultivation into new lands. Table 5.4 sets down the main trends of growth of output, labor, and labor productivity in the three sectors of the economy.

The low contribution of capital to the output growth is visible in the stagnation we see in the number of animals employed by the sector, in relationship to labor and the area under cultivation, and on the share of animal output in total output. In Great Britain, for example, animal products contributed 75 percent to output from 1905 to 1914, as compared to 59 percent for the period from 1865 to 1874, whereas in Portugal, the share of animal products in output remained relatively stable during the same period at a much lower level, namely, about 25 percent of total output. The difference in the intensity of animal use in farming has been pointed out as a major reason for British higher productivity levels as compared to France. As France's animal production was proportionally similar to that of Portugal, it seems very plausible that the scarcity of farm animals goes a long way toward explaining

---

[19] Crafts 1985; Lains and Pinilla, eds. 2009.

Portugal's backwardness in its most important productive sector, but French farmers enjoyed better conditions nevertheless as they had a ratio of arable land per worker of 5.4 hectares compared to 3.7 hectares in Portugal, and the same figure for Britain was 9.8 hectares per worker (O'Brien and Keyder 2011). Setting aside the structural problems mentioned earlier, Portugal's agricultural sector contributed in a positive way to the country's economic growth until 1900. Thanks to the growth in agricultural labor productivity, farm wages were able to rise without significant price increases in farm output and food production could expand without too much pressure on labor, which allowed the transformation of the structure of employment in favor of the industrial and services sectors, where labor productivity tended to be higher.

The mostly positive trends in Portuguese agriculture came to a halt by 1900, in terms of overall growth of output and input productivity (see Table 5.4). The protection by tariffs, quotas, and price guarantees conceded to wheat and other grains is part of the explanation for this output growth slowdown, because the protected sectors soon reached a ceiling of productivity gains. By favoring grain production over other products, such as wine and cattle, protectionism diverted resources away from sectors in which Portugal was more efficient, such as wine, mostly by driving grain prices down in relation to the others. It is quite possible that the regime of grain protection started in 1889 and confirmed with a new legislation (*Lei da Fome*) ten years later, also contributed to lower farm earnings. The data shows that the protectionist law seems to have spurred nationwide grain output during the years from 1867 to 1902, insofar as the increase of cultivated land was not accompanied by an increase in cattle production. However, it is necessary to keep in mind the fact that the extensive nature of Portuguese agricultural growth depended not only on the relationship of the costs of farming-capital goods, namely cattle, and grain, but also on the relationship of the latter and the land and labor prices. While there was an abundance of labor and land for clearing in relation to capital, and consequently, while the relative costs favored the first two productive factors over the last, we cannot expect to see growth of farming production greater than the application of capital.

The performance of the Portuguese agricultural sector during 1870–1900 was quite an achievement, both in terms of the historical experience of the country, and in terms of what happened elsewhere in Europe (Federico 2008). Truly, part of that growth was due to the fact that agriculture was recovering from the deep depression registered in the 1850s and which had been a consequence of a severe disease in the vines. The growth of output was a consequence of the growth of inputs, with capital expanding slightly slower than land and labor, as well as of the growth of total factor productivity. Portugal went through a long period of civil wars and political unrest until well into the mid-nineteenth century, and the capacity of the government to control the whole territory was something relatively recent by 1870. But since then the country went through a period of sustained institutional development, marked by the increase of the role of the state in the economy and investments in social overhead capital, such as roads and railways, and in education. Such transformations were crucial for the agricultural sector, and the most important example in this respect is the contribution of the railway network for the growth of wheat output in the southern regions of Santarém and Alentejo, from where cereals were transported by rail to the Lisbon market.[20] But the changes in the institutional framework were very limited, and that certainly affected the pace of structural change in the Portuguese agriculture and the economy at large. Yet we need to take into account the possibility that agricultural expansion was not far from the growth potential for the period and thus that it was not seriously constrained by the slow pace of institutional change.

The agricultural sector was less protected in general than industry, as it happened elsewhere in Europe, with the exception of wheat, which was the only main agricultural produce that was traded internationally. Wheat tariffs were first reintroduced in 1865 and were heightened considerably in 1889 and 1899. Protection led to a considerable expansion of wheat output, which also led to the increase of the area under cultivation. The expansion of wheat output in the 1890s was a major contribution to the growth of total agricultural output. Domestic wheat output expanded rapidly and this time that expansion was followed by a small revolution in production methods, which involved the increasing use of chemical fertilizers, draft animals, and mechanical threshing. Railways were also increasingly used as a means of transportation as wheat travelled further away to be sold at larger urban markets, as mentioned. During the period of growth from about 1870 to 1900, there was an increase in the growth of agricultural exports, particularly, of wine, live animals, fish preserves, and cork. Wine accounted for as much as 45.3 percent of total exports in 1870–1879 and still for 34.4 percent in 1905–1914 (see later).

There is an episode that shows how the development of agriculture after 1870 was markedly different from that of the previous decades, which was the reaction of the wine sector to phylloxera, a disease in the vines that occurred precisely in the 1860s and 1870s. This episode

---

[20] For the expansion of the railway network since 1856, see Silveira *et al.* 2011.

is relevant as it compares favorably to the lack of response of the wine sector to the other spread of disease that occurred in the 1850s. In fact, the wine sector managed to react to the phylloxera disease that attacked vines in many parts of the country since the late 1860s. And that was made possible by the rapid substitution of the existent vines by new ones imported from the Americas which were immune to the phylloxera insect. This implied a large and coordinated effort by the state and by the owners of vines, which did not occur in previous episodes of widespread diseases in agricultural production. The fight against the disease led to important changes in the structure of wine output, as well as in the regional distribution of vines, which led to the increase in the share of lower quality wines and the output of southern regions of the country. This transformation led to substantial gains because there was an increasing demand for lower quality wines, in both the domestic and the international markets. Portuguese wines were exported to France during the 1880s in order to fill the gap in the production of wine in France which was also affected by phylloxera. This demonstration of flexibility and investment capacity to change output according to changes in factors of production was new in Portugal's agricultural sector and is the outcome of the slow changes that had been occurring since around 1870. The fact that the exports and the domestic economy, because of industrialization, were expanding was certainly favorable to that process of change, as they implied continuing growth of demand.

On the negative side of such an episode lies the fact that the new wines did not improve on quality and also there were no important developments in marketing, neither in other sectors linked to wine such as bottling and production of cork bottle stoppers and glass bottles. These were direct consequences of the low quality of output, as wine was sold mainly in bulk and not bottled. Output from other areas of the agricultural sector also expanded. That was the case with wheat output where expansion was due to the growth of domestic demand and occurred in a context of free trade and increasing imports. Output from other smaller sectors also expanded, namely olive oil, rye, potatoes, and meat but their contribution to total output did not change significantly. As a matter of fact, the structure of Portugal's agricultural sector remained virtually unchanged in the three decades between 1870 and 1900, and certainly one main feature of the development of the sector and the persistence of its degree of backwardness.

In order to explain the growth of agricultural output, we also have to take into account the fact that Portugal entered its first phase of sustained industrialization during the period from 1870 to 1913 when industrial output expanded at 2.5 percent per year. This was a relatively high rate compared to Portugal's past experience, but not extraordinary in western

European terms (Reis 1993: Chapter 4). The achievements of industrialization were only moderate also because the point of departure was very low. Moreover, the growth of the industrial sector was very much dependent on tariff protection and state intervention, and tariffs were among the highest in Europe. Protection helped shape the structure of the Portuguese industrial sector against its pattern of comparative advantage but the fact is that presumably industrial growth would have been slower without high tariffs. The growth of the industrial sector was the driving force for the growth of incomes and domestic demand, from which the agricultural sector clearly benefited.

## Paths of industrialization

The nineteenth century was the century of industrialization in all of Europe, including its periphery and Portugal was no exception. Backwardness and slow agricultural transformation was compatible with the growth of industrial output, catering mainly to domestic consumption of basic manufactured goods, such as textiles, olive oil, flour, and other processed foods, and a few tools and machinery for daily use. Industrialization in the periphery was to a large extent dependent on protection, but tariff policy was not its main driver. In the case of Portugal, the period before and after mid-century were in many aspects different, as the appeasement that followed the 1851 military coup, on the one hand, and the growth of the international economy on the other, changed considerably the context for the growth of the sector. The two periods are also clearly distinct in terms of the necessary quantitative information and thus the scope of the analysis also differs substantially, as we need to resort more to indirect information regarding the first half of the century.

### The early steps

In many aspects, the analysis of the development of Portuguese industry during the first half of the nineteenth century is still tributary to earlier works of authors that had contemporary worries about national economic conditions in comparison to what was happening elsewhere in Europe.[21] According to such authors, manufactures had somehow prospered since the consulate of the marquis de Pombal, who implemented protectionist measures and led the state to intervene directly in some industrial ventures, during the second half of the eighteenth century, and that

[21] Balbi 1822; Neves 1983 [1820]. See Chapter 4.

prosperity would have lasted down to the French invasions and the end of the Brazilian empire. This interpretation has been under revision for a long time now, as we have shown earlier, but it still reminds us that we need to look at the period of the British industrial revolution in order to understand what happened with the industrial sector in Portugal.[22] Pombal's royal manufactures marked a difference in the industrial context, as they tended to be larger and probably used machinery beyond what was the norm in the rest of the sector, which was clearly more dependent on small manufacturing units in many instances working in counter-cycle to the activity in the agriculture, which remained the most important activity for the population at large. These manufactures did not survive, in fact, the end of state protection after the turn of the century. Yet it is not clear what happened to the several, albeit smaller, manufacturing establishments spread across the country, and which satisfied the demand for industrial and consumer goods related to food, clothing, housing, and leisure. And there may be a close connection between such activity and what happened during the nineteenth century, when industrialization gained some momentum. In order to assess the development of national industrial production in the nineteenth century, we need to keep in mind the emerging complexity of the sector, which was no longer limited to the few establishments easily detectable by the official statistics on royal factories and export trade. It is also important to note that domestic production was capable of satisfying almost totally the domestic demand for manufactured goods, as imports in this period were necessarily small.

This perspective on Portuguese industry follows what has been established for other European countries, where foreign trade accounted for a small part of output. Indeed, international trade in raw materials, as well as in intermediate and manufactured goods, represented a relatively small proportion of the industrial output of most European countries. Substantial development was certainly witnessed in some markets mostly connected with cotton textiles, coal and iron, especially in Great Britain. The lion's share of Portugal's industrial production went toward domestic consumption, and responded to the market conditions prevailing there. Regarding supply, favorable conditions relied on the capacity of the sector to attract labor and capital. As for demand, the sector evidently depended on demand for essential consumer goods, such as foodstuffs (namely flour or wine), textiles, and clothing. Ultimately, Portuguese industry relied much more on events and developments in the agricultural sector than on what happened abroad or in terms of economic policies.

[22] Macedo 1982; Pedreira 1994.

Gaps in the knowledge about the performance of individual royal factories and industrial exports have only recently been explicitly identified – paving the way for a myriad of interpretations drawing on new data. In many cases, these interpretations are not compatible, and there is much room for further research (Pedreira 2005).

Data for the evolution of the industrial sector in the early nineteenth century is very scarce and we need to avoid incomplete models. One such model, available from the historiography, draws conclusions on the state of manufacturing based on the evolution of foreign trade and the increase in the number of royal factories. Accordingly, toward the end of the eighteenth century, the growth of exports would have implied an increase in industrial output, further helped by intervention on the royal manufactures.[23] Thus, it was the need to substitute imports of luxury items such as textiles made of silk or glassware, and other goods such as naval construction, rope, iron goods, and woolens, and to find new sources of revenue for the state that drove the intervention in the sector and brought about public investment in factories and thus an increase in industrial output. The same line of argument, where industrial output growth is proxied by the level of state intervention and foreign trade, is also employed to detect another positive period of growth, between 1812 and 1826, which would have been reversed in the following decade up to 1835, and in this year the cycle would have turned upward once more (Godinho 1955: 280). However, we need to take into account the possibility that the overall effect of public investment in manufactures was limited (Pedreira 1988: 279–280). In fact, even if we cannot assess the dimension of the country's industrial sector, nor, therefore, the weight that the royal factories had in the total, we must also consider what happened to the smaller units serving the needs of local markets.[24] According to one account, the number of factories doubled during the period between the surveys of 1813 and 1822, but that may have been just a "modest resumption of activities [that] did not truly generate a new industrializing impulse (...), the transformation went clearly beyond a modest restart of work."[25] What can be concluded from the deductions made earlier is that the first decades of the nineteenth century were unfavorable for the growth of those industrial sectors in which international trade played an important role. With the emergence of problems in the colonial markets for industrial output, the structure of the Portuguese industrial sector had to experience changes. Given that the sectors

[23] Godinho 1955; Pedreira 1988.
[24] On wool manufacturing in the early nineteenth century in the city of Portalegre, see Matos 1999: 456–462.
[25] Pedreira 1988: 280–281. See also Custódio 1983.

concerned with external trade were also probably more advanced than the industrial sectors that supplied the domestic market, the negative impacts of the contraction of these industrial activities were possibly manifold. However, this impact will always be limited to the relatively smaller scale of these sectors. In effect, a much more important part of Portugal's industrial sector, involved in the supply of consumer goods for the domestic market, was not directly affected by the convulsions of the international markets.

Based upon the same model in which the fluctuations of industrial output are inferred from fluctuations in external trade and domestic prices, the existence of greater industrial growth following the liberal victory in 1834 has been pointed out.[26] This conclusion follows the view of contemporary observers. In fact, there are some strong indicators of the recovery of industrial activity that illustrate some differences with the previous decades. To support the idea of industrial progress during the same period, other authors point to the rapid growth of cotton thread imports from 1834 onwards and of woven cotton from 1842. Moreover, steam engines were introduced in factories after 1835 and their number increased to 70 by 1852, with a total power output of 983 horsepower. These figures are extremely low, however. In the United Kingdom there were approximately 10,000 steam engines with a total energy output of 100,000 hp in 1838. The use of steam as a power source in Portugal was first tried in the maritime connections between Lisbon and Porto at the beginning of the 1820s but they only became regular from 1837 on.[27] Just like the countries from which they were imported, in Portugal steam engines were used mainly in foundries, cotton mills, milling, and in the manufacture of paper, that is, the sectors that were more receptive to innovations in terms of the motive power used. Yet alternative energy sources continued to predominate in most industrial sectors. Advances in the use of steam engines remained slow for many years and in 1881 there were still only 328 steam engines across the country, yielding around 7,000 hp.

The idea of industrial progress in this period is confirmed by an "industrialization index" for 1835–1845, based on the number of industrial establishments created in Lisbon and Oporto. Certainly this is only a partial indicator, as it does not provide levels of output or of employment, but it is nevertheless significant when taken into consideration jointly with other available information. In fact, between 1801 and 1813 an average of three establishments were created each year; between 1814

[26] Godinho 1955. See also Macedo 1982b: 281.
[27] Justino 1989: 127–128; Custódio 1983.

and 1825, the number increased to 13 per year, to 19 between 1826 and 1834, and to 46 per year between 1835 and 1845. Thus, 506 of the 863 factories existing in the two cities in 1845 had been established in the previous ten years. Some of the "factories" that had been founded since the beginning of the century had disappeared in the meantime, particularly during the period of the French invasions; in spite of this, the growth shown here reveals the strong possibility of an increase in the creation of industrial units dating from the mid 1830s.[28] For the remainder of the decade, we also have scattered information regarding the establishment of larger industrial establishments, such as new large textile factories in the city of Lisbon and on its outskirts (Torres Novas and Alenquer), which was associated with large increases in the import of both cotton thread and cloth, adding to the notion that industrial production was clearly growing. A new large tobacco factory in Lisbon (Xabregas) was also established in this period. In the 1820s out of a total of 11,810 industrial workers in the country, 61 percent were employed in large factories. The above positive trends in larger scale manufacturing may be confirmed by the evolution in the number of industrial workers in Lisbon and Porto in units with more than ten workers. In fact, during the period from 1814–1815 to 1829–1830, the total number of industrial workers in Lisbon and Porto increased only slightly from 2,018 to 2,278. This reflects a sharp increase in Porto, which was counterbalanced by a decline in Lisbon caused by the end of imperial preference in Brazil (see Table 5.5). Thereafter, the total number of workers doubled to 5,522 in 1845 and again to 10,029 in 1852. With respect to the number of industrial workers throughout the country, there is information for the 1820s and for the years 1845 and 1852. This shows that the number of industrial workers employed in units of ten or more increased from a total of 7,257 during the 1820s, to 12,874 in 1845, and to 15,897 in 1852.[29] Table 5.6 shows the evolution of the industrial population structure during the nineteenth century, enabling us to see a few important consistencies, such as with textiles, which retained its dominant position for the entire century.

The overview we have presented so far on the evolution of the industrial sector in the first half of the nineteenth century clearly depicts some positive trends in many of the sector's aspects. We need to recall that this period was marked by the end of colonial preference in Brazil and by continued military and political instability. According to the traditional view, the industrial sector reportedly suffered a great deal because of these events. Some historians

---

[28] Serrão 1980: 79–81. See also Godinho 1955: 245–246.
[29] Castro 1978: 27–28; Custódio 1983: 44, 52.

Table 5.5 *Population and industrial units in Portugal, 1814–1852*

| | Industrial population | | | | | Industrial units | | | | |
|---|---|---|---|---|---|---|---|---|---|---|
| | Units with more than ten workers | | | | | Units with more than ten workers | | | | |
| | Lisbon | Porto | Lisbon and Porto | Country | Total | Lisbon | Porto | Lisbon and Porto | Country | Total |
| 1814–15 | 1283 | 735 | 2018 | 7257* | | 45 | 37 | 82 | 258* | 1569* |
| 1829–30 | 909 | 1369 | 2278 | | 11 810* | 36 | 72 | 108 | | |
| 1845 | 2641 | 2881 | 5522 | 12 874 | | 62 | 91 | 153 | nd | |
| 1852 | 5012 | 5017 | 10 029 | 15 897 | | 73 | 172 | 245 | 386 | 863 |

*1820.

*Sources:* For Lisbon and Porto (Justino 1989: 148). For the country (Justino 1989: 84; Pedreira 1993: 70; Lains 1990: 36).

Table 5.6 *Composition of industrial work, 1815–1910 (percent)*

|  | Pedreira (1994) | Lains (1995) | Lains (1995) | Rodrigues and Mendes (1999) | Lains (1995) |
|---|---|---|---|---|---|
|  | 1815–25 | 1845 | 1852 | 1896 | 1910 |
| Cotton | 31.3 | 31.4 | 35.4 | 25.5 | 33.7 |
| Woolens | 12.3 | 24.5 | 26.3 | 19.4 | 16.6 |
| Linen | 1.6 | 2.2 | 2.7 |  | 4.3 |
| Hats | 9.9 |  |  | 3.7 |  |
| Leather | 13.9 |  |  | 1.9 |  |
| Food | 2.9 | 5.4 | 5.3 | 3.7 | 7.3 |
| Cork |  | 0.8 | 1.2 | 9.5 | 7.4 |
| Tobacco |  | 4.3 | 9.4 | 10.4 | 6.6 |
| Metals | 10.0 | 7.0 | 5.8 | 6.2 | 6.1 |
| Paper | 3.9 | 9.8 | 7.6 | 3.2 | 2.7 |
| Ceramics | 14.3 | 14.7 | 6.7 | 5.9 | 4.1 |
| Soaps |  | 0.5 | 0.5 |  | 1.2 |
| Tinned fish |  |  |  | 10.1 | 9.9 |
| Totals | 100.0 | 100.0 | 100.0 | 100.0 | 100.0 |

*Source:* Lains 2005: 270.

mentioned earlier went as far as arguing that Portuguese industrialization was virtually stopped because of them. The available information that we gathered, although patchy, points toward another interpretation of slow but steady growth. In fact, from the mid 1830s, Portuguese industry experienced a period of relative expansion, a conclusion that is supported by less contested quantitative data. This tenuous industrial boom was part of a confirmed tendency that had its origins in the second half of the eighteenth century, and which the difficult years of the early nineteenth century had only temporarily interrupted. Portuguese industry thereafter came to experience a period of increased prosperity from 1850, continuing to provide for the needs of the domestic market.

### Industrial growth after 1851

For the years following the 1851 coup that put an end to the troubled times of the first half of the century, there is enough statistical information on industrial output and labor force, which allows us to identify overall trends and establish comparisons with other countries. We can thus delve more deeply into the factors of growth and backwardness of Portugal vis-à-vis its foreign competitors.[30] European industrialization was not characterized by spurts of growth, nor did it depend on a few leading sectors such as those where innovation was faster in the British industrial revolution (Crafts and Harley 2000). European industrialization resulted from advances and growth in many sectors, which were, in turn, driven by changes in capital intensity, the use of new technologies, new methods of labor organization, and to a large extent by each country's capacity to adapt to changes in the international markets and to attract foreign technology and capital (Crouzet 1990). Moreover, there was a certain geographical pattern in which peripheral countries appear late on the industrialization scene (Pollard 1994). Due to its peripheral position, and low levels of human and physical capital, as well as natural resources, such as coal and iron, Portugal could have hardly caught up with the first wave of industrialization, which occurred around 1830, or even after. That being said, these factors could have been imported from abroad, but that did not occur also in most European countries until industrialization was well underway, later in the century.

Despite the mid-century advances, when most of the economies of north-western Europe had already achieved considerable industrial development, Portugal remained essentially agrarian and economically backward. Industry had, in fact, progressed from where it had been at the beginning of the century, but that progress was clearly insufficient to bring meaningful change to the structure of the country's economy. From around 1850 on, growth among the more industrialized countries showed ever-greater links to foreign trade and investment, as well as more and more migration to the New World. These three factors bolstered industrial specialization at the national level and greatly enhanced overall productivity as well as industrial productivity in particular. The countries that stayed abreast of these developments saw their productivity and income per capita converge in a way that had never been witnessed before (Broadberry and O'Rourke 2010).

Notwithstanding its import barriers, Portugal managed to take part in the changes that were underway in the international economy by the mid-century, including borrowing funds in international markets.[31] Portugal thus benefitted from foreign investment, mostly through the issue of sovereign debt abroad, and other forms of lending to the state. These financial dealings were coupled with renewed exports to Brazil, as well as considerable emigration to that destination. At the same time, the Portuguese economy benefitted from the import of foodstuffs, essential

---

[30] Cabral 1981; Lains 1995 and 2005; Pereira, M. H. 1983; Reis 1993.
[31] Esteves 2003; Mata 1993; Reis 1994 and 2003. On Ireland and Britain, see Ó Gráda 2001: 314–321.

Table 5.7  *Growth of industrial output, 1854–
1911 (annual peak to peak growth rates, percent)*

|           | Growth rates |
|-----------|--------------|
| 1854–1861 | 2.49         |
| 1861–1873 | 2.26         |
| 1873–1890 | 1.86         |
| 1890–1900 | 2.66         |
| 1900–1911 | 2.44         |

*Source:* Lains 2005: 274.

to feed the country's burgeoning population, along with intermediary goods for industrial purposes. All in all, the portion of the country's economy that was directed toward the outside flourished and became more modern. Still, this was not enough to accelerate Portugal's industrial development. Industrial production went from about 12 percent of GDP in 1850 to about 27 percent in 1910. This was the outcome of a growing industrial output on the order of 2.6 percent per year, while the agrarian sector grew at only 0.7 percent per year during these same years (Lains 2007: 136). We can identify three main cycles in the evolution of Portuguese industry, namely, between 1851 and 1870, with an annual growth of 1.4 percent until 1870, between 1870 and 1890, with a growth rate of 2.5 percent per year, and between 1890 and 1914, where growth reached 3 percent per year. Productivity of industrial labor also performed well from 1870 to 1900, as did productivity in farm labor (see Table 5.7).

Portugal's industrial development was therefore not sensitive to banking or financial crises, such as those that occurred in 1846, 1876, and, later, in 1891. These were rather severe crises and they had a great impact on domestic political and social life, but they affected to a much smaller degree or not at all the industrial output, as this sector relied very little on borrowing in the markets, which, incidentally, was also largely the case throughout the rest of Europe.[32] Portugal had some of the strictest import barriers of Europe. It is difficult to assess the effects of protectionism on the country's industrial growth, as measuring those effects depends on the type and scale of growth that would have occurred had the economy been more open to foreign competition. Most probably, the industrial sector would not have performed as well as it did, and the agrarian sector would have performed better. The final outcome of that path would have pivoted on whether or not certain areas of agriculture would have been

[32] Lains 2003, 2007; Reis 1993.

able to attain higher productivity levels than the levels achieved in industry under the regime of protection. Obviously, some industrial sectors might have emerged by targeting export markets, but considering the overall backwardness of the country, and its poor competitiveness vis-à-vis foreign producers, that whole alternative scenario seems unlikely.

The literature has also looked at the role of the state to explain industrial backwardness. It has been pointed out that the state put too much pressure on capital markets in order to cover for persistent public deficits, and thus entrepreneurs had to face higher borrowing costs. However, we should note that there were no crowding-out effects, that is, interest rates in Portugal did not rise significantly as a result of demand for domestic borrowing by the state. This belief is corroborated by the fact that the demand for investment would be less than the supply of savings, as attested by the success of public debt issues, and by the range of financial applications related to the state.[33] The persistently low levels of literacy and schooling have also been advanced by several historians as major causes of industrial backwardness. Poor schooling may be associated with poor productivity of labor in industry. Many of the tasks in industries such as weaving and textiles were carried out less efficiently in Portugal because the workforce was less able to learn and adapt to the new methods of production. Perhaps this same argument can be extended to management, where poorer literacy also existed (Reis 1993). The relationship between industrial labor productivity, literacy, and human capital is currently an area of research interest, and evidence about the Portuguese case may shed some light on the issue. However, whether because of low levels of human capital or other reasons, the fact remains that Portugal's industrial labor productivity was on average about half that of Great Britain around 1900. Since the wage differential was similar, the lower productivity level cancelled any advantage of a cheaper labor force (Reis 1993).

Although we had to look at the first and second parts of the century through different lenses due to differences in data availability, it is possible to draw some general conclusions regarding the whole period. Perhaps the most important features of industrial development in Portugal are slow but steady growth, in terms of output and labor productivity, and the fact that the sector was able to keep up with the increasing domestic consumption of primary goods, namely, food and clothing. This somewhat demonstrates that the pattern of demand drove production. The progress that was achieved should not, however, hide the challenges that Portugal's industry was unable to overcome. Perhaps one

---

[33] Lains 2003c; Esteves 2003.

of the best indicators of the problems that the Portuguese industrial sector faced is the fact that its level of exports remained rather limited throughout the century, which is particularly significant in a context of thriving international trade.

## The foreign sector

Throughout Europe foreign trade expanded rapidly over half a century to 1913, and Portugal was no exception. In fact, from mid-century to the outbreak of World War I, Portuguese exports and imports by value increased roughly four-fold, with the trend of growth rate being approximately 2.5 percent per year. The corresponding figure for volumes is only slightly higher at 2.8 percent per year (Lains 2003). As elsewhere in the industrializing world, Portuguese foreign trade expanded more rapidly than national output and yet, the growth of Portuguese exports lagged behind that of other countries in the European periphery, such as the Scandinavian countries, Italy, Spain, and Hungary. Moreover, Portuguese exports remained essentially agricultural and there was very little industrial development based on exports. Portugal's export performance is necessarily related to the poor performance of the rest of the economy. The growth of exports depends on the capacity of the export sector to compete in the international markets and that capacity is a function of the productivity levels of the labor force employed in the export sector and thus of the average labor productivity of the country and thus to its level of income per capita. The relationship between exports and economic growth has received much attention in the literature and two opposing perspectives may be singled out. One is the export-led growth theory, based on the hypothesis according to which open markets and international specialization are factors of growth; the other is the dependence theory, according to which closed markets and import substitution are the levers of growth. Even though the two theories depart from opposing hypotheses, both postulate that the rate of economic growth of a less developed country can be enhanced by the right choice of trade-related policy measures, either free trade or protection. Moreover, both theories assume that the role of exports is paramount.

The growth in export volume is divided into six sub-periods of nearly one decade each (see Table 5.8). The relatively high growth rate for 1842–1856 is probably overstated because 1842 may be a low point in the cycle. During the following decade, from 1856 to 1866, export volume growth registered a slowdown, which was reversed in the years from 1866 to 1886. These were decades of exceptional growth. Between 1886 and 1913 the growth rates for export volumes returned to the levels

Table 5.8 *Growth of trade, 1842–1913 (1910 prices)* *(peak to peak yearly growth rates, percent)*

| Exports | | Imports | |
|---|---|---|---|
| 1842–1856 | 2.9 | 1843–1856 | 1.8 |
| 1856–1865 | 1.6 | 1856–1867 | 1.9 |
| 1865–1874 | 4.9 | 1867–1875 | 4.0 |
| 1874–1886 | 3.4 | 1875–1890 | 3.6 |
| 1886–1898 | 1.6 | 1890–1900 | 0.6 |
| 1898–1910 | 1.6 | 1900–1913 | 2.9 |
| 1856–1913 | 2.0 | 1856–1913 | 2.3 |

*Note:* Figures in the last row are trend growth rates.
*Source:* Lains 1995: 29 and 122.

of the initial decade of 1856–1866. In spite of the high growth rates of the years 1866–1886, the Portuguese performance for 1855–1913 stood around the median for Europe as a whole. Compared to more successful small countries, the growth of exports from Portugal lagged in the periods following 1886 and in particular after 1895. The changing rhythm of the period after 1886 was associated with important shifts in the composition and direction of Portuguese exports.

The upturn in the international economy from the mid-nineteenth century on gave a boost to Portugal's foreign sector, which performed better than the country's overall economy. Portugal was more open to the outside in 1914 than it had been in 1850 and certainly in 1807. This greater openness not only spurred exports and imports of goods and services, but also allowed larger flows of international capital into the country, as well as emigration, particularly to the New World. As Portugal delved further into the international economy, its production became more specialized in goods that could compete better in the world market. In doing so, it increased its exports of primary products, including wine or minerals, as well as its imports of manufactures, foodstuffs, and raw materials. In this context, the trade balance became increasingly negative, which was an outcome of the need to make up for the backwardness of a country that was poorer than most of its trading partners. For many years Portugal was able to cope with this situation, as the trade deficit could be offset by inflows of foreign capital, emigrants' remittances, and, later in the century, by the revenue derived from re-exporting goods from the African colonies.[34]

---

[34] On Brazilian remittances, see Esteves and Khoudour-Castéras 2011; on Portuguese capital exports to the African colonies, see Mata 2007.

Growth in the foreign sector was also linked to the country's growing liberalism, but this did not prevent governments from imposing some restrictions on foreign trade, for tax purposes, to protect certain economic sectors, and in some extreme cases, because of the need to counter the trade deficit. In the nineteenth century, Portuguese political and economic liberalism and trade protectionism coexisted peacefully, like elsewhere in Europe.

Historians have wondered if peripheral countries, in Europe or elsewhere, could have obtained additional advantages by raising import barriers even more. In fact, those countries entered international markets with a handicap, as they had to compete from weaker positions and in sectors where international demand expanded slower, had lower productivity, and less capacity for growth. Some of these countries were able to overcome these hindrances, like the Scandinavian countries, ultimately developing buoyant primary exports, but these were the exception. The influence of the foreign sector and the specialization in primary products for export has received vast attention from researchers working on the performance of the Portuguese economy from 1850 to 1913.[35] According to that view, after about 1840, Britain aimed to secure external markets for its manufactures. For that it imposed free-trade policies on Portugal and in exchange allowed imports of raw materials and foodstuffs therefrom. The increase in exports thus reportedly led to an inflated expansion to Portugal's agricultural sector, and at the same time brought stagnation to the industrial sector, which had to face foreign competition without the cushion of the earlier protectionist policy. The negative effects of the excessive dependency on foreign trade was felt mostly from the early 1880s onwards, since despite the upturn in the agricultural sector there was a gradual loss of market share to other countries that had higher levels of productivity, especially those with abundant natural resources, especially countries in Latin America (Pereira 1983: 319–320). This loss of foreign market share could not be compensated by domestic consumption, due to the stagnation caused by the deindustrialization of the Portuguese economy, a bitter fruit of "external dependence." The view that the Portuguese economy was shaped by external relations does not take into account the fact that the sector only weighed about 7.5 percent of national output in 1900.[36]

The existence of close ties between fluctuations of Portuguese exports and foreign demand must be further investigated. In the world markets of

[35] Cabral 1979 and 1981; Pereira 1983; Sideri 1978. See also Fontoura and Valério 2000 and Lains 2003.
[36] Esteves 2003; Bairoch 1976.

the second half of the nineteenth century, demand for food and raw materials was closely related to fluctuations in national incomes and industrial production of the most industrialized nations, including Great Britain, France, Germany, and the United States, which together formed the core of the world economy. However, in the six decades running up to 1913, Portuguese exports did not fluctuate according to global demand. The explanation for this is that Portugal occupied a small and unimportant position in world trade, and at the same time Portugal's supply of primary products was not aligned with world demand for those primary goods.

In fact, most of Portugal's products amounted to a very small share in the total supply from all exporters, usually less than 5 percent. This means that fluctuations of Portuguese exports by value were rather isolated from the ups and downs of global demand. The country's exports essentially comprised primary sector products that the core nations lacked, namely from the mid-nineteenth century on. Yet the type of products that Portugal exported was not amongst those for which demand grew fastest among industrialized nations. For example, Britain's imports, which were driven by rising income, comprised increasing amounts of wheat, meat products, cattle for slaughter, milk products, and eggs. Of these, Portugal exported in large quantities only beef cattle. Britain's demand for all the other Portuguese exports of foodstuffs, such as wine, olive oil, salt, fruit, and vegetables, grew at a slower pace. The same happened with raw materials destined for industry. Britain's demand for industrial imports increasingly turned to timber, mineral oils, rubber, and paper pulp, items that were not abundant in Portugal. Export growth was relatively high since 1846, but increased in the period from 1865 to 1886, to decline thereafter. Overall, Portugal's exports grew slightly below the European average and also below imports (see Table 5.8).

Portuguese exports were comprised almost exclusively of items derived from agriculture. Even under the best possible circumstances, it would be difficult for a country as geographically and economically small as Portugal to have much diversity in its resources. This, in turn, meant that the chances of having a range of products that could enjoy a comparative advantage over others in the global marketplace were fairly slim, and we should not be surprised with Portugal's limited range of exports at the time. The same situation existed in other countries, too, such as Denmark and Sweden. The relative success in those countries shows that a limited range of exports does not necessarily lead to adversity in export performance, nor does it mean that a limited exporting sector will necessarily perform poorly. Even though the degree of concentration of exports in Denmark and Sweden was comparable to Portugal's, the growth of the export sectors in both those countries was among the fastest in Europe in the second half of the nineteenth century. The difference there rested in the variation in the type of products their exports were concentrated on, and in the way their national economies responded to export stimuli. Denmark specialized in exporting cereals, as long as the world market for cereals remained favorable, until 1870, butter, fresh meat, and eggs. Sweden specialized in sawn lumber, paper and paper pulp, iron, and steel. Not only did these products enjoy a growing demand around the world, notably in Great Britain, but their production had external effects in other sectors which these two Scandinavian countries managed to take advantage of. Portugal, on the other hand, specialized in exports for which global demand grew at a slower pace, or even fell, or whose production had external effects that, aside from being small, were only partially exploited. Importantly, the products cited earlier for Denmark and Sweden, with the exception of iron and steel, belonged to the agricultural sector. Therefore, the notion that specialization in farm products is necessarily unfavorable for the export sector of a country should be discarded, especially as the second half of the nineteenth century was generally good for farming exports in the global markets.

Changes in the composition or the distribution of exports from Portugal have to be explained, especially because they were associated with the decline in the rhythm of overall economic growth (Table 5.9). In seeking to explain such changes, we touch on some of the most fundamental problems in Portugal's export sector. Indeed, we need to understand whether the drop in exports after 1886 was due to the fall in demand for the kind of products Portugal was specialized in, or whether there were changes in the structure of demand, toward higher quality goods, which Portuguese exporters were not able to meet. We also need to look at the performance of exports to the protected markets in the African colonies. Qualitative changes in external demand were equally important for the weak response of some Portuguese exports. In fact, exports such as olive oil, wine, fruits and vegetables, and wool had low levels of quality and these products were driven out of the global market, which grew ever more demanding, and sought better quality products from other parts of Europe and the world. Exports of cork bottle stoppers are a good example of this. Throughout the period under consideration, stoppers consistently represented less than 10 percent of all the cork exported from Portugal, by volume. Clearly Portugal could have benefitted more if cork production had been greater, and certainly this was possible from the demand side. Indeed, despite the high import barriers which the principal cork-consuming countries erected to protect their own industries, there was a large demand for this item worldwide. But Portugal failed to exploit that

Table 5.9 *Composition of exports, 1840–1914 (percent of total exports)*

| | 1840–1849 | 1850–1859 | 1860–1869 | 1870–1879 | 1880–1889 | 1890–1899 | 1900–1909 | 1905–1914 |
|---|---|---|---|---|---|---|---|---|
| Wax | 1.3 | 1.9 | 3.9 | 3.1 | 0.6 | 0.3 | 0.4 | 0.4 |
| Hides and skins | 0.3 | 0.2 | 0.5 | 0.6 | 0.7 | 0.8 | 0.9 | 0.9 |
| Wool | 1.4 | 1.6 | 2.1 | 1.4 | 0.9 | 0.7 | 0.5 | 0.4 |
| Cork | 2.1 | 2.5 | 3.6 | 4.4 | 8.9 | 9.3 | 8.8 | 9.4 |
| Wood | – | – | 0.5 | 0.7 | 0.5 | 0.4 | 3.6 | 2.6 |
| Minerals | – | – | 7.1 | 7.8 | 5.4 | 5.3 | 3.9 | 3.4 |
| **Raw materials** | **5.1** | **6.2** | **17.7** | **18.1** | **17.0** | **16.9** | **18.1** | **17.1** |
| Live animals | 0.4 | 1.3 | 5.5 | 8.7 | 7.4 | 7.3 | 13.0 | 10.6 |
| Fresh and salted fish | 0.7 | 0.7 | 0.8 | 1.3 | 1.2 | 1.3 | 1.4 | 1.9 |
| Fruits and vegetables | 8.3 | 7.9 | 8.8 | 9.3 | 6.7 | 7.8 | 8.0 | 7.2 |
| Grains | 1.0 | 1.2 | 1.0 | 0.3 | 0.0 | 0.2 | 0.1 | 0.1 |
| Salt | 2.3 | 2.7 | 1.8 | 1.5 | 1.0 | 0.6 | 0.4 | 0.3 |
| **Foodstuffs** | **12.7** | **13.8** | **17.9** | **21.1** | **16.3** | **17.2** | **22.9** | **20.1** |
| Canned Fish | – | – | – | 0.1 | 2.1 | 4.3 | 5.5 | 6.4 |
| Flour | 0.8 | 0.8 | 0.3 | 0.1 | 0.2 | 0.5 | 0.8 | 1.0 |
| Olive oil | 2.8 | 5.1 | 4.3 | 2.5 | 0.7 | 1.2 | 1.8 | 1.8 |
| Port wine | 37.7 | 37.7 | 37.1 | 35.3 | 26.6 | 24.4 | 17.7 | 17.8 |
| Madeira wine | 7.1 | 3.7 | 1.3 | 2.1 | 2.6 | 2.8 | 2.3 | 1.9 |
| Common wine | 6.6 | 10.5 | 6.5 | 7.9 | 22.8 | 16.4 | 13.5 | 14.7 |
| **Processed foodstuffs** | **54.2** | **57.8** | **49.5** | **48.0** | **55.0** | **50.1** | **41.6** | **43.6** |
| Textiles | 13.2 | 6.1 | 2.7 | 1.8 | 0.7 | 4.4 | 5.0 | 4.3 |
| Footwear | 0.1 | 0.2 | 0.6 | 0.9 | 0.7 | 0.3 | 0.4 | 0.3 |
| Cork manufactures | 0.1 | 0.1 | 0.3 | 0.8 | 2.2 | 2.8 | 3.0 | 3.0 |
| Iron manufactures | 0.8 | 0.7 | 0.5 | 0.6 | 0.4 | 0.5 | 0.4 | 0.4 |
| **Manufactures** | **14.2** | **7.1** | **4.1** | **4.1** | **4.0** | **8.0** | **8.8** | **8.0** |
| **Other** | **13.8** | **15.1** | **10.8** | **8.7** | **7.7** | **7.8** | **8.6** | **11.2** |

*Notes:* Data are for 1842, 1843, 1848, 1851, 1855–1856, 1861, and 1865–1914.
*Source:* Lains 1992: appendix c.

niche market. Spanish bottle corks, for example, secured 86 percent of the market in the United States (1908–1910), equivalent to nearly all of the corks that Portugal sold to Great Britain. Incidentally, the latter was the only market with a considerable dimension for Portugal (Lains 2006).

Portugal's underperformance in foreign markets can also be understood by the country's low capacity to negotiate trade treaties with its major trading partners. Spain and Italy, for example, obtained the most-favored-nation clause from France, allowing them to pay half the import duties on corks that Portugal paid. The lack of negotiation power may have been caused by the fragmented nature of operations prevailing among Portugal's cork producers, preventing them from acting as a bloc in world markets. And it should be stressed that Portugal produced and exported about half of all the cork consumed in the world. The growth of Portugal's wine exports also lagged behind total world demand for wines. For example, even though exports to France expanded rapidly up to 1886, Portugal's share of that market was steadily eroding, falling from 15 percent in 1876 to 6 percent in 1888. Common wine, that is wine with less than 30 percent alcohol content, sold to Britain ranged between 200 and 300 thousand gallons on average between 1876 and 1898. This was unimpressive when compared to total wine exports from Spain and France, which together exceeded 6 million gallons in 1876 and 9 million in 1898. Moreover, Portuguese wines, including fortified wines, represented 50 percent of the British market in 1811–1820, and declined thereafter to 37 percent in 1841–1850 and 21 percent in 1891–1896 (Sideri 1978: 336), a significant fall in the share of what was its largest foreign customer. The reason for this fall stems from Portugal's low competitiveness but also partly, as we shall see later, from Britain's weak interest in doing business with Portugal's wine producers. This dwindling interest was driven, on the one hand, by the increasing specialization of Britain's own high-quality exports, like specific machine parts, certain types of cloth, and yarns for weaving, which demanded trading partners with markets that were large enough to make the profits of doing business there sufficiently attractive. On the other hand, German and North American exporters were more competitive in smaller and poorer markets, compared to the British, as they were willing to adapt to the particular needs of those markets. Hence, in the second half of the nineteenth century, the Portuguese market was a more appropriate outlet for specialized German and American goods, and these two trading partners gradually took over much of the business with Portugal that had earlier been conducted with Britain.

The decline of British interest in Portugal's trade was already visible as early as 1860, when the Anglo-French trade treaty was signed. This treaty launched the free-trade movement across continental Europe and was of paramount interest to the British government. With that treaty, French wines gained preferential treatment over Portuguese and Spanish wines, in stark disregard of the most-favored-nation status granted to the two countries in earlier treaties. Portugal protested against this arrangement, but the British government did not change its position. In 1866, Portugal signed a new treaty with France and offered Britain the most-favored-nation status in return for rescinding the preferential treatment of French wines in British markets, which would have extended to Britain the same tariff reductions prescribed in the French-Portuguese trade agreement. The negotiations between Europe's oldest allies dragged on for ten more years, and in 1876 Portugal finally granted the most-favored-nation status to Britain without getting anything in return. Britain's specific position in these affairs largely derived from the declining importance of the Portuguese market for British exports. For Britain to extend equal treatment to Portugal for wine sales was certainly not in the best interest of France, either, which for commercial and political reasons was far more important to Great Britain.

The reduction in the growth rate of exports after the mid 1880s was not due to any decline in global demand for the kind of products in which the Portuguese export sector was specialized. In fact, world demand for Portuguese exports evolved less favorably than that for other more sophisticated primary products. Countries that specialized in exports of frozen meat or butter fared better than those such as Portugal that specialized in low-quality wines, raw cork, or cattle. This led, inexorably, to the loss of markets and further exacerbated the country's low productivity. The loss of market shares was thus a consequence of the country's inability to diversify exports within the same kind of sectors. Diversification depended on the industrial transformation of farm products or on the improvement in the quality of some of the merchandise sold abroad in an effort to hold on to existing foreign markets, which were becoming ever more demanding. The dismal negotiating power of the successive governments and, for that matter, of exporters themselves, even in those areas where they held a sizeable share of the world market, such as cork, contributed to the shrinking number of agents importing Portuguese goods.

### Trade policy

The nineteenth century arrived with a host of troubles in the finances and affairs of the state, and addressing these matters called for an increase in tax collection. As taxes were one of the leading sources of state revenue, customs duties were one of the favorite targets of reform measures, seeking above all to broaden the tax base. The possibility of introducing changes in tariff schedules was, however, restricted by the stipulations of the 1810 trade agreement between Portugal and Great Britain, which was to remain in effect for twenty-five years. This treaty established a maximum tariff of 12 percent to be levied on imports. As soon as it expired, in 1835, a committee was formed in the government to study the way forward. The efforts of Parliament, as well as those of the committee, were interrupted by the revolution of September 1836. However, in the midst of the considerable ideological disagreement that emerged from the discussions of the constitutional framework of the new liberal regime, the new government pursued the work begun before the revolution and announced a new tariff schedule in 1837, which basically followed the guidelines laid down before the conflict.[37]

The 1837 tariff implied an increase in import duties on average from 15 to 30 percent, inaugurating a period of high duties that remained in effect during the remainder of the century. In 1843, a new tariff was issued, and average rates fell, but only slightly, to 24 percent.[38] The purpose of the customs duties was mainly to increase state revenue, but the truth is that the 1837 tariff was also protectionist to some degree, for certain sectors of industry. It is, however, unclear whether the protectionist effect was felt in other areas of the economy, as high rates were imposed on several intermediate goods, hampering national production across a broad range of sectors. In addition, some of the products subjected to taxes were not even produced domestically. Nevertheless, many sectors benefitted from the import barriers and the lower influx of goods that resulted from it. Still, determining the impact of the 1837 tariff schedules and the following ones on the country's industrial performance remains a challenge. No doubt, the new tariffs gave considerable breathing room to Portugal's manufacturing sector, which recovered considerably, as we have shown earlier in the chapter.

Portugal's customs duties were changed by new rules in 1852, and again in 1892, but these reforms were never as influential as has been argued, as they came about in moments when international prices were counteracting their effects, a situation to which their creators were certainly sensitive. From 1837 to 1852, international prices fell considerably, making the customs rates introduced in 1837, and raised for some items in 1841, excessive by the time the new rules were issued in 1852. It thus became possible to lower tariffs without dealing with the larger issue of actually shifting national policies. Forty years later the situation was reversed. When Portugal abandoned the gold standard, in 1891, and the international environment turned sour, the price of imports in Portugal soared. Now the tariffs could rise without implying higher protectionism. The tariff schedule of 1892 certainly did not represent a return to protectionism, but it was nothing more than an economic, and

---

[37] Bonifácio 1991; Serrão 1980.     [38] Bairoch 1976. See also Bonifácio 1991: 251.

largely political, adjustment aimed at maintaining the status quo in customs policy. In 1837 the tariffs ceased to stand at roughly 15 percent of imports. Following that date Portugal embraced protectionism and did not let it go until the eve of World War I (Lains 2006).

A few comparisons with the situation in other countries confirm the protectionist character of Portugal's customs policies. For example, tariffs on cotton yarn and cotton and wool manufactures imports in 1875 and 1895 were surpassed (in Europe) only by the tariffs for cotton manufactures in Spain and Russia in 1895 (Lains 2006: 247). At the same time, a British commission charged with studying the levels of protectionism among that country's principal trading partners published a list for the year of 1902, a year in which Portuguese tariffs were fairly low, on average, identifying Portugal as one of the most protectionist countries of all – outdistanced only by Russia and the United States. Portugal was on a par with the backward, but also large, Spanish economy. This comparison is all the more significant if we bear in mind that the smaller the economy of a country, the slimmer the chances of success for a protectionist customs policy, since there is a faster exhaustion of the capacity for absorption in the domestic protected market, as well as the inevitable greater need for imports because of the reduced range of domestic resources. Similarly to what was happening in most European countries, in Portugal the revenue flowing from customs duties represented a significant portion of the state budget. Since it was collected in a few, well-defined places around the country, it was easily controlled and supervised, and foreign trade was thus a tax base that was greatly favored by governments. On the other hand, given the great variety of incomes of persons and companies, taxing personal and business income was such a vast and complex activity that only a relatively advanced state apparatus at the political, social, and economic levels had the ability to run it well. It is thus easy to understand why even in the early twentieth century, only five countries were operating systems of personal income taxation that were in any way comparable to what we know today (Lains 2006).

In a coherent industrial protectionist system, tariff levels should be set according to whether the imported good is an input or a finished product. As such, raw materials should pay low duties, as they do not jeopardize the industries that will use them, while manufactures are subject to higher fees, in order to defend the prices and output of domestic industries. At first glance, this scaling of import tariffs seems to have been taken into account in Portugal's customs policies, but upon closer inspection, the policies pursued appear to be somewhat confused and ill defined. The lack of clear consistency in the protectionist policies leads us to suspect that they may have been designed to cater for the demands of relatively antagonistic interests, without a previous compromise between or among them. It goes without saying that the construction of a protectionist system will always invite pressure from interested agents defending their own business. In the period under consideration, the state was merely a mediator, evidently concerned only about ensuring revenue to manage its teetering public accounts. The level of protectionism varies in proportion to the influence of the pressure groups involved, and reveals which industry's lobbyists had the upper hand at a given moment. The more dispersed the consumers, the harder it was to make claims vis-à-vis central government authorities, as organizational costs tend to be greater. Consumers of final products are thus usually at a disadvantage when it comes to obtaining political favor compared to consumers of intermediary goods, in other words, industries. The amount of cohesion among the latter is certainly greater, not only because there are fewer of them and they can communicate with greater ease, but because they have greater economic leverage vis-à-vis the authorities.

The only relatively significant farming products to receive attention in customs policies (although ignored from 1865 to 1889) were grain, more specifically wheat. But actual grain protection stemmed not from import barriers, but from the price floor in the domestic market, forcing millers to import wheat. This price-floor regime was introduced in 1889 and strengthened ten years later. Tariff revenue from wheat imports went directly into state coffers. Although grain protectionism in Portugal was thus only indirectly derived from actual import tariff schedules, we should add some further observations on this that may shed some light on the conclusions drawn in the preceding section about the foreign sector. Grain production grew at a faster pace during the years of grain protection, essentially from 1885 on, than in the years immediately before, namely, during a time of free trade. Some caveats here are that cereal production did *not* grow more rapidly than wine production or animal husbandry, which together made up most of Portugal's gross agricultural production, from 1846 to 1912; nor was this growth matched by overall agricultural production, which was a consequence of the slowing rates of growth in those other two sectors, which may have fallen off precisely because production shifted to grain.

The protection of wheat farmers, who operated almost exclusively in the vast estates of the southern region of Alentejo, does not seem to arise in response to any serious agricultural crisis in that region, nor does it reflect any special suitability of its soils for wheat production. Rather, it appears to be the result of a successful lobby that appealed to the state's financial needs. Protectionism was thus driven by pressure groups and fiscal concerns within the government, and not necessarily by an economic rationale. It is no coincidence that the government's greatest attention was focused on a sector concentrated in the hands of a few wealthy landowners rather than on more widespread and popular sectors, such as wine production, fruit growing, or animal husbandry. In fact, wheat accounted for the largest share of food imports and domestic production did not satisfy that demand, making it a good candidate for raising income from taxes. The policy of industrial protectionism was also linked to strong interest groups operating in that sector, and it is equally true that the easier the agreements struck between industrialists and the governments, the greater the problems related to substitution of imports of manufactures. The high tariffs did not reduce to any great extent the purchases from abroad, and the Treasury did not take its eyes off of such an important source of tax revenues. Regarding the form of the import barriers erected in Portugal during this period, the absence of an impact on domestic industrial production (the most protected sector) comes as little surprise. The relationship between the growth index for Portuguese industrial output and the degree of customs restrictions is somewhat of a paradox. Despite the gradual rise in the average *ad valorem* tariffs from 1855 to 1897, the growth rate for industrial output was *below* that of the rate in the following period, from 1897 to 1913.

As mentioned earlier, the effects of the variations in tariffs on the economy must be examined in terms of effective protection. Only then can we accurately itemize the additional costs for the industries that were obliged to purchase intermediary products from abroad, underpinning the higher tariffs, which might or might not outstrip the benefits of greater protection on the final product. The same rationale holds for the case in which the trend is for falling tariffs. Similarly to what happened with agriculture, industrial protectionism not only failed to promote growth in the sector but it seems to have spawned an industrial structure that was disconnected from the potential of the country's secondary sector. In effect, industrial protectionism helped diverting resources to sectors in which Portugal was ill-suited to compete with foreign producers, and ultimately resulting in the need to tax imports of manufactures that were difficult to substitute with domestic production. Comparing the advantages for Portugal's manufacturers relative to foreign manufacturers, with the levels of protectionism that afforded those advantages, we can see just how customs policies had a negative impact on the country's economic structure in the second half of the century. The sectors that benefitted from higher nominal protection were not those in which Portugal enjoyed greater comparative advantage. A good example is the case of woolens and cotton cloth, which benefitted from considerable protection, even though a Portuguese worker produced only 15–25 percent of the value of his counterpart in Great Britain. We can see, therefore, that protectionism's contribution to sustained industrial growth targeted in large measure areas in which domestic production had less trouble competing with imports in the short term (Lains 2006: 253).

As industrial growth under a protectionist regime is, of course, limited by the size of the domestic market, in small countries such as Portugal that rule is especially important. Having exhausted the internal capacity to absorb production, boosting sales of industrial products depended on the ability to price products competitively in the foreign markets. The protectionist regime in effect throughout this period diverted resources to industrial undertakings in which the country had no clear advantages over the leading foreign competition. As a result, having saturated the domestic market for cotton cloth at the end of the nineteenth century, this sector suffered a crisis for lack of any foreign outlet. In the same vein, we see a lack of coherence in the fact that spinning had *effectively* greater protection than weaving, even though it was an activity in which larger countries enjoyed greater advantage. It is also noticeable that when the industries related to weaving briefly enjoyed protection, in 1892, some of the labor was replaced by machinery. An in-depth study of Portuguese industry would certainly detect other examples of protected industries unsustainable in Portugal because of an inability to compete abroad. With the data we have before us at the moment we can reach the same sort of conclusion comparing industrial specialization in Portugal with that of small nations in northeastern Europe.

In contrast with the case of Portugal, the successful industrialization in Scandinavia, the Netherlands, and Switzerland in the nineteenth century was due mainly to the development of highly specialized niche markets that appeared as a result of mass production based on coal and steel underway in the powerful economies, such as Great Britain and Germany. Rather than striving to compete in industrial sectors dominated by large countries with many resources and vast domestic markets, these small economies chose to concentrate in industrial sectors in which the large countries were less competitive. For example, the Belgian and Swiss textile industries specialized in certain "semi-manufactures," such as linen and silk thread and carded wool, which competed favorably with large-scale producers in Britain and France, where mechanization and mass production were fundamental. Holland and Denmark exploited niche industries in the processing of national and imported food items, steel, and textile threads from imported raw materials. In these cases, the key was to compete in areas that depended on specialized manual labor, thereby offsetting the advantages of mass production and machinery.

The most progressive industries in these small countries in Europe's northwest were also closely tied to the type of natural resources present. One of the most important industries in Sweden – and that with the greatest contribution to industrial growth – was the sawing of lumber, naturally exploiting the country's vast forests. Industrial specialization in Portugal was very different. Thanks to the protectionism in place during the period under study, there was an excessive concentration of resources in industries that were simply not sustainable in global markets, as we have seen earlier. Favorable factors that helped other countries and that Portugal lacked included large markets, abundant capital properly allocated, and technical and scientific know-how. However, the comparison between Portugal and other small European countries that enjoyed greater success in the last quarter of the century should not be taken too far, as the latter were closer to core countries and had relevant differences in terms of ecological conditions, culture, transmission of ideas and experience, investors, and capital.

The higher levels of income and the rents provided by tariffs attract new capital into the protected sector, as agents seek the best opportunities for doing business. As capital enters sectors, competition increases and profits tend to decline. If the entry of capital was limited by institutional constraints, investors would probably be willing to pay a premium in order to get into the sector, because the added expenses would be offset by the higher profits, which then become reduced in effective terms. As a result, in the medium term, that is, a period of time sufficient to attract new investment, protected sectors will tend to show profits on a par with those in non-protected areas. This is why it makes little sense to maintain a regime of protection for a long time, as it loses its effectiveness. However, agents in the protected sectors tend to oppose reforms, not because they obtain higher real returns, but because lowering tariffs brings transition costs in the form of loss of the capital initially invested. Only a strong central government can impose the reform of a system based on the concession of privileges. In other words, it is hard to compensate the sectors that will incur the transition costs. Evidently, in Portugal political powers were unable to rise to that challenge, even though it would have been in their interest to do so. The ability to control public expenditure and reduce the deficit and debt was certainly one of the greatest challenges of the Portuguese governments of the liberal era.

### Financial liberalism

The financial needs of the Portuguese state grew considerably throughout the eighteenth century, but were seriously worsened during the wars with

France at the end of the century. The debts thus accumulated were to be solved during the new liberal regime and to a large extent marked its course (Silveira 1987: 511). As a consequence of war expenditures, the government of Queen Mary issued in 1796 Portugal's first public loan, at the amount of 4,000 million *réis* and, in that same year, the Church ceased to be exempt from the income tax of 10 percent or *decima*.[39] Data on public accounts for the period before 1846 is, however, scanty and not fully comparable. Moreover, this was a period of large price fluctuations, which renders the analysis of the series in constant price terms more difficult. Table 5.10 gathers the available information on public revenue, expenditures, and debt, as well as on price indices, from which some conclusions can be drawn. First, we may gauge the extent to which the period of war in the late eighteenth and early nineteenth centuries was accompanied by a sharp rise in expenditure, but also a considerable drop in public revenue. The first effect was felt with the direct cost of fielding the troops, the second with the high costs resulting from the disruptions to the economy and public administration, in which the tax base shrank and tax collection, itself, was interrupted. Military spending as a percentage of public expenditure rose from 56 percent in 1800 to 70 percent in the following year. The return to peace in 1802 allowed the military spending to level off, along with total public spending.

The war triggered the state's second round of public borrowing. Public accounts data for the following years are limited to data on state revenue for just a few years, and it is thus impossible to be certain about the financial impact of the French invasions. Still, the information we have for public revenue reveals a sharp fall during the decade if we look at deflated values. Public revenue was also directly affected by the end of the Portuguese-Brazilian Empire, reflecting the weight of taxation on commerce with the Empire on the whole. Between 1796–1806 and 1816–1822, customs duties collected from Brazilian trade fell by 200 million *réis* (in 1827 prices), and between 1816–1822 and 1827 they fell less than 100 million *réis*, about 10 percent over this entire period of almost a quarter of a century (Pedreira 1994: 364). Clearly, the rise of public debt and deficit came mainly from the participation in the French wars and the consequent "plunging income from agriculture, industry, and commerce" (Capela 1993: 239). An example of the weight of war expenses can be seen in the levy of the extraordinary war tax in February 1808, which raised the huge sum of 2,936 million *réis*. The state's total revenue in the years leading up to the French invasions were only 5,000–7,000 million *réis* per year, while Table 5.10 shows

---

[39] See Chapter 3. See also Martins 1988b: 28–29.

Table 5.10 *State revenues and expenditures, 1800–1846 (million* réis*)*

|  | Expenditure | Revenue | Deficit | Expenditure | Revenue | Deficit |  |
|------|-------------|---------|---------|-------------|---------|---------|------------|
|  | Current prices | | | 1863/1867 prices | | | Price index |
| 1800 | 11,967 | 10,627 | 1,340 | 8,236 | 7,314 | 922 | 145.3 |
| 1801 | 13,011 | 9,859 | 3,152 | 7,958 | 6,030 | 1,928 | 163.5 |
| 1802 | 10,082 | 9,511 | 571 | 6,329 | 5,970 | 358 | 159.3 |
| 1804 |  | 11,045 |  |  | 6,805 |  | 162.3 |
| 1805 |  | 11,200 |  |  | 7,170 |  | 156.8 |
| 1810 |  | [8,500] |  |  | 4,665 |  | 182.2 |
| 1811 |  | [11,000] |  |  | 5,419 |  | 203.0 |
| 1812 | 8,018 | 8,121 | −103 | 4,341 | 4,397 | −56 | 184.7 |
| 1817 | 11,533 | 10,436 | 1,097 | 9,219 | 8,342 | 877 | 125.1 |
| 1820 | 8,519 | 7,873 | 646 | 12,927 | 11,951 | 976 | 65.9 |
| 1821 | 7,038 | 6,820 | 218 | 10,615 | 10,287 | 329 | 66.3 |
| 1822 |  |  | 1,607 |  |  | 2,090 | 76.9 |
| 1827 | 8,996 | 6,600 | 2,396 | 11,578 | 8,494 | 3,084 | 77.7 |
| 1828 | 14,899 | 11,030 | 3,869 | 21,750 | 16,102 | 5,648 | 68.5 |
| 1835 | 12,744 | 9,902 | 2,842 | 15,171 | 11,788 | 3,383 | 84.0 |
| 1836 | 13,077 | 9,491 | 3,586 | 15,928 | 11,560 | 4,368 | 82.1 |
| 1837 | 11,271 | 9,294 | 1,977 | 17,077 | 14,082 | 2,995 | 66.0 |
| 1838 | 11,845 | 9,693 | 2,152 | 19,546 | 15,995 | 3,551 | 60.6 |
| 1839 | 11,128 | 9,693 | 1,435 | 16,810 | 14,642 | 2,168 | 66.2 |
| 1840 | 11,327 | 9,916 | 1,411 | 15,820 | 13,849 | 1,971 | 71.6 |
| 1841 | 10,511 | 9,381 | 1,130 | 14,185 | 12,660 | 1,525 | 74.1 |
| 1842 |  |  |  |  |  |  | 68.8 |
| 1843 |  |  |  |  |  |  | 62.4 |
| 1844 | 11,064 | 9,224 | 1,840 | 20,007 | 16,680 | 3,327 | 55.3 |
| 1845 |  |  |  |  |  |  | 51.9 |
| 1846 | 10,805 | 9,400 | 1,405 | 17,260 | 15,016 | 2,244 | 62.6 |

*Sources:* Silveira 1987: 527; Reis 1996: 37; for prices: Godinho 1955: 81–85 (cereals only); Justino 1988–1989, vol. II: 14; Macedo 1982: 209 (for 1804); Marques 1973, vol. II: 24 (for 1805); Hespanha 1993: 224 (for 1810 and 1811); Marques 1981: 536–537 (for 1820 and 1822).

revenue in the range of 8,200–11,000 million *réis* for the years 1810–1812. Thus, that extraordinary tax raised the state's revenue by a proportion of somewhere between a quarter and a half, which was an exceptional effort on the part of taxpayers. The largest part of the war tax came from the sale of the Church's gold and silver, *c.* 1,330 million *réis*. From the commanderies (*comendas*) of the military orders 374 million *réis* were collected, and the remainder was obtained from "commerce" (619 million *réis*) and the administrators of the *décimas* in Lisbon and the provinces (464 million *réis*) (Capela 1993: 237–238).

The available information on expenditure is even scarcer, but we may surmise an evolution that parallels what we see for revenue. In 1812, the year immediately after the French invasions, public accounts had reached a real value much lower than where they had stood a decade earlier. This was due essentially to the fact that the Portuguese currency had not been devalued. But aside from this, in this same year the state had nearly managed to balance its financial affairs, and carried a budget that was only slightly negative. Still, military expenses made up 78 percent of all public spending, rising from 60 percent in 1802. With such a substantial reduction in spending, in real terms, along with the rise in the amount spent with the armed forces, it is natural that spending in other sectors fell. Regarding public finances, the period of the Napoleonic Wars compares well to the years that followed, and from the period 1812–1817 onwards public spending more than doubled, in real terms (see Table 5.10). Revenue also climbed considerably, but proportionately less, and as a result, in 1817, when Gomes Freire conspired against Beresford, public spending, including expenditure on the armed forces, increased considerably, as did the deficit. Until 1820 revenue and expenditure continued to rise, but the deficit more or less flattened out, and then dropped in the following year.

Between 1821 and 1822 the public deficit returned and lasted through most of the rest of the century. The state Budget had to be presented annually to the *Cortes* which was a relevant institutional change that led to changes in public accounting methods. According to the scarce data that is available, the negative balance for public finances increased to *c.* 2,000 million *réis* in 1822 and the deficit continued to worsen until 1827, standing at about a third of total revenue in that year. These years saw considerable political unrest due to two successive counter-revolutionary coups, and in the 1827–1829 period the deficit peaked at outstanding levels. If the public deficit is a good reflection of the general performance of Portugal's economic affairs, we must conclude that matters were even worse in the wake of the 1820 revolution than during the French invasions. In other words, the loss of public revenue stemming from the end of the trade monopoly with Brazil and the war, along with the soaring military spending, had less grievous consequences than the disruptions that came with the regime change in 1820 and the subsequent political upheavals. Naturally, the budget is vulnerable to a shifting political scene, in light of the government's control of the purse strings and the spending agenda pursued. There is better information about public accounts for the years following the civil war that shows that public finances in the early years of Maria II's liberal government were in a very sorry state of affairs. This was mostly due to the debt accumulated during the war. But the government took no visible steps to control the deficit, allowing it to fester and grow even worse, reaching 4,368 million *réis* in 1836, whereupon it dropped to 3,551 million *réis* in 1838, and still further for a while, but then climbed again during the governments of Costa Cabral. The deficit registered after 1835 was not due wholly to the civil war. Part of the problem resided in the fact that the state maintained a large standing army to please the supporters of the liberal cause. In addition, as mentioned earlier, there were sporadic moments of improvement in public finances after 1838, when the Portuguese state regained a measure of credibility in international markets, which recovered from the French wars.[40]

In fact, this was a period of greater ease in securing foreign loans, and because of that, the state's financial problems lost some of their urgency. Portugal's credibility in international financial markets was aided by its return to internal political tranquility, which lasted throughout the 1830s. This was also precisely the decade witnessing a return to normality of international financial markets, which was probably not a coincidence. Nevertheless, the problem of financing the Portuguese state's undertakings did not disappear. The persistent troubles called for substantive institutional changes, notably with the structure of taxation, and in particular, the levy of direct taxes, which probably did not keep up with the recovery of personal income and economic upturn that followed the return of peace. The late adoption of tax reform may well have served as a stumbling block to further economic development. An alternative interpretation is that the tardiness of reform was a result of the fact that economic development proceeded faster than what the country was used to, and efforts to instill a new legal framework could not stay abreast of the rapid change. Either way, the deteriorating public finances should not be seen as an indicator of a deteriorating economy. As we shall see later, the Portuguese economy may have managed to recover rather rapidly from the consequences of the civil war.

The country's financial distress would remain a thorn in the side of successive governments for the rest of the nineteenth century, and is recorded in the chronic deficits and steadily burgeoning debt. This drove public policy, but its true impact has been exaggerated. Aside from plaguing the state's administrators, neither the deficit nor the debt necessarily caused a bad economic situation. The most important consequences of budgetary indiscipline were to keep an upward pressure on prices and interest rates, and, in fact, Portugal saw no significant inflation after 1835, and interest rates, although higher than in the more advanced

[40] Silveira 1987; Reis 1996: 25.

countries of Europe, were not really too high. This view is justified insofar as the role of the state while being the principal debtor in the country's financial markets did not necessarily overlap with private investment. There are cases in which bankers sought even greater borrowing on the part of the state, as only this could serve as an outlet for a portion of savings. The main reason to infer that neither the deficit nor the debt was the root of economic distress is that this was the mechanism that brought foreign capital into the country throughout most of the nineteenth century. Moreover, the most difficult foreign borrowing was obtained by private entities, or at least without resorting to any state guarantees, similarly to what we see in the rest of Europe.

In broad terms, public expenditure of the Portuguese state, relative to GNP, was not excessive when compared to other European countries. What happened is that the "modernization" of the country had costs, and it was easier for the state to pick up the bill. The greatest problem with regard to balancing the books sprang from the struggle to raise taxes and to stretch their revenue far enough to cover expenses. Tax hikes demanded a series of instruments that the public administration was still lacking, and that only came into being, through considerable effort, later in the nineteenth century. Examining the creation of these instruments is the best way to grasp the extent of the problem. Meddling in the form of taxation provoked an outcry from citizens, but such tampering was justified in some cases, like in the case of civil war, as we see with the *Patuleia* uprising (1846–1847). This introduced a fundamental contradiction in the affairs of the nation, which was to separate economic modernization from administrative modernization. The deficit and public debt were consequences of this "marching out of step," but were perhaps preferable to the alternative, which was to oppose them. Policy reforms aimed at restructuring the state budget were naturally affected by dissension among the various political interests that emerged victorious from the civil war of 1832–1834.[41]

### Public debt and the banking system

Along these same lines, some institutions were entrusted with holding funds belonging to the state. It was in this context that the Bank of Lisbon came into being in 1821, marking the beginning of the banking system of Portuguese liberalism. This was followed in 1846 with the transformation of that bank into the Bank of Portugal, and a host of dealings related to the issue of coinage and paper money, and tobacco contracts.[42] Among the

---

[41] Mata 1993, 2005; Esteves 2003.    [42] Lains 2002 and the bibliography cited therein.

main privileges granted by the state to the Bank of Lisbon were the rights to accept deposits, make loans, discount letters of credit and other paper instruments, and, most importantly, a monopoly on the emission of paper money backed by the state treasury.[43] In return for these privileges, the bank had the duty to amortize the paper money issued by the state in 1796. Paper money was formally terminated by decree from July 23, 1834, but it continued in circulation. Full redemption never occurred, and in 1850 a Special Amortization Fund was created for the purpose.[44] Paying down this loan had been, until then, under the supervision of an Interest Committee (*Junta de Juros*), and this shift of responsibility for a part of the public debt was the first step in a series of similar transfers away from the state and into the hands of the private sector. It is also against this backdrop that we see the creation of the Board of Public Credit (*Junta de Crédito Público*) in 1837. While this body was not really an element of the government or state, it was charged with ensuring the availability of funds for paying interest or amortizing public debt, which is to say, with servicing the debt. Some years later the Caixa Geral de Depósitos (the state-owned savings bank) would be created – the first central institution accepting deposits from private citizens.

The state's option to borrow from the private sector called for a clearer definition of its prerogatives in matters of public monies. To this end, the 1822 Constitution prescribed that the allocation of public revenue had to be approved by the government and the *Cortes*, and that the settlement of state obligations required the signature of the Public Treasurer (*secretário de Estado da Fazenda*). It further stipulated that the collection of public revenue be centralized in the Public Treasury, and that these funds be supervised by duly appointed auditors (*Contadorias do Tesouro*). The Constitution also ordered governments to apply its own revenue when incurring any new public debt (Martins 1988b: 40–41). The 1822 Constitution thus gave the state sufficient power to control the financial institutions to which it entrusted public monies. The decades following the creation of the Bank of Lisbon were marked, as a result, by the relation between the state and the financial interests of the bank's shareholders. Despite the power of money, history tells us that in the first half of the nineteenth century the state kept the upper hand.

The *Maria da Fonte* uprising in April 1846 and the civil war that ensued which lasted for more than a year led to upheavals that once again had consequences on the state's finances.[45] The insecurity triggered distrust regarding the paper money in circulation and an immediate run on the

---

[43] Reis 1996: 78; Lains 2002.
[44] Marques 1973. See also Costa 1992 and Justino 1994.     [45] Reis 1996; Capela 1997.

Bank of Lisbon, realizing the fears of the bank's administrators, although it must be said that the political crisis was not the only source of financial straits facing the bank (Reis 1996: 179). In addition to this, there had already been signs of trouble as early as late September 1845, when the government had been unable to meet its scheduled payment of 800 million *réis* to the Companhia Confiança Nacional, a leading financial syndicate founded a year earlier. In order to obtain an extension on this payment, the government had turned over shares of public debt that were due precisely in the first semester of 1846. That company had accepted the shares in good faith as a guarantee that carried more weight than the contract they had with the government, but it forced the company to cover the *décima* (income tax) and various other taxes involved in paying off the loan it had made to the state.

Due to the political turmoil and its inability to keep its promises, in May 1846 the government decreed a three-month suspension of redemption on Bank of Lisbon paper currency and on payment of the promissory notes of the Companhia Confiança Nacional. This suspension was later extended on two occasions. All this forced the government to recognize its responsibilities and the difficulties resulting from the creation of those two institutions. In effect, the state had increased its debt burden and was far in arrears in its servicing of that debt. On June 8, 1846, the payment due date for the shares held by the Companhia Confiança Nacional, the government of the duke of Palmela circulated an ordinance to the Bank of Lisbon and other financial institutions asking for their help in paying the expenses of the public service. The state's financial distress was back and brought a new era of state investment dependency on foreign and domestic private sources of money.

In Portugal, as elsewhere in Europe, enlarging the state's functions was one of the cornerstones of liberalism in the nineteenth century.[46] Despite the large gap vis-à-vis the core countries, the Portuguese state made relevant contributions to the transformation of the economy, although that implied a soar in public debt. In fact, the state largely invested in infrastructure, such as roads, railways, ports, utilities, communications, schools, and other social institutions. Portugal's low starting level of development was visible in the lack of infrastructure. The only decent road in the 1850s was the one that connected the two main cities, Lisbon and Porto, leaving the rest of the country nearly isolated. There were no canals worthy of mention, and the only large port was in Lisbon, which made it cumbersome for merchants to travel and to trade by sea. The level of illiteracy in the mid-century was close to 90 percent, as there were few

---

[46] Cardoso and Lains 2010; Mata 1988; Pedreira 1993; Reis 1993.

private schools and no state school system. Thus, in order to face these challenges, it was necessary to rely to a great extent on revenue from taxes on property, business transactions, and certain types of income, as well as borrowing from the private sector, whether from banking syndicates or through the sale of various public debt securities, both in Portugal and abroad. Against the largest of these loans, the state authorized the issue of paper under regimes of both competition and monopoly, or negotiated other contracts regarding certain commercial monopolies. These concessions were mechanisms by which the state effectively underwrote the debt involved. Still another means by which the state guaranteed the payment of these several instruments was through the creation of banks, namely the Companhia Confiança Nacional and Bank of Lisbon (which later would become Bank of Portugal), that received an agreed amount of income in return for servicing the interest payments on a determined part of the public debt, or for amortizing it altogether (Mata 2008).

After these decades of financial unrest, the *Regeneração* uprising of 1851 was followed by a considerable effort to put the state's finances back onto an even keel. These were in large measure the toils of Fontes Pereira de Melo. In the end, balancing the books meant adhering to the gold standard, in 1854. Aside from this, there were a number of other important steps: the regulation of public audits (1863), which centralized and unified the state's accounting system; the founding (1864) of the Banco Nacional Ultramarino (National Overseas Bank) and the Companhia Geral do Crédito Predial Português (Portuguese Building Credit Company), providing mortgages based on the sale of debentures. In 1867, the new legislation for joint-stock companies allowed firms to be chartered without prior government approval, and this was another sign of liberalization of the economic and financial systems. In that same year a new Civil Code was introduced, providing the framework of a modern society, in contrast with that inherited from the *Ancién Régime*. But social problems were still ahead and in the very next year a popular revolt arose. All of these reforms came to a halt in early 1868 with the *Janeirinha* revolt opposed to a sweeping tax reform that ultimately was not implemented. From then on, financial reforms were frozen. Still, the forward strides of the financial market from 1870 onwards engendered substantial changes in the institutional functioning of banking and other financial services in Portugal. From 1870 up to mid 1876, the Portuguese banking system enjoyed a period of fast growth, and saw the creation of many banks, including Caixa Geral de Depósitos, a public bank that collected the deposits of public administration. This period was, however, interrupted by a short but deep financial crisis due to a bank run provoked by a sharp depreciation of Spanish bonds held by Portuguese citizens (Mata 1993: 35–37).

The banking crisis that triggered the moratorium on payments of August 18, 1876, was a great setback for banking in Portugal, and called for state intervention. Thus, treasury bonds turned out to be one of the best investments available on the market. Between 10th and 16th August 1876, three banks in the North (in Porto, Viana do Castelo, and Braga) suspended payment on their notes. On the 18th the Banco Lusitano de Lisboa followed suit. There followed a run on the Bank of Portugal, which was unable to redeem in metal all of the paper currency in circulation immediately. This was due in large part to the fact that it had sent much of its gold reserves to the banks in the North, through its affiliate in Porto. The government stepped in and declared a general moratorium on the redemption of paper currency across the nation. A few days later, on the 28th of August, the Bank of Portugal was in a position to redeem its paper, and the government of Fontes arranged the necessary funds from foreign lenders to cover the country's bank debts, paying in gold the debts that were attached, essentially, to the inactive contracts realized with a banking consortium in 1872, and for a few other matters. This operation was carried out with the collaboration of the Bank of Portugal, acting as the lender of last resort – a function that it would be called upon to exercise time and again in the near future. The relative speed with which Porto's banks recovered was due to the Bank of Portugal's abundant gold reserves. The favorable foreign trade balance afforded by the bank's considerable reserves also impacted the public debt situation, which enjoyed a period of respite, without needing to turn so frequently to short-term borrowing to meet its obligations.

The 1876 banking crisis did not take a serious toll on the rest of the economy, because in Portugal only a fraction of production (in agriculture, industry, and foreign trade) depended on lending from banks or national lending institutions. In light of the country's financial conditions and the weak links between banking and agriculture (and business, in general), natural in a country where financial services were still embryonic, we should not be surprised by the statement, that "not in politics, commerce, shipping, industry, nor in agriculture was there any great shock [as a result of the banking crisis]." The events of 1876 *did* reveal that the banking system needed greater regulation, and as would be vehemently argued in the coming years, the Bank of Portugal should have a monopoly on issuing paper money for the entire country, and not only for Lisbon, as it had had until then (Martins 1954: 50).

### Debt, crisis, and recovery

Following thirty years of rule of the *regeneradores* in Portuguese government, in 1886, the political left took power for the next four years and new priorities were set. The new government formed by the *Partido Progressista* had as finance minister Mariano de Carvalho, who showed from the outset that he wanted to change the financial system instituted by the right. Presenting his first state budget in Parliament in the beginning of 1887, the minister outlined an ambitious plan that implied sweeping reforms of the three institutions controlling the main sources of state revenue. First, he wanted to replace import duties on tobacco, the single largest item of state revenue, by reinstating a state monopoly. Second, Carvalho aimed at increasing the government's control over the Bank of Portugal, the largest joint-stock bank, which had the monopoly of issuing notes in Lisbon. Third, the Junta do Crédito Público, the committee that issued state bonds and made the payments to the public, was to be stripped of its supervisory functions, perceived as making it too independent from the government, and the supervision of the public debt was made directly the responsibility of the Ministry of Finance. Carvalho had his sights set on changing three of the more important pillars of the financial system built by the *regeneradores* across several decades. In order to fund the creation of the state monopoly over tobacco, the finance minister had to seek parliamentary authorization for a public loan of up to 7,200 million *réis*. The lower chamber of parliament, in which the government had a majority vote, approved this operation in May 1888. The total cost of indemnities paid by the government for the expropriation of the tobacco companies was slightly below the limit for the loan granted by Parliament but they nevertheless reached the astonishing sum of 6,333 million *réis*.[47] This suggested the doubling of the government deficit to 11,526 million *réis* in the fiscal year 1888–1889 (see Figures 5.2 and 5.3). This one budgetary heading increased to account for 23 percent of total state expenditure; and because the loan was not offset by any increase in state revenue, the public deficit increased from 6,887 to 11,998 million *réis* (Mata 1993: 53–54, 157–159, 189, 218). This was the true cost of the change of direction initiated by the new *progressista* government. Carvalho was able to go ahead with his plan because his ultimate purpose was to use the revenue from the state monopoly to fund public debt.

Mariano de Carvalho's revolutionary plans were ambitious but were met with little opposition from the *Regeneradores* because there was some consensus about the need to increase state control of financial institutions dealing with public debt and monopolies – at least that is what we can infer from the fact that Carvalho's reforms were not

[47] Mata 1993: 157–159, 218; Ramos 1994.

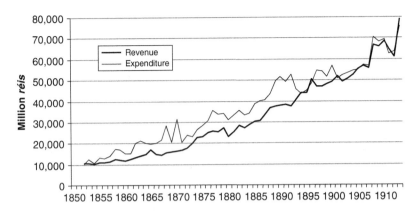

Figure 5.2  Government revenue and expenditure, 1852–1913
Source: Lains 2008b: 490.

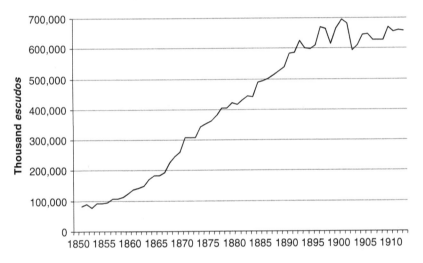

Figure 5.3  Public debt, 1851–1913
Source: Lains 2008b: 491.

reversed when the *regeneradores* regained full control of the government ten years later. In early 1887, the three 3 percent bonds were quoted at a historic high of 82.6 percent (implying a real interest rate of 3.63 percent); in September of the previous year, the issue price was 69.6 percent (a real interest rate of 4.31 percent). The average

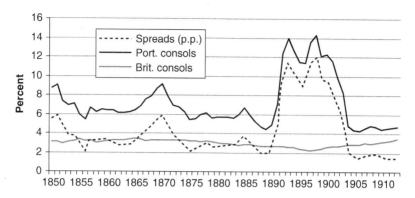

Figure 5.4 Yields of British and Portuguese consoles, 1850–1913
Source: Lains 2008b: 492.

interest for public debt in the secondary market, in 1880–1889, was 5 percent (domestic) and 5.6 percent (foreign), as compared to 3 percent for British consoles. The difference between these rates is a measure of the premium on Portuguese public debt, which had been declining since 1854–1859 from a maximum of 3.7 percent in the 1850s (for both domestic and foreign debt). According to an estimate, in the primary market the interest rate deviated substantially from that of the secondary market in 1890–1899, reaching 11.9 percent (domestic) and 9.3 percent (foreign). The two markets converged thereafter. The domestic premium reached a minimum in 1900–1910 at 2.5 percent, whereas the foreign premium, given by the exchange risk after Portugal left the gold standard in 1891, was estimated at 3 percent (Esteves 2003). The spread between the Portuguese and the British consoles declined from its 1885 peak of 3.78 to 2.28 percent in 1887 (see Figure 5.4). Moreover, between the fiscal years of 1885–1886 and 1886–1887, the state's effective revenue increased by 10 percent, while the deficit decreased by 25 percent, from around 9,400 to 7,100 million *réis* (see Figure 5.2). The markets reacted positively to the reforms and there was an improvement in the state's credit rating and the reasonable quotation for its funds. Between 1886 and 1889, the average price of Portuguese bonds in the secondary market in London increased by 33 percent and in Lisbon by 29 percent.[48] The spread of Portuguese consoles reached a historical low of 1.83 percent in 1889 (see Figure 5.4).

[48] Esteves 2003; Mata 1993.

The Portuguese finance minister did not have the time to raise the funds needed to carry out his plan on the tobacco monopoly, as he was ousted from government in November 1889, following a financial scandal, and the entire government fell shortly thereafter. Carvalho exceeded his powers as finance minister and promised to provide financial assistance to a bankers' syndicate, without consulting the prime minister and leader of his party, Luciano de Castro. The syndicate had been formed in 1881 with the aim of providing the city of Porto with a direct link to the Spanish rail network through Salamanca (Pinheiro 1987). The government collapsed because of the ambition of the minister of foreign affairs, Barros Gomes. He had provoked the British government by publishing the "rose-colored map" with the Portuguese southern African colonies carved out from coast to coast, including the area that would became Rhodesia, and moving troops accordingly. This triggered an ultimatum from the British government in January 1890, which provoked outrage in Portugal, leading to the fall from power of the *Partido Progressista* and, ultimately, to a decade-long interruption of the bipartisan system that had governed the country since 1870. The fall of the *progressista* cabinet was followed by a period of increasing political instability, marked by high levels of unrest in the streets against not only the two main parties, but also against the monarchy, led by the emerging republican forces.

### The 1891 crisis

At the height of political instability, a financial crisis emerged in 1891, when the Bank of Portugal's reserves declined to a point that it ceased to provide the market with the exchange that was requested, which "came from the export of produce, from Brazilian remittances and from funds that the Treasury had obtained abroad through the realization of credit operations." According to one account, "[b]y the end of April [1890], the Bank had only managed to purchase £1,564,384 [7,040 million *réis*] while it had sold £2,664,114 [11,989 million *réis*]. Additionally, the foreign loans obtained by the Bank had declined by 2,000 million *réis*". Accordingly, there was an excess demand for gold amounting to 6,949 million *réis*, consisting of the 2,000 million *réis* reduction in the Bank of Portugal's credit ceiling abroad and the deficit of 4,949 million *réis* between the value of the gold that the Bank had provided to the market and the value that it had managed to purchase (Reis 2007). In order to balance external accounts, and in the absence of any other means of foreign payment, it became necessary to export gold. A country that, thanks to exports, to emigrant remittances, and to foreign credit, had traditionally been a receiver of gold coins was now forced to export 21,535 million *réis* worth of gold. This was a considerable proportion of the country's monetary circulation (Reis 1991). Suspension occurred because the state suffered a liquidity crunch in the spring of 1891 and had to ask the Bank of Portugal to issue notes in order to be able to lend it fresh funds. Since the Bank was unable to acquire additional gold with which to back these notes, it had to suspend payments in gold until the state paid back its debts – which never happened.

In November 1890, the finance minister attempted, unsuccessfully, to raise a loan with foreign creditors in order to pay for the coupon that was due in that date. In the meantime, the London stock market had been shaken by the problems facing the Baring Brothers' Bank, whose business was mainly with Latin American countries: it was also the Portuguese state's main banker in the City. It was at this point that the Count of Burnay, the financier whom Mariano de Carvalho opposed, offered a "temporary loan" of 13,500 million *réis*, negotiated with the *Comptoir d'Escompte* and based on the mortgage of the revenue from the state's tobacco monopoly. This was not fresh money, however, as it implied the reallocation to the *Comptoir d'Escompte* of Burnay's credits with the Portuguese state, as well as the revenues from the tobacco monopoly which belonged already to the state.[49] It should be added that this sort of financial operation was typical of the time. The tobacco contract was finally signed in February 1891 but the finance minister did not seek the necessary approval from the Parliament, and it also did not have political support from the two main political parties. The main reason for the opposition to the new contract was the fact that the majority of the members of the monopoly's administrative body were foreigners. Even so, the contract was approved by law on March 23, 1891. With some difficulty, the new government managed to pay the interest on the external debt in 1891. The state's receipts from the new tobacco contract rose to 5,011 million *réis* in 1891–1892, which represented a substantial increase relative to the customs revenues of the last year of the free trade regime, during which the tobacco duty collected by customs amounted to just 2,829 million *réis*. But the state's total revenue remained unchanged because other income declined by roughly the same amount (Mata 1993: 136). As a result, in May 1891 the government accepted the need to suspend the currency's convertibility for a period of sixty days.

Mariano de Carvalho was reinstated as finance minister and his first act was to present to Parliament in June 1891 a series of wide-ranging reforms, as many had attempted before him. The reforms included,

[49] On Burnay, see Mata 2010.

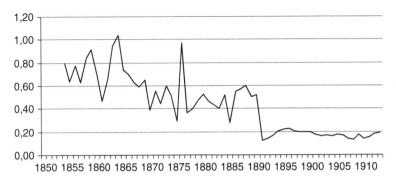

Figure 5.5  Bank of Portugal gold reserves/circulation, 1854–1913
Source: Lains 2008b: 499.

among many aspects, a revision of the contract with the Bank of Portugal, in order to introduce silver coins, and thus a bimetallic standard, and the reintroduction of a monopoly in the alcohol industry. The plan was defeated in Parliament by an odd, cross-party alliance. But the proposed reforms served to mask more serious measures, which, since they did not need parliamentary approval, Carvalho carried out anyway. On July 9, 1891, he signed a decree extending the suspension of the currency's convertibility, introduced as a temporary measure two months earlier. This same decree confirmed the Bank of Portugal as the country's only issuing bank, and granted it the right to replace the Porto banks' notes with its own. Portugal's abandonment of the gold standard opened the way for the state to finance itself through the issuing of banknotes. Of all the measures to solve the crisis that Carvalho had at his disposal, this was probably the one that had the fewest domestic and external implications. His overriding objective was to halt the steady decline in the Bank of Portugal's gold reserves (see Figure 5.5). In December 1891, a new statute increased the fiduciary circulation limit to 38,000 million *réis*, which could be raised further by reinforcing the Bank's capital reserves. The statute also increased the government's Bank of Portugal current account credit limit from 2,000 million to 6,000 million *réis* for the financial year 1891–1892. The change made to the regulation of the Bank in 1887 was now having an effect.

But the powerful minister's time was running out and he was to be soon replaced by Oliveira Martins, an independent intellectual that had long criticized the financial policy of the two main parties, paving the way for a more radical solution to the financial crisis. Once again, the main challenge that the new minister faced was how to service the state's domestic and foreign debts, but the path that he chose was not the only one available to him, nor was it necessarily the best (Ramos 1994: 203–208). The finance minister had spent several years contesting what he described as the *regenerador* or *fontista* policy, which involved maintaining unbalanced state budgets that were financed through the public debt. According to him, this policy had failed to create the necessary internal wealth, but it did serve to make bankers and government officials wealthier. Now that he was finance minister, Martins saw the opportunity to introduce changes. His remedy was to increase taxes to balance the state's accounts, rather than resorting to further debt issues. At the beginning of 1892, he put this plan into action by addressing the only immediately accessible and secure source of taxation: the earnings of public debt bonds. It was a highly unpopular move that no one had previously dared to venture, and it delivered a profound blow to the Portuguese financial system, changing rules that had been considered sacrosanct for almost forty years. With this measure, the state's credit rating suffered, both inside the country and abroad, as did the monetary circulation, the banking system, and thousands of individuals whose savings were held in debt bonds, purchased in the Junta do Crédito Público and in public treasury bonds acquired in the Lisbon stock exchange.

The government's margin for maneuver was not large, but there was still some flexibility. Although the tobacco monopoly's earnings had already been allocated, the state still had some secure sources of income that could be used to guarantee loans. Still available, too, was the revenue from import duties, which were used by Hintze Ribeiro's *regenerador* government in 1902 as a means to restore financial stability (Esteves 2003). Despite all the difficulties, the Portuguese state was still able to oppose more direct control of government accounts by representatives of foreign bondholders, unlike Greece some years later. In Portugal's favor was not the fact that it had a higher degree of solvency than Greece, but that the international political scene was advantageous. Oliveira Martins reported to Parliament that the state had large amounts of credit at its disposal, from banks and other companies – credit that had been granted to assist these institutions in previous periods of crisis. Unlike in 1876, however, in 1891 the state was forced to seek assistance from the Bank of Portugal, using legal means to pay and increase fiduciary circulation.

To worsen an already difficult situation, the loan, which had been anticipated during the tobacco contract negotiated with Henry Burnay in February 1891, had failed to fully materialize, as the markets no longer wished to lend to the Portuguese state on the terms that it was able to offer. Unwilling to recoup its credits and guarantees, and unable to resort to domestic or foreign credit, the only alternative left to the minister of finance was to increase the state's revenue. In order to do so, Martins proposed to revive a 1880 law, which would increase the tax on the earnings of civil servants, including those employed by corporations and charities, whether or not they were subsidized by the state, from 3 to 10 percent. He also proposed to increase the tax on earnings from internal debt bonds, and all the various types of credit titles, from 3 to 30 percent. Finally, he suggested a pact with the foreign creditors. The 10,000 million *réis* deficit was thus resolved through this single set of measures. Apparently, Martins preferred to default, albeit only partially, on the domestic debt and to negotiate with creditors afterwards.

In Parliament, the minister proposed that there should be no interference in the interest rates payable on the external debt, and that interest on the internal debt should not be taxed at more than 10 percent. He believed that it was possible to balance the budget by "fixing the debt at a convenient level and seeking other, fairer taxes with greater coverage." Reducing public debt was not an absolute priority. He felt it was more important to ensure that the sacrifices that were being imposed on the population to fight the financial crisis affecting the country were fair. Martins' proposal to tax the interest earned on foreign debt bonds would undermine the state's ability to obtain new foreign loans. This was an opinion that was shared by other members of Parliament, and was eventually supported by the Parliament's finance committee. Oliveira Martins' budget was approved by the chamber on February 13, 1892, and passed on to the finance committee. Two days later, it was returned to the chamber in the form of a parliamentary bill. The finance committee had limited the 30 percent tax to earnings from interest over internal public debt, exempting earnings from foreign debt from taxation and leaving all other national bonds subject to a 10 percent tax on interest earnings. With this important change, the minister's bill was accepted by the members of both major parties and passed into law on February 26, 1892. The only three republican representatives in Parliament voted against it.

The prime minister, José Dias Ferreira, however, wanted to go even further, and Oliveira Martins left the government in disagreement. In late May 1892, Ferreira managed to obtain the complete agreement of Parliament's finance committee, controlled by the *regeneradores*, which had been denied to Oliveira Martins. On June 13, 1892, he decreed that interest payments on foreign debt paid in gold should be reduced to one-third, with the remainder being paid in Bank of Portugal notes after the deduction of the 30 percent tax that had been applicable to all interest earnings paid in Portugal since February 1892. These combined measures reduced the nominal interest paid to foreign bondholders from 3 to 1 percent. Unlike Martins, Ferreira made no reference to the rights of foreign creditors – Martins had attempted to reach an agreement over the part of their interest payments that was now to be paid in Portuguese currency. The reaction in Paris was negative, particularly as foreign creditors (who saw their interest rates reduced by 66 percent) were more affected than domestic creditors (who suffered only a 30 percent reduction), even though they managed to be paid in gold. The impact of Dias Ferreira's measures was huge and the price of Portuguese bonds sold abroad fell to between 20 and 30 percent of the par value in the 1892–1902 period (Esteves 2005).

The *Regenerador* party finally returned to power in February 1893. Its leader, Serpa, was unable to lead the government and the younger Hintze Ribeiro was appointed as prime minister. An initial plan to contemplate foreign bondholders was to allocate revenue from colonial customs. However, because of the extreme sensitivity of the public in matters concerning the colonies, the plan was abandoned. Instead, the new *regenerador* government had to confirm the previous decree of June 13th, that one-third of the interest payments to foreign bondholders would be made in gold; he consigned half of all customs revenue (in excess of 11,400 million *réis*, without the tax revenue from tobacco and grain), and he agreed to share any gains from the decrease in the gold premium once it had fallen to less than 22 percent. This kind of procedure was a common request from the London-based Council of Foreign Bondholders to other peripheral governments (Esteves 2005: 321). As customs revenue rose, foreign creditors received payments amounting to 2,446 million *réis*. These arrangements were not enough to fully satisfy foreign bondholders. French interests in that council wanted direct control of public revenue, including the entire customs revenue. On the other hand, German and British representatives were willing to accept a roll-over in exchange for gaining control over the Portuguese African colonies. Yet the Portuguese government did not give in and negotiations stalled for the next nine years. In 1903, an agreement was finally signed which meant that the outstanding debt was cut by 38 percent and the maturity of the remaining capital was extended to ninety-nine years at an interest of 3 percent. This was a partial victory of the Portuguese government of the time, as interest payments were substantially reduced, but access to international capital markets was virtually closed since then.

The most striking conclusion from this analysis of the 1891 financial crisis in Portugal is that at no time did the national government express serious concerns about the reaction of foreign markets to any of the measures brought in to deal with it. The decision to default on the payment of government debt to foreign bondholders in 1892 required a radicalization of political life. It began with the accession to power of the *Partido Progressista*, in 1886, and the appointment of a succession of finance ministers from the left. These ministers wanted to revise the policy that had been followed for decades by the right-wing *Partido Progressista*, and to change the way public finances were handled in Portugal. The radicalization of political life was further enhanced by the rise to power of Martins and Dias Ferreira, who had never been engaged directly in party politics and followed policies that would dramatically change the conducting of state business. When Dias Ferreira, following Oliveira Martins' initial move, decided to default on foreign bondholders, he showed no concern about the effects of such a measure on the country's capacity to raise further loans in international capital markets.

### The recovery

Although the options available to the Portuguese government in 1891 were limited, default was not the only possible course of action. In order to avoid defaulting, however, the government would have had to call in the payment of many private debts to the Bank of Portugal, to increase taxation, or to drastically reduce the money supply. These alternative means of solving the crisis would have had even more serious consequences for the economy and thus for the political stability of the country as a whole – the public was not prepared to accept a severe contraction in economic activity in order to satisfy foreign lenders. The decision to default was not uncommon among governments at the periphery of the international financial system, and the Portuguese decision was not an exceptional one. Indeed, events in Portugal during the crucial years from 1891 to 1892 demonstrate the power of a peripheral government to avoid complying with the rules of the game. The most important tool at the disposal of lenders was their ability to suspend their loans to defaulting governments. The fact that a large share of the country's trade involved Britain, Brazil, and Portugal's African colonies, whereas most foreign loans were raised in Paris and Berlin, diminished the ability of lenders to retaliate by limiting access to international trade. Portugal's experience during the 1891–1892 crisis points to the weaknesses of the international financial markets when it came to the enforcement of sovereign debt repayment. The government of a peripheral country could simply choose to default if the consequences were less harmful to domestic economic and political interests than the alternative fiscal measures.

In any event, a new era started with the crisis, as the lack of access to international capital markets and the low level of domestic savings compelled governments to rebalance the budget. The public deficit was substantially reduced and financed by issuing money, as Portugal was then out of the gold standard, and thus the Bank of Portugal could print money freely. Nevertheless, we have to take into account the fact that governments managed to keep money creation under control, despite the continuing political instability. And such control is pretty much visible in the available financial indicators that show a decline in the deficit from 1.5 percent of GDP in 1854–1891 to 0.3 percent in 1891–1914, and only small increases in money supply, inflation, and public debt (Lains 2007). The performance of the financial sector was accompanied by a relatively positive performance in the economy too, as we have seen earlier in this chapter. The rotating form of government, an understanding between the leaders of the major parties, returned and lasted until the end of the monarchy, in October 1910. The monarchy did not fall because of financial troubles, which at that moment were not terribly serious, nor was it the result of any sort of economic problem. It fell because the slow but steady growth in the standard of living of the citizenry throughout the nineteenth century was not accompanied by any improvement in political representation. The greatest promise of representation came from the Republicans – even though in time they would not deliver on that promise (Ramos, Vasconcelos, and Monteiro 2010). In any event, for the development of the Portuguese economy, what proved to be most important were the events taking place in the international economy.

The slow pace of economic growth in the decades up to 1914 went together with the slow development of institutions and infrastructures. Moreover, recent work on heights has concluded that Portugal's standard of living declined in comparison to the more developed economies in Europe, as industrialization gained momentum by mid-nineteenth century and particularly after 1870, due to low investment levels in human capital.[50] But there were some positive signs in institutional development. First, the control of the state over the territory increased significantly and was universally achieved by the eve of the War. Second, literacy rates rose in significant ways and, at the same time, mortality fell and urbanization increased. Third, the financial system became more developed and widespread. Finally, there was an important effort in building railways, roads, and other infrastructures, mainly up to the 1890s. Such developments were made possible by increasing government deficits that were financed either domestically or in the international capital markets. Such positive economic and institutional developments were nevertheless insufficient and Portugal failed to

---

[50] See Stolz, Baten, and Reis 2013.

catch up to the levels of income per capita of the front-runners. But half a century of slow but sustained growth led the Portuguese economy to a higher degree of maturity, in terms of its structure and overall productivity levels. Those changes proved to be fundamental for the response to the distresses provoked by World War I.

# 6    Patterns of convergence, 1914–2010

The main feature of the Portuguese economy in the twentieth century was both a rapid transformation and a slow but consistent catching-up to the living standards of the European forerunners. The convergence of the Portuguese income per capita and productivity levels commenced soon after the end of World War I and continued throughout the Republican regime, which lasted until 1926, in spite of the high levels of political instability. During those early years, economic growth was to a large extent linked to tariff protectionism and to direct state intervention in the economy. That process was not unique to Portugal, as it occurred in most of the poorer European periphery, where rates of economic growth increased to unprecedented levels.[1] World War II led to an inevitable halt in economic growth, but Portugal's neutrality spared the country deeper consequences and created opportunities for the expansion of a few economic sectors, namely those linked to exports. The post–World War II years were the best ever for the Portuguese economy, which saw levels of income and productivity converge faster with those recorded in Europe's most advanced countries, namely in the major industrial powers. This convergence trend was shared by most peripheral countries in Europe, regardless of their political regime, and lasted until 1973.[2] During the golden years or growth, Portugal and the rest of Europe had economic policies which tended to foster a greater opening to the outside, and a greater presence of the state in the economies. In terms of the structure of the economy, faster growth led to a swift industrialization of the country, an increase in the weight of the services sector, a decline in the importance of agriculture, and an increase in the weight of foreign trade, and higher participation of foreign capital in national investment.

---

[1] For the interwar period, see Feinstein *et al.* 1997. See also Aldcroft 2006, Broadberry and O'Rourke, eds. 2010, Di Vittorio 2002, Chapters 10–12, and Lains 2007b.
[2] For twentieth-century Portugal, see Amaral 2010, Corkill 1999, Lains 2003a, Lains and Silva, eds. 2005, vol. 3, Lopes 1996, Mateus 1998, Neves 1994 and 1996, and Rosas, ed. 1994; and for Europe, see further Crafts and Toniolo, eds. 1996 and Eichengreen 2007.

Political discontent and the colonial wars led to yet another revolution, in 1974, which immediately followed the year of the international crisis caused by the end of the Bretton Woods system and the soar in oil prices in the world markets. A period of political instability ensued, lasting until 1976 or 1977, and in this year Portugal applied to join the European Communities, which it eventually did in 1986. The first decade after joining the EEC was mostly favorable in economic terms, but problems arose from the mid 1990s onwards, as competition from Eastern Europe and changes in the global economy worsened the overall environment of economic development for Portugal. This chapter deals with the main trends of the Portuguese economy, analyzed through the angle of the international institutional framework and its effects in domestic economic policies. The role of the state expanded during the century, but increasingly so within the international institutions that Portugal joined soon after the end of World War II, which made state intervention compatible with a market economy open to outside competition.

Changes in the external conditions for Portuguese economic growth throughout the century are associated with transformations in the international and European economies. But domestic conditions for the growth of the Portuguese economy have also changed substantially. Although the consequences of changes in industrial, monetary, and fiscal policies, as well as the overall political conditions, have largely been accounted for by the literature, less attention has been paid to changes in the structure of the economy and the consequences that those changes may have had in the potential for growth. The Portuguese economy went through an intensive process of structural transformation during the two decades prior to 1973. While in 1950 Portugal was largely an agrarian economy, with about 50 percent of the population employed in the agricultural sector, by 1973 the growth of the industrial and the services sectors had substantially transformed the economy. The sheer shift of labor from agriculture to the other sectors of the economy was a source of growth, as the labor productivity in agriculture was about half that of industry and services. The potential gains in terms of growth accruing from shifts of resources to industry were thus much reduced after two decades of intense industrialization and the growth of the service sector. High levels of investment in human and physical capital were the main instruments for rapid economic growth up to 1973. The fact that Europe was expanding rapidly was also of considerable help. After 1973, however, the overall conditions for growth were less favorable, as most of the gains from structural change had already been reaped. The fact that the European economy slowed down imposed further restrictions on rapid growth. More importantly, the Portuguese economy opened up to the external world more rapidly during the last decades of the century, for which accession to the EEC in 1986 was, of course, of paramount importance. The increasing degree of openness implied that the economy had to evolve according to its pattern of comparative advantages, which led to an overall reduction in the growth of factor productivity, income per capita, and convergence to the levels of the more developed European economies. After two decades of intensive growth, the Portuguese economy was substantially altered and, despite the fact that the potential effect of structural change on economic growth eventually died out, the various forms of capital and capacities acquired in the period of rapid growth pushed the economy into a stage of growth at higher levels. This phase of higher growth came to a halt by the end of the century in a context of increasing exposure to the international economy, which is a paradox that can only be explained partially at this stage.

## The economic consequences of World War I

World War I ended the period of expansion of the world economy of the second half of the nineteenth century. The conflict involved a considerable amount of human, economic, and financial resources, and had dire consequences both at the international and national levels. In broad terms, the war was linked with the closing of borders, which eventually led to the rise of authoritarian regimes in a few European countries and in other parts of the world. Across many regions, nineteenth-century economic liberalism, which was a fact despite varying degrees of tariff protection, gave way to economic and financial protectionism and the increase of the intervention of the states in the national economies. As a result, once the war was over, the international economic environment looked very different from what it had looked like before 1914. The most important effect of protectionism was that the recovery of national economies that occurred in most countries immediately after the war was not accompanied by the recovery of international economic relations. In fact, World War I put a halt to international trade, as well as foreign investment and European and Asian emigration to the Americas, and within Europe. Change in international economic relations furthermore forced national economies to readjust in order to replace imports of raw materials and foodstuffs. In addition, the military effort of the countries directly involved in the hostilities led to an increase in production in the arms sector. In industrialized Europe, imports of certain raw materials and foodstuffs were replaced by synthetic products, which affected exporters of primary products leading to import substitution policies in the tropical areas. These structural changes hindered the return to the patterns of international trade that had prevailed throughout the nineteenth century.[3]

Aside from the change in the international division of labor brought about by the war, many European governments, including Portugal's, financed the military effort by raising the internal public debt and increasing the amount of money in circulation, as well as by taking out loans abroad. Among European countries, only Great Britain remained on a relatively firm footing financially, as its war effort had mostly been paid through the increase in taxation and domestic borrowing. This financial stability allowed Britain to extend war loans to its continental allies. Like other European allies, Portugal received loans from Britain as soon as it joined the War, in March 1916. At the end of the War, Great Britain was creditor of all of its continental allies, and a debtor of the United States. The debtor countries, facing serious financial difficulties, demanded war reparations from Germany, settled by the Versailles Treaty in 1919.[4]

From the early 1920s on, European economies regained momentum, financial stability returned slowly, and some degree of international political cooperation under the League of Nations ensued. Europe slowly returned to a monetary system, the *gold-exchange standard*, a replication of the nineteenth-century gold standard system, under which central bank reserves of member nations could be composed of gold as well as of other currencies linked to this commodity. This system, recommended by the 1922 Genoa Conference, aimed to address the scarcity of gold reserves in Europe. The new standard was first adopted in the countries hit hardest by inflation during the war, namely Germany, Austria, and Hungary, then by the new countries arising from the Treaty of Versailles, and, finally, by Western allies. The 1924 Dawes Plan restructured the payment of war reparations by Germany through the extension of American private loans to Weimar, loans that the German government could then use to repay its debts to Allied countries who had taken out loans with Great Britain (de Cecco 1995).

The key question arising from the return to the new version of the gold-exchange standard was the definition of a complex set of exchange rates for the different currencies. Because the war had influenced the value of these currencies in different ways, it was no longer possible to return to pre-1914 parities without jeopardizing the relative competitiveness of the countries involved. The countries that had remained neutral soon

---

[3] Eloranta and Harison 2010; Findlay and O'Rourke 2007, Chapter 8; Feinstein *et al.* 1997.
[4] Feinstein *et al.* 1997; See also Keynes 1995.

returned to pre-war parities, like Sweden, in 1922, the Netherlands and Switzerland, in 1924, and Denmark and Norway, in 1928. The United Kingdom, which had managed to remain on a healthy financial footing, as mentioned earlier, also returned to parity before 1926. Most of the remaining allies in the European continent, including France and Italy, adopted the gold standard between 1923 and 1926, with parities ranging from one-tenth to one-third of their pre-war value. The countries defeated in the war were the most affected by it, and Germany, Poland, Austria, and Hungary, hit by hyperinflation, chose parities that were well below 1 percent of what they had been before the war. Lastly, Portugal, Romania, Bulgaria, Greece, and Yugoslavia returned to parities between 3 and 9 percent of their pre-war values. The range of new parity alignments illustrates how hard it was to find a new equilibrium in the international exchange markets. The gold-exchange standard was thus reinstated in a context of instability, and any change in the main flows of international finance would be enough to trigger a crisis. In October 1929, the New York stock market crashed and the Great Depression followed. These events affected the outflow of financial resources to Europe, and had a particularly severe impact, as the continent was still recovering from the imbalances caused by the War. The Great Depression, which affected many parts of Europe, can therefore ultimately be seen as an extension of the financial disruptions arising from the War.[5]

### Post-war growth

Despite its peripheral position and relatively low degree of involvement, the Portuguese economy was severely affected by the Great War, particularly through its direct effects on domestic finances and the international economy. First, exports from mainland Portugal and re-exports from the colonies shrank because of the contraction in international markets. Second, there was a disruption of inward capital flows and emigrant remittances from Brazil and, eventually, the flow of emigrants to Brazil was also interrupted. Finally, imports of industrial inputs, like charcoal, as well as raw materials, manufactures, and agricultural products, like wheat, also declined significantly. The war also considerably affected the country's finances, as it was financed mostly by printing money and taking out war loans from Britain, which caused high levels of inflation and an upsurge in the external debt. Portugal had one of the highest inflation levels in Europe in the decade after the war. The political consequences of

---

[5] Feinstein *et al.*1997: 46. See for Italy's financial recovery, during the advent of Fascism, Zamagni 1993: 243–255.

Table 6.1 *Monetary and fiscal indicators for Portugal, 1854–1945*

| | GDP Deflator (annual growth %) | Exchange Rate (annual growth %) | Money Supply (annual growth %) | Total Public Debt (annual growth %) | Budget Deficit (−) / Surplus (+) (% of GDP) |
|---|---|---|---|---|---|
| 1854–1891 | 0.39 | 0.00 [(1)] | 3.23 | 5.12 | −1.5 |
| 1891–1914 | 0.92 | 0.69 | 0.68 | 0.46 | −0.3 |
| 1914–1918 | 58.81 | 8.68 | 21.37 | 11.29 | −6.8 |
| 1918–1924 | 30.84 | 60.28 | 37.68 | 41.70 | −8.7 |
| 1924–1929 | −3.33 | −4.17 | 5.20 | 3.48 | −3.3 |
| 1929–1939 | −0.10 | 1.85 | 6.21 | −2.84 | +0.9 |
| 1939–1945 | 15.22 | −1.58 | 27.77 | 5.54 | −0.9 |

[(1)]Portugal was on the gold standard from 1854 to 1891.
*Source:* Lains 2007.

the unstable economic and financial situation were particularly acute in Portugal because of the political turmoil stemming from the turbulent end of the monarchy and the transition to the Republican regime.[6]

The magnitude of the financial problems was particularly striking. Between 1914 and 1918, state expenditure nearly tripled, in nominal terms, while revenue rose by only about 50 percent, and in order to finance the increase in the deficit, public debt increased by about 50 percent. At the same time, the money supply increased twofold. The impact on inflation was dramatic, though it was protracted for two years. In fact, Portugal's rate of inflation in 1918 was not far from that of most European countries (see Table 6.1). Between 1920 and 1924, however, prices in Portugal rose almost threefold, thus considerably more than anywhere else in Europe, except in the countries struck by hyperinflation, like Finland, and most notably Germany and Austria.[7]

No other country directly involved in the war depended as heavily on external financial sources to balance its external accounts and Portugal was particularly vulnerable to international financial shocks caused by the war. Indeed, emigrant remittances and earnings from colonial re-exports weighed so heavily in the balance of payments that their abrupt decline led to both an increase in the external debt and protectionist measures. Another consequence of Portugal's participation in the war since 1916 was the rise of state expenditure, financed mostly through even more

[6] Afonso and Aguiar 2005; Lains 1998, 2007a; Mateus 1998. See also Batista *et al.* 1997.
[7] Feinstein *et al.* 1997: 39. See also Aldcroft 2006 and Di Vittorio 2006.

borrowing and monetary emission, which had the inevitable effect of fueling inflation. Considerable political unrest was another factor propelling the state's finances into disarray. All these elements pushed the country into an inflationary spiral, far outstripping the difficulties expected to come with the war effort.

Political instability was the norm in Portugal's First Republic (1910–1926), with a high turnover of governments lasting on average only two months. A relative normality was nevertheless achieved by 1922, under prime minister António Maria da Silva, whose government stayed in power for nearly two years. A set of legislative changes pulled the country back onto a firmer financial footing. In February 1922, taxes were raised considerably in the context of a fiscal reform, and the public deficit was thus substantially reduced. In the following year, import tariffs were also raised and customs regained their traditional role as a major source of public funding. In 1924, a foreign reserve fund was created, imposing the retention with the tax authorities of 50 percent of gold and foreign currency earnings from exports. The new fund eased the pressure over the reserves managed by the Bank of Portugal, allowing it to concentrate further on managing the country's monetary policy.[8]

In 1925, the banking system underwent a reform, and the government took on a higher degree of supervision over banks, as the stabilization of the economy largely depended on putting the financial sector under control. The Bank of Portugal gained regulatory powers and was barred from making commercial loans in the two leading markets, Lisbon and Porto, thus enhancing its central bank functions. In the context of the same reform, the Caixa Geral de Depósitos, the state savings bank, was allowed to undertake commercial discount operations, paving the way for an expansion of its activities and for the possibility of using its funds other than through the issuing of state bonds.[9] The 1925 reform also imposed stricter rules on banking activities by raising the capital requirements for all banking firms, including those already in operation. The capital requirements were defined in relation to the price of gold to counterbalance the depreciation in the Portuguese currency. The task of overseeing the banking sector, previously entrusted with the Commerce Ministry, was passed on to the Finance Ministry (Reis 1995b: 488). Nevertheless, the consolidation of the country's finances was left unfinished. When the reforms were underway, the economy was recovering and a relative rebalancing of public accounts and the external deficit were being achieved, another military coup occurred, in May 1926, and

[8] Gomes and Tavares 1999; Mata and Valério 1996; Valério 1994: 473–474.
[9] Lains 2002–2011, vol. 2; Reis 1995.

political unrest ensued. Though the reasons behind the coup were mainly political, the new regime, which eventually transformed into a dictatorship, used the financial situation to justify it.

A major issue the new regime had to deal with was the war debt to Great Britain. According to the Treaty of Versailles, Portugal's payments to Britain were contingent upon Germany's payment of reparations. Since the reparations, totaling 49.5 million pounds sterling, had not been repaid, in the early 1920s the Portuguese government suspended the payments of interest to Britain. Because of this, in 1922 Britain added the unpaid interest payments to the main debt, thus raising the initial nominal value from 22 up to 23.5 million pounds sterling by December 1926 (Valério 1994: 419–420). This was a considerable amount of money, certainly when bearing in mind that in 1929 Portuguese exports stood at around 10 million pounds, and emigrant remittances at 5–7 million.[10] In December 1926, the war debt was forgiven by Britain and early in 1927, the Portuguese government opened negotiations with the League of Nations for a 12-million-pound loan. Negotiations eventually failed because of the stringent conditions imposed by the lenders, which included foreign control over part of the country's tax revenue. The conditions imposed by the League of Nations were less humiliating than those imposed by private lenders in some Balkan and Middle Eastern countries before 1914. But the truth is that in spite of its troubled financial history in the nineteenth century, Portugal's public revenue had never been under foreign control. Conversely, Greece had already been under this regime in the late nineteenth century. And it was now once again subjected to it after obtaining two loans from the League of Nations, in 1924 and 1927, which imposed foreign interference in its banking and tax systems, as well as in the stabilization of the drachma (Dertilis and Costis 1995: 462). The turmoil surrounding the terms of the 1927 loan paved the way to the ascendancy of future dictator, Oliveira Salazar, as finance minister, in April 1928.

### The rise of dictatorship

Salazar changed the course of the country's financial policy, promoting changes that reaped financial stability and helped the recovery of the Portuguese economy.[11] The new policies were undoubtedly assisted by the gradual balancing of the country's external accounts, which in turn helped balance public accounts. Salazar continued reform efforts, and

[10] Rosas, ed. 1994: 140; Telo 1994: 782–783.    [11] Salazar 1997; Telo 1994.

even followed some of the measures suggested in the report of a reform commission appointed by the previous government, which he had led himself. Among the most important reforms is that of 1928, which imposed budgetary discipline on all ministries, whose budgets came under the strict control of the new Finance Ministry. The new finance minister pursued further in redressing the role of the state in managing the economy, in a succession of steps that earned him the reputation of a deacon of financial rigor and discipline. In 1929, Salazar introduced a new tax law that allowed the state to recover revenue from the taxes affected by inflation. In that same year, the state-owned savings bank, Caixa Geral de Depósitos, which was by then already one of the largest deposit banks in the country, was empowered also as an investment bank and instrument of the state's economic policy. It also took over from the Bank of Portugal the management of public funds for agricultural loans, and was given additional funds to extend credit in the industrial, urban construction, and public works sectors. Ten years later, Caixa handled about 70 percent of market share in deposits (Reis 1995a, 1995b). In that same year, 1929, following fascist Italy, the Portuguese government launched a campaign to foster national wheat output, the *Campanha do Trigo*, which led to the regulation of internal wheat prices, through tariffs and price subsidies, and a new protectionist customs tariff was put in place.

In 1930, the relations between Portugal and the colonies were regulated by new legislation, with constitutional force, the *Acto Colonial*, which protected colonial trade and reinstated the earlier role the colonies had played in the financing of the Portuguese balance of payments. The new colonial system was based on the control of the monetary flows between Portugal and Africa, rather than only the control of trade in goods. The government in Lisbon imposed highly restrictive policies in the colonies, which had to balance their budgets and foreign trade deficits, and that was achieved rapidly, in 1931 severely affecting the African economies. The government did not want to lose control of the internal and external finances of its colonies and the colonies would not be allowed to become a burden for the metropolitan finances. Moreover, the obligation to send colonial produce to be re-exported through Lisbon was replaced by exchange controls whereby earnings in foreign currency from African exports had to be deposited in the Bank of Portugal, in exchange for Portuguese escudos and other colonial currencies. Domestic imports into the colonies could be paid in escudos, in Portugal, and imports from foreign countries had to be paid for in foreign currencies provided, within certain limits, by the Portuguese government.[12]

---

[12] Clarence-Smith 1985; Ferreira 2005; Lains 1998.

In 1931, Portugal joined the gold-exchange standard, which was already in place across most of Europe, and under which the pound sterling became a reserve currency, in addition to gold. However, when Great Britain withdrew from the system, Salazar followed suit, indexing the Portuguese escudo to the pound. Finally, in 1935, Salazar laid out the first economic plan for state investment, which was called *Lei de Reconstituição Económica*.[13] The legal and institutional changes brought about by Salazar had an overall positive impact in redressing public accounts and in the economy, although the new finance minister was also surfing the overall recovery of the international economy and the financial and monetary stabilization of the late 1920s, which had positive effects on the external accounts and, indirectly, on public debt and deficit. Portugal's external equilibrium depended on three main opposing factors, namely, the level of remittances from emigrants, mainly in Brazil, earnings from re-exports of goods from the African colonies and, finally, movements of capital. The benefits from the African colonies for Portugal's balance of payments were probably high from the start. They were undoubtedly important, since 1948, time from which data for the balance of payments are available. Albeit increasing slightly between 1924 and 1931, emigrant remittances fell substantially after 1931, when the Brazilian government imposed a ban on capital exports. The end of capital exports from Brazil ultimately led to a drop of Portuguese emigration there by about two-thirds.[14] As for capital movements, the evidence shows that the stabilization of the escudo and the decline in inflation levels attracted foreign capital to Portugal once again, particularly, the capital that had fled the country during the war, which was then returning to the country. It is likely that what happened in Portugal is similar to what happened in France and Italy when dealing with their exchange rate and inflation issues. In 1928, British investments in Portugal reached 21 million pounds, and 25 million in the colonies. In 1929, Portuguese expatriates had between 60 and 70 million pounds invested abroad, and that figure doubled in the following year. Portugal's balance of payments thus improved considerably since 1930. The Government's financial position also improved, as it managed to halt spending and recover some revenue. Between 1928 and 1929, the public budget was finally balanced (Mata and Valério 2003b).

The recovery of trade at the international level was stalled by protectionist measures and by the financial imbalances that marked the world in

[13] See Nunes and Valério 1983. See also Confraria 2005.
[14] For the colonies, see Alexandre 2011 and Lains 1998; and for remittances, see Baganha 1988 and Chaney 1986.

this period. As such, Europe's post-war recovery during the 1920s was based on thin ground, and eventually was halted by the New York stock exchange crash, in October 1929, and the Great Depression that followed. The impact of the Great Depression on the European economies varied in intensity and depended to a large extent on the degree of involvement of each country with the international economy and, particularly, with the international flows of capital. The 1929 crash and the Great Depression led to a decline in capital exports from the United States to countries such as Germany or Austria, which were then struggling to pay war reparations and the allies that were receiving the reparations were thus less able to pay for their war loans. That was one of the most important ways of spreading of the depression, but Portugal was relatively withdrawn from those channels, due to its relatively small participation both in the war and in reparations. Moreover, as the largest economies had governments that engaged in contractionist policies to redress the external accounts and thus furthered the negative consequences of the depression that started in the United States, the Portuguese government had the financial capacity to somehow engage in expansionist policies (Eichengreen 1992). That certainly was one of the main reasons for the successful ascendency of Salazar as a powerful finance minister and, ultimately, in 1932, as prime minister and dictator.

As the Great Depression ended up dominating events in the following decade, the signs of economic and financial recovery that had preceded it were less noted. In Portugal, during the remaining years leading to the outbreak of World War II, there was a consolidation of the dictatorial government, which implied fierce political repression in the metropolis as well as in the African colonies, but also by an overall improvement of macroeconomic conditions, and increase in public investment in infrastructures, such as roads, railways, energy production and distribution, namely electricity, which was followed by new private investment, in particular, in large-scale industries (Map 6.1). All these economic transformations were reflected in the data for industrial and total output growth.[15]

Growth in the interwar period was achieved through productivity gains within agriculture and industry, as well as by moving factors to construction and services (Lains 2007). Productivity gains were obtained in sectors that we may classify as traditional. Yet Portugal was such an underdeveloped country in the European context that the relatively simple pattern of structural change that took place could and did have a significant impact on overall economic growth. Structural changes occurred in a context of increased tariffs and other forms of protection

---

[15] See Aldcroft 2006 and Lains 2012 for a comparison of Portugal with the rest of the poor European periphery in this period.

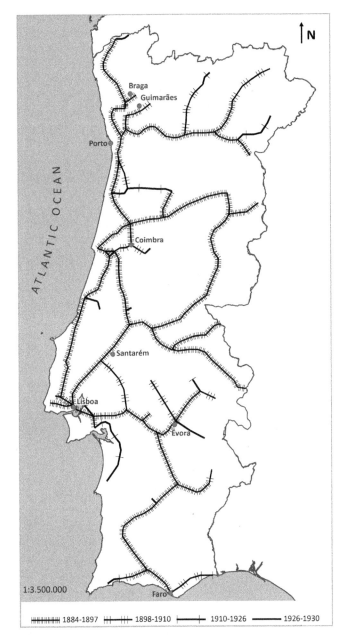

Map 6.1 The railway network, 1884–1930

from external competition and output growth was directed toward the domestic market. This was possible thanks to the existence of favorable conditions in the balance of payments that allowed higher levels of investment, which occurred despite the slowing down of the international economy. Literature shows that scholars have paid a lot of attention to the financial and monetary distress of the interwar period and to the decline in the growth of international transactions in goods, services, and capital, and migration flows. Less attention has been paid to what happened to domestic output, which in many cases expanded fast. The implications of these findings on Portugal are not that protection is good for growth in any case, as it refers only to the situation in which the international economy stagnated and Portuguese producers benefited from exploring further the possibilities provided by the growth of domestic demand and by state protection. Such an outcome was made possible by higher levels of domestic savings and investment. Probably, the higher intensity of growth that occurred in Portugal during the interwar period was made possible by the fact that the country was backward but not too backward. That would mean that the Portuguese economy had achieved by 1914 some degree of development and industrialization. That would have made a difference and would help explain why the success on the periphery of Europe was possible. Growth before 1950 was necessary for the country to achieve the minimum social and economic capabilities in order to take full benefits of the international economic boom during the golden age of growth, when the economy opened up and benefited from the exploitation of external markets and capital imports.

## The golden age of growth

In the aftermath of World War II, there was a crucial change in the way economic policy was conducted at both the national and the international levels. The intervention of national governments in the economies increased substantially but, more importantly, steps were taken since earlier phases regarding the coordination of such policies, particularly in what their financial implications were concerned.[16] The new international economic order was first set in the international conference led by the United States and British governments, held at Bretton Woods, in 1944. The conference laid the basis for the recovery of international trade by providing the financial means to cover bilateral financial imbalances between countries, for which the International Monetary Fund and the World Bank were created (Steil 2013). As soon as the war ended

---

[16] Crafts and Toniolo 2010; Eichengreen 2007; Houpt et al. 2010.

and the perils from the Cold War began to emerge, the Western governments, led by Washington, furthered the recovery by setting the Marshall Plan, in 1947, which lent dollars to the countries with limited reserves in foreign currency, and the constitution of the OEEC, one year later, which imposed on the receiving countries the abolition of tariffs and other barriers to international trade. In 1950, the European Payments Union was established. The leadership of the United States, closely followed by the United Kingdom and, after some initial reluctance, France and other European governments, stimulated effective cooperation among a large number of countries and paved the way to a rapid recovery of the economies devastated by the war, as well as the reconstruction of the international economy (De Long and Eichengreen 1993).

The new institutional arrangements eventually impacted only on Western Europe, as the continent became divided by the *iron curtain*. The contrast with the aftermath of World War I is striking, but the conditions were also quite different, both economically and from the point of view of the strategic interests of the parties involved. While multiple factors had shaped the new worldwide setting, two were particularly important. The first was the fact that the United States had accumulated a vast share of the world's gold reserves, thereby allowing that country to leverage international financial markets, at least in the North Atlantic region. The second factor was linked to the need to contain Soviet expansion, which required the recovery of the economic conditions in Europe and, in particular, in Germany occupied by France, Britain, and the United States, as military strength was closely linked to the state of the economy. And Germany's late-nineteenth- and early-twentieth-century industrial history clearly showed to policy makers the extent to which national economic recovery had to be intimately linked to the recovery of international trade. European integration would become associated with three main international political components that went beyond the United States' aim to ensure Germany's recovery, namely strong cooperation between states, further economic integration at the international level, and the coordination of national public policies. Early in this political process, the United States became less and less engaged with European integration, as Washington's attention was driven toward problems elsewhere, such as the Korean War, and European integration proceeded as an internal affair. But the United States certainly paved the way for the successful coordination of economic policies.[17]

---

[17] Bordo and Teixeira 1995.

*The Marshall Plan and its aftermath*

The Marshall Plan or, in its official designation, the European Recovery Program, involved financial assistance from the United States to overcome difficulties in financing the balance of payments of the receiving countries. The latter were in turn forced to lower their trade barriers, so that international trade could pick up quickly. The amounts involved in this plan were modest when compared to the daunting needs of the European economies in terms of investment. Nevertheless, from the very beginning the spirit of this endeavor conveyed a clear sign of what would follow in terms of European integration. Portugal was among its sixteen founding countries. The degree of each country's participation in the Marshall Plan and the OEEC varied according to its importance in the international economic sphere. At first, the Portuguese government was unenthusiastic and refused to participate. According to the official version, the country did not need outside help for its development.[18] Salazar would, however, be forced to reconsider his earlier stance because of the deterioration of Portugal's balance of payments after the war. Indeed, gold and foreign currency reserves, which had accumulated considerably during the war, had then fallen to unsustainable low levels. The problems in the balance of payments in 1947 and 1948 resulted from weak exports coupled with the drain on currency reserves to pay for food imports. These financial woes thus forced the government to accept the Marshall Plan and to become a member of the OEEC. This put a definite end to the economic autarky that characterized the interwar period. But the Portuguese government faced the liberalization of international commercial relations with caution, not unlike other European countries, as we shall see later. The amount of US aid that Portugal received was small when compared to total domestic investment, and nearly two-thirds of the funds were used for the purchase of American consumer goods, notably wheat. The aid was nevertheless relevant in terms of the need to finance the balance of payments and cover for the trade deficits that Portugal had with industrialized Europe. And the fact remains that the decisions taken regarding the lowering of trade barriers and how the Marshall Aid would be spent somehow shaped Portugal's economic policy thereafter. The Portuguese government, a dictatorship unaligned with the rest of Western Europe, undoubtedly became integrated in terms of its economic policy.[19]

By the time it joined the OEEC, the Portuguese government's economic policy was still essentially framed by the 1935 *Lei de Reconstituição*

---

[18] Lains 2003c, Chapter 6; Rollo 2007.     [19] Milward 1992; Rollo 1994, 2007.

*Económica* which was to remain in effect until 1950. The Act revealed the government's priorities and provided a framework for public as well as private investment and sought to promote the building of infrastructure and create or reinforce specific industrial sectors believed to be strategic for the national economy, and served as an umbrella for the multiple mechanisms of state economic intervention created or reinforced during the years of autarky in the 1930s, and it laid out principles that would later be included in a set of more detailed economic plans. The first of these plans was launched for the period 1953–1958. Both the 1935 Act and the plans launched since the 1950s insisted upon the need for public intervention in infrastructure building, in the development of agriculture, and in a swift industrialization, by focusing on heavy industry.[20] The economic plans, along with the participation in the OEEC, constituted the backbone of the *Estado Novo* economic policy practically until its very end. These macro-level economic policies were attended by other measures that proved to be of great importance as well, including policies aimed at curbing inflation, introducing price controls on certain essential items, and instruments for balancing the public accounts and maintaining the value of the *escudo*. Ultimately, membership of the OEEC became a milestone in Portugal's alignment with the institutions for international economic cooperation and commercial regulation, giving the country an outward-looking view, although not jeopardizing the policies aimed at a new economic specialization and structural transformation. The Portuguese economy enjoyed a number of features that actually favored this form of state intervention and ultimately led to higher rates of GDP growth. Chief among these were a unified central state, albeit authoritarian, a relatively good transport, energy, and irrigation infrastructure, and even a few more advanced industrial sectors. Furthermore, there was an exceptional accumulation of gold, foreign currency, and other financial assets in the Bank of Portugal and in the rest of the banking system, all of which translated into improvements in the balance of payments. These circumstances were especially welcome in a country whose future rapid industrialization would depend on imported raw materials and equipment, the payment of which could never be covered by exports, emigrant remittances, or any other forms of payment. Portugal was therefore relatively well prepared to take part in the new international economic order that would emerge from Bretton Woods.

[20] Lains 2003c; Rosas, ed. 1994.

## The EFTA unexpected guess

By the late 1950s, much had changed since the early steps taken in the days of the Marshall Plan. Despite their structural differences, the creation of the European Coal and Steel Community (ECSC), in 1951, the European Economic Community (EEC), in 1957, and the European Free Trade Association (EFTA) in 1959, revealed a concern with the international coordination of national economic policies and thus allowing for open frontiers. The ECSC was a supranational authority with regulatory powers over the production and trade of steel and coal, and its very existence underlined the need to revitalize sectors that were crucial for the industrial sector of the member countries, namely West Germany, France, the Benelux, and Italy. Its main task consisted of assessing the surplus production of Belgium and the earnings that would accrue to Germany for boosting its lower cost of production. This assessment indicated the need to shut down a portion of Belgium's production units and allow Germany to increase its production, and, thus, its exports. This policy of resource reallocation naturally burdened Belgium with costs, and the labor force laid off had to be transferred to other sectors. This process was pursued through the granting of subsidies to the Belgian industry, paid for mostly by Germany, the very country that was benefiting from this scheme. This is an example of what would become the norm during the process of European integration, namely, the transfer of funds to the sectors negatively influenced by the opening to international markets. This first step toward European integration was clearly politically motivated, and indeed this is what led the government of West Germany to accept funding the subsidies awarded under the auspices of the coal and steel treaty. The EEC had interests and principles similar to those of its forerunner. The ECSC had been politically important and represented an institutional innovation in terms of cooperation between states, but its economic consequences were less significant, since it only aimed to regulate specific markets. The link between the two international institutions, which strove for the competitive modernization of their member states, was not the product of mere chance, but rather of the influence of external factors. The governments of the different countries wished to intervene in the sectors they felt were essential for economic development, but without resorting to outright protectionist measures that could hinder international trade. France is the best example of success in this regard, while Great Britain is an outlier.[21]

---

[21] See Coppolaro and Lains 2013. See also, for Portugal's economic conditions, Lopes 1996, Neves 1996, and Pintado 2002.

These early steps toward European integration were restricted to a very select group of countries, and an examination of the reasons behind the newly created institutions reveals why the group was kept so small. Europe's peripheral countries were excluded mostly because their integration potential was low, which is all the more striking if one bears in mind the goals of the ECSC, and especially of the EEC. In the Portuguese case, political issues also played their part, since accepting a dictatorial regime would have been strange in institutions that followed democratic principles. But economic issues ended up mattering the most in the decision to keep Portugal apart. First, Portugal lacked a significant production of coal and steel. Second, it was far from being a crucial trade partner of the founding member countries. Finally, when the Common Agricultural Policy was later established, from the early 1960s onward, the opening of agricultural markets within the European Communities implied the strengthening of the policy of subsidies that founding member states provided to their farmers, and which became coordinated and paid through Brussels via the Common Agricultural Policy.

Great Britain chose not to join the ECSC and the EEC because its trade in coal and steel with the Six was relatively small, and because joining the coal and steel common policy meant the nationalization of the sector under a supranational body that the British government was unwilling to give powers to. Yet under British leadership, a number of Western European countries outside the EEC, including Portugal, the unexpected guest, joined to form the European Free Trade Association (EFTA), with the goal of dismantling trade barriers among its members and to jointly negotiate tariff reductions with the EEC countries.[22] Portugal's participation in EFTA made it an exceptional case, since it was the only non-industrialized member admitted. As a consequence, the Portuguese government was forced to scrap import barriers, but was nevertheless able to negotiate special clauses that allowed for that process to progress slower than in other member countries, thereby affording some breathing room for industrial sectors that were still in their infancy. Additionally, some markets were secured for certain transformed agricultural exports, as Portugal was able to have them classified as industrial products, thereby benefitting from lower import duties in the markets of its EFTA partners (Lopes 1996). Soon after, Portugal finally joined the remaining Bretton Woods institutions, namely the International Monetary Fund, in 1961, and the General Agreement on Tariffs and Trade, in 1962 (Bordo and Teixeira 1995). In that same year, in the context of the beginning of the colonial wars, Salazar's government created the *Espaço Económico*

---

[22] Leitão 2000, 2007; Rollo 2007.

*Português*, which intended to be a single market with a single currency within the Portuguese empire, but that failed in most of its main objectives (Ferreira 2005).

Accession to EFTA had a stronger influence on Portuguese exports in the early 1960s, but exports to the EEC countries nevertheless continued to grow quickly. The main reason behind this was the fact that during this period Germany and France were the engines that drove Europe's economy, in terms of sheer size and pace of growth. But unlike the EEC, which had more sweeping ambitions, EFTA's goals were limited to removing trade barriers over industrial products, thus leaving the issue of agricultural protection aside. This looked more promising for an economy with a high share of the GDP depending on the agricultural sector. Only in the 1960s, because of the leap in industrialization and industrial exports, would the Portuguese agricultural sector for the first time actually lose labor force, and the share in total output declined. The decision to join EFTA reflected expectations that membership would be favorable to the economy through a boost in exports. This seems plausible enough since aside from the direction of economic policy or state measures for direct industrial intervention, certain industrial sectors exporting to Europe had been improved during the 1950s. Portugal enjoyed some comparative advantages in the latter, namely manual-labor-intensive sectors, since labor was cheaper than in most of its trade partners. Portugal was a successful exporter of cork, wine, canned fish, fruits and vegetables, and a few other products, including textiles, but the last one mainly to the colonies (Lains 2003c). While exports increased significantly after 1960, industrial output also expanded quickly, particularly in the sectors that received state protection, especially basic industries like cement, chemicals, and energy. Despite the fact that these industries catered mainly to the domestic market, there still was a wide growth margin. In fact, during the following years and up to 1973, the country had a very high growth rate and converged at a quick pace to the level of GDP of Europe's industrialized core.

### State intervention and economic growth

The Estado Novo was strongly interventionist in terms of economic policy, since its earlier phases, and that was enhanced during the later period of the regime. Economic policy materialized in several ways, but certainly one that was of utmost relevance, particularly in political terms, were the *Planos de Fomento* which were regularly published for the years 1953–1958, 1959–1964, 1965–1966, and 1967–1973 (a fifth plan was already in the making for 1974–1979, when the regime ended). These economic plans were shaped on similar plans from France, a country to which economists in Portugal had close links then, and constituted mainly guidelines for public investment, which governments hoped that private investors would follow (Almodovar and Cardoso 1998: 114–119). And they were very ambitious. The 1953–1958 plan defined investment priorities that would amount to about 40 percent of total investment in Portugal during the period, with a public contribution from the state of about one-third of the total. The relevance of the plans increased thereafter, both in terms of the guidelines for investment, but also in terms of economic regulation. The weight of public investment is even larger in the second plan for 1959–1964, which amounted to roughly 20 percent of the country's total investment. The economic plans were accompanied by monetary and financial policies, which were relatively orthodox, with a strong control on public deficit, inflation, and exchange rate fluctuations. The times were relatively easy in this field, as the country went through a relatively favorable period of balance of payments financing, due to the large size of remittances from Portuguese emigrants in Europe, and also due to capital imports, in the EFTA context.[23]

Yet, Portugal's growth model would be under severe criticism. It was a far cry from the pessimism of the late 1940s and early 1950s, since it became clear that the Portuguese economy was actually growing. But a few doubts about the future of the country in an increasingly competitive international environment still lingered. Some worried that the model followed by Portugal would put the country's economic future at risk because it was based on protectionist policies in certain sectors at the expense of others, which made the country dependent on a set of very specific factors subject to change at any given moment. In broad terms, the model that was criticized relied on low-wage industrialization. This was based on an artificial low cost of living, which, in turn, was based upon low price fixing of agricultural produce at the national level. This was dangerous, the critics wrote, because it hindered the country's agricultural development. Industry, they claimed, would still benefit from low-cost raw materials from the colonies, not because of decolonization, something that crossed the minds of few people in the early 1960s, but because the low prices would jeopardize the colonies' own development. It is worth noting that this criticism called into question the priorities set out in Salazar's development model. The criticism was not aimed at the ideological form of his regime, but rather at his specific economic policies. In other words, no one really opposed state intervention in economic

---

[23] Nunes and Brito 1990; Lopes 1996.

affairs or especially in industry.[24] The whole notion of state intervention in the economy was well accepted by critics, who looked up to the contemporary example of France and other European nations. Critics of the regime were now questioning, especially from the late 1960s onwards, the effects of economic policies on the distribution of national income and the concentration of wealth in the hands of the industrialists who benefitted from the state's protection. The first signs of concern regarding the regional imbalances brought about by industrialization also emerged in this period. Yet the fact was that inequality, as measured by wage distribution, increased during the first decade of industrialization, but then declined toward the end of the regime, following the classical inverted-U Kuznets curve (Lains *et al.* 2012).

Rapid industrialization during the golden age of growth inevitably meant the decline in the share of agricultural output in GDP, as well as the worsening of the level of *relative* economic conditions of those engaged in the primary sector. On the other hand, during the same period there was a sharp increase in migration of agricultural labor to Lisbon, Porto, and the city of Setúbal, to the south, urban centers that increased steeply in terms of population, in many instances under dismal conditions, and to emigration toward Western European countries that were also undergoing a period of rapid economic expansion.[25] The transformation of the structure of the economy and the harsh conditions that it imposed on large stretches of the population have been interpreted in the historical literature as a direct consequence of the dictatorship, leading to a sharp criticism of the regime and it is worth exploring here that debate. The debate has implicit in it a counterfactual situation in which an agrarian reform that would redistribute large estates in the south and enclose small holdings in the north, would create better conditions for agriculture, and thus allow an expansion of output, factor productivity, and wages in the sector.[26] Yet that counterfactual does not take into account what would be the consequences of a larger agrarian sector in the overall performance of the economy, as productivity increases in agriculture were certainly harder to achieve than in manufacturing or, for that matter, services. Investment in agriculture between 1960 and 1973 was sufficient only to compensate for the loss of labor to the cities and foreign countries. This explains the slow growth of agricultural production. When compared with Europe's leading countries, and bearing in mind indicators like the productivity of agricultural labor rather

---

[24] For industrial policy, see Confraria 1994, 1999, and 2005; Moura 1973; Nunes and Brito 1990.
[25] For outward emigration, see Baganha 2003 and Leite 1994. See also Badia *et al.* 2012.
[26] Pereira 1983, 2001; Rosas 2000.

than total production, the conclusions to be drawn about Portuguese agriculture are quite different. The pattern of growth observed in the first half of the twentieth century, where a backward agricultural sector could contribute positively to overall growth, changed in a dramatic way after 1960. The main factor behind that change was the rapid growth of manufacturing. Due to the fact that employment in the agricultural sector fell more rapidly than output, there were improvements in labor productivity and also in the productivity of land of the main crops, such as wheat, other cereals, as well as animal output. Moreover, investment in the agricultural sector expanded at a slower pace than investment in industry in a systematic way. Due to the fact that industrial productivity growth expanded at rates that the agricultural sector could not follow, there was probably no place for economic policies that could have diminished the pace of structural change without consequences in the overall rate of economic growth. But there were also no relevant policies that would compensate for the loss of income either. The agricultural sector, despite its shortcomings in comparison to other parts of Europe, managed to obtain considerable labor and capital productivity gains during parts of the period analyzed in this chapter. Such overall productivity gains implied that investments in the agricultural sector could compete favorably with investments in other sectors of the economy.[27]

The debate on the consequences of the economic policies followed by the government in Portugal became increasingly more ideological, during the late 1960s, as the intensity of the political opposition increased, as the Salazar regime approached its end. However, the course of economic policy was not seriously challenged and continued marked by tight monetary policy, strong intervention in the economy through legislation and public investment, and the continuation of opening up of the borders. The major weakness of these polices was the cost of the colonial wars that increased steeply in the late 1960s and early 1970s. The rise in industrial export, emigrant remittances, and imported capital balanced Portugal's external accounts, with low levels of inflation and relatively stable exchange rates. The favorable balance of payments allowed for the adoption of policies of low interest rates and a balanced state budget, in turn encouraging both private and public investment. In the industrial sector, private investment opportunities closely followed the footsteps of structural transformations reflected in domestic demand boosted by a rising standard of living and increased foreign demand. The services sector grew in a similar fashion, catering to the growing needs of a dynamic economy, notably in banking and other financial services, business, health care, and

[27] Lains 2009; Martins 2005; Soares 2005.

education. In the context of a relatively favorable macroeconomic situation, the state was now able to allocate funds for programs aimed at further industrialization, either through direct intervention or through protectionist mechanisms. The fact that the country was now in a phase of greater openness to the outside world in no way blocked these policies. As we saw earlier, negotiations with EFTA left room for such actions. Eventually, however, Portugal would adopt policies that were very much in line with those followed by other European countries. State intervention in Portuguese industry was channeled for the most part into seemingly basic sectors, such as energy production and transport. Without state protection the country would hardly have witnessed such a rapid expansion of the national electric power network or an increase in cement production, steel works, chemical fertilizers, and chemicals in general. These were not new sectors in the country, and their growth depended largely on previous experience mostly accumulated during the interwar years.[28]

Data for the balance of payments between Portugal and its colonies exist only from 1964 onwards, but since the balance of payments for the empire (Portugal plus the colonies) was positive for most of the period from 1950 to 1971 and, up to 1965 the income account of Portugal alone was in deficit the overall surplus was attributable to the contribution of the colonies. From 1965 onwards, the colonies retained their surpluses with Portugal. But by then Portugal ran a surplus with foreign countries and the relative importance of the colonies declined. From 1967 onwards contributions from emigrant remittances surpassed the colonies as sources of foreign exchange, and the contribution of the colonies to Portugal's foreign earnings had been dwarfed by 1973. In fact, the contribution of the colonies to Portugal's balance of payments can be correlated to their share in Portugal's trade. During the 1960s, the share of the colonies in the Portuguese exports was 24 percent, which represented 4 percent of Portugal's GDP and a slightly higher percentage of the industrial output. The contribution to the balance of payments was equivalent to about 1.8 percent of GDP, in 1964. The overall financial benefits of the colonies may have surpassed the official transfers of foreign currency by a large margin. According to one estimate, in 1957, total benefits from the Portuguese colonies amounted to 6 percent of Portugal's GDP and this is probably an upper limit (Lains 1998: 257). But the extent to which colonial supplies of foreign currency made a contribution to Portuguese economic growth is debatable. Portugal had an investment gap due to a low level of domestic savings, which had

---

[28] Confraria 2005; Lopes 1996; Lopes 2005; Neves 1996; Mateus 1998.

to be filled either by capital imports or by invisible earnings from abroad, and in that macroeconomic context the contribution of the colonies may have had an important role. Given that exports of capital from Portugal to the colonies remained low in the early 1960s, the low level of domestic savings was hardly imputable to the empire. In the 1960s, emigrant remittances contributed to the *overvaluation* of the escudo and thereby favored imports, particularly of capital goods, and thus a more capital intensive pattern of growth. In the 1950s and 1960s, Portugal had the lowest capital-output ratio of the southern European countries. Thus the bias in favor of capital-intensive growth was probably not a major problem and the country's favorable balance of payments position arising from colonial revenues and emigrant remittances had probably a net positive effect on the Portuguese economy (Lains 1998). Colonial wars started in Angola in 1961 and pushed the expenditures with the colonies up to 26 percent of Portugal's public budget, from 1961 to 1974, and the share of the military in that budget to 85 percent, which imposed a severe contraction of investment expenditures in the African economies. The manning of this military effort represented 6 percent of Portugal's total labor force. The consequences of the expenditures on colonial wars for the Portuguese economy are difficult to analyze. The cost of the war was certainly high, representing 8 percent of GNP throughout the 1960s, a proportion that is higher than even the more optimistic estimates of the gains from the colonies in the late 1950s. Yet the increase in government spending induced by the war may have fostered the growth of demand for industrial goods, as well as the growth of domestic consumption, by reversing the tight fiscal policies that the governments had maintained since the early 1950s.

Portuguese industrial exports were sold on protected markets in Africa and certainly that had effects upon the industrial structure of the metropolis. Capital exports to the colonies remained low until the 1950s and only thereafter did they affect metropolitan financial markets. Emigration followed closely the pattern of capital exports and its effects should also be taken into account. Yet, the shares of the domestic industrial output, investment, and population that were diverted by colonial protectionism were probably too low to make a large difference in the pattern and rate of Portuguese economic growth. Portuguese economic and industrial growth has been dependent historically on the possibility of financing an adverse balance on the current account in order to sustain imports of industrial inputs and food. That is basically why the foreign currency obtained through the sale of tropical products from the colonies made a positive contribution to metropolitan economic growth. The importance of the colonies for the economy was, however, being reduced by the early

1960s when Portugal increased its trade, investment, and emigration links with industrial Europe and when the colonies became increasingly dependent on imports of industrial inputs and capitals from foreign countries. The contribution of the colonies as a source of external financing of the Portuguese economy faded away by the 1960s onwards and, contemporarily, the wars of independence created a heavy burden for the Portuguese government's finances.

The *Estado Novo* was not so much noted by the fact that to a greater or lesser extent it was a corporative regime, but rather by the fact that it had managed fairly successfully to enforce its guidelines across a vast network of public and private institutions. This strong level of state intervention was not unique in Europe, nor was it at odds with the gradual opening up of economies to the outside, and in many ways actually made this transition easier. The actions of economic authorities were somehow driven by economic intervention, either through investment in select sectors or through the regulation of markets. These efforts often created conflicts amongst private-sector agents. However, the *Estado Novo*'s corporative policies could also be described as politicized economy, similarly to what would happen in the near future during the first decade of democracy after the 1974 revolution. Despite the implications of the industrial policy, in a certain way, the control of production was exercised only at the level of installed capacity, while the prices were actually controlled outright.

The apparent coherence of the economic policy started to wane toward the end of the regime, during the consulate of Salazar's successor, Marcello Caetano, whose governments lasted from 1968 to 1974. This later period of the dictatorship started under the tune of changes and in some aspects changes were really needed as the regime had become quite atavistic in many instances. But, as the truly meaningful changes, namely the reestablishment of democracy and the end of the colonial war, failed to materialize, the period was marked by a high level of political uncertainty that ended up affecting also economic policy. The most important challenge for Caetano's government was the mounting costs of the wars in the African colonies, which accrued to half of total government expenditures in the early 1970s. That was followed by an unprecedented rise in inflation, further aggravated by the changes in the international context as a consequence of the demise of the Bretton Woods system and the rise of oil prices. Yet in spite of the worsening of some economic indicators, the country's economy continued on a path of healthy growth. Meanwhile, the first enlargement of the European Communities, in 1973, to the United Kingdom, Ireland, and Denmark, ultimately undermined the role of EFTA, and Portugal's European context also worsened, notwithstanding the commercial agreement with the Six, previously signed in 1972 (Leitão 2007a and b).

The two decades following World War II were an exceptional time for Europe, a golden age of opportunities. This was a period of rapid economic recovery for the Continent from years of high protectionism and two devastating wars. The corrective measures put in place were cautious and coordinated at the international level, and matched the specific needs of the period. This accounts for Europe's successful economic recovery during these years. It also goes a long way toward explaining Portugal's strong economic growth between 1945 and 1973. Other factors also helped the country respond positively to the challenges it faced, namely the greater ability to save and invest, at both the state and private sector levels, the benefits reaped from the structural transformation of the economy, under which resources for agriculture, a less productive sector, were reallocated into industry and services, an increased competitiveness in foreign markets and, finally, the implementation of economic, financial, and monetary policies that gave stability and traction to these favorable changes. The list of benefits is long, but we need to focus on what is most important, and certainly the most important influence came from the events that unfolded in Europe and the rest of the world until 1973, when numerous changes occurred.

## Democracy and European integration

The sharp rise in oil prices in the winter of 1973 led to the end of two decades of worldwide economic growth. In Portugal, in spite of the crisis, the first months after the April 1974 revolution brought about a new wave of optimism regarding the country's future. Regardless of the optimism associated with revolutions, in 1974, the Bank of Portugal indeed held a comfortable amount of reserves in gold and foreign currency. Hopes of a swift recovery were, however, short-lived, as the trade deficit increased substantially in relation to the pre-1974 level, and it was not offset by emigrant remittances, an influx of foreign capital, or by revenue from tourism. The economic policy after the revolution was largely determined by short-term constraints. Portugal had not for a long time experienced a similar hardship with its balance of payments as it did during the second half of the 1970s and early 1980s, which limited to a great extent economic policy options. In the 1960s, inflation had been rising slowly but, from October to December 1973, oil prices quadrupled and in 1974 inflation peaked at 20 percent for the first time in many decades. Inflation was only one of the many problems Portugal was facing then, and the list further included the economic and financial constraints arising from the colonial wars in Africa, which impacted severely on the state's finances, as well as on the labor force, a crisis in the agricultural sector due to a halt in investment and productivity growth and which impacted on the external trade deficit, the weakening of industrial growth, and the difficulties in paying for the emerging social security system and for an extensive program of official price controls. Thus, the new democratic governments had little headroom to correct what were then considered the main negative economic and social consequences of the dictatorial regime, whatever the strength of the diagnoses that were presented by the wide spectrum of political forces that emerged after the April 1974 *coup*. One main tool that was rapidly put into place was the devaluation of the country's currency in order to put a check on imports and promote exports, mainly of industrial goods. But the check on imports depressed domestic investment, given its dependence on the purchase of intermediate goods from abroad. And the promotion of exports by devaluation meant an added stimulus for leaving the traditional features of the export sector unchanged (Lopes 1996, 2005).

The institutional framework of the *Estado Novo* inherited by the new democratic regime was rather a rigid one, particularly in what regards the ability to adjust to the new inflationary environment. This was another form of institutional "eurosclerosis," not unlike what happened elsewhere in a number of democratic Western European countries where "coordinated capitalism," driven by the dialogue between governments, trade unions, and business representatives, was not able to adapt to the post-1973 inflationary period.[29] Thus, in Portugal, the policy of fixing price of essential goods that was in place since the late 1960s, became unsustainable as inflation rose even more, yet the government did not stop or even change it. Yet some of the policies inherited from the *Estado Novo* went uncontested by the governments that followed the 1974 coup. The earlier provisional governments were too fragile to deal with the opposition that the necessary price adjustments would trigger. Subsequent governments, in 1975, did not challenge the price and wage control policies because this fitted in with their left-wing policy models. Moreover, they had to deal with the fact that wage in the civil service had not been raised for a long time, and thus decided to raise them and to establish the first national minimum wage. This convoluted period was worsened by the massive influx of populations from the colonies, the drop in emigration to Europe, and the resulting decline

---

[29] Eichengreen 1996, 2007. Sweden is a good case to show the effects of the 1973 crisis on coordinated capitalism. See Magnusson 2000: 257–263.

in remittances, as well as the negative impact of the international recession on Portuguese exports and foreign capital inflows. These negative trends were amplified by the flight of capital, especially as the political situation and confidence in stability eroded. The slowdown of economic growth led to a decline in state revenue and a worsening of the public deficit (Lains 2003c: Chapter 6).

These earlier years of the new regime were marked by another *coup* held on March 11, 1975, and led by General Spínola who was briefly the first president of the republic of the new regime, which failed and was followed by a radicalization of Portuguese politics. The *Movimento das Forças Armadas* gained momentum, established the *Conselho da Revolução*, and soon after decreed the nationalization of the banking sector and of a considerable number of large industrial firms. The enormous change in the ownership of a wide part of the Portuguese economy has been studied in many different ways, but it is hard to conclude about its ultimate impacts on the structure and growth of the economy. Probably the impact was more of a political than of an economic nature and certainly it was less relevant than the impact of the international crisis.[30] In fact, the changes in the international economic environment at the world level and, particularly, at the European level, clearly dominated the Portuguese economy in the years to come (Lains 2003). In 1973, the United Kingdom, Ireland, and Denmark finally joined the European Communities, after almost a decade of indecisions and negotiations, but the crisis that followed the oil price hikes rapidly changed the rules of engagement, particularly where Britain was concerned. In fact, the economic depression that unfolded led to a considerable decline in the potential – and, ultimately, real – gains that the new members could draw from the enlarged common market, whereas the costs of joining, notably with financing the Common Agricultural Policy, remained unchanged. At the same time, the other governments of the European Communities reacted to the weakening of the international economy and the rising inflation and unemployment by increasing the levels of protection and state intervention at the national level. The increase in state protectionism was still allowed, as Brussels did not have the power to intervene in matters concerning market regulation and the subsidizing of firms at the national level. The second half of the 1970s was thus an unfavorable era for market integration within the European Communities.[31] Meanwhile, on the backstage, the integration of European institutions was moving

---

[30] The best study on the 1975 nationalizations and the privatizations that followed later from the 1990s onwards is still Sousa and Cruz 1995.

[31] For a survey, see Dinan 2005. See also Marsh 2011.

forward, albeit slowly. The most relevant changes were the formal constitution of regular meetings of heads of state and government, the
European Council, and the signing of the Lomé Convention, the trade
agreement with African and Caribbean countries, both in 1975; the first
direct elections for the European Parliament and the creation of the
European Monetary System, in 1979; and the increasing role of the
European Court of Justice. These advances were considerable, but
more were still to follow, as the problems caused by the international
recession forced a change in the paradigms of governance and European
integration.

*Closing the political gap*

It was in the context of grand diplomatic stalling and less visible institutional change in the European Communities that negotiations with
Portugal and Spain took place. In 1977, the Socialist government led
by Mário Soares applied for membership and negotiations officially
started in October 1978, but only began *de facto* in 1980 and lasted
until 1984 (Vilaça 2000). The duration of the negotiations was
a consequence of both political and economic domestic difficulties, but
also of the stalemate in European integration. Furthermore, Portugal was
undergoing changes at the political and economic level. In fact, in 1979
a new government with a more liberal stance rose to power and paved the
way for a reduction in the weight of the state in the economy, as well as the
reversal of the 1975 nationalizations. In 1979, too, Margaret Thatcher
became prime minister and introduced a radical change in British
economic policy regarding the role of the state and trade unions. These
changes were also followed in other countries, albeit in a less radical way.
Eventually, even Europe's center-left political forces also recognized the
need for a shift in paradigm. In 1981, the newly elected French president
François Miterrand formed a coalition government with socialists and
communists that started by following left-leaning economic policies, less
worried with public budget deficits and inflation and, consequently, in
favor of currency devaluations to protect the domestic market from
imports and to push for exports. Two years later, however, the French
government changed tack, as inflation and the public deficit were going
out of control, which would ultimately imply the withdrawal from the
European Monetary System and thus imperil a crucial tool of the efforts
to recast European integration.[32] This change of course was followed by
other European governments and led to a convergence with British

---

[32] Borzel 2005; Neal 2007.

policies and a reduction of the divide within the Communities. By 1983, Germany, Italy, Belgium, the Netherlands, and Denmark were governed by liberal parties, which replaced Social-Democratic parties, associated with economic policies that in the past had achieved growth but were by then seen as responsible for economic stagnation. This change was clearly linked to the dissemination of the idea that a new paradigm of economic policy and of state intervention in the economy was needed. In 1984, the British quarrel with Brussels was solved at the European Council held in Fontainebleau, where London was granted partial compensations for the funds it transferred to Brussels for the Common Agricultural Policy. Finally, in 1985, the Single European Act was signed, opening the doors to the enlargement of the Communities to Spain and Portugal. The timing of the accession cannot be understood without taking into consideration such European developments.

Yet domestically, the first half of the eighties was also politically unstable as the largest political parties failed to win an absolute majority in Parliament or to form stable coalitions. In these years a major overhaul of Portuguese politics was going on, following closely what was happening elsewhere in Western Europe, toward a more liberal perspective of governance, characterized by privatizations, allegedly more market-friendly politics, and a reduction in the influence of trade unions in politics, and the IMF interventions and the increasing role of the Bank of Portugal in politics were of paramount relevance.[33] The first coalition government of the two leading Socialist and Social-Democrat parties, in 1982, which ultimately allowed for a politically significant revision of the Constitution in the same year abolishing the last institutional heritage from the 1974 carnation revolution, namely, the *Conselho da Revolução*, designated and formed by the military. Probably the most important change introduced was the reversal of the constitutional norm that barred the privatization of the banks and large industrial sectors that had been nationalized at the height of the revolutionary period. The return to a relative normality would, however, be hindered by the economic and financial problems caused by the second oil shock of 1979 and the recession it triggered across Europe. Moreover, the problems in balancing the external accounts, as well as the government budget, led to financial distress which ultimately implied a second intervention of the International Monetary Fund in 1982–1983, following the one of 1977. The story of these interventions is still to be made and it has to be taken into

---

[33] These are conclusions of an ongoing project entitled "History of the Bank of Portugal, 1974–2000."

consideration that they were motivated by financial needs, but also politically. In 1983, Mário Soares' *Bloco Central* government had to introduce significant spending cuts and tax rises and negotiate a restructuring of its foreign debt to correct the external deficit. This financial crisis eventually led to a convergence of the efforts of the two leading parties, which increased the country's bargaining power vis-à-vis the European Communities. Yet in 1985 one of the governing parties elected a new leader who ultimately put an end to the coalition government, but nevertheless allowed it to sign the adhesion treaty. This is a very clear sign of the extent of the domestic consensus on European integration.

Portugal's adhesion negotiations were helped by the fact that the set of demands from the Communities was rather straightforward and relatively simple to obtain due to the domestic political advancements in the first decade of democracy. The most important negotiations surrounded the issues of financial compensation for agriculture and fisheries, as well as the integration of the *acquis communautaire*, that is, the incorporation of European legislation in the Portuguese legal framework, and the lowering of trade barriers between Spain and Portugal which were by then still in place, despite a bilateral trade agreement signed in 1980. The Portuguese negotiators did not try to change the way policies were steered because of the country's size but also because of the fact that the Communities were recognized as institutionally more mature. The enlargement was soon followed by the introduction of the "Delors packages," which would strongly benefit new member states financially but were the outcome of internal discussions in the Commission where the Portuguese government had a relatively minor role. It was therefore a windfall rather than a demand from Lisbon. Yet the financial assistance undoubtedly served to dispel any remaining doubts among voters about adhesion. Passive acceptance of membership was rewarded with gains derived from the smooth recovery that the European economy was enjoying at the time of Portugal's accession.[34]

Throughout much of the negotiations, expectations about the outcomes of accession were largely positive. A few people on the left of the political spectrum, who viewed the Communities from the perspective of the dispute between capitalism and socialism, were nevertheless somewhat skeptical.[35] Furthermore, a number of liberal economists pointed out the difficulties of adjustment in the Portuguese economy in the context of a higher exposure to the markets.[36] But broadly speaking, the

---

[34] See Hibou 2005. On Portugal, see Lobo and Lains, eds. 2007, Pinto and Teixeira, eds. 2002, and Vasconcelos and Seabra, eds. 2000.
[35] *Não ao Mercado Comum (. . .)* 1980.
[36] See *Conferência Internacional* 1977 and *Conferência Internacional* 1980.

perspective provided by economists that advised both the governments and the Bank of Portugal, some of whom came from abroad, which had an increasingly important role in the design of economic policy, was favorable.[37] This stance was strengthened after 1986, when optimistic forecasts regarding the moment when Portugal would bridge the gap with the more advanced nations and reach the same level of well-being emerged. In the following years, and up to the mid 1990s, the Portuguese economy experienced a boom in the context of the deepening of European integration that followed the signing of the Maastricht Treaty, the Stability and Growth Pact, and the beginning of the Economic and Monetary Union (EMU). Meanwhile, in 1992, following domestic problems, the Spanish government devalued the peseta by 22 percent and the currency's EMS fluctuation band was increased from 3 to 15 percent. Portugal also found it necessary to make some exchange rate adjustments, but on a smaller scale. At the time, these adjustments were evaluated positively. The next decisive step toward deeper integration was abolition of the remaining trade barriers and other forms of protectionism of national markets. In 1995, the socialists came back to power and declared Portugal's commitment to the Maastricht criteria, which called for strict budgetary discipline and reduction of the public debt, thus reinforcing the will to keep the country in tune with economic and monetary integration. The European Monetary Union triggered a considerable surge in economic relations among member states, especially in the trade of goods and services, as well as capital flows.

The Euro was introduced in two phases: in 1999, when exchange rates within the monetary union were fixed, and in 2002, when the new physical coins and notes were put into circulation. Mainly under pressure from Spain, the implementation of the monetary union was accompanied by economic intervention mechanisms through the creation of the Cohesion Fund or the so-called Delors Package II, which doubled the funds of the first package.[38] This new arrangement helped to open the Union to the outside world and represented a very significant step in its history. However, the monetary union also ensued at a time of sharp recession in Spain and slower growth in Portugal. The worsening economic situation in two of the countries benefiting from cohesion funds should not be linked to greater integration alone, as there were many

---

[37] The economists Richard Ekaus, Paul Krugman, and Robert Solow, among others, visited Lisbon for a few times between 1975 and 1977 to advise on economic policy. See Krugman 2008 and Lopes 2008.
[38] Powell 2005: 200–201; Lains 2007.

factors in the equation. The truth is that the capacity of the Iberian governments to respond was steadily eroding.

In sum, Portugal's accession to the European Communities was followed by policy measures that in some ways sought to offset the risks of a backward country joining a union of more advanced economies. The nature of these policies was quite different from that of the EFTA period. Policies now reflected funding provided by the Community intended to stimulate public and private investment in priority areas, including restructuring the agricultural sector, promoting communication infrastructure, and investing in labor force training. These targets were broader than EFTA's, and were less direct, leaving more to the decision-making power of private individuals and companies. It was certainly a watershed in the design of economic policies, and allowed for a better adaptation of Portuguese agriculture to foreign competition, growth in transport infrastructure, among others, and an upgrading of human resources. There were other, macroeconomic spinoffs too, as the Community's structural funds were also applied to the current account balance. Once again, however, not every effect of the Common Agricultural Policy and structural funds was positive, but ultimately the benefits almost certainly outweighed the costs. This is precisely what we need to assess in detail by looking at output and productivity trends throughout the whole century.

## Growth in the twentieth century

The evolution of the Portuguese economy during the twentieth century can now be studied in depth as a whole thanks to the amount of data that economic historians have been collecting about the main macroeconomic aggregates.[39] In fact, we have enough good data to depict trends and fluctuations of income per capita, the pace at which the Portuguese economy converged to the levels of the more developed European economies, as well as to identify the main sources of growth, namely investment in physical and human capital and factor productivity, and to make a thorough analysis of changes in the structure of the economy. The extent of these transformations is quite considerable and the Portuguese economy had one of the most significant overhauls of Europe, from West to East, as it went from a mainly agricultural society, with relatively little participation in the international economy, and little social protection and high levels of illiteracy and absolute poverty, to a service economy, socially and politically advanced. It still

---

[39] For quantitative sources for the twentieth century, see Batista *et al.* 1997, Lains 2003c, appendix, Pinheiro, ed. 1997 and Valério, ed. 2001.

Table 6.2 *Growth of real income per capita on the European periphery, 1913–2009 (annual growth rates, percent)*

|  | Portugal | Spain | Greece | Ireland | European core |
|---|---|---|---|---|---|
| 1913–1929 | 1.35 | 1.65 | 2.45 | 0.33 | 1.39 |
| 1929–1938 | 1.28 | −3.53 | 1.50 | 0.87 | 1.16 |
| 1938–1950 | 1.56 | 1.48 | −2.72 | 0.94 | 1.00 |
| 1950–1973 | 5.47 | 5.63 | 5.99 | 2.98 | 3.55 |
| 1973–1986 | 1.52 | 1.31 | 1.75 | 2.47 | 2.01 |
| 1986–1998 | 3.45 | 2.65 | 1.39 | 5.42 | 1.88 |
| 1998–2009 | 1.00 | 2.80 | 3.30 | 3.50 | 1.31 |

*Note:* European core is the average of Belgium, Denmark, France, and Germany (West Germany up to 1991). Great Britain, Italy, Netherlands, Norway, and Sweden.
*Source:* Pereira and Lains 2012.

remains one of the most backward economies in the region, but one where structural similarities with the forerunners are considerably more important than the dissimilarities.

Table 6.2 shows the growth of GDP per capita in Portugal and other peripheral countries of Europe and northern Europe. The first feature to note in the table is the favorable performance of the Portuguese economy during the first half of the century, which was above that of the average of the more advanced countries as well as of peripheral countries. This was caused by several elements, most importantly the fact that other peripheral countries were undergoing serious political disruptions. In Spain, the civil war that spanned from 1936 to 1939 had deep economic consequences, as did the Nazi occupation during World War II and the civil war that followed in Greece. In Ireland, independence in 1922 was followed by a period of international isolation, which deeply affected its economy due to its previous strong ties with Britain.[40] In Portugal, the problems ensuing from the advent of the Republican regime and later of dictatorship were of a much smaller scale than in those countries, and this largely accounts for differences in the economic performance of the peripheral countries in this period.

In order to identify the pattern of convergence of the Portuguese economy toward the more developed European economies, we can represent the country's GDP per capita as a percentage of an average for a sample of nine more advanced countries. This measure of

[40] Crafts and Toniolo, eds. 1996; Di Vittorio 2002. On Ireland, see also Lains 2008a.

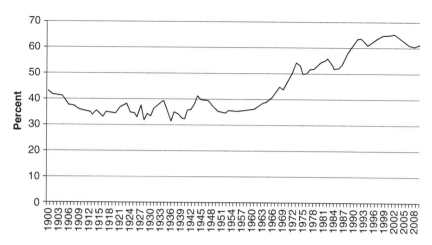

Figure 6.1 Portugal's convergence to the European core's GDP per capita, 1900–2009
Source: See Table 6.2.

convergence shows a slight increase in the gap of income per capita in the beginning of the twentieth century, up to the end of World War I, followed by a very slow recovery to 1945, and a sharp decline in the aftermath of World War II. From the early 1950s onwards, however, Portugal's GDP per capita increased faster than that of the other countries in the table and the gap was partially closed from about 35 to about 55 percent (see Figure 6.1). After 1973, convergence stalled again for slightly more than a decade, to recover in the years up to the early 1990s, when Portugal's GDP per capita was still about 65 percent of the average of the nine core countries, and remained at that level for the rest of the period. Growth in the post-war period up to 1973 occurred in countries under different political environments, including full democracies, socialist regimes closed to the more dynamic West and closely linked to the Soviet Union, or, as was the case of Portugal, Spain and, partially, Greece, market-oriented dictatorships increasingly integrated within Western Europe. From this range of experiences, it is clear that the nature of the political regime can only partially explain the speed of growth and convergence in this period. In the Western European periphery, Ireland was the exception until 1973, because of its close links to Britain, one of the least dynamic economies of the core countries. The reasons why Britain lagged behind are certainly related to the fact that it did not actively engage in European integration up to the end of the golden age of growth. It is important to study

Portuguese economic growth in a comparative framework, as it will lead us to a better set of conclusions regarding the *proximate* causes of growth, of which Salazar's economic policies are just a part.

After 1973, the pace of economic growth in Western Europe declined substantially and this downturn still needs to be the subject of further examination, as current explanations are not thorough enough, which stems from the fact that it is hard to come up with an explanation that covers such a wide array of national experiences. In the East, economic downturn came somehow later, in the 1980s, as these economies were not as dependent on the international settlements led by Bretton Woods and on middle east oil, but was much more severe, eventually leading to the fall of the socialist regimes there.[41] The best single explanation for the downturn which was already mentioned earlier in the chapter is that the domestic institutions that accounted for success prior to 1973 were unable to adapt to the new international situation that required greater flexibility.[42] In this regard, Ireland must be singled out once again as atypical, but this time in a positive way, as it resumed growth more rapidly than the rest of the West. The reason may be because there the state had not been as much as a factor of growth prior to 1973 and thus had less opportunity to develop atavistic interests. Britain, on the other hand, managed to dismantle faster the interventionist state, albeit at a high social cost, especially since the 1980s, thereby easing the transition to a period when institutional flexibility became more important. The 1973 downturn was particularly pronounced in Portugal, due to the political unrest provoked by the 1974 *coup*, in which we have to include the end of the African empire, in 1975. Moreover, the oil crisis and the change in the international economic order that preceded it with the end of Bretton Woods had to have a larger impact on an economy such as the Portuguese, due to its fragilities that stemmed from the traditional dependence on external sources of financing, such as returns from the re-export of colonial products, emigrant remittances, or capital imports. In fact, the international context had a major impact on the fluctuations of the Portuguese economy, a feature that we can clearly detect for the twentieth century, but which was certainly also present in previous centuries.[43] We need, however, to look also at changes in the domestic conditions of growth, including the evolution of investment in physical and human capital and technological change.

---

[41] Crafts and Toniolo 1996, 2010; Maddison 2001; Temin 2002.
[42] Eichengreen 1996, 2007.    [43] Lains 2003a; Lopes 1996.

*Growth accounting*

Economic growth is the outcome of different sources, including inputs or factors of production, namely labor force and the human capital it embodies in terms of education and on-the-job training; investment in physical capital, including infrastructure, machinery, and technology; and increases in the levels of productivity gained in the use of such factors. The sources of economic growth of a given country can be measured by using a simple production function that relates output with inputs, and data from national accounts, in what became known in the literature as growth accounting. These growth accounting exercises provide good grounds for the debate on the role of technology and institutional factors in nations catching up or falling behind, depending on the extent to which institutions affect the growth of total factor productivity. Different sources of growth can be associated with differences in the potential or sustainability of economic growth over time. Growth that depends on increases in the number of workers or their workload is more constrained than growth that is more dependent on investment, and both are more limited than growth based on the expansion of knowledge or factor productivity, as growth of the labor force and of investment have higher opportunity costs.[44] The distinction between inputs and growth of total factor productivity as sources of growth can be useful, but it does bring several problems with it. First, as productivity growth is measured as a residual, its correct measurement depends on the accuracy of the model. Second, it is not clear how that residual should be interpreted as it embodies a technological effect, which is also embodied in the growth of human and physical capital. Third, the distinction between input and factor productivity contribution to growth does not highlight the contribution of institutions, governments, and infrastructures as these factors affect both the growth of inputs and the growth of labor and capital productivity. Despite these shortcomings, the fact is that we can gain some insights into the causes of economic growth by estimating changes in the relative contribution of inputs and technology across time and across countries. Investment in physical capital made a large contribution to growth in Southeast Asia during thirty years following World War II. In the socialist regimes of the Soviet bloc, the expansion of economic activity was typically dependent more on capital investment than on technological advancements, imposing a higher burden on savings and thus on consumption levels and reaching more easily the limit.[45]

---

[44] For the development of these concepts, see Maddison 2001 and Crafts 2009.
[45] Crafts 2009; Ritschl 1996.

Table 6.3 *Sources of Portuguese economic growth, 1910–2009 (annual growth rates, percent)*

|  | Labor | Human capital | Capital | Total factor productivity | GDP |
|---|---|---|---|---|---|
| 1910–1934 | 0.33 | 0.70 | 0.42 | 0.72 | 2.17 |
| 1934–1947 | 0.44 | 0.38 | 1.30 | −0.02 | 2.09 |
| 1947–1973 | 0.23 | 0.82 | 2.58 | 1.53 | 5.17 |
| **1973–1990** | 0.02 | 1.61 | 1.74 | 0.56 | 3.93 |
| 1990–2000 | 0.73 | 1.27 | 0.80 | 1.50 | 3.17 |
| 2000–2009 | −0.03 | 0.80 | −2.46 | −0.10 | 0.89 |
| **1990–2009** | 0.38 | 1.09 | 1.41 | 0.70 | 2.14 |

*Source:* Pereira and Lains 2012.

Growth accounting estimates for Portugal are available for the twentieth century (see Table 6.3).[46] Total factor productivity expanded rather slowly in the first half of the century, increased significantly during the golden age years, from 1947 and 1973, at an annual rate of 1.53 percent, slowed down again after 1973, to regain speed later on, from 1990 to 2000, and slowing down again in the first decade of the new Millennium. According to the same accounts, growth before 1950 was largely due to the increase in labor, as well as human capital, and especially physical capital, which expanded particularly fast in the years between 1934 and 1947. This was due to considerable investment in public infrastructure and strong private investment in industry and agriculture (Table 6.3, third column). Total factor productivity growth between 1990 and 2000 may be attributed to the impact of European integration, and the slowdown after 2000 reflects what happened to factor productivity and investment in physical capital. Disentangling the different components of growth provides us with clues about the relative importance of investment, labor, and factor productivity, and this clearly enhances our understanding of the reasons behind fluctuations in the rates of growth. Our understanding of the decline of growth in the post-1973 period has to deal with explanations for the decline in total factor productivity and not as much with what happened in terms of the growth of inputs, in particular physical and human capital, which continued to expand at fast rates. Growth accounting is, however, essentially descriptive, and in order to find causal links more detailed research needs to be carried out, even if reaching definitive conclusions regarding the true

---

[46] Comparable estimates are available from Amaral 1998, Mateus 1998, and Neves 1996. For estimates on agriculture in Portugal during the nineteenth century, see Chapter 5.

Table 6.4 *Output and productivity growth by sector, 1950–2009 (annual growth rates, percent)*

|  | 1950–1973 | 1973–1990 | 1990–1999 | 2000–2009 |
|---|---|---|---|---|
| Agriculture |  |  |  |  |
| Output | 1.3 | 1.2 | 1.5 | −0.4 |
| Employment | −2.2 | −2.8 | −3.7 | −0.6 |
| Productivity | 3.5 | 4.0 | 5.2 | 0.2 |
| Industry |  |  |  |  |
| Output | 7.6 | 2.5 | −3.3 | −0.2 |
| Employment | 1.8 | 1.8 | −8.0 | −2.0 |
| Productivity | 5.8 | 0.7 | 4.7 | 2.2 |
| Services |  |  |  |  |
| Output | 6.0 | 3.7 | 3.9 | 1.8 |
| Employment | 1.6 | 3.8 | 2.9 | 1.3 |
| Productivity | 4.4 | −0.1 | 1.0 | 0.5 |
| Total GDP |  |  |  |  |
| Output | 5.7 | 2.9 | 3.4 | 0.9 |
| Employment | 0.2 | 1.7 | 0.8 | 0.2 |
| Productivity | 5.5 | 1.2 | 2.6 | 0.7 |

*Source:* Pereira and Lains 2012.

causes behind economic growth and, in particular, behind fluctuations in the level of economic activity, may prove difficult.[47]

### Sectoral growth

The analysis of output and labor productivity growth by sectors, that is, agriculture, industry, and services, for the years 1910–2009, provides further clues to understanding the main trends of the evolution of the Portuguese economy (see Table 6.4). After a period of slow growth, agricultural output expanded fast during the period from 1930 to 1950, which was mainly due to the protection extended to domestic wheat output and agriculture in general, from 1929 onward. Yet in the following decades, agricultural growth declined, as the effects of protection began to dwindle and the sector was unable to export. Yet, as population employed in the sector started declining since about 1950, labor productivity increased at a fast pace, between 3.5 and 5.2 percent per year. Agricultural growth was, however, mainly labor intensive, with little additional capital investment.

[47] For further discussion on growth trends later in the century, see Amaral 2010, Banco de Portugal, ed. 2009, Franco, ed. 2008, Lains, ed. 2009, Pereira and Lains 2012, and Teixeira *et al.*, eds. 2014.

The agricultural sector remained under state protection through the regulation of supply markets, price controls, and public investment in infrastructure. The resilience of Portugal's agricultural sector, until about 1960, was a consequence of the growth of domestic demand for agricultural products, protection from foreign competition, and public policies that imposed price controls and promoted investment in infrastructures. But it was also the outcome of the fact that the potential for output and productivity growth remained comparatively large until later on, as compared to the European countries where industrialization had started earlier. In fact, in certain periods of time, the levels of labor productivity in some agricultural sectors were higher and could increase faster than levels in some branches of the industrial or the service sectors. Structural change within the primary sector could bring more productivity gains, thus the shift of resources from agriculture to industries such as low value-added textiles. It was only with the rapid industrialization in the 1960s and increasing imports of agricultural products, that that changed in a significant way. The increase in agricultural imports did not put too much pressure on the external accounts, because of the growing inflow of emigrant remittances and capital imports. Moreover, the Portuguese agricultural sector, despite its shortcomings, managed to obtain considerable labor and capital productivity gains during parts of the period analyzed in this chapter. Such overall productivity gains implied that investments in the agricultural sector could compete favorably with investments in other sectors of the economy (Lains 2009b).

After 1960, agricultural output growth slowed down but as the labor force employed declined in absolute terms, labor productivity grew very fast. The fall in the labor force was mainly due to the expansion of the industrial sector and its capacity to attract labor from agriculture. The development of the agricultural sector is an important factor for the development of the rest of the economy, to the extent that it may be a source of increase of domestic consumption of manufacturing goods, as well as services, such as transport or banking. Yet, in the post–World War II period, in a context of rapid economic change at the national and international levels, industrialization depended on much more than just higher levels of domestic demand from the agricultural sector. Given that employment was influenced by factors exogenous to agriculture, we may conclude that under conditions of steady growth in production, the migration of labor to the other sectors drove changes in its productivity, rather than the other way around. Changes in agriculture thus depended on changes in the rest of the economy, and not the opposite.[48]

[48] Lains 2009; Soares 2005.

As to the industrial sector, output growth was relatively high since 1910 and peaked in the years 1950 to 1973 at 7.6 percent per year, as did labor productivity in the same years, at 5.8 percent. The output of basic industries, including metallurgic and energy production, reached an annual growth rate of 15.5 percent in the 1958–1966 period, chemicals and rubber grew at close to 10 percent per year in the two decades from 1953 to 1973, amounting to an unprecedented sevenfold increase in output (Lains 2003c: Chapter 6). After 1973, industrial growth slowed down and this was associated with a change in the reasons behind the transformation of the sector. In fact, the share of manufacturing with higher levels of capital intensity started declining. No major changes in the composition of the Portuguese industry occurred, but the trends of change reversed in that same year. For example, the sector of food, beverages, and tobacco, whose importance had dropped to 21 percent of transformed industrial output in 1973, started to rise thereafter. The same change occurred in textiles, clothing, and footwear, although the turnaround came slightly earlier, in 1966. Even though the sectors of food, beverages, tobacco and textiles, clothing, and footwear grew at more modest rates until 1973, their contribution to total industrial output growth was similar to that of the more capital-intensive sectors, due to the fact that their share in total output was considerably higher. As such, the contribution of these sectors to industrial growth still rose from 1973 on, and the textiles contributed with about 40 percent of industrial growth in the 1980–1990 period.

Thus, in order to understand the ups and downs in the rates of growth of Portugal's industrial sector, we need to look at all sectors, from the more modern to the more traditional manufactures. The growth of industry was mainly driven by the domestic market, then followed by exports and, finally, by import substitution. However, the contribution of domestic demand to growth varied across sectors, and this period witnessed the emergence of manufactures catering mostly to export markets, like textiles. The role of exports also changed during the years for which this type of disaggregated data on demand is available. Indeed, exports grew between 1959 and 1964, and again between 1970 and 1974, and possibly also in the following decades, for which no similar estimates exist, and a rising domestic demand is also noteworthy, while the contribution of import substitution fell. Prominent among the industries principally serving the domestic market were the sectors of metalworking, basic metallurgy, non-metallic mineral products, and consumer goods of food and clothing. In the export sectors we find industries making intensive use of abundant resources, like textiles and pulp and paper. Differing rates of growth in the sector were not driven by the demand mentioned earlier. As a result, the sectors in which domestic demand outweighed exports, that is, metallic products, basic metallurgy, and non-metallic mineral products, grew as quickly as pulp and paper, where the main demand came from abroad. We may likewise observe that the changing market weights do not move in parallel with rising and falling output.

Bearing all this in mind, we can argue that the shape of demand for industrial output, both domestic, including demand from agriculture, and external, did not set the pace for Portugal's industrial expansion in an obvious way, at least not in the years with a stronger growth, which ended in 1973. By this we intend not to dismiss the role of demand in the industrialization process, but only to put it in perspective. Demand factors certainly determined the structure of the country's industry, but did not set the pace of growth of output. For example, the fact that textiles and food remained so important in the structure of the sector for so many years is strongly linked to Portugal's low income per capita and to the resulting weak demand for other, less essential consumer goods, such as domestic appliances or cars. Changes in the weight by sector toward rising industrial output accompany the falling average rate of the country's industrial growth, from 8.6 percent per year, between 1956 and 1973, to under 3 percent, in the 1973–1990 period, even though this growth continued to outperform that of the rest of Europe. It is difficult to assess the opportunity costs triggered by the state's interference in the early days of industrialization. We can nevertheless contend that state policies led to the creation of a range of infrastructure, such as basic industries, public works, and electric power supply that helped the remaining industrial sectors, especially those connected to light industries. Along this line of thinking, it is worth recalling that the success of certain future exporters may be related to the very policy of import substitutes. In light of the relevance that foreign markets historically have among small, open, developing economies, Portugal's industrialization should follow the pattern of advantages seen elsewhere regarding outward trade. However, compared with other small European countries, by 1978 Portugal was still among those that were less open to the outside.

By the early 1970s, the level of capital per worker in Portugal was still relatively low when compared with that in the rest of Europe, and this disadvantage was higher in terms of human capital than physical capital. The relationship between skills and wealth is less clear than the one between physical capital and wealth. Socialist Yugoslavia, for example, while having a GDP per capita similar to that of Portugal, recorded in 1970 considerably higher levels of schooling and labor qualification, in fact close to the levels seen in Western Europe. These differences highlight the fact that training a skilled workforce depends less on wealth than on physical capital training. This is important in terms of the prospects for international specialization of a country like Portugal, since it suggests that the development of comparative advantages based on skilled labor can be less costly in terms of resources than the development of comparative advantages in physical capital-intensive sectors. Further, later we will discuss the reasons behind the success of manufactures linked to skilled labor-intensive sectors and that have performed successfully in international markets.

Factor endowments clearly reflect in a country's structure of industrial production and employment. Sectors with a more intensive use of unskilled labor prevail in Portugal, similarly to what happens across Southern Europe. Industries that make less use of capital in their production account for the largest share of industrial production, and, in this respect, the Portuguese case is relatively extreme, especially regarding the distribution of labor. The structure of the industrial sector is increasingly reflected in the structure of exports, as the country continued to open to the outside. As a result, Portugal specialized in export products which are unskilled labor-intensive. Exceptions to this rule exist, as certain exports are produced by highly skilled labor, and these sectors have grown over the years. The fact that the comparative advantages of Portuguese industry are concentrated in sectors that are more unskilled-labor-intensive, albeit increasingly more specialized, is not necessarily a negative factor for the future of Portugal's industry. In some areas, the country reached a relatively strong standing in foreign markets. These sectors include manufactures of leather, wood, textiles, clothing and footwear, and non-metallic minerals. In addition to these sectors, Portugal also has some comparative advantages in specific areas, such as office machinery and electric appliances.

The variety of Portugal's industrial specialization can be revealed by data on exports, which show that Portugal had comparative advantages in many sectors, including some that employ a highly skilled labor force. Industries such as chemical fertilizers, electric wires and cables, and electric-powered industrial machinery are among these. The years of rapid industrialization in the 1960s and 1970s were marked by the development of specific sectors of basic industry. In a small and increasingly open economy, their success depended on their ability to compete in the space where they could expand to international markets. But the latter were transformed by the 1973 and 1979 oil crises, and increasingly competitive, thus presenting an additional challenge for a peripheral country with little bargaining power. There were probably few alternatives to the path of rapid post-war industrialization followed by

Portugal. Despite the abundance of cheap labor, capital-intensive investments could be rational, since even though capital was relatively scarce at the macroeconomic level, it was not necessarily so at the micro level. This may have been the case because interest rates were held down by the government, and also because investment opportunities were not abundant, which in many instances meant that the supply of capital was higher than demand for it. The shortage of business initiatives in industry was closely linked to the high-risk nature of investment in most of them, which were in little explored areas, given the infancy of most of the industries in question. The cases of the Lisbon shipyards, Lisnave, and the Sines petrochemical complex, sponsored by direct or indirect state intervention, are good examples of the rise in the output of equipment goods and large-scale investment. The profitability of these investments, however, depended on the ability these sectors had to export, and thus on their competitiveness, as the domestic market was insufficient.[49]

The services sector acted as a shock absorber for the cyclical fluctuations of growth in the other sectors of the economy (see Table 6.4). Services' output thus grew slower than industry between 1950 and 1973, and faster between 1973 and 1990. Yet in terms of labor productivity the story is slightly different, as it declined in both sectors after 1973, which was a major feature of the period.[50] Looking at the employment figures also yields some interesting conclusions. Between 1950 and 1973, the overall growth of employment in Portugal was very low, at only 0.2 percent per year, which translated in to a relatively high growth rate in the productivity of labor. However, in the following period, from 1973 until 1990, employment growth rose to an annual rate of 1.7 percent, and labor productivity in those same years was very low. These two opposing trends were due, on the one hand, to large-scale emigration toward Europe in the decades up to 1973 and, on the other, to the return of Portuguese citizens from the African colonies, after they gained independence in 1975 (Amaral 2010). Overall employment growth since 1973 occurred mostly in the services sector, as the growth rate increased from 1.6 percent per year in 1950–1973 to 3.8 percent in 1973–1990. In the following decades, overall employment growth retreated from those levels. The labor force employed in agriculture fell during the whole period after 1950, as the economy gained momentum, first pulled by rapid industrialization and, after 1973, by the growth of both industry and services.

---

[49] Pintado 2002; Ribeiro et al. 1987.    [50] Pintado 2002; Lains 2003c.

*After the golden age*

Changes in the growth rate of GDP can be explained by changes in the rate of growth of labor and capital, and changes in total factor productivity. In the last quarter of the twentieth century, the observed contraction in the rate of growth of industrial output was mainly due to the decline in total factor productivity growth. After 1973, there was a substantial fall in the contribution of total factor productivity growth that was, in part, due to the increased rate of growth of human capital offsetting the reduction in physical capital growth. The contribution of capital to total output growth declined only slightly and the decline in the rate of growth of total output can be ascribed mainly to the decline in the contribution of total factor productivity growth. Thus, explaining the fall in total factor productivity growth goes a long way toward understanding such an important turn in the performance of the Portuguese economy in the last decades of the twentieth century. Changes in the growth of productivity at the aggregate level can be attributed to changes in productivity growth in each of the sectors or economic areas, or to the transfers of resources from low-performing sectors to higher-performing ones. Less-developed countries had production and employment structures that differed from those of more advanced countries. This is explained by the greater size of the agricultural sector at the outset, but also by the differences among industrial sectors. In earlier development phases, there is a tendency for larger textile and food-producing sectors, and smaller sectors for chemicals, machinery, and advanced, technology-intensive industries.

Differences in the structure of output can be linked to the availability of natural resources, levels of domestic savings and investment, and different elasticities of demand. Structural change can be driven by rising demand for investment goods, to the detriment of consumer goods, in periods of greater investment, and can be caused by a greater use of intermediary products in agriculture and industry. The fall of factor productivity growth in the industrial sector, after 1973, may also be explained by shifts in the structure of the output. For example, Portugal's industrial labor productivity was comparatively higher in traditional sectors, namely, textiles, wearing apparel, leather and footwear, wood products, paper, and electrical appliances. These were the sectors where Portugal had comparative advantages in the international markets. Yet productivity growth after 1973 was below the average for industry. Thus, the rise in exports could be associated with a declining growth of total factor productivity in the sector or that the short-term gains accruing from specialization along comparative advantages were offset by the losses accruing from the specialization in sectors with lower growth potential.[51] The impact of changes in the structure of labor employment in total labor productivity can also be measured by breaking down the growth of aggregate productivity into three components. The first is an intra-industry effect, which refers to changes of productivity within each sector; the second is the static effect, which measures the gains accruing from the shift of resources toward sectors with productivity *levels* above the average; and the dynamic effect, which measures the impact of resources shifting to sectors with productivity growth *rates* above the average. We have data on this type of analysis for the periods from 1953 to 1990 and from 1979 to 2002.

Accordingly, during 1960–1973 and 1979–1990, structural change had a negative impact on productivity growth. This was the result of rising employment in the textile sector, which had lower than average *levels* and *growth rates* of labor productivity (Lains 2004). Between 1979 and 1990, a transfer of resources to sectors with lower productivity levels took place. Gains from structural change were largely due to the transfer of resources from agriculture to industry and services, as well as transfers within the services sector. Because of this, few gains resulted from structural changes in the industrial sector, because the structure depended on factors that did not vary significantly during those periods, such as natural resources and the levels of physical and human capital, and patterns of domestic and international demand for industrial products. Moreover, the dynamic effect was also negative in 1986–1994 and 1994–2002, and impacted negatively in labor productivity growth by –53.5 percent in the first period and –39.1 percent in the second period. In other words, in Portugal labor was leaving the industries, in both manufacturing and services, with above average productivity growth.[52]

The transformation of Portugal's economic structure in terms of employment had a positive impact on the growth of aggregate labor productivity during the golden age that followed World War II. After 1973, that impact fell sharply and eventually disappeared altogether, as much of the labor employed in agriculture transferred to the industrial and services sectors. The changes in the structure of wage labor thus greatly contributed to the slowdown in labor productivity growth since 1973. The impact of structural change was different in the industrial sector. The rapid rise of industrial labor productivity in the years before 1973 was not clearly linked to structural changes in industrial employment, i.e., in those areas with higher levels or higher rates of labor productivity growth. In other words, regarding the existence of a structural bonus effect in manufacturing, the table shows mixed results.

---

[51] Barbosa *et al.* 1999: 282–284. See also Pessoa 2014.    [52] Lains 2008a; Pessoa 2014.

After 1973, we see negative effects that vary according to the way structural changes in labor moved to the industrial areas with levels and rates of productivity growth below the average of the manufacturing sector. This is partly explained by the fact that this sector presented significant differences in the levels and rates of labor productivity growth. These differences were caused by fluctuations within the country's manufacturing sector in terms of capital and labor skills.

To better understand the economic downturn after 1973, the causes of the performance of labor productivity in the industrial sector must be taken into consideration, as must the causes behind the negative structural effect, which are probably linked to the structure of investment in human and physical capital in the industrial sector. Such difficulties must be included in our evaluation of the country's economic growth during the last quarter of the century. The reallocation of resources from agriculture to industry, and then to services, is, in relative terms, more important for less industrialized countries, for which it is especially important to pre-visualize and define the goal of structural change vis-à-vis the country's economic challenges. In addition, this process has less of an impact as poorer countries conform to a pattern of structural change more similar to that of developed economies, in which the impact of that change on economic growth probably ends up fading as well. In less developed economies, structural change can thus be a source of economic growth or contraction. Economies develop in stages involving different types of structural change, and this has an impact on the rate of the overall growth of economies. In the first phase, agriculture dominates the economy and the increase in aggregate productivity is driven by the slow growth of productivity in this sector. In the second phase, the country becomes industrialized, and the increase in aggregate productivity is driven by the transfer of resources into sectors with higher productivity levels. The positive effect of this resource transfer does not depend exclusively on the fact that the productivity is growing more rapidly in the industrial sector than elsewhere in the economy; it also results from the fact that the *level* of industrial productivity is higher than in other sectors. The third phase of economic growth witnesses a surge in the services sector that generally has a tendency to have lower productivity levels and growth rates than in the industrial sector. Thus, growth in the services sector can have a slowing effect on overall economic growth. But the effects of structural change on economic growth can be equally important for the transformations that occur in the agricultural, industrial, and services sectors. Europe's peripheral countries, and in particular Portugal, have undergone major transformations as different sectors adapted to changes in patterns of demand, both domestically and internationally.

The transformation of the structure of the Portuguese economy in terms of employment shares had a positive impact in the growth of aggregate labor productivity during the golden age. After 1973, that impact was substantially reduced and eventually disappeared as labor was largely reallocated out of the agricultural sector into the industrial and services sectors. Thus changes in the structure of labor employment did contribute significantly to the downturn in labor productivity growth. Within the industrial sector, structural change had a different impact. The rapid growth of industrial labor productivity registered in the years up to 1973 was not clearly associated with changes in the structure of industrial employment toward industrial branches with higher levels or higher growth rates of labor productivity. In the following decade, changes in the structure of labor employment were directed toward industrial branches with levels and growth rates of labor productivity lower than the manufacturing sector average. This outcome stems from the fact that Portugal's manufacturing sector embodied important differences in levels and growth rates of labor productivity. The causes behind such differences are related to differences in capital endowments and labor skills across the Portuguese manufacturing sector.

As the world economy at large lost momentum in the last quarter of the twentieth century for reasons that go beyond simple explanations due to the variety of cases, the room for growth and convergence in Europe became much smaller. Yet in certain periods of time some economies in the European periphery still managed to expand faster than the average and thus bridge at least partially the gaps in income and productivity levels in relation to the more advanced economies. Such gains were to a certain extent associated with changes in European economic policies that favored economic integration, that is, relevant increases in international trade and capital and, albeit less intensively, migration of workers. That happened both after the EU enlargement to the south and the east, from the mid 1980s onwards. However, the close association between the deepening of European integration and economic convergence in the periphery has somehow disappeared in the first decade of the new millennium and the case of Portugal is certainly paradigmatic of that.

## The climacteric and beyond

Economic history is not about measuring the spirit of economic agents regarding historical landmarks, but it is possibly true to argue that there is a generalized pessimism about the growth potential for the Portuguese economy in the first decade of the new millennium, precisely when the Economic and Monetary Union, created in 1992 and fully implemented in 1999 with the launching of the euro, was supposed to bring large benefits to the whole of the Eurozone (Marsh 2011). Large benefits were expected of the monetary union due to the reduction of transaction costs, financial integration, and interest rates (Barbosa *et al.* 1999). Yet expectations were not fulfilled and the initial optimism was replaced by pessimism regarding the prospects for growth of the Portuguese economy and also, to a certain extent, the prospects for European integration and that is clearly reflected in many studies carried out by international organizations that look after the state of the world and the European economies.[53] The post-euro pessimism is in stark opposition from what could be expected by the analysis of what happened after comparable moves toward more integration at the national and international levels, such as those which happened after Bretton Woods, the Marshall Plan, the creation of the EEC, and successive enlargements, or what happened in Portugal after the 1974 coup, the accession to the European Communities in 1986, or to the Economic and Monetary Union in 1992, which we have analyzed in this chapter. As a backward economy in the context of a more developed region, standard growth theory would predict that the Portuguese economy would continue to converge to the levels of factor productivity and income per capita of the more advanced countries in Europe. Convergence would occur in a context of open borders, as the flow of workers, capital, knowledge, and trade in goods and services would lead to bridging the gap between the levels of factor productivity and the structure of the Portuguese economy, and those of the more advanced countries in Europe and elsewhere. That is the main lesson of convergence that we may find in the economic history of Europe and large stretches of the rest of the world since the Industrial Revolution and which we have reviewed in this book. Moreover, as we have shown in this chapter, the twentieth century, taken as a whole, was a period of overall convergence of income levels, although with relevant fluctuations.

Thus, since about 2000, the Portuguese economy has diverged albeit slightly from the rest of Europe and we need to understand whether that divergence will once again be reversed or not.[54] One possible explanation is that the country's growth potential is hindered by institutional under-development and the lack of political will to change the judicial system, labor market legislation, or excessive rents in a few quasi-monopolistic

---

[53] OECD 2013. See, for this period, Banco de Portugal, ed. 2009 and Lains, ed. 2009.
[54] Banco de Portugal, ed. 2009; Franco, ed. 2008; Lains, ed. 2009; Pereira 2011; Teixeira *et al.*, eds. 2014.

sectors. There are certainly a good number of institutional problems that need to be solved, but not clear is the extent to which economic growth slowdown is due to them or other factors. Moreover, the view that laggard institutions are the main cause of slow growth is hardly compatible with the long-term view presented in the current book, even if we consider just the twentieth century. In fact, whatever gauge we use, it seems clear that Portugal's level of institutional development in 2000 was considerably higher than half a century before during the heyday of the golden age. In the first place, the country became a full-fledged democracy, which means that economic policy options are politically and socially sustained for longer periods as there is no risk of rupture in the political environment.[55] Second, the levels of literacy of the population at all levels have increased significantly, virtually closing the gap to the rest of Europe, which means that institutions on which the economy depends are now staffed by a more educated labor force. That is relevant not only for the public sector, but also for the private sector, as is the case with banking and other financial institutions. A similar argument can be developed in what regards health levels of the population which have increased at a very rapid speed throughout the second half of the twentieth century and particularly in the last quarter. In what regards the international economic setting, Portugal's institutional development is also notable, as a consequence, most of all, of its full integration in the European Communities and the European Union that followed. Even though institutional development is unquestionable, it is necessary to take into account too that this is certainly a moving target, as similar developments occurred elsewhere in the world and particularly in Europe, the region that is more relevant for Portugal.

In determining what lies behind poor economic performance, we should not take as causes of backwardness factors that are merely associated with it, as it is necessary to investigate different possibilities regarding causality. Bad institutions may hinder growth, but backwardness may also be a cause behind poor institutional development. For example, if backwardness is related to lower levels of literacy, this in turn can be associated with lower institutional performance which implies significant investment in human capital (Cameron 1997: 3–5). If causality is not taken into account, we cannot but reach the conclusion that economic policies in Portugal have been wrong throughout the century and that the right options have not been followed, for sociological reasons or because of the mentality of businessmen, politicians, or even the population more broadly. Whatever the role institutions may have in blocking growth

---

[55] On democracy and economic growth in Southern Europe, see Maravall 1997.

potential, it is very unlikely that they are the sole cause for the climacteric observed since the turn of the century.

Growth slowdown after 2000 may also be related to the impact of the deepening of European integration on Portugal's economy. In fact, recent developments in economic geography cast doubts on the ability of less developed areas reaping net benefits from participating in a wider market, without trade barriers for products, capital, and people, and full openness to international competition, and catching up to the more advanced areas. Open borders mean that the national economy has to adapt to a new international environment and that economic sectors that are not competitive internationally have to close or adapt, whereas sectors that are able to compete can prosper and new sectors may also emerge. Yet it may be the case that the output gains from the emerging or new sectors do not compensate for the losses stemming from the sectors that are driven out of production. One expected outcome from the abolition of trade barriers is the concentration of activity in areas that provide better infrastructure and that are already well endowed with technological development and the like.[56] The intensification of globalization in the last two decades, which was accompanied by the emergence of new industrial exporters, such as China or India, increased competition in the sectors which formed an important part of Portugal's industrial output, such as textiles and electronics. And these industries suffered a severe blow, particularly since China joined the World Trade Organization, in 2001 (St. Aubyn 2014:70–71).

One relevant explanation for the drop in growth rates derives from the analysis of the impact of structural change of the economy, as there was an increase in the share in GDP of sectors with lower than average levels of productivity, such as social services, including education and health. On the other hand, lower productivity growth may also be related to a decline in the rate of human capital accumulation, as literacy and secondary schooling fully get to total population in the relevant age brackets. Also, investment in basic infrastructure, such as roads or ports, has probably reached a ceiling in terms of overall impact on growth, as the country moved from a very backward situation to levels closer to those of the wealthier European countries. Economic policy during the years 1990 onwards was also fundamentally pro-cyclical and that may have exacerbated structural imbalances, both at the level of the public budget and the external account, which ultimately constrained growth.[57] Finally, by joining the euro, exporters lost competitiveness, to the extent

---

[56] Krugman and Venables 1995. See, for Portugal, Amador *et al.* 2009 and Marques 2009.
[57] Gaspar and St. Aubyn 2009; Lopes 2005.

that the new currency was overvalued, and domestic producers had to face increased levels of competition from abroad. Moreover, the low interest rates that the Portuguese economy had to face, as determined by the Eurozone monetary policy, had a negative impact on domestic savings and led to a high level of external borrowing (Martins 2009). All the above are hypotheses that need to be further analyzed and the most likely outcome is that no single cause will ever emerge as more significant. If that is so, if economic problems derive from a large array of causes, we then need to conclude that the best way to characterize the difficulties of the Portuguese economy to grow have to be related to the general context and, in particular, to the important changes that occurred in the international economy since the launching of the euro.[58] But does that mean that the Portuguese economy cannot converge in a context where an autonomous fiscal and monetary policy is absent? The answer to that question is related to our interpretation of how European integration has worked out similar problems across its history.

We need to recall that the Portuguese economy since as far back as the end of World War II was increasingly opened to the international economy, as a consequence of successive abolition of barriers to trade of many kinds, including tariffs, quotas, domestic price protection, or other legislative arrangements. The destruction of such barriers had several important marks which as we have mentioned throughout this chapter were virtually completed by the creation of the Economic and Monetary Union, following the 1992 Maastricht Treaty. It was not a smooth process and on some occasions there were periods of reversal, the most important of which was certainly the one that followed the 1973 international economic crisis and the 1974 military coup in Portugal. It is also worth noting that the abolition of barriers to trade was not necessarily followed at all times by an increase in the intensity of economic relations with the outside world; that intensity also depended on the speed of growth of both the domestic and international economies. Yet certainly the main trend was that of an increasing degree of openness for Portugal accompanied by the growth of foreign trade, capital flows, and international migration. Moreover, we can also conclude that the increase in the degree of participation in the international economy was met by changes in the structure of the Portuguese economy akin to its set of comparative advantages. That was quite clear during the years from 1960 to 1973 (and beyond), when the agricultural sector with no export capacity shrunk considerably and resources, that is, labor and capital, moved toward the

[58] See Pereira and Lains 2012: 115–124. See also Aguiar-Conraria *et al.* 2012 and Blanchard 2007.

manufacturing sector and in particular to sectors with a high export performance. A similar period of structural change following the country's pattern of comparative advantages occurred during the short-lived boom in the aftermath of the accession to the European Communities to the mid 1990s. From then on, the contribution of structural change up to economic growth and, in particular, the contribution of foreign trade, dwindled significantly. Then started the period in which trade openness ceased to be accompanied by the adaptation of the domestic economy to competition from abroad and higher levels of growth and convergence. The understanding of these changes is a major issue in the study of the Portuguese economy and, for that matter, of integration and convergence of the less developed areas in the European Union, and thus no final answer to that puzzle can be provided without further investigation.

Yet we may note here, following what has been stated throughout the present chapter, the possible relevance of the contribution of economic policy to the adaptation or lack thereof of the Portuguese economy to increasing levels of openness. In fact, up to the more recent times, successive steps in the reduction of trade barriers were accompanied by domestic or European policies that helped the needed changes in the structure of output. This occurred either by keeping protection to some sectors in the context of wider liberalization, as it occurred during the textile "revolution" in the 1960s, or during the 1986–1995 short boom when structural change was considerably helped by the two waves of structural funds designed by the European Commission during Jacques Delors' presidency. Moreover, during those days when trade openness and economic growth went hand in hand, Portuguese governments maintained their ability to use fiscal and monetary policy, which ended up having some positive effects and not only in the short term. One such circumstance was during the late 1970s and early 1980s, in the context of high inflation rate levels, when a crawling-peg was introduced for the exchange rate, implying a slow and predictable devaluation of the domestic currency, the *escudo*, which promoted exports and domestic demand for domestic producers (Lopes 2008: 26). After 1992 and, particularly, after 1999, as the Economic and Monetary Union was bringing more integration to Europe, not only did transfers from Brussels remain at the same level as before, but also the national government lost its capacity to intervene in the economy and also there was a perverse effect of monetary policy of the European Central Bank on Portugal's external accounts and government deficit, due to the sharp fall in the cost of borrowing from the international capital markets.

Higher factor productivity is naturally needed for higher growth and it will certainly be associated also with changes in the structure of output toward sectors with higher levels or growth rates of productivity. That transformation may stem from economic policies which will have to be European, as national economic policies are restricted within the European Union and the Eurozone. By the end of the twentieth century, the Portuguese economy was clearly backward in terms of social and economic indicators, such as income per capita levels, labor productivity, demographic indicators, literacy and schooling years, or economic infrastructure. Its structure of economic activity also lagged behind significantly, especially in the industrial sector. But the Portuguese economy also shows an accumulated experience of institutional development and greater competitiveness in foreign markets. The last twenty years have shown that the openness to the outside, from an institutional point of view, was not a sufficient condition for the economy to follow a path of unequivocal convergence.

What lessons can we learn from these developments? It is hard to determine what actions would need to be taken to ensure that the opening to the outside would bring about progress in the country's productivity and revenue. The international specialization of the Portuguese economy in 2010 was perhaps less favorable to growth than the specialization that existed in 1992, as since then the weight of some sectors with lower labor and capital productivity increased. This transformation, which will need to be reverted, was the consequence of an adaptation to a more competitive world. In the history of the European Communities such costs of growth have been partially offset by public policies. But such policies may be harder to implement as enlargement to 25 countries, in 2004, raised the number of regions and countries competing for that support. It is therefore difficult to envision a quick solution for the problems experienced by a poor country adapting to greater integration with wealthier and more developed countries, in terms of industry, services, and capital markets. One could even argue that there is no solution and that any effort to correct the processes already underway will only exacerbate the challenges that Portugal faces.

# Conclusion

This book is about the economic history of a small country at the southwestern European periphery, with borders dating back to the twelfth century, and which was for a long period of time at the center of an empire with settlements across Asia, South America, and Africa. The study is based on a large body of literature which has focused on the evolution of political, institutional, demographic, and economic settings within a long period of state formation and consolidation. In spite of the scarcity of quantitative information, most of all regarding the medieval and early modern periods, we were able to provide a coherent account that responds to the fundamental questions about when, how, and why the economy expanded, stagnated, or contracted, and about changes of the country's role in the world economy. All countries matter in a way or another, but Portugal, the country we have studied here, matters in many ways that are particularly relevant. European economic history is also about what happened in its peripheral regions.

It is our contention that the present study highlights in a relevant way the vagaries of long-term institutional and economic development in the European periphery. Our research shed light on the reasons why empires are formed and the economic consequences they may have in the metropolitan economies, as well as on the role of economic and financial transactions at international level, and movements of population and urbanization. The book is also relevant for understanding the degree to which political stability influenced the pace of economic growth.

With fixed borders for more than eight centuries, Portugal provides a case study for which we can observe several dimensions considering the steadiness of space and political order. Since late medieval times, Portugal seldom experienced warfare in its domestic front, at a time when international relations in Europe were shaped by military confrontations that are at the root of state formation. Even the Dynastic Union of 1580 was not the fruit of conquest, but an enforcement of the rights of Philip II of Spain to the throne of Portugal. The secession in 1640, however, became a milestone in the political history of the country. Historians today may recognize it as a part of a long-term political movement that shaped European history, whereby the hegemony of Spanish Habsburg composite monarchy was undermined. In this respect, Portugal's history parallels that of the United Provinces, and diverges from the Catalonian experience. Therefore, critical moments of conflict, like the Restoration War and the War of the Spanish Succession, did not endanger the territorial integrity. That outcome was made possible by diplomatic alignments that ensured the military protection of the Atlantic powers, particularly the one that became the leading economy in the nineteenth century. Thus, diplomacy was a significant device in Portugal's fixed borders, which ensured the endurance of an institutional framework, whose key features laid down the foundations of an early modern state. Yet, the same alignments also put the country further away from central Europe, a region that experienced fast growth in the nineteenth century. Hence, stability of the borders and state formation seem to have been at least a neutral factor for economic growth.

The stability of the territory went hand in hand with demographic features, which also singles out this case study. From the sixteenth to the eighteenth century, population growth can be compared to that of the leading northwestern countries, displaying an annual average rate close to 0.4 percent. However, while in England population vitality went together with a steady increase in urbanization rates, in Portugal there was a fall in the percentage of urban dwellers. The question is why Portugal followed a different path. One of the answers lies probably in the role of the empire in providing an escape to Malthusian constraints in the English case, which did not occur in the Portuguese case.

Like England, Portugal had one of the long-lasting empires, whose commercial dynamics and volume of trade per capita was also parallel to that of other European colonizers. A discussion of the linkage between colonial expansion and long-term growth needs to take Portugal's experience into account because it offers evidence that causes that may have been sufficient elsewhere, although present in Portugal did not promote conditions for economic growth. On the one hand, the connection between colonial expansion and military might seems to be absent in Portugal; on the other hand, the empire pushed domestic revenue up, but did not underpin conditions to gains of productivity, as happened in England, where the increase of domestic sectors' output responded to aggregate demand, including the demand from colonial settlements.

The expanding markets in the Portuguese colonies were mostly supplied with re-exports of European goods, generating a wealthy *entrepôt* trade and rents but without propelling specialization and higher demand of domestic labor and capital.

We have looked above all to the dynamics of institutional and economic transformation, going beyond narratives based on the observation of successive crises thus cutting with a more traditional historiography where the relevance of crises and failures tend to be overemphasized. Crises did occur in Portugal, of course, and were sometimes severe, but they were most frequently just part of a larger process of historical change, which is what we really need to explain. We are often reminded that Portugal lagged behind the steps of countries larger in population and natural resources and more powerful in military or political terms. Yet, that is just part of the story, as peripheral and smaller countries also saw very important transformations at all levels, and in particular in their economies. We have emphasized economic transformation and focused our analysis on the major trends throughout the centuries, particularly the evolution of population, agriculture, industry, and services, as well as the evolution of the institutional framework, public finances, banking, and foreign trade.

We have shown that the Portuguese population experienced moments of stagnation and contraction, the most dramatic of which came with the Black Death in the late fourteenth century. Between 1500 and 1800 the Portuguese population grew at a rate only slightly lower than that of northeastern Europe, and faster than in the Mediterranean area. In the eighteenth century, perhaps for the first time since the beginning of the overseas expansion, emigration to Brazil, in response to the gold mining rush, caused a population decline in mainland Portugal for thirty years, up to the 1730s. A similar flow of emigration occurred in the second half of the nineteenth century and, again, in the third quarter of the twentieth century. These migration cycles had different causes, which responded to events in the world economy, whether in the case of migration to the empire, to Europe, or to other parts of the world, and they were part of population flows that were taking place elsewhere in Europe. However, the idea that Portugal can be characterized as a country of emigrants does not fit into the early modern period, and from the sixteenth to the end of the eighteenth century, the number of inhabitants grew threefold. This demographic pressure actually led to a gradual increase in the area under cultivation in the kingdom and changes in the rural landscape over the centuries reflect the slow dissemination of the population across the countryside. We concluded that the yield obtained from the land also increased over the long term, albeit with short-run fluctuations. In the nineteenth century, Portugal still kept large stretches of arable land uncultivated, and during the first half of the twentieth century land was being cleared for the plantation of forests, particularly in the mountainous regions. Increasing the area of cultivated land and turning pastures into cultivated areas introduced some tensions in terms of "internal colonization," and perhaps put downward pressure on the earnings of agricultural labor. Thus gains in output were achieved through the addition of labor and the tilling of more land, and the revenue obtained through these factors was modest.

From early times the agricultural activity was closely linked to the international markets. In the Middle Ages, Portugal imported grain and exported wine and olive oil, a trade pattern that would continue in the centuries to come. Foreign trade of agricultural produce expanded slightly in the following centuries, encouraged by the signing of trade treaties with major commercial partners, under which primary goods, transformed or not to varying degrees, would be exchanged for manufactures. The Methuen Treaty (1703), the end of the monopoly over Brazilian trade (1810), and the tariff-reduction treaties signed throughout the remainder of the nineteenth century fostered the internationalization of the economy. But the growth of Portuguese agriculture was not driven by exports and outward-looking policies. It was much more a response to domestic population dynamics, settlement patterns, the capacity for innovation, climate conditions, and the presence or absence of war. Development in agriculture did not follow the more positive course that prevailed elsewhere in Great Britain or the Low Countries, where there were important structural transformations and productivity of land and labor increased substantially. These transformations allowed for faster urbanization growth in the eighteenth and nineteenth centuries. Contrarily, after a significant increase in the sixteenth century, urbanization in Portugal slowed down and, from the 1700s to the 1800s, fell slightly, in a similar pattern to the Netherlands but different to the one experienced in Spain and Italy.

The slow pace of urbanization from about 1600 onwards mirrors the diffusion of industrial labor in the rural areas. Industrial activities spread across the country according to population settlement patterns, and some manufactures also concentrated in and around urban centers, or close to sources of energy, such as charcoal and water, and transport infrastructure. In fact, manufacturing developed mostly in the form of rural domestic units responding to the demand of a low income population. The situation somewhat changed with protectionist policies in the seventeenth and eighteenth centuries, and with the development of external trade, notably with the empire which was a source of primary goods for re-exports and domestic consumption, as well as outlets for exports. From the nineteenth century onwards, international competition increased significantly, both in the European and in the domestic markets, which had to face the lower prices of manufacturing imports. These challenges were not exclusive to Portugal, as international economic growth brought together trading nations with different abilities and, as a result, different types of specialization. Fortunes rose and fell among these many trading partners over time, and did not always adversely affect Portugal. Short-term setbacks were counter-balanced in the long run, pulling the country ever closer to the international sphere. Importantly, Portuguese industry was relatively well diversified, which put it on a good footing for considerable growth in the nineteenth century, and especially throughout the twentieth century, when it outpaced the rates of growth elsewhere in Europe.

Imperial relations defined the structure of external trade from the sixteenth century up to the twentieth century. This structure was marked by re-exports of colonial products, with successive cycles dominated by different staples, namely pepper, sugar, gold, and later on cotton, coffee, and cocoa. As a result, the trade balance became sensitive to competition with other European powers when they established their own overseas empires. The seventeenth century set in regularly negative trade balances, which persisted thereafter. For many decades, these imbalances were offset by the influx of Brazilian gold that arrived in such quantities that Portugal became one of Europe's leaders in terms of money supply per capita. One of the puzzles facing historians and economists studying the eighteenth century is to fully grasp the consequences of this cash surplus and its impact on GDP, which reached new heights precisely in the years when the inflow of gold reached its peak.

The insertion of Portugal's foreign relations into the European context has often been neglected by historians, since the overseas expansion was a high-profile event, and one that had an obvious impact on world economy. The fleets that sailed from Portugal's shores, the exotic cargos they brought back, the wealth of the monarch and private individuals who amassed fortunes, have sparked the imagination of generations, both in Portugal and abroad far more than the mundane reality of economic activity, which was mostly that of agriculture, sometimes little beyond the subsistence level, and the manufacturing of items of low standards. Portugal ruled with varying degrees of intensity over its overseas possessions which had an important role on the country's foreign trade, as well as on the financing of the State and the activity of merchants and coastal cities, of which Lisbon is certainly the most relevant example. But important as it was in shaping external relations and the way the state was financed, the empire was only part of the country's economic activity and it was seldom dominant in terms of the contribution to economic evolution.

Portugal maintained high trade deficits for centuries, and balance was achieved when borders were closed. The persistence of deficits is largely a consequence of recurrent financing difficulties that threatened the country's economic and political stability. Yet, such instability should be seen as a direct consequence of Portugal's participation in the international economy, and ultimately affecting the country's productivity levels in relation to those of its main trading partners. Foreign debt and the chronic problems incurred in servicing it continue to overwhelm Portugal's economic performance.

The building of the fiscal state was less affected by the State's inability to manage tax collection than by the institutional consequences of the colonial system. The easy access royal coffers had to rents extracted from key imperial products may have contributed to smooth tensions between the king and other social bodies competing for fiscal resources, such as the aristocracy and the Church, right from the beginning of overseas expansion. Indeed, continental and intercontinental trade gave rise to a fair share of public revenue. Therefore, and despite the fact that a large part of domestic production still hinged on agriculture, the State's financial wealth in the Portuguese *Ancién Régime* mostly depended on customs duties and monopolies on a few colonial trades. Taxes levied on agriculture and internal trade did not have the same weight as revenue from external activities, even after the enforcement of an income tax that became a permanent part of the fiscal system from 1640 until the nineteenth century. After the 1850s, the State's reliance on external trade lessened due to increasing effectiveness in taxing internal economic activity. The century was especially characterized, however, by the rise in public borrowing, as fiscal revenue was insufficient to meet the State's expenditure needs. Difficulties in funding the State were a long-term issue and the solutions implemented did not have a definitive character, leading ultimately to the fall of the monarchy and the rise of a republican regime after 1910.

The twentieth century was to a great extent defined by the external context, following the severe consequences of the two world wars, and the positive influence of European integration. For a brief period of time, following World War II, it seemed that all causes of backwardness had changed into causes of growth of the Portuguese economy, but that paradox is solved by the long-term perspective we present in this book. In fact, in 1950, at the beginning of that golden age of growth, the Portuguese economy had already reached a level of maturity that allowed the benefits of European integration, whereas in 1973, at the end of that same age, it was still burdened by levels of relative backwardness that made harder the adjustment to the new phase of globalization.

Population, agriculture, industry, foreign trade, public finances, and state building are key issues to provide a thorough overview of a country's economy at any given moment, as well as reliable information to track its path. The ambition to do so is not new, and the current work makes good use of such earlier efforts by continuing to explore some of the themes they have put forward. If Economic History is a global topic that deals with the advancement of economic activity across time and space, political regimes, and national boundaries, does it still make sense to engage in the study of a country of the European periphery such as Portugal? We hope that the present book has answered this question positively, because global economic history needs surveys of histories at a national level, which would enable us to cross-check variables and identify those that are necessary and sufficient for economic growth in any circumstances.

At the beginning of the period studied here, Portugal's level of development was probably not too different from elsewhere on the European continent and yet at the end of the period, the country is one of the less developed economies in Europe. A crucial question that we may derive from that fact for Portuguese and European economic history is when that divergence commenced and the reasons that we may attribute to it. As we look back to the whole period studied here, the moment that sorts out as the most crucial one for the beginning of divergence is the second half of the seventeen century, which coincided eventually with the restoration of Portugal's independence from Spain in 1640. This was the epoch of nation-state formation, following the peace of Westphalia, when economic development became more dependent on state and military power. Apparently the Portuguese economy failed to surf that wave in a satisfactory way and from then on lost its relative position in Europe and the world and that certainly marked its development in the following centuries. As it was noted in the book, backwardness does not imply absence of growth, and the Portuguese economy did expand considerably in the last three centuries considered in the book, albeit at differing rates of expansion. Most certainly, economic growth in Portugal will continue, following what happened with special vigor in the twentieth century, but backwardness compared to European greater powers will not be fully overcome soon, as the first decade of the millenium allows us to realistically predict.

# References

Acemoglu, D. and J. A. Robinson. 2012. *Why Nations Fail? The Origins of Power, Prosperity and Poverty.* New York: Crown Publishers.

Afonso, Óscar and Álvaro Aguiar. 2005. "A Internacionalização da Economia." In *História Económica de Portugal,* edited by Pedro Lains and Álvaro Ferreira da Silva, vol. III, 305–341. Lisbon: Imprensa de Ciências Sociais.

Aguiar-Conraria, Luís, Fernando Alexandre, and Manuel Correia Pinho. 2012. "O Euro e o Crescimento da Economia Portuguesa: Uma Análise Contrafactual." *Análise Social* 42 (2): 298–321.

Aldcroft, Derek H. 2006. *Europe's Third World. The European Periphery in the Interwar Years.* Aldershot: Ashgate.

Alden, Dauril. 1968. *Royal Government in Colonial Brazil, with Special Reference to the Administration of the Marquis of Lauradio, Viceroy, 1769–1779.* Berkeley: University of California Press.

Alegria, M. Fernanda, João Carlos Garcia, and F. Relaño. 1998. "Cartografia e Viagens." In *História da Expansão Portuguesa,* edited by Francisco Bethencourt and Kirti Chaudhuri, vol. I, 26–61. Lisbon: Círculo de Leitores.

Alencastro, Luís Filipe de. 2000. *O Trato dos Viventes. Formação do Brasil no Atlântico Sul.* São Paulo: Companhia das Letras.

Alexandre, Valentim. 1993. *Os Sentidos do Império. Questão Nacional e Questão Colonial na Crise do Antigo Regime Português.* Porto: Edições Afrontamento.

Alexandre, Valentim. 2011. "The Colonial Empire." In *Contemporary Portugal. Politics, Society, Culture,* edited by António Costa Pinto, 2nd edn, 73–94. New York: Boulder.

Allen, Robert C. 1999. "Tracking the Agricultural Revolution in England." *The Economic History Review* 52 (2): 209–235.

Allen, Robert C. 2001. "The Great Divergence: Wages and Prices in Europe from the Middle Ages to the First World War." *Explorations in Economic History* 38 (4): 411–447.

Allen, Robert C. 2008. "The Nitrogen Hypothesis and the English Agricultural Revolution: A Biological Analysis." *The Journal of Economic History* 68 (1): 182–210.

Allen, Robert C. 2009. *The British Industrial Revolution in Global Perspective.* Cambridge: Cambridge University Press.

Almeida, Luís Ferrand de. 1973. *A Colónia do Sacramento na Época da Sucessão de Espanha.* Coimbra: Universidade de Coimbra.

Almeida, Luís Ferrand de. 1992. "A Propósito do Milho 'Marroco' em Portugal nos Séculos XVII e XVIII." *Revista Portuguesa de História* 27: 103–143.

Almodovar, António and José Luís Cardoso. 1998. *A History of Portuguese Economic Thought*. London: Routledge.

Álvarez Nogal, Carlos and Leandro Prados de la Escosura. 2007. "The Decline of Spain (1500–1850): Conjectural Estimates." *European Review of Economic History* 11: 319–366.

Álvarez Nogal, Carlos and Leandro Prados de la Escosura. 2013. "The Rise and Fall of Spain, 1270–1850." *The Economic History Review* 66 (1): 1–37.

Amador, João, Sónia Cabral, and Luca D. Opromolla. 2009. "Um Retrato do Comércio Internacional Português." In *A Economia Portuguesa no Contexto da Integração Económica, Financeira e Monetária*, edited by Banco de Portugal, 263–337. Lisbon: Banco de Portugal.

Amaral, Luciano. 1998. "Convergência e Crescimento Económico em Portugal no Pós-Guerra." *Análise Social* 33 (4): 741–776.

Amaral, Luciano. 2010. *Economia Portuguesa. As Últimas Décadas*. Lisbon: Fundação Manuel dos Santos.

Amaral, Luciano. 2012. "Institutions, Property, and Economic Growth: Back to the Passage from the *Ancien Régime* to Liberalism in Portugal." *Análise Social* 67 (1): 28–55.

Amaral, Luís Carlos. 1994. *São Salvador de Grijó na Segunda Metade do Século XIV. Estudo de Gestão Agrária*. Lisbon: Cosmos.

Amaral, Luís Carlos. 2007. *Formação e Desenvolvimento do Domínio da Diocese de Braga no Período da Reconquista (Século IX-1137)*, PhD diss., University of Porto.

Amorim, Inês. 1997. *O Mosteiro de Grijó. Senhorio e Propriedade, 1560–1720 (Formação, Estrutura e Exploração do seu Domínio)*. Braga: s.n.

Amorim, Maria Norberta. 1999. "O Minho: Comportamentos Demográficos através da Informação Paroquial." *Ler História* 3: 9–43.

Amzalak, Moses B.1928. *A Economia Política em Portugal: o Diplomata Duarte Ribeiro de Macedo e os seus Discursos sobre Economia Política*. Lisbon, Academia das Ciências de Lisboa.

Antunes, Cátia. 2004. *Globalization in the Early Modern Period. The Economic Relationship between Amsterdam and Lisbon, 1640–1705*. Amsterdam: Aksant.

Antunes, Cátia. 2008. "The Commercial Relationship between Amsterdam and the Portuguese Salt-Exporting Ports: Aveiro and Setúbal, 1580–1715." *Journal of Early Modern History* 12 (1): 25–53.

Araújo, Ana Cristina *et al.* 2007. *O Terramoto de 1755. Impactos Históricos*. Lisbon, Livros Horizonte.

Arruda, José Jobson de. 1980. *O Brasil no Comércio Colonial*, São Paulo, Ática.

Azevedo, João Lúcio.1921. *História dos Cristãos-novos Portugueses*. Lisbon: Livraria Clássica.

Azevedo, João Lúcio. 1929. "Organização Económica." In *História de Portugal*, edited by Damião Peres, vol. II, 419–433. Barcelos: Portucalense Editora.

Azevedo, João Lúcio. 1973. *Épocas de Portugal Económico*, 3rd edn. Lisbon: Clássica Editora.

Azevedo, João Lúcio. 1990. *O Marquês de Pombal e a sua Época*, 2nd edn. Lisbon: Clássica Editora.

Badia-Miró, Marc, Jordi Guilera, and Lains, Pedro. 2012. "Regional Incomes in Portugal: Industrialization, Integration and Inequality, 1890–1980." *Journal of Iberian and Latin American Economic History* 30 (2): 225–244.

Baganha, Maria Ioannis. 1988. "Social Marginalization, Government Policies and Emigrant Remittances, Portugal 1870–1930." In *Estudos e Ensaios. Em Homenagem de Vitorino Magalhães Godinho*, 431–449. Lisbon: Sá da Costa.

Baganha, Maria Ioannis. 2003. "Portuguese Emigration after World War II." In *Contemporary Portugal. Politics, Society and Culture*, edited by António Costa Pinto and António Costa, 139–158. New York: Boulder.

Bairoch, Paul. 1976. *Commerce Extérieur et Développement Économique de l'Europe au XIXe siècle*. Paris: Mouton.

Bairoch, Paul. 1989. "Les Trois Révolutions Agricoles du Monde Développé: Rendements et Productivité de 1800 à 1985." *Annales Économies Sociétés Cultures* March–April: 317–353.

Balbi, Adrien. 1822. *Essai Statistique sur le Royaumme de Portugal et d'Algarve*. Paris: chez Reych Gravier, libraires.

Banco de Portugal, ed. 2009. *A Economia Portuguesa no Contexto da Integração Económica, Financeira e Monetária*. Lisbon: Banco de Portugal.

Barata, Filipe Themudo and António Castro Henriques. 2011. "Economic and Fiscal History." In *The Historiography of Medieval Portugal (c. 1950–2010)*, edited by José Mattoso, 261–281. Lisbon: Instituto de Estudos Medievais, FCSH.

Barbosa, António Pinto, ed. 1999. *O Impacto do Euro na Economia Portuguesa*. Lisbon: Publicações D. Quixote.

Barreto, José, ed. 1986. *Sebastião José de Carvalho e Melo: Escritos Económicos de Londres, 1741–1742*. Lisbon: Biblioteca Nacional.

Barrett, Ward. 1990. "World Bullion Flows, 1450–1800." *The Rise of Merchant Empires. Long Distance Trade in the Early Modern World, 1350–1750*, edited by J. D. Tracy, 224–254. Cambridge: Cambridge University Press.

Barros, Henrique da Gama. 1956. *História da Administração Pública em Portugal nos Séculos XII a XV*, 11 vols., 2nd. Lisbon: Sá da Costa.

Barros, João de. 1919. *Geografia d'Entre Douro e Minho e Trás-os-Montes*. Porto: Biblioteca Pública Municipal do Porto.

Batista, Dina, *et al.* 1997. New Estimates for Portugal's GDP, *1910–1958*. Lisbon: Banco de Portugal.

Beirante, Ângela. 1981. *Santarém Quinhentista*. Lisbon: s. n.

Beirante, Ângela.1993. "A Reconquista Cristã." In *Nova História de Portugal. Portugal das Invasões Germânicas à Reconquista*, edited by Joel Serrão and A. H. de Oliveira Marques, vol. II, 253–363. Lisbon: Editorial Presença.

Bensaúde, Joaquim. 1942. *A Cruzada do Infante D. Henrique*. Lisbon: Agência Geral das Colónias.

Berend, Iván T. and György Ránki.1982. *The European Periphery and Industrialization, 1780–1914*. Cambridge: Cambridge University Press.

Bethencourt, Francisco. 1994. *História das Inquisições. Portugal, Espanha e Itália*. Lisbon: Círculo de Leitores.

Bethencourt, Francisco and Kirti Chaudhuri, eds. 1998. *História da Expansão Portuguesa*, vols. I-III. Lisbon: Círculo de Leitores.

Bethencourt, Francisco and Diogo Ramada Curto, eds. 2007. *Portuguese Oceanic Expansion, 1400–1800*. Cambridge: Cambridge University Press.

Bicalho, Maria Fernanda, Júnia Ferreira Furtado and L. M. Souza, eds. 2009. *O Governo dos Povos*. São Paulo: Alameda, 2009.

Blanchard, Olivier. 2007. "Adjustment within the Euro: The Difficult Case of Portugal." *Portuguese Economic Journal* 6 (1): 1–21.

Blussé, Leonord and Femme Gaastra, eds. 1981. *Companies and Trade*. Leiden: University of Leiden Press.

Boissellier, Stéphane. 2003. *Le Peuplement Médiéval dans le Sud du Portugal*. Paris: Centre Culturel Calouste Gulbenkian.

Bonifácio, M. Fátima. 1991. *Seis Estudos sobre o Liberalismo Português*. Lisbon: Editorial Estampa.

Bonney, Richard, ed. 1995. *Economic Systems and State Finance*. Oxford, Oxford University Press.

Bonney, Richard, ed. 1999. *The Rise of the Fiscal State in Europe, c. 1200–1815*. Oxford: Oxford University Press.

Bonney, Richard and W. Mark Ormrod. 1999. "Introduction: Crises, Revolutions and Self-Sustained Growth: Towards a Conceptual Model of Change in Fiscal History." In *Crises, Revolutions and Self-Sustained Growth. Essays in European Fiscal History, 1130–1830*, edited by W. M. Ormrod, M. Bonney e R. Bonney, 1–21. Stanford: Shaun Tyas.

Bordo, Michael D. and Fernando Teixeira dos Santos. 1995. "Portugal and the Bretton Woods International Monetary System." In *International Monetary Systems in Historical Perspective*, edited by Jaime Reis, 181–208. London: MacMillan.

Borzel, Tanja A. 2005. "Europeanization: How the European Union Interacts with Its Member States." In *The Member States of the European Union*, edited by S. Bulmer and C. Lequesne, 45–69. Oxford: Oxford University Press.

Bouza-Álvarez, Fernando. 2008. *D. Filipe I*. Lisbon, Temas e Debates.

Boxer, Charles R. 1951. "English Shipping in the Brazil Trade, 1640–1654." *The Mariner's Mirror* 37 (3): 197–230.

Boxer, Charles R. 1957. *The Dutch in Brazil, 1624–1654*. Oxford: Oxford University Press.

Boxer, Charles R. 1962. *The Golden Age of Brazil, 1695–1750*. Berkeley: California University Press.

Boxer, Charles R. 1969. "Brazilian Gold and British Traders in the First Half of the Eighteenth Century." *The Hispanic American Historical Review* 49 (3): 454–472.

Boyajian, James. 1983. *Portuguese Bankers at the Court of Spain, 1620–1650*. New Brunswick: Rutgers University Press.

Boyajian, James. 1993. *Portuguese Trade in Asia under the Habsburgs, 1580–1640*. Baltimore: The John Hopkins University Press.

Braga, Isabel Drummond. 1998. "A Produção Artesanal." In *Nova História de Portugal. Portugal. Do Renascimento à Crise Dinástica*, edited by Joel Serrão and A. H. de Oliveira Marques, organized by João Alves Dias, vol. 5, 182–194. Lisbon: Editorial Presença.

Braudel, Fernand. 1966. *Le Mediterranée et le Monde Mediterranéen à l'Epoque de Philippe II*, 2nd edn. Paris: Armand Colin.

Braudel, Fernand. 1982–1984. *Civilization and Capitalism, 15th–18th Century*. 3 vols. New York: Harper and Row.

Brewer, John. 1989. *The Sinews of Power. War, Money and the English State, 1688–1783*. New York: Alfred A. Knopf.

Broadberry, S. and B. Gupta. 2006. "The Early Modern Great Divergence: Wages, Prices and Economic Development in Europe and Asia, 1500–1800." *The Economic History Review* 59 (1): 2–31.

Broadberry, Stephen and Kevin O'Rourke. 2010. *The Cambridge Economic History of Modern Europe*, 2 vols. Cambridge: Cambridge University Press.

Cabral, Manuel Villaverde. 1979. *Portugal na Alvorada do Século XX*. Lisbon: A Regra do Jogo.

Cabral, Manuel Villaverde. 1981. *O Desenvolvimento do Capitalismo em Portugal no Século XIX*, 3rd edn. Lisbon: A Regra do Jogo.

Cameron, Rondo. 1997. *A Concise Economic History of the World. From Paleolithic Times to the Present*, 3rd edn. New York: Oxford University Press.

Campbell, Bruce M. S. 2010. "Nature as Historical Protagonist: Environment and Society in Pre-industrial England." *Economic History Review* 63 (2): 281–314.

Canabrava, Alice. 1984. *O Comércio Português no Rio da Prata, 1580–1640*. Belo Horizonte: Itatiaia.

Capela, José Viriato. 1993. *Política, Administração Pública, Economia e Finanças Públicas Portuguesas, 1750–1820*. Braga: Universidade do Minho.

Capela, José Viriato. 1997. *Política de Corregedores: a Actuação dos Corregedores nos Municípios Minhotos no Apogeu e Crise do Antigo Regime, 1750–1834*. Braga: Universidade do Minho.

Cardim, Pedro. 1998. *As Cortes e Cultura Política no Portugal do Antigo Regime*. Lisbon: Edições Cosmos.

Cardoso, José Luís. 1989. *O Pensamento Económico em Portugal nos Finais do Século XVIII: 1780–1808*. Lisbon: Editorial Estampa.

Cardoso, José Luís, ed. 1990. *Memórias Económicas da Real Academia das Ciências de Lisboa, para o Adiantamento da Agricultura, das Artes e da Industria em Portugal, e as suas Conquistas*. Lisbon: Banco de Portugal.

Cardoso, José Luís. 2001. *História do Pensamento Económico Português. Temas e Problemas*. Lisbon: Livros Horizonte.

Cardoso, José Luís. 2005. "Política Económica." In *História Económica de Portugal, 1700–2000. Séc. XVIII*, edited by Pedro Lains and Álvaro Ferreira da Silva, vol. I, 345–367. Lisbon: Imprensa de Ciências Sociais.

Cardoso, José Luís. 2007. "Pombal, o Terramoto e a Política de Regulação Económica." In *O Terramoto de 1755. Impactos Históricos*, edited by Ana Cristina Araújo *et al.*, 165–182. Lisbon: Livros Horizonte.

Cardoso, José Luís and Pedro Lains. 2010. "Public Finance in Portugal, 1796–1910." In *Paying for the Liberal State. The Rise of Public Finance in Nineteenth-Century Europe*, edited by José Luís Cardoso and Pedro Lains, 251–278. Cambridge: Cambridge University Press.

358    References

Carlos, Ann M. and Stephen Nicholas. 1988. "Giants of an Earlier Capitalism: The Chartered Trading Companies as Modern Multinationals." *Business History Review* 62: 398–419.

Carrara, Angelo Alves. 2007. *Minas e Currais: Produção Rural e Mercado Interno em Minas Gerais, 1674–1807.* Juiz de Fora: Editora da UFJF.

Carrara, Angelo Alves and Ernest Sánchez Santiró, eds. 2012. *Guerra e Fiscalidade na Ibero-América Colonial, Séculos XVII-XIX.* Juiz de Fora-Cidade do México: Editora da UFJF-Instituto Mora.

Carreira, António. 1983a. "A Companhia de Pernambuco e Paraíba. Alguns Subsídios para o Estudo da sua Acção." *Revista de História Económica e Social* 11: 55–88.

Carreira, António. 1983b. *As Companhias Pombalinas: de Grão-Pará e Maranhão e Pernambuco e Paraíba.* Lisbon: Editorial Presença.

Carreira, António. 1988. *A Companhia Geral do Grão-Pará e Maranhão (O Comércio Intercontinental Portugal-África-Brasil na Segunda Metade do Século XVIII),* 2 vols. São Paulo: Companhia Editorial Nacional.

Carvalho, Rómulo. 1979. *Relações entre Portugal e a Rússia no Século XVIII.* Lisbon: Sá da Costa.

Castro, Armando. 1978. *História Económica de Portugal,* 3 vols. Lisbon: Caminho.

Chalmeta, Pedro.1994. "An Approximate Picture of the Economy of al-Andalus." In *The Legacy of Muslim Spain,* vol. 2, edited by Salma Khadra Jayyusi, 741–758. Leiden: Brill.

Chaney, R. 1986. *Regional Emigration and Remittances in Developing Countries. The Portuguese Experience.* New York: Praeger.

Cipolla, Carlo. 1991. *Between Two Cultures. An Introduction to Economic History.* New York: W. W. Norton.

Cipolla, Carlo. 2003. *Before the Industrial Revolution. European Society and Economy, 1000–1700,* Routledge, Reprint of 3rd edn.

Clarence-Smith, Gervase.1985. *The Third Portuguese Empire, 1825–1975. A Study in Economic Imperialism.* Manchester: Manchester University Press.

Clark, Gregory. 2007. *A Farewell to Alms – A Brief Economic History of the World.* Princeton: Princeton Univ Press.

Clark, Peter. 2009. *European Cities and Towns, 400–2000.* New York: Oxford University Press.

Clavero, Bartolomé.1986. "Enfiteusis: que Hay en un Nombre." *Anuario de Historia del Derecho Español* 56: 467–519.

Clemens, P. G. E. 1976. "The Rise of Liverpool, 1665–1750." *The Economic History Review* 29 (2): 211–225.

Cluny, Isabel. 2003. "A Diplomacia Portuguesa e a Guerra da Sucessão de Espanha." In *O Tratado de Methuen. Diplomacia, Guerra, Política e Economia,* edited by José Luís Cardoso *et al.,* 51–71. Lisbon: Livros Horizonte.

Coelho, António Borges.1986. *Quadros para uma Viagem a Portugal no Século XVI,* 2 vols. Lisbon: Caminho.

Coelho, Maria Helena da Cruz. 1989. *O Baixo Mondego nos Finais da Idade Média.* Lisbon: Imprensa Nacional-Casa da Moeda.

Coelho, Maria Helena da Cruz. 1996. "Concelhos." In *Nova História de Portugal. Portugal em Definição de Fronteiras, 1096–1325. Do Condado Portucalense à Crise do Século XIV*. Organized by Maria Helena da Cruz Coelho and Armando L. de Carvalho Homem, vol. 3, 554–584. Lisbon: Presença.

Coelho, Maria Helena da Cruz and Armando L. de Carvalho Homem, eds. 1996. *Portugal em Definicão de Fronteiras (1096–1325)*. *Do Condado Portucalense à Crise do Século XIV*, vol. 3. Lisbon: Presença.

Coelho, Maria Helena da Cruz and Joaquim Romero Magalhães. 2008. *O Poder Concelhio. Das Origens às Cortes Constituintes: Notas de História Social*, 2nd edn. Coimbra: Centro de Estudos e Formação Autárquica.

Coffman, D'Maris, Adrian Leonard and Larry Neal, eds. 2013. *Questioning Credible Commitment: Perspectives on the Rise of Financial Capitalism*. Cambridge: Cambridge University Press.

Coimbra, Carlos. 1938. "O Infante D. Henrique e o Descobrimento do Caminho Marítimo para a Índia." *I Congresso de História da Expansão Portuguesa no Mundo*. Lisbon: Sociedade Nacional de Tipografia.

*Colecção de São Lourenço*. 1973. *edição de Elaine Sainceau*, vols. I e IV. Lisbon: Junta de Investigação do Ultramar.

*Conferência Internacional sobre Economia Portuguesa (I)*. 1977. 2 vols. Lisbon: Fundação Calouste Gulbenkian.

*Conferência Internacional sobre Economia Portuguesa (II)*. 1980. 2 vols. Lisbon: Fundação Calouste Gulbenkian.

Confraria, João. 1994. "Continuity and Change in Portuguese Industrial Policy." In *Europe's Economic Challeng*, edited by P. Bianchi, K. Cowling and R. Sugden, 104–113. London: Routledge.

Confraria, João. 1999. "Portugal: Industralization and Backwardness." In *European Industrial Policy. The Twentieth Century Experience*, edited by J. Foreman-Peck and G. Federico, 268–295.Oxford: Oxford University Press.

Confraria, João. 2005. "Política Económica." In *História Económica de Portugal. O Século XX*, edited by Pedro Lains and Álvaro Ferreira da Silva, vol. 3, 397–421. Lisbon: Imprensa de Ciências Sociais.

Congost, Rosa. 2003. "Property Rights and Historical Analysis. What Rights? What History." *Past and Present* 181: 73–106.

Coppolaro, Lucia and Pedro Lains. 2013. "Portugal and European integration, 1947–1992: An Essay on Protected Openness in the European Periphery." *E-Journal of Portuguese History* 11 (1): 61–81.

Corkill, David. 1999. *The Development of the Portuguese Economy. A Case of Europeanization*. London: Routledge.

Cortesão, Jaime. 1940a. *Teoria Geral dos Descobrimentos Portugueses*. Lisbon: Seara Nova.

Cortesão, Jaime. 1940b. "A Economia da Restauração." In *Congresso do Mundo Português*, vol. VII, 671–687. Lisbon: Seara Nova.

Cortesão, Jaime. 1979. *História dos Descobrimentos Portugueses*, 4th edn., 3 vols. Lisbon, Círculo de Leitores.

Cortesão, Jaime. 1984. *Alexandre de Gusmão e o tratado de Madrid*. Lisbon: Livro Horizonte, 3 vols.

Costa, Fernando Dores. 1992. *Crise Financeira, Dívida Pública e Capitalistas, 1796–1807*. Master diss., Lisbon: Universidade Nova de Lisboa.

Costa, Fernando Dores. 2003. "A Participação Portuguesa na Guerra de Sucessão de Espanha: Aspectos Militares." In *O Tratado de Methuen. Diplomacia, Guerra, Política e Economia*, edited by José Luís Cardoso *et al.*, 71–96. Lisbon: Livros Horizonte.

Costa, Fernando Dores. 2004a. "Milícia e Sociedade." In *Nova História Militar de Portugal*, edited by Manuel Themudo Barata and Nuno Severiano Teixeira, vol. II, 68–111. Lisbon: Círculo de Leitores.

Costa, Fernando Dores. 2004b. *A Guerra da Restauração, 1641–1668*. Lisbon: Livros Horizonte.

Costa, Fernando Dores. 2010. *Insubmissão: Aversão ao Serviço Militar no Portugal do Século XVIII*. Lisbon: Imprensa de Ciências Sociais.

Costa, Fernando Dores and Jorge Pedreira. 2005. *D. João VI*. Lisbon: Círculo de Leitores.

Costa, João. 2010. *Palmela nos finais da Idade Média. Estudo do Códice da Visitação e Tombo de Propriedades da Ordem de Santiago de 1510*, Unpublished MA dissertation, Universidade Nova de Lisboa.

Costa, João Paulo Oliveira e. 2009. *Henrique, o Infante*. Lisbon: Esfera dos Livros.

Costa, João Paulo Oliveira e, José Rodrigues Damião and Pedro Aires Oliveira. 2014. *História da Expansão e do Império Português*. Lisbon: Esfera dos Livros.

Costa, Leonor Freire. 1993. "A Construção Naval." In *História de Portugal. No Alvorecer da Modernidade, 1480–1620*, edited by José Mattoso, organized by Joaquim Romero Magalhães, vol. III, 292–310. Lisbon: Círculo de Leitores.

Costa, Leonor Freire. 1997. *Naus e Galeões na Ribeira de Lisboa. A Construção Naval para a Rota do Cabo no Século XVI*. Cascais: Patrimonia Historica.

Costa, Leonor Freire. 2002a. *Império e Grupos Mercantis. Entre o Oriente e o Atlântico (Século XVII)*. Lisbon: Livros Horizonte.

Costa, Leonor Freire. 2002b. *O Transporte no Atlântico e a Companhia Geral do Comércio do Brasil, 1580–1663*, 2 vols. Lisbon: Comissão Nacional para as Comemorações dos Descobrimentos Portugueses.

Costa, Leonor Freire. 2003. "Da Restauração a Methuen: Ruptura e Continuidade." In *O Tratado de Methuen. Diplomacia, Guerra, Política e Economia*, edited by José Luís Cardoso *et al.*, 31–50. Lisbon: Livros Horizonte.

Costa, Leonor Freire. 2005. "Relações Económicas com o Exterior." In *História Económica de Portugal (1700–2000). O Século XVIII*, edited by Pedro Lains and Álvaro Ferreira da Silva, vol. I, 263–264. Lisbon: Imprensa de Ciências Sociais.

Costa, Leonor Freire. 2006. "Privateering and Insurance: Transaction Costs in Seventeenth-Century European Colonial Flows." In Atti delle "Settimane di Studi," *Ricchezza del Mare, Ricchezza dal mare, secc XIII-XVII*, Istituto Internazionale di Storia Economica F. Datini, edited by Simonetta Cavaciocchi, 703–726. Prato: Le Monnier.

Costa, Leonor Freire. 2009. "Fiscal Innovations in Early Modern States: Which War Did Really Matter in the Portuguese Case?" *Working Paper* n. 40. Lisbon: Gabinete de História Económica e Social.

Costa, Leonor Freire. 2013. "Portuguese Resilience in a Global War. Military Motivation and Institutional Adaptation in the Sixteenth-and-Seventeenth-Century Cape Route." In *Global History of Trade and Conflict since 1500*, edited by Lucia Cappolaro and Francine Mckenzie, 38–60. New York: Palgrave Macmillan.

Costa, Leonor Freire and Mafalda Soares da Cunha. 2006. *D. João IV*. Lisbon: Círculo de Leitores.

Costa, Leonor Freire, Maria Manuela Rocha and Rita Martins de Sousa. 2013. *O Ouro do Brasil*. Lisbon: Imprensa Nacional-Casa da Moeda.

Costa, Leonor Freire, Maria Manuela Rocha and Tanya Araújo. 2011. "Social Capital and Economic Performance: Trust and Distrust in Eighteenth Century Gold Shipments from Brazil." *European Review of Economic History* 15 (1): 1–27.

Costa, Leonor Freire, Maria Manuela Rocha e Paulo Brito. 2014. "Money Supply and the Credit Market in Early Modern Economies: The Case of Eighteenth-Century Lisbon." *Working Paper* no. 52. Lisbon: Gabinete de História Económica e Social.

Costa, Leonor Freire, Nuno Palma and Jaime Reis. 2015. "The Great Escape? The Contribution of the Empire to Portugal's Economic Growth, 1500–1800." *European Review of Economic History* 19 (1): 1–22.

Crafts, Nicholas. 1985. *British Economic Growth during the Industrial Revolution*. Oxford: Clarendon Press.

Crafts, Nicholas. 2009. "Solow and Growth Accounting: A Perspective from Quantitative Economic History." *History of Political Economy* 41 (annual suppl): 200–220.

Crafts, Nicholas and Gianni Toniolo, eds. 1996. *Economic Growth in Europe since 1945*. Cambridge: Cambridge University Press.

Crafts, Nicholas and C. Knick Harley. 2000. "Simulating the Two Views of the British Industrial Revolution." *Journal of Economic History* 60 (3): 819–841.

Crafts, Nicholas and Gianni Toniolo. 2010. "Aggregate growth, 1950–2005." In *The Cambridge Economic History of Modern Europe*, edited by Stephen Broadberry and Kevin O'Rourke, vol. 2, 296–332. Cambridge: Cambridge University Press.

Crouzet, François. 1990. *Britain Ascendant. Comparative Studies in Franco-British Economic History*. Cambridge: Cambridge University Press.

Crouzet, François. 2000. *A History of the European Economy 1000–2000*, University of Virginia Press.

Cuenca Esteban, Javier. 2004. "Comparative Patterns of Colonial Trade: Britain and Its Rivals." In *Exceptionalism and Industrialization. Britain and Its European Rivals, 1688–1815*, edited by Leandro Prados de la Escosura, 35–68. Cambridge: Cambridge University Press.

Cunha, Mafalda Soares da. 1990. *Linhagem, Parentesco e Poder. A Casa de Bragança, 1384–1483*. Lisbon: Fundação da Casa de Bragança.

Custódio, Jorge. 1983. "Introdução à Memória sobre os Meios de Melhorar a Indústria Portuguesa." *Memória sobre os Meios de Melhorar a Indústria Portuguesa de Acúrsio das Neves*, 7–72. Lisbon: Ed. Querco.

Davis, Ralph. 1962. *The Rise of the English Shipping Industry in the Seventeenth and Eighteenth Centuries*. London: Macmillan.

De Cecco, M. 1995. "Central Bank Cooperation in the Inter-War Period: A View from the Periphery." In *International Monetary Systems in Historical Perspective*, edited by Jaime Reis, 113–114. London: MacMillan.

De Long, J. Bradford and Barry Eichengreen. 1993. "The Marshall Plan: History's most Successful Adjustment Program." In *Postwar Economic Reconstruction and Lessons for the East Today*, edited by R. Dornbusch, W. Nölling and R. Layard, 189–230. Cambridge (Mass.): MIT Press.

De Vries, Jan. 1984. *European Urbanization 1500–1800*. London: Methuen.

De Vries, Jan. 1994a. "The Industrial Revolution and the Industrious Revolution." *Journal of Economic History* 5 (2): 249–271.

De Vries, Jan. 1994b. "Population." In *Handbook of European History, 1400–1600. Late Middle Ages, Renaissance and Reformation. Structures and Assertions*, edited by Thomas A. Brady, Heiko A. Oberman, James Tracy, vol. 1, 1–50. Leiden: E. J. Brill.

De Vries, Jan. 2003. "Connecting Europe and Asia: A Quantitative Analysis of the Cape Route Trade, 1497–1795." In *Global Connections and Monetary History*, edited by Dennis O. Flynn and Arturo Giraldez, 35–106. Ashgate: Aldershot.

De Vries, Jan. 2008. *The Industrious Revolution: Consumer Behavior and the Household Economy, 1650 to the Present*. New York: Cambridge University Press.

De Vries, Jan. 2009. "The Economic Crisis of the Seventeenth Century after Fifty Years." *Journal of Interdisciplinary History* 11 (2): 151–194.

De Vries, Jan and Ad Van der Woude. 1997. *The First Modern Economy. Success, Failure and Perseverance of the Dutch Economy, 1500–1815*. Cambridge: Cambridge University Press.

Dertilis, G. and K. Costis. 1995. "Banking, Public Finance, and the Economy: Greece, 1919–1933." In *Banking, Currency, and Finance in Europe between the Wars*, edited by C. H. Feinstein, 458–471. Oxford: Clarendon Press.

Devy-Vareta, Nicole. 1986. "Para uma Geografia Histórica da Floresta Portuguesa. Do Declínio das Matas Medievais à Política Florestal do Renascimento (séc. XV e XVI)." *Revista da Faculdade de Letras – Geografia*, Série I, 1: 5–37.

Dias, João Alves. 1984. "Uma Grande Obra de Engenharia em Meados do Século XVI. A Mudança do Curso do Tejo." *Nova História. Século XVI* 1: 66–82.

Dias, João Alves. 1985. "Um Documento Financeiro do Século XVII." *Nova História* 3–4: 107–148.

Dias, João Alves. 1996. *Gentes e Espaços. Em Torno da População Portuguesa na Primeira Metade do Século XVI*, vol. I. Lisbon: Fundação Calouste Gulbenkian.

Dias, João Alves. 1998. "População." In *Nova História de Portugal. Portugal. Do Renascimento à Crise Dinástica*, edited by Joel Serrão and A. H. de Oliveira Marques, organized by João Alves Dias, vol. 5, 11–52. Lisbon: Presença.

Dias, Luís Carvalho. 1954. "Os Lanifícios na Política Económica do Conde de Ericeira." *Boletim da Federação Nacional dos Industriais de Lanifícios* 44: 8–60.

Dinan, Desmond. 2005. *Ever Closer Union*. London: Palgrave MacMillan.

Disney, Anthony. 1978. *Twilight of the Pepper Empire: Portuguese Trade in Southwest India in the Early Seventeenth Century*. Cambridge (Mass.): Harvard University Press.

Disney, Anthony. 2009. *A History of Portugal and the Portuguese Empire*, 2 vols. Cambridge: Cambridge University Press.

Di Vittorio, António, ed. 2006. *An Economic History of Europe. From Expansion to Development*. London: Routledge.

*Do Sítio de Lisboa, sua Grandeza, Povoação e Comércio, etc. Diálogos de Luís Mendes de Vasconcelos*, (1803 [1608]), facs. ed., Lisbon.

Domingues, Francisco Contente. 2007. "Science and Technology in Portuguese Navigation: The Idea of Experience in the Sixteenth Century." In *Portuguese Oceanic Expansion, 1400–1800*, edited by Francisco Bethencourt and Diogo Ramada Curto, 460–478. Cambridge: Cambridge University Press.

Drelichman, Mauricio. 2005. "The Curse of Moctezuma: American Silver and the Dutch Disease." *Explorations in Economic History* 42 (3): 349–380.

Duarte, Luís Miguel. 1995. "A Actividade Mineira em Portugal durante a Idade Média (Tentativa de Síntese)." *Revista da Faculdade de Letras – História* 12: 75–111.

Duby, George. 1977. *L'Économie rurale et la vie des campagnes dans l'occident médiéval. France, Angleterre, Empire, IXe-XV siècles*, vol. 2. Paris: Flammarion.

Dupâquier, Jacques. 1997. "Les vicissitudes du peuplement (XV-XVIII siècles)." In *Histoire des Populations de l'Europe*, edited by J. P Bardet and J. Dupâquier, 239–261. Paris: Fayard.

Duplessis, Robert S. 1997. *Transitions to Capitalism in Early Modern Europe*. Cambridge: Cambridge University Press.

Durães, Margarida. 2004a. "Uma Comenda Nova. O Senhorio de Adaúfe: Propriedade e Exploração Agrícola (sécs. XVI-XIX)." In *Actas do III Congresso Histórico de Guimarães: D. Manuel e a sua Época*, 229–251. Guimarães: s.n.

Durães, Margarida. 2004b. "Estratégias de Sobrevivência Económica nas Famílias Camponesas Minhotas: os Padrões Hereditários (sécs. XVIII-XIX)." Paper presented at *XIV Encontro Nacional de Estudos Populacionais*. Minas Gerais: Associação Brasileira de Estudos Populacionais.

Durand, Robert. 1982. *Les Campagnes Portugaises entre Douro et Tage aux XII^e et XIII^e Siècles*. Paris: Fundação Calouste Gulbenkian.

Ebert, Christopher. 2008. *Between Empires: Brazilian Sugar in the Early Atlantic Economy 1550–1630*. Leiden: Brill.

Eichengreen, Barry. 1992. *Golden Fetters. The Gold Standard and the Great Depression, 1919–1939*. Oxford: Oxford University Press.

Eichengreen, Barry. 2007. *The European Economy since 1945. Coordinated Capitalism and Beyond*. Princeton: Princeton University Press.

Elliott, J. H. 1991. *El Conde-Duque de Olivares. El Político en una Época de Decadencia*, 6th edn. Barcelona: Editoral Crítica.

Eloranta, Jari and Mark Harrison. 2010. "War and Disintegration, 1914–1950." In *The Cambridge Economic History of Modern Europe*, edited by Stephen Broadberry and Kevin O'Rourke, vol. 2, 133–155. Cambridge: Cambridge University Press.

Emmer, Peter C. 2003. "The First Global War: The Dutch versus Iberia in Asia, Africa and the New World, 1590–1609." *E-Journal of Portuguese History* 1 (1): 1–14.

Engerman, Stanley. 1995. "Mercantilism and Overseas Trade, 1700–1800." In *The Economic History of Britain since* 1700, edited by Roderick Floud and Donald McCloskey, 2nd edn., vol. I, 182–204. Cambridge: Cambridge University Press.

Epstein, Stephen L. 2000. *Freedom and Growth. The Rise of States and Markets in Europe, 1300–1750.* London: Routledge.

Ericeira, conde da (D. Luís de Meneses). 1945 [1679]. *História de Portugal Restaurado,* int. and notes by Álvaro Dória, vols. I–IV. Porto: Livraria Civilização Editora.

Esteves, Rui Pedro. 2003. "Looking Ahead from the Past: The Inter-Temporal Sustainability of Portuguese Finances, 1854–1910." *European Review of Economic History* 7 (2): 239–266.

Esteves, Rui and David Khoudour-Castéras. 2011. "Remittances, Capital Flows and Financial Development during the Mass Migration Period, 1870–1913." *European Review of Economic History* 15 (3): 443–474.

Falcão, Figueiredo. 1859. *Livro em que se Contém toda a Fazenda e real Património dos Reinos de Portugal, Índia e Ilhas Adjacentes.* Lisbon: Imprensa Nacional.

Farinha, António Dias. 1989. "O interesse pelo Norte de África." In *Portugal no Mundo,* edited by Luís de Albuquerque, vol. 1, 101–112. Lisbon: Publicações Alfa.

Farinha, António Dias. 1998. "Norte de África." In *História da Expansão Portuguesa,* edited by Francisco Bethencourt and Kirti Chaudhuri, vol. I, 118–136. Lisbon: Círculo de Leitores.

Federico, Giovanni. 2008. *Feeding the World: An Economic History of Agriculture, 1800–2000.* Princeton: Princeton University Press.

Feinstein, Charles H., Peter Temin and Gianni Toniolo. 1997. *The European Economy between the Wars.* Oxford: Oxford University Press.

Felice, Emanuele. 2011. "Regional Value Added in Italy, 1891–2001, and the Foundation of a Long-term Picture." *Economic History Review* 64 (3): 929–950.

Ferlini, Vera Lúcia Amaral. 1988. *Terra, Trabalho e Poder: o Mundo dos Engenhos no Nordeste Colonial.* São Paulo: Brasiliense.

Fernandez-Armesto, Felipe. 2007. "The Portuguese Expansion in a Global Context." In *Portuguese Oceanic Expansion, 1400–1800,* edited by Francisco Bethencourt and Diogo Ramada Curto, 480–511. Cambridge, Cambridge University Press.

Ferreira, Ana Maria. 1995. *Problemas Marítimos entre Portugal e a França na Primeira Metade do Século XVI.* Cascais: Patrimonia Historica.

Ferreira, Manuel Ennes. 2005. "O Império e as Relações Económicas com África." In *História Económica de Portugal, 1700–2000. O Século XX,* edited by Pedro Lains and Álvaro Ferreira da Silva, vol. 3, 343–371. Lisbon: Imprensa de Ciências Sociais.

Findlay, Ronald and Kevin O'Rourke. 2007. *Power and Plenty. Trade, War, and the World Economy in the Second Millennium.* Princeton: Princeton University Press.

Fisher, H. E. S. 1971. *The Portugal Trade. A Study of Anglo-Portuguese Commerce, 1700–1770.* London: Methuen.

Fisher, H. E. S. 1981. "Lisbon, Its English Merchant Community and the Mediterranean in the Eighteenth Century." In *Shipping, Trade and Commerce.*

*Essays in Memory of Ralph Davis*, edited by P. L. Cottrell and D. H. Aldcroft, 23–44. Leicester: Leicester University Press.

Fonseca, Hélder Adegar. 2005. "A Ocupação da Terra." In *História Económica de Portugal, 1700–2000. O Século XIX*, edited by Pedro Lains and Álvaro Ferreira da Silva, vol. 2, 83–118. Lisbon: Imprensa de Ciências Sociais.

Fonseca, Hélder and Jaime Reis. 2011. "The Limits of Agricultural Growth in a Fragile Eco-system. Total Factor Productivity in Alentejo, 1750–1850." In *Growth and Stagnation in European Historical Agriculture*, edited by Mats Olsson and Patrick Stensson, 167–194. Turnhout: Brepols.

Fonseca, Jorge. 1990. "Propriedade e Exploração da Terra em Évora nos Séculos XVIII e XIX." *Ler História* 18: 111–138.

Fonseca, Jorge. 1995. "Um Lavrador Setecentista e o seu 'Livro de Memórias.'" *Almansor* 13: 127–151.

Fonseca, Luís Adão. 2005. *D. João II*. Lisbon: Círculo de Leitores.

Fontoura, Paula and Nuno Valério. 2000. "Foreign Economic Relations and Economic Growth in Portugal: A Long Term View." *Economies et Sociétés* 3: 175–206.

Francis, A. David. 1966. *The Methuens and Portugal, 1691–1708*. Cambridge: Cambridge University Press.

Franco, Francesco, ed. 2008. *Challenges Ahead for the Portuguese Economy*. Lisbon: Imprensa de Ciências Sociais.

Freire, Dulce and Pedro Lains, eds. (forthcoming). *An Agrarian History of Portugal, 1000–2000*. Leiden: Brill.

Freitas, Gustavo de. 1951. *A Companhia Geral do Comércio do Brasil, 1649–1720. Subsídios para a História Económica de Portugal*. São Paulo: Coleção da *Revista de História*.

Freitas, Jorge Penim. 2007. *O Combatente durante a Guerra da Restauração. Vivência e Comportamentos Militares ao Serviço da Coroa Portuguesa, 1640–1668*. Lisbon: Prefácio.

Galego, Júlia and Suzanne Daveau. 1986. *O Numeramento de 1527–1532. Tratamento Cartográfico*. Lisbon: Centro de Estudos Geográficos.

Galor, Oded. 2005. "From Stagnation to Growth: Unified Growth Theory." In *Handbook of Economic Growth*, edited by Philippe Aghion & Steven Durlauf, vol. 1, 171–293. Amsterdam: Elsevier/North Holland.

Garcia, João Carlos. 1986. "Os Têxteis no Portugal dos Séculos XV e XVI." *Finisterra. Revista Portuguesa de Geografia* 21: 327–344.

Gaspar, Jorge. 1970. "Os Portos Fluviais do Tejo." *Finisterra. Revista Portuguesa de Geografia* 5: 153–204.

Gaspar, Vítor and Miguel St. Aubyn. 2009. "Política Orçamental, Ajustamento ao Euro e Crescimento em Portugal e Espanha." In *Sem Fronteiras. Os Novos Horizontes da Economia Portuguesa*, edited by Pedro Lains, 67–89. Lisbon: Imprensa de Ciências Sociais.

Gil, Maria Olímpia da Rocha. 1965. *Arroteias no Vale do Mondego durante o Século XVI. Ensaio de História Agrária*. Lisbon: Instituto de Alta Cultura.

Godinho, Vitorino Magalhães. 1955. *Prix et Monnaies au Portugal, 1750–1850*. Paris: Armand Colin.

Godinho, Vitorino Magalhães. 1962. *A Economia dos Descobrimentos Henriquinos.* Lisbon: Livraria Sá da Costa Editora.

Godinho, Vitorino Magalhães. 1978a. *"L'Émigration Portugaise (XV-XX Siècles).* Une Constante Structurale et les Réponses aux Changements du Monde." *Revista de História Económica e Social* 1: 5–32.

Godinho, Vitorino Magalhães. 1978b. *Ensaios II. Sobre História de Portugal,* 2nd edn. Lisbon: Sá da Costa.

Godinho, Vitorino Magalhães. 1982–1984. *Os Descobrimentos e a Economia Mundial,* 2nd edn., 4 vols. Lisbon: Presença.

Godinho, Vitorino Magalhães. 1990. *Mito e Mercadoria, Utopia e Prática de Navegar: Séculos XIII-XVIII.* Lisbon: Difel.

Godinho, Vitorino Magalhães. 2008. *A Expansão Quatrocentista Portuguesa,* 2nd edn. Lisbon: Dom Quixote.

Goldstone, Jack A. 1991. *Revolution and Rebellion in Early Modern World.* Barkley, Los Angeles: University of California Press

Gomes, Costa. 1883. *Collecção de Leis da Dívida Pública Portuguesa.* Lisbon: Imprensa Nacional.

Gomes, Miguel Costa and José Tavares. 1999. "Democracy and Business Cycles: Evidence from Portuguese Economic History." *European Review of Economic History* 3 (3): 295–321.

Gonçalves, Iria. 1964. *Pedidos e Empréstimos Públicos em Portugal durante a Idade Média.* Lisbon: Ministério das Finanças.

Gonçalves, Iria. 1989. *O Património do Mosteiro de Alcobaça.* Lisbon: Universidade Nova de Lisboa.

Gonçalves, Iria. 2010. "O espaço rural." In *História da Vida Privada em Portugal. A Idade Média,* edited by Bernardo de Vasconcelos e Sousa, vol. I, 39–53. Lisbon: Temas e Debates.

Goris, J. A. 1925. *Études sur les colonies marchandes meridionales à Anvers de 1488 à 1567: Portuguais, Espagnols, Italiens.* Lovaina: Librairie Universitaire.

Grafe, Regina. 2012. *Distant Tyranny. Markets, Power and Backwardness in Spain, 1650–1800.* Princeton: Princeton University Press.

Gregório, Rute Dias. 2007. *Terra e Fortuna: os Primórdios da Humanização da Ilha Terceira (1450–1550).* Lisbon, Centro de História de Além-Mar, FCSH-Universidade Nova.

Guedes, Max Justo. 1990. *História Naval Brasileira. As Guerras Holandesas no Mar,* vol. II/ IA. Rio de Janeiro: Serviço de Documentação Geral da Marinha.

Haber, Stephen and Herbert S. Klein 1997. "The Economic Conseqeunces of Brazilian Independence." In *How Latin America Fell Behind: Essays on the Economic Histories of Brazil and Mexico, 1800–1914,* edited by Stephen Harber, 243–259. Stanford: Stanford University Press.

Hajnal, John. 1965. "European Marriage Patterns in Perspective." In *Population in History,* edited by D. V. Glass and D. E. C. Eversley, 101–143. London: Edward Arnold.

Hamilton, Earl F. 1934. *American Treasure and the Price Revolution in Spain, 1501–1650.* Cambridge (Mass.): Harvard University Press.

Hanson, Carl A. 1982. "Monopoly and Contraband in the Portuguese Tobacco Trade, 1624–1702." *Luso-Brazilian Review* XIX (2): 149–168.

Hanson, Carl A. 1986. *A Economia e Sociedade no Portugal Barroco, 1668–1703*. Lisbon: Publicações D. Quixote.

Hecksher, Eli F. 1954. *An Economic History of Sweden*. Cambridge (Mass.): Harvard University Press.

Henriksen, Ingrid. 2009. "The Contribution of Agriculture to Economic Growth in Denmark, 1870–1939." In *Agriculture and Economic Growth in Europe since 1870*, edited by Pedro Lains and Vicente Pinilla, 117–147. London: Routledge.

Henriques, António Castro. 2008. *State Finance, War and Redistribution in Portugal, 1249–1527*. PhD diss., University of York.

Henriques, António Castro. 2014a. "Plenty of Land, Land of Plenty. The Agrarian Output of Portugal (1311–1320)." Working paper, Faculdade de Economia, Universidade do Porto.

Henriques, António Castro. 2014b. "The Rise of a Tax State: Portugal, 1371–1401." *E-Journal of Portuguese History*, 12 (1): 49–66.

Hespanha, António Manuel. 1982. *História das Instituições. Época Medieval e Moderna*. Coimbra: Livraria Almedina.

Hespanha, António Manuel. 1989. "O Governo dos Áustria e a Modernização da Constituição Política Portuguesa." *Penélope* 2: 50–73.

Hespanha, António Manuel. 1993. "Os Poderes do Centro: a Fazenda." In *História de Portugal. O Antigo Regime*, edited by José Mattoso and organized by António Manuel Hespanha, vol. IV, 202–239. Lisbon: Círculo de Leitores.

Hespanha, António Manuel. 1994. *As Vésperas do Leviathan. Instituições e Poder Político. Portugal (Século XVII)*. Coimbra: Almedina.

Hespanha, António Manuel. 2004. "As Finanças da Guerra." In *Nova História Militar de Portugal*, edited by Manuel Themudo Barata and Nuno Severiano Teixeira, vol. II, 176–190. Lisbon: Círculo de Leitores.

Hibou, Béatrice. 2005. "Greece and Portugal: Convergent or Divergent Europeanization?" In *The Member States of the European Union*, edited by S. Bulmer and C. Lequesne, 229–253. Oxford: Oxford University Press.

Houpt, Stefan, Pedro Lains and Lennart Schön. 2010. "Sectoral Developments, 1945–2000." In *The Cambridge Economic History of Modern Europe*, edited by Stephen Broadberry and Kevin O'Rourke, vol. 2, 333–359. Cambridge: Cambridge University Press.

Israel, Jonathan. 1989. *Dutch Primacy in the World Trade, 1585–1740*. Oxford: Oxford University Press.

Johnson, Harold. 1987. "Portuguese Settlement, 1500–1580." In *Colonial Brazil*, edited by Leslie Bethel, 1–38. Cambridge: Cambridge University Press.

Justino, David. 1981. "Crise e Decadência da Economia Cerealífera Alentejana no Século XVIII." *Revista de História Económica e Social* 7: 29–80.

Justino, David. 1988–1989. *A Formação do Espaço Económico Nacional. Portugal, 1810–1913*, 2 vols. Lisbon: Vega.

Justino, David. 1994. *História da Bolsa de Lisboa*. Lisbon: Bolsa de Valores de Lisboa.

Keynes, John Maynard. 1995. *The Economic Consequences of the Peace*. London: Penguin Classics.

Kindleberger, Charles P. 1991. "The Economic Crisis of 1619 to 1623." *The Journal of Economic History* 51 (1): 149–175.

Klein, Herbert S. 1999. *The Atlantic Slave Trade. New Approaches to the Americas.* Cambridge: Cambridge University Press.

Klein, Herbert S. 2010. *The Atlantic Slave Trade.* Cambridge: Cambridge University Press.

Krugman, Paul. 2008. "Outside Advice, Then and Now." In *Challenges Ahead for the Portuguese Economy,* edited by Francesco Franco, 231–236. Lisbon: Imprensa de Ciências Sociais.

Krugman, Paul and Anthony J. Venables. 1995. "Globalization and the Inequality of Nations." *The Quarterly Journal of Economics* 110 (4): 857–880.

Labourdette, Jean-François. 1988. *La nation française à Lisbonne de 1669 a 1790. Entre colbertisme et liberalisme.* Paris: Fondation Calouste Gulbenkian.

Laet, J. 1925. *História ou Anais dos Feitos da Companha Privilegiada das Índias Ocidentais desde o seu Começo até ao Fim do Ano de 1636,* 2 vols. Rio de Janeiro: Biblioteca Nacional.

Lains, Pedro. 1990. *A Evolução da Agricultura e da Indústria em Portugal, 1850–1913. Uma Interpretação Quantitativa.* Lisbon: Banco de Portugal.

Lains, Pedro. 1991. "Foi a Perda do Império Brasileiro um Momento Crucial do Subdesenvolvimento Português?" *Penélope* 5: 151–163.

Lains, Pedro. 1995. *A Economia Portuguesa no Século XIX. Crescimento Económico e Comércio Externo 1851–1913.* Lisbon: Imprensa Nacional-Casa da Moeda.

Lains, Pedro. 1998. "An Account of the Portuguese African Empire, 1885–1975." *Journal of Iberian and Latin American Economic History* 16: 235–263.

Lains, Pedro. 2002–2011. *História da Caixa Geral de Depósitos, 1876–2010,* 3 vols. Lisbon: Imprensa de Ciências Sociais.

Lains, Pedro. 2003a. "Catching-up to the European Core: Portuguese Economic Growth, 1910–1990." *Explorations in Economic History* 40: 369–386.

Lains, Pedro. 2003b. "New Wine in Old Bottles: Output and Productivity Trends in Portuguese Agriculture, 1850–1950." *European Review of Economic History* 7 (1): 43–72.

Lains, Pedro. 2003c. *Os Progressos do Atraso. Uma Nova História Económica de Portugal, 1842–1992.* Lisbon: Imprensa de Ciências Sociais.

Lains, Pedro. 2004. "Structural Change and Economic Growth in Portugal, 1950–1990." In *Explorations in Economic Growth,* edited by S. Heikkinen and J. L. van Zanden, 321–340. Amsterdam: Aksant.

Lains, Pedro. 2005. "A Indústria." In *História Económica de Portugal, 1700–2000,* edited by Pedro Lains and Álvaro Ferreira da Silva, vol. 2, 259–281. Lisbon: Imprensa de Ciências Sociais.

Lains, Pedro 2006. "Protectionism and Portuguese Industrialization." In *Classical Trade Protectionism,* edited by Jean-Pierre Dormois and Pedro Lains, 242–264. London: Routledge.

Lains, Pedro. 2007. "Growth in a Protected Environment: Portugal, 1850–1950." *Research in Economic History* 24: 121–163.

Lains, Pedro. 2008a. "The Portuguese Economy in the Irish Mirror, 1960–2002." *Open Economies Review* 19 (5): 667–683.

Lains, Pedro. 2008b. "The Power of Peripheral Governments: Coping with the 1891 Financial Crisis in Portugal." *Historical Research* 81: 485–506.

Lains, Pedro, ed. 2009a. *Sem Fronteiras. Os Novos Horizontes da Economia Portuguesa.* Lisbon: Imprensa de Ciências Sociais.

Lains, Pedro. 2009b. "The Role of Agriculture in Portuguese Economic Development, 1870–1973." In *Agriculture and Economic Growth in Europe since 1870,* edited by Pedro Lains and Vicente Pinilla, 333–352. London: Routledge.

Lains, Pedro. 2012. "The Burden of Backwardness: The Limits to Economic Growth in the European Periphery, 1830–1930." In *Alan S. Milward and a Century of European Change,* edited by F. Lynch, F. Guirao and S. M. Ramirez Perez, 221–239. London: Routledge.

Lains, Pedro and Álvaro Ferreira da Silva, eds. 2005. *História Económica de Portugal, 1700–2000,* 3 vols. Lisbon: Imprensa de Ciências Sociais.

Lains, Pedro and Vicente Pinilla, eds. 2009. *Agriculture and Economic Development in Europe since 1870.* London: Routledge.

Lains, Pedro, Ester G. da Silva and Jordi Guilera. 2012. "Wage Inequality and Open Economy Forces: Portugal, 1944–1984." *Scandinavian Economic History Review* 61 (3): 287–311.

Lampe, John R. and Marvin R. Jackson. 1982. *Balkan Economic History, 1550–1950. From Imperial Borderlands to Developing Nation.* Bloomington: Indiana University Press.

Landes, David S. 1998. *The Wealth and Poverty of Nations. Why Some Are So Rich and Some So Poor.* London: Little, Brown and Co.

Lane, Frederic. 1973. *Venice, a Maritime Republic.* Baltimore: Johns Hopkins University Press.

Langhans, Franz-Paul. 1949. *A Casa dos Vinte e Quatro em Lisboa.* Lisbon: Imprensa Nacional.

Lapa, J. R. Amaral. 1968. *A Bahia e a Carreira da Índia.* São Paulo: Companhia Editora Nacional.

Leitão, Nicolau Andresen. 2000. "Portugal's European Integration Policy 1947–1972." *Journal of European Integration History* 7 (1): 25–35.

Leitão, Nicolau Andresen. 2007a. *Estado Novo, Democracia e Europa, 1947–1986.* Lisbon: Imprensa de Ciências Sociais.

Leitão, Nicolau Andresen. 2007b. "A Flight of Fantasy? Portugal and the First Attempt to Enlarge the European Economic Community, 1961–1963." *Contemporary European History* 16 (1): 71–87.

Leite, Joaquim da Costa. 1994. *Portugal and Emigration, 1855–1914.* PhD diss., Columbia University.

Livi-Bacci, Massimo. 1999. *La Population dans l'Histoire de l'Europe.* Paris: Éditions du Seuil.

Livi-Bacci, Massimo. 2002. "500 Anos de Demografia Brasileira: Uma Resenha." *Revista Brasileira de Estudos de População* 19 (1): 141–159.

Lobo, Marina Costa and Pedro Lains, eds. 2007. *Em Nome da Europa. Portugal em Mudança, 1986–2006.* Cascais: Princípia.

Lodge, Richard. 1933. "The English Factory at Lisbon." *Transactions of the Royal Historical Society* XVI: 211–247.

Lopes, F. Fernandes. 1938. "Em Favor do Plano Henriquino das Índias." *I Congresso de História da Expansão Portuguesa no Mundo.* Lisbon: Sociedade Nacional de Tipografia.

Lopes, José Silva. 1996. *A Economia Portuguesa desde 1960*. Lisbon: Gradiva.

Lopes, José Silva. 2005. "Finanças Públicas." In *História Económica de Portugal, 1700–2000. O Século XX*, edited by Pedro Lains and Álvaro Ferreira da Silva, vol. 3, 265–304. Lisbon: Imprensa de Ciências Sociais.

Lopes, José Silva. 2008. "Introduction." In *Challenges Ahead for the Portuguese Economy*, edited by Francesco Franco, 25–31. Lisbon: Imprensa de Ciências Sociais.

Lopez, Robert S. 1971. *The Commercial Revolution of the Middle Ages, 950–1350*. Englewood Cliffs, New Jersey: Prentice Hall.

Macedo, Jorge Borges de. 1982a. *A Situação Económica no Tempo de Pombal. Alguns Aspectos*, 2nd edn. Lisbon: Moraes Editores.

Macedo, Jorge Borges de. 1982b. *Problemas de História da Indústria Portuguesa no Século XVIII*, 2nd edn. Lisbon, Querco.

Macedo, Jorge Borges de. 1989. "Diplomacia, Agricultura e Comércio Transitário: Factores Subalternizados no Estudo do Tratado de Methuen." In *Nova Economia em Portugal. Estudos em Homenagem a António Manuel Pinto Barbosa*, 75–93. Lisbon: Universidade Nova de Lisboa.

Macedo, Jorge Borges de. 1990. *O Bloqueio Continental. Economia e Guerra Peninsular*, 2nd edn. Lisbon: Gradiva.

Macedo, Jorge Braga, Álvaro Ferreira da Silva and Rita Martins de Sousa. 2001. "War, Taxes and Gold: The Inheritance of the *Real*." In *Transferring Wealth and Power from the Old to the New World: Monetary and Fiscal Institutions in the 17th through the 19th Centuries*, edited by Michael Bordo and Roberto Cortés-Conde, 187–230. Cambridge: Cambridge University Press.

Maddalena, Aldo de. 1981. "La Europa Rural." In *Historia Económica de Europa. Siglos XVI y XVII*, edited by Carlo Cipolla, vol. II, 214–276. Barcelona: Ariel.

Maddison, Angus. 2001. *The World Economy. A Millennial Perspective*. Paris: OECD.

Madureira, Nuno. 1997. *Mercado e Privilégios. A Indústria Portuguesa entre 1750 e 1834*. Lisbon: Editorial Estampa.

Madureira, Nuno Luís and Ana Cardoso de Matos. 2005. "A Tecnologia." In *História Económica de Portugal, 1700–2000. O Século XVIII*, edited by Pedro Lains and Álvaro Ferreira da Silva, vol. 1, 123–144. Lisbon: Imprensa de Ciências Sociais.

Magalhães, Joaquim Romero. 1970. *Para o Estudo do Algarve Económico durante o Século XVI*. Lisbon: Edições Cosmos.

Magalhães, Joaquim Romero. 1988. *O Algarve Económico, 1600–1773*. Lisbon: Estampa.

Magalhães, Joaquim Romero. 1993. "As Estruturas da Produção Agrícola e Pastoril." *História de Portugal. No Alvorecer ba Modernidade, 1480–1620*, edited by José Mattoso and organized by Joaquim Romero de Magalhães, vol. 3, 243–281. Lisbon: Círculo de Leitores.

Magalhães, Joaquim Romero. 1998a. "Articulações Inter-regionais e Economias-mundo." In *História da Expansão Portugues*, edited by Francisco Bethencourt and Kirti Chaudhuri, vol. I, 308–337. Lisbon: Círculo de Leitores.

Magalhães, Joaquim Romero. 1998b. "A Construção do Espaço Brasileiro." In *História da Expansão Portugues*, edited by Francisco Bethencourt and Kirti Chaudhuri, vol. II, 28–64. Lisbon: Círculo de Leitores.

Magalhães, Joaquim Romero. 2012. *No Portugal Moderno. Espaços, Tratos e Dinheiros.* Coimbra, Imprensa da Universidade de Coimbra.

Magnusson, Lars. 2000. *An Economic History of Sweden.* London: Routledge.

Maia, Fernanda Paula. 1991. *O Mosteiro de Bustelo: Propriedade e Produção Agrícola no Antigo Regime.* Porto: Universidade Portucalense.

Malanima, Paolo. 2009. *Pre-Modern European Economy. One Thousand Years (10th–19th Centuries.* Leiden: Brill.

Malanima, Paolo. 2013. "When Did England Overtake Italy? Medieval and Early Modern Divergence in Prices and Wages." *European Review of Economic History* 17 (1): 45–70.

Maravall, José María. 1997. *Regimes, Politics and Markets. Democratization and Economic Change in Southern and Eastern Europe.* Oxford: Oxford University Press.

Marcos, Rui Figueiredo.1997. *As Companhias Pombalinas: Contributo para a História das Sociedades por Acções em Portugal.* Coimbra: Almedina.

Marques, André Evangelista. 2008. *O Casal. Uma Unidade de Organização Social do Espaço no Entre Douro e Lima (906–1200).* Noia: Editorial Toxosoutos.

Marques, A. H de Oliveira. 1973. *História de Portugal,* 2 vols. Lisbon: Palas Editores.

Marques, A. H. de Oliveira. 1978. *Introdução à História da Agricultura em Portugal.* Lisbon: Cosmos.

Marques A. H. de Oliveira. 1985. *História de Portugal. Das Origens ao Renascimento,* vol. 1., 12th edn. Lisbon: Palas Editores.

Marques, A. H. de Oliveira. 1987. *Nova História de Portugal. Portugal na Crise dos Séculos XIV e* XV, edited by Joel Serrão and A. H. de Oliveira Marques, vol. 4. Lisbon: Presença.

Marques, A. H. de Oliveira, ed. 1998. *Nova História da Expansão Portuguesa. A Expansão Quatrocentista,* edited by Joel Serrão and A. H. de Oliveira Marques, vol. 2. Lisbon: Editorial Estampa.

Marques, A. H. de Oliveira and João José Alves Dias. 2003. *Atlas Histórico de Portugal e do Ultramar Português.* Lisbon: Centro de Estudos Históricos.

Marques, Alfredo. 1988. *Política Económica e Desenvolvimento em Portugal, 1926–1959. As Duas Estratégias do Estado Novo no Período de Isolamento Nacional.* Lisbon: Livros Horizonte.

Marques, Guida. 2002. "O Estado do Brasil na União Ibérica: dinâmicas políticas no Brasil no Tempo de Filipe II de Portugal." *Penélope* 27: 7–35.

Marques, Helena. 2009. "Concorrência Externa e Especialização Internacional." In *Sem Fronteiras. Os Novos Horizontes da Economia Portuguesa,* edited by Pedro Lains, 165–193. Lisbon: Imprensa de Ciências Sociais.

Marques, João Francisco. 1989. *A Parenética Portuguesa e a Restauração, 1640–1668. A Revolta e a Mentalidade,* 2 vols. Porto: Instituto Nacional de Investigação Científica.

Marques, José. 1988. *A Arquidiocese de Braga no Século XV.* Lisbon: Imprensa Nacional-Casa da Moeda.

Marreiros, Maria Rosa Ferreira. 1996b. "Os Proventos da Terra e do Mar." In *Nova História de Portugal. Portugal em Definição de Fronteiras (1096–1325). Do Condado Portucalense à Crise do Século XIV,* edited by Maria Helena da Cruz Coelho e Armando Luís Carvalho Homem, vol. 3, 400–475. Lisbon: Presença.

Marsh, David. 2011. *The Euro. The Battle for the New Currency*. New Haven: Yale University Press.

Martins, Conceição Andrade. 1988. "Os Ciclos do Vinho do Porto: Ensaio de Periodização." *Análise Social* 24 (1): 391–429.

Martins, Conceição Andrade. 1990. *Memória do Vinho do Porto*. Lisbon: Instituto de Ciências Sociais.

Martins, Conceição Andrade. 1998. *Vinha, Vinho e Política Vinícola em Portugal. Do Pombalismo à Regeneração*. PhD diss., Évora: Universidade de Évora.

Martins, Conceição Andrade. 2003. "O Tratado de Methuen e o Crescimento do Comércio Vinícola Português na Primeira Metade de Setecentos." In *O Tratado de Methuen (1703). Diplomacia, Guerra, Política e Economia*, edited by José Luís Cardoso *et al.*, 111–130. Lisbon: Livros Horizonte.

Martins, Conceição Andrade. 2005. "A Agricultura." In *História Económica de Portugal, 1700–2000. O Século XIX*, edited by Pedro Lains and Álvaro Ferreira da Silva, vol. 2, 219–258. Lisbon: Imprensa de Ciências Sociais.

Martins, Joaquim Pedro de Oliveira. 1954. *Política e Economia Nacional*. Guimarães: Guimarães Editora.

Martins, Manuel Mota Freitas. 2009. "A Política Monetária Europeia e a Economia Portuguesa." In *Sem Fronteiras. Os Novos Horizontes da Economia Portuguesa*, edited by Lains, Pedro, 31–57. Lisbon: Imprensa de Ciências Sociais.

Mata, Maria Eugénia. 1988. "As Três Fases do Fontismo: Projectos e Realizações." In *Estudos e Ensaios em Homenagem a Vitorino Magalhães Godinho*, 413–430. Lisbon; Sá da Costa.

Mata, Maria Eugénia. 1993. *As Finanças Públicas Portuguesas da Regeneração à Primeira Guerra Mundia*. Lisbon: Banco de Portugal.

Mata, Maria Eugénia. 2005. "O Capital." In *História Económica de Portugal, 1700–2000*, edited by Pedro Lains and Álvaro Ferreira da Silva, vol. 2, 153–187. Lisbon: Imprensa de Ciências Sociais.

Mata, Maria Eugénia. 2007. "Foreign Joint-stock Companies Operating in Portuguese Colonies on the Eve of the First World War." *South African Journal of Economic History* 22 (1–2): 74–107.

Mata, Maria Eugénia. 2008. "The Role of Implicit Contracts: Building Public Works in the 1840s in Portugal." *Business History* 50 (2): 147–162.

Mata, Maria Eugénia. 2010. "Portuguese Public Debt and Financial Business before World War I." *Business and Economic Horizons* 3 (3): 10–27.

Mata, Maria Eugénia. 2012. "From Pioneer Mercantile State to Ordinary Fiscal State, Portugal 1498–1914." In *The Rise of Fiscal States: A Global History, 1500–1914*, edited by Bartolomé Yun-Casalilla, and Patrick O'Brien, 215–232. Cambridge: Cambridge University Press.

Mata, Maria Eugénia and Nuno Valério. 1996. "Monetary Stability, Fiscal Discipline and Economic Performance. The Experience of Portugal since 1854." In *Currency Convertibility. The Gold Standard and Beyond*, edited by Jorge Braga de Macedo, B. Eichengree and Jaime Reis, 204–227. London: Routledge.

Mata, Maria Eugénia and Nuno Valério. 2003a. *História Económica de Portugal. Uma Perspectiva Global*, 2nd edn. Lisbon: Presença.

Mata, Maria Eugénia and Nuno Valério. 2003b. "Finances Publiques et Structure de l'Etat au Portugal, 1851–1988." *Économies et Sociétés*, 115–162.

Mateus, Abel.1998. *Economia Portuguesa desde 1910*, 2nd edn. Lisbon: Verbo.

Mathias, Peter. 1979. "Credit, Capital and Enterprise in the Industrial Revolution." *The Transformation of England: Essays in the Economic and Social History of England in the Eighteenth Century*, 88–115. New York: Columbia University Press.

Mathias, Peter.1993. *The First Industrial Nation. The Economic History of England, 1700–1914*, 2nd edn. New York: Routledge.

Matos, Ana Maria Cardoso de. 1999. *Ciência, Tecnologia e Desenvolvimento Industrial no Portugal Oitocentista. O Caso dos Lanifícios no Alentejo*. Lisbon: Editorial Estampa.

Matos, Artur Teodoro de. 1980. *Transportes e Comunicações em Portugal, Açores e Madeira, 1750–1850*. Ponta Delgada: Universidade dos Açores.

Mattoso, José. 1985. *Identificação de um País. Ensaio sobre as Origens de Portugal, 1096–1325*, 2 vols. Lisbon: Estampa.

Mattoso, José. ed. 1992–1994. *História de Portugal*. 8 vols. Lisbon: Círculo de Leitores.

Mattoso, José and Armindo de Sousa. 1993. *História de Portugal. A Monarquia Feudal, 1096–1480*, edited by José Mattoso, vol. 2. Lisbon: Círculo de Leitores.

Mauro, Frédéric.1983. *Le Portugal, le Brésil et l'Atlantique au XVIIᵉ Siècle, 1570–1670*. Paris: Fondation Calouste Gulbenkian.

Maxwell, Kenneth. 1991. *Conflicts and Conspiracies: Brazil and Portugal, 1750–1808*. Cambridge: Cambridge University Press.

Maxwell, Kenneth. 1995. *Pombal, Paradox of the Enlightenment*. Cambridge: Cambridge University Press.

Mello, Evaldo Cabral. 1998. *Olinda Restaurada. Guerra e Açúcar no Nordeste, 1630–1654*. Rio de Janeiro: Topbooks.

Mello, Evaldo Cabral. 2002. *O Negócio do Brasil. Portugal, os Países Baixos e o Nordeste, 1641–1669*. Lisbon: Comissão Nacional para as Comemorações dos Descobrimentos Portugueses.

Melo, Arnaldo Rui Azevedo de Sousa. 2009. *Trabalho e Produção em Portugal na Idade Média: o Porto, c. 1320 – c. 1415*. PhD diss., Braga, Universidade do Minho.

Mendels, Franklin. 1972. "Proto-industrialization. The First Phase of the Industrialization Process." *Journal of Economic History* 32 (2): 241–261.

Meneses, Avelino de Freitas de. 2001. "A Exploração da Terra." In *Nova História de Portugal. Portugal. Da Paz da Restauração ao Ouro do Brasil*, edited by Joel Serrão and A. H. de Oliveira Marques, organized by Avelino de Freitas de Meneses, vol. VII, 226–263. Lisbon: Presença.

Milward, Alan. 1992. *The European Rescue of the Nation-State*. London: Routledge.

Milward, A. and Saul, S. B. 1973. *The Economic Development of Continental Europe, 1780–1870*. London: George Allen and Unwin.

Milward, A. and Saul, S. B. 1977. *The Development of the Economies of Continental Europe, 1850–1914*. London: George Allen and Unwin.

Miranda, Flávio. 2014. "Portuguese Traders in Atlantic Europe in the Middle Ages." *E-Journal of Portuguese History* 12 (1):119–130.

Miranda, Susana Münch. 1994. *A Fazenda Real na Ilha da Madeira (Segunda Metade do Século XVI)*. Lisbon: Instituto de História de Além-Mar.

Miranda, Susana Münch. 2009. "Centre and Periphery in the Administration of the Royal Exchequer of Estado da India, 1517–1640." *E-Journal of Portuguese History* 7 (2): 1–14.

Miranda, Susana Münch. 2011. "A Fiscalidade no Estado da Índia: Configuração e Dinâmicas, 1510–1640." In *Los Ambitos de la Fiscalidad: Fronteras, Território y Percepción de Tributos en los Impérios Ibéricos, siglos XV–XVIII*, edited by Luis Salas, 107–123. Madrid: Ministerio de Economia y Hacienda, Instituto de Estudios Fiscales.

Mokyr, Joel. 1994. "Technological Change, 1700–1830." In *The Economic History of Britain since 1700–1860*, edited by Rodrick Floud and Deirdre McCloskey, 12–43. Cambridge: Cambridge University Press.

Mokyr, Joel. 2009. *The Enlightened Economy: Britain and the Industrial Revolution, 1700–1850*. London: The Penguin Books.

Monteiro, Nuno Gonçalo. 1996a. "A Sociedade Local e os seus Protagonistas." In *História dos Municípios e do Poder Local. Dos Finais da Idade Média à União Europeia*, edited by César Oliveira, 29–55. Lisbon: Círculo de Leitores.

Monteiro, Nuno Gonçalo. 1996b. "O Espaço Político e Social Local." In *História dos Municípios e do Poder Local. Dos Finais da Idade Média à União Europeia*, edited by César Oliveira, 121–136. Lisbon: Círculo de Leitores.

Monteiro, Nuno Gonçalo. 2001. "Identificação da Política Setecentista. Notas sobre Portugal no início do Período Joanino." *Análise Social* 35 (4): 961–987.

Monteiro, Nuno Gonçalo. 2003. *O Crepúsculo dos Grandes. A Casa e o Património da Aristocracia em Portugal, 1750–1832*, 2nd edn. Lisbon: Imprensa Nacional-Casa da Moeda.

Monteiro, Nuno Gonçalo. 2005a. "A Ocupação da Terra." In *História Económica de Portugal (1700–2000). O Século XVIII*, edited by Pedro Lains and Álvaro Ferreira da Silva, vol. 1, 67–91. Lisbon: Imprensa de Ciências Sociais.

Monteiro, Nuno Gonçalo. 2007a. "Regime Senhorial e a Revolução Liberal." In *Elites e Poder. Entre o Antigo Regime e o Liberalismo*, edited by Nuno G. Monteiro, 179–312. Lisbon: Imprensa de Ciências Sociais.

Monteiro, Nuno Gonçalo. 2007b. "Nobility and Aristocracy in Ancien Régime Portugal, Seventeenth to Nineteenth Centuries." In *The European Nobilities in the Seventeenth and Eighteenth Centuries*, 2nd edn, edited by H. M. Scott, vol. I, *Western and Southern Europe*, 256–284. Houndmills: Palgrave Macmillan.

Monteiro, Nuno Gonçalo. 2008. *D. José. Na Sombra de Pombal*. Lisbon: Temas e Debates.

Moreira, Cristina and Jari Eloranta. 2011. "Importance of 'Weak' States during Conflicts: Portuguese Trade with the United States during the Revolutionary and Napoleonic Wars." *Journal of Iberian and Latin American Economic History* 29 (3): 393–423.

Moreira, Manuel A. Fernandes. 1990. *Os Mercadores de Viana e o Comércio do Açúcar Brasileiro no Século XVII*. Viana do Castelo: Câmara Municipal de Viana do Castelo.

Moreira, Maria João Guardado. 2008. "O século XVIII." In *História da População Portuguesa*, edited by Teresa Ferreira Rodrigues, 247–287. Porto: Edições Afrontamento.

Moreira, Maria João Guardado and Teresa Rodrigues Veiga. 2005. "A Evolução da População." In *História Económica de Portugal (1700–2000). O Século XVIII*, edited by Pedro Lains and Álvaro Ferreira da Silva, vol. 1, 35–65. Lisbon: Imprensa de Ciências Sociais.

Morineau, Michel. 1985. *Incroyable Gazettes et Fabuleux Métaux (XVI–XVIII siècles)*. Paris: Editions de la Maison des Sciences de l'Homme.

Mota, Salvador Magalhães. 2000. *O Senhorio Cisterciense de Santa Maria de Bouro: Património, Propriedade, Exploração e Produção Agrícola, 1570–1834*. PhD diss., Porto: Universidade do Porto.

Moura, F. Pereira de. 1973. *Por Onde Vai a Economia Portuguesa?* Lisbon: Dom Quixote.

Moutokias, Zacarias. 1988. *Contrabandoy Control Colonial en el Siglo XVII*. Buenos Aires: Centro Editor de America Latina.

Munro, John H. 1992. *Bullion Flows and Monetary Policies in England and the Low Countries, 1350–1500*. Hampshire: Variorum-Ashgate.

Murteira, André. 2010. "A Carreira da Índia e as Incursões Neerlandesas no Índico Ocidental e em Águas Ibéricas de 1604–1608." In *O Estado da Índia e os Desafios Europeus. Actas do XII Seminário Internacional de História Indo-Portuguesa*, edited by João P. Oliveira e Costa and V. L. Gaspar Rodrigues, 457–501. Lisbon: Centro de História de Além Mar.

*Não ao Mercado Comum. Efeitos Globais da Adesão à CEE e Alternativa*. Lisbon: Edições Avante.

Nardi, Jean Baptiste. 1996. *O Fumo Brasileiro no Período Colonial, Lavoura, Comércio e Administração*. São Paulo: Editora Brasiliense.

Nash, R. C. 2001. "The Economy." In *The Seventeenth Century: Europe 1598–1715*, edited by Joseph Bergin, 11–49. Oxford: Oxford University Press.

Neal, Larry. 2007. *The Economies of Europe and the European Union*. Cambridge: Cambridge University Press.

Neal, Larry and Jeffrey G. Williamson, eds. 2014. *The Cambridge History of Capitalism*, 2 vols. Cambridge: Cambridge University Press.

Neto, Maria Margarida Sobral. 1993. "A Persistência Senhorial." In *História de Portugal. No Alvorecer da Modernidade, 1480–1620*, edited by José Mattoso and organized by Joaquim Romero de Magalhães, vol. 3, 165–175. Lisbon: Círculo de Leitores.

Neto, Maria Margarida Sobral. 1997. *Terra e Conflito. Região de Coimbra. 1700–1834*. Viseu: Palimares Editores.

Neves, João César das. 1994. *The Portuguese Economy: A Picture in Figures. XIX and XX Centuries*. Lisbon: Universidade Católica Editora.

Neves, João César das. 1996. "Portuguese Post-War Growth: A Global Approach." In *Economic Growth in Europe since 1945*, edited by Nicholas Crafts and Gianni Toniolo, 329–354. Cambridge: Cambridge University Press.

North, Douglass. 1981. *Structure and Change in Economic History*. New York: W. W. Norton.

North, Douglass. 1990. *Institutions, Institutional Change and Economic Performance*. New York: Cambridge University Press.

North, Douglass and Barry Weingast. 1989. "Constitutions and Commitment: Evolution of the Institutions Governing Public Choice in Seventeenth-Century England." *Journal of Economic History* 49 (4): 803–832.

Nunes, Ana Bela and José Maria Brandão de Brito. 1990. "Política Económica, Industrialização e Crescimento." In *Nova História de Portugal. Portugal e o Estado Novo, 1930–1960*, edited by Joel Serrão and A. H. de Oliveira Marques, organized by Fernando Rosas, vol. XII, 306–351. Lisbon: Editorial Presença.

Nunes, Ana Bela and Nuno Valério.1983. "A Lei de Reconstituição Económica e a sua execução: um exemplo dos projectos e realizações da política económica do Estado Novo." *Estudos de Economia* 3 (3): 331–359.

O'Brien, Patrick. 1982. "European Economic Development: The Contribution of the Periphery." *Economic History Review* 35 (1): 1–18.

O'Brien, Patrick. 1988. "The Political Economy of British Taxation, 1660–1815." *The Economic History Review* 41 (1): 1–32.

O'Brien, Patrick. 2005. "Final Considerations: Aristocracies and Economic Progress under the Ancien Régime." In *European Aristocracies and Colonial Elites: Patrimonial Management Strategies and Economic Development, 17th–18th Centuries*, edited by Paul Jansens and Bartolomé Yun Casalilla, 247–263. Manchester: Ashgate.

O'Brien, Patrick and Caglar Keyder 2011. *Economic Growth in Britain and France, 1780–1914. Two Paths to the Twentieth Century*. New York: Routledge.

O'Brien, Patrick and Leandro Prados de la Escosura. 1998. "The Costs and Benefits for Europeans from Their Empires Overseas." *Revista de Historia Económica* 16 (1): 29–89.

O'Brien, Patrick and Philip A. Hunt. 1999. "England, 1485–1815." In *The Rise of the Fiscal State in Europe, c. 1200–1815*, edited by Richard Bonney, 52–100. Oxford: Oxford University Press.

Ó Gráda, Cormac. 2001. *Ireland. A New Economic History, 1780–1939*. Oxford: Clarendon Press.

O'Rourke, Kevin. 2006. "The Worldwide Economic Impact of the French Revolutionary and Napoleonic Wars, 1793–1815." *Journal of Global History* 1 (1): 123–149.

OECD. 2013. *Portugal. Reforming the State to Promote Growth*. Paris: OECD.

Ogilvie, Sheilagh. 2000. "The European Economy in the Eighteenth Century." In *The Eighteenth Century: Europe 1688–1815*, edited by T. C. W. Blanning, 91–130. Oxford: Oxford University Press.

Ogilvie, Sheilagh and Markus Cerman, eds. 1996. *European Proto-industrialization*. Cambridge: Cambridge University Press.

Olival, Fernanda. 2001. *As Ordens Militares e o Estado Moderno. Honra, Mercê e Venalidade em Portugal, 1641–1789*. Lisbon: Estar Editora.

Olival, Fernanda. 2004. "Structural Changes within the 16th-Century Portuguese Military Orders." *E-Journal of Portuguese History* 2 (2): 1–20.

Oliveira, António de. 1971–1972. *Vida Económica e Social de Coimbra de 1537 a 1640*, 2 vols. Coimbra: Universidade de Coimbra.

Oliveira, António de. 1990. *Poder e Oposição Política em Portugal no Período Filipino, 1580–1640*. Lisbon: Difel.

Oliveira, António de. 2002. *Movimentos Sociais e Poder em Portugal no Século XVII*. Coimbra: Instituto de História Económica e Social.

Oliveira, Aurélio de. 1979. *A Abadia de Tibães, 1630/1680–1813. Propriedade, Exploração e Produção Agrícola no Vale do Cávado durante o Antigo Regime*, 2 vols., PhD diss., Porto: Universidade do Porto.

Oliveira, Aurélio de. 1980. "A Renda Agrícola em Portugal durante o Antigo Regime (séculos XVII-XVIII). Alguns Aspectos e Problemas." *Revista de História Económica e Social* 6: 1–56.

Oliveira, Aurélio de. 1981. "Rendas e Arrendamentos da Colegiada de Nossa Senhora da Oliveira de Guimarães, 1648–1731." In *Actas do Congresso de História de Guimarães e sua Colegiada*, vol. II, 99–121. Guimarães: s.n.

Oliveira, Aurélio de. 1989. "Economia e Conjuntura Agrícola no Portugal de Seiscentos: O Exemplo de Entre-Douro-e-Minho, 1600–1650." *Penélope* 3: 129–146.

Oliveira, João Nunes. 1990. *A Produção Agrícola de Viseu entre 1550 e 1700*. Viseu: Câmara Municipal.

Oliveira, João Nunes. 2002. *A Beira Alta de 1700 a 1840: Gentes e Subsistências*. Viseu: Palimage.

Ormrod, David. 2003. *The Rise of Commercial Empires. England and Netherlands in the Age of Mercantilism, 1650–1770*. Cambridge: Cambridge University Press.

Osório, Helen. 2007. *O Império Português no Sul da América: Estancieiros, Lavradores e Comerciantes*. Porto Alegre: Editora da UFRGS.

Palma, Nuno and Jaime Reis. 2016. "From Convergence to Divergence: Portuguese Demography and Economic Growth, 1500–1850." Groningen Growth and Development Centre. Research Memorandum.

Pamuk, Sevket. 2009. *The Ottoman Economy and Its Institutions*. Farnham: Ashgate.

Parker, Geoffrey. 2013. *Global Crisis: War, Climate Change and Catastrophe in the Seventeenth Century*. New Haven: Yale University Press.

Parker, Geoffrey and Leslie Smith, eds. 1978. *The General Crisis of the Seventeenth Century*. London: Routledge.

Pedreira, Jorge M. 1988. "Agrarismo, Industrialismo, Liberalismo: Algumas Notas sobre o Pensamento Económico Português, 1780–1820." In *Contribuições para a História do Pensamento Económico em Portugal*, edited by J. L. Cardoso, 63–83. Lisbon: Publicações D. Quixote.

Pedreira, Jorge M. 1993. "La Economia Portuguesa y el fin del Imperio Luso-brasileño, 1800–1860." In *La Independencia Americana. Consecuencias Económicas*, edited by Leandro Prados de la Escosura and Samuel Amaral, 219–252. Madrid: Alianza.

Pedreira, Jorge M. 1994. *Estrutura Industrial e Mercado Colonial. Portugal e Brasil, 1780–1830*. Lisbon: Difel.

Pedreira, Jorge M. 1995. *Os Homens de Negócio da Praça de Lisboa de Pombal ao Vintismo, 1755–182. Diferenciação, Reprodução e Identificação de um Grupo Social*. PhD diss., Lisbon: Universidade Nova de Lisboa.

Pedreira, Jorge Miguel. 1998. "O Sistema das Trocas." In *História da Expansão Portuguesa*, edited by Francisco Bethencourt and Kirti Chaudhuri, vol. 4, 213–301. Lisbon: Círculo de Leitores.

Pedreira, Jorge M. 2000. "From Growth to Collapse: Portugal, Brazil, and the Breakdown of the Old Colonial System, 1760–1830." *Hispanic American Historical Review* 80 (4): 839–864.

Pedreira, Jorge M. 2003. "Diplomacia, Manufacturas e Desenvolvimento Económico." In *O Tratado de Methuen (1703). Diplomacia, Guerra, Política e Economia*, edited by José Luís Cardoso *et al.*, 131–156. Lisbon: Livros Horizonte.

Pedreira, Jorge M. 2005. "A Indústria." In *História Económica de Portugal, 1700–2000. O Século XVIII*, edited by Pedro Lains and Álvaro Ferreira da Silva, vol. 1, 177–208. Lisbon: Imprensa de Ciências Sociais.

Pedreira, Jorge M. 2007. "Costs and Financial Trends in the Portuguese Empire, 1415–1822." In *Portuguese Oceanic Expansion, 1400–1800*, edited by Francisco Bethencourt and Diogo Ramada Curto, 49–87. Cambridge: Cambridge University Press.

Pereira, Álvaro Santos. 2009. "The Opportunity of a Disaster: The Economic Impact of the 1755 Lisbon Earthquake." *The Journal of Economic History* 69 (2): 466–499.

Pereira, Álvaro Santos. 2011. *Portugal na Hora da Verdade. O Que Fazer para Vencer a Crise Nacional*. Lisbon: Gradiva.

Pereira, Álvaro Santos and Pedro Lains. 2012. "From an Agrarian Society to a Knowledge Economy? The Rising Importance of Education to the Portuguese Economy, 1950–2009." In *Higher Education in Portugal 1974–2009. A Nation, a Generation*, edited Guy Neave and Alberto Amaral, 109–134. London: Springer.

Pereira, António dos Santos. 2003. *Portugal, o Império Urgente (1475–1525). Os Espaços, os Homens e os Produtos*, 2 vols. Lisbon: Imprensa Nacional-Casa da Moeda.

Pereira, João Cordeiro. 1983. *Para a História das Alfândegas em Portugal no Início do Século XVI. Vila do Conde. Organização e Movimento*, Lisbon, Universidade Nova de Lisboa.

Pereira, João Cordeiro. 2003. *Portugal na Era de Quinhentos*. Cascais: Patrimonia Historica.

Pereira, Miriam Halpern. 1983. *Livre-Câmbio e Desenvolvimento Económico, Portugal na Segunda Metade do Século XIX*, 2nd edn. Lisbon: Sá da Costa Editora.

Pereira, Miriam Halpern. 2001. *Diversidade e Assimetrias: Portugal nos Séculos XIX e XX*. Lisbon: Imprensa de Ciências Sociais.

Peres, Damião. 1933. *História de Portugal*, vol. III. Porto: Portucalense Editora.

Peres, Damião. 1983. *História dos Descobrimentos Portugueses*, 3rd edn. Porto, Vertente.

Persson, Karl Gunnar. 2010. *An Economic History of Europe. Knowledge, Institutions and Growth, 600 to the Present*. Cambridge: Cambridge University Press.

Persson, Karl Gunnar. 2014. "Markets and Coercion in Medieval Europe." In *The Cambridge History of Capitalism*, edited by Larry Neal and Jeffrey G. Williamson, 225–266. Cambridge: Cambridge University Press.

Pessoa, Argentino. 2014. "Structural and Technological Change in the European Periphery." In *Structural Change, Competitiveness and Industrial Policy. Painful Lessons from the European Periphery*, edited by A. A. C. Teixeira, E. G. Silva and R. P. Mamede, 105–132. Abingdon: Routledge.

Pfister, Ulrich and Georg Fertig. 2010. *The Population History of Germany: Research, Stratagies and Preliminary Results*. Working Paper 2010–2035. Max Planck Institute for Demographic Research.

Philips, Carla Rahn. 1993. "The Growth and Composition of Trade in the Iberian Empires, 1450–1740." In *The Rise of Merchant Empires. Long Distance Trade in the Early Modern World 1350–1750*, edited by James D. Tracey, 34–101. Cambridge: Cambridge University Press.

Philips, Carla Rahn and William D. Phillips. 1997. *Spain's Golden Fleece. Wool Production and the Wool Trade from Middle Ages to the Nineteenth Century*. Baltimore: John Hopkins University Press.

Pinheiro, Maximiano, ed. 1997. *Séries Longas para a Economia Portuguesa. Pós II Guerra Mundial*, 2 vols. Lisbon: Banco de Portugal.

Pintado, V. Xavier. 2002. *Structure and Growth of the Portuguese Economy*, 2nd edn. Lisbon: Imprensa de Ciências Sociais.

Pinto, António Costa and Nuno Severiano Teixeira, eds. 2002. *Southern Europe and the Making of the European Union*. Boulder: Social Sciences Monographs.

Pinto, Virgílio Noya. 1979. *O Ouro Brasileiro e o Comércio Anglo-Português*. São Paulo: Companhia Editora Nacional.

Pollard, Sidney. 1994. *Peaceful Conquest. The Industrialization of Europe, 1760–1970*. Oxford: Oxford University Press.

Polónia, Amélia. 2007. *A Expansão Ultramarina numa Perspectiva Local: o Porto de Vila do Conde no Século XVI*, 2 vols. Lisbon: Imprensa Nacional-Casa da Moeda.

Pomeranz, Kenneth. 2000. *The Great Divergence. China, Europe, and the Making of the Modern World Economy*. Princeton: Princeton University Press.

Possamai, Paulo C. 2006. *A Vida Quotidiana na Colónia do Sacramento (1715–1735)*. Lisbon: Livros do Brasil.

Powell, Charles. 2005. "A Adesão Espanhola à União Europeia Revisitada." In *Portugal, Espanha e a Integração Europeia. Um Balanço*, edited by Sebastian Royo, 191–216. Lisbon: Imprensa de Ciências Sociais.

Prados de la Escosura, Leandro.1988. *De Imperio a Nación. Crecimiento y Atraso Económico en España, 1870–1930*. Madrid: Alianza Universidad.

Prados de la Escosura, Leandro. 2003. *El Progreso Económico de España, 1850–2000*. Bilbao: Fundación BBVA.

Prestage, Edgar. 1935. *Memórias sobre Portugal no Reinado de D. Pedro II*. Lisbon: E. Prestage.

Price, J. M. and Paul G. E. Clemens. 1987. "Revolution of Scale in Overseas Trade: British Firms in the Chesapeake Trade, 1675–1775." *The Journal of Economic History* 47 (1): 1–43.

*Prices Wages and Rents in Portugal 1300–1910*, directed by Jaime Reis, http://pwr-portugal.ics.ul.pt/

Quental, Antero de. 1982. "Causas da Decadência dos Povos Peninsulares nos Últimos Três Séculos." In *Antero de Quental. Prosas Sócio-Políticas*, edited by Joel Serrão, 255–296. Lisbon, Imprensa Nacional.

Ramos, Rui, Bernardo Vasconcelos Sousa, and Nuno Monteiro. 2009. *História de Portugal*. Lisbon: Esfera dos Livros.

Rau, Virgínia. 1951a. *A Casa dos Contos*. Coimbra: Universidade de Coimbra.

Rau, Virgínia. 1951b. *A Exploração e o Comércio do Sal de Setúbal*. Lisbon: s.n.

Rau, Virgínia. 1954. "Subsídios para o Estudo do Movimento dos Portos de Faro e Lisboa durante o século XVII." *Anais da Academia Portuguesa da História* 5:199–277.

Rau, Virgínia.1961. *Estudos de História Económica*, Lisbon: Ática.

Rau, Virgínia. 1968. *Política Económica e Mercantilismo na Correspondência de Duarte Ribeiro de Macedo (1668–1676)*. Do Tempo e da História, 20.

Rau, Virgínia. 1971. *O Açúcar de São Tomé no Segundo Quartel do Século XVI*. Lisbon: Centro de Estudos da Marinha.

Rau, Virgínia. 1982. *Sesmarias Medievais Portuguesas*, 2nd edn. Lisbon: Editorial Presença.

Rau, Virgínia.1983. *Feiras Medievais Portuguesas. Subsídios para o seu Estudo*, 2nd edn. Lisbon: Editorial Presença.

Rau, Virgínia. 1984. *Estudos sobre a História do Sal Português*. Lisbon: Editorial Presença.

Reis, Jaime. 1991. *A Evolução da Oferta Monetária Portuguesa, 1854–1912*. Lisbon: Banco de Portugal.

Reis, Jaime. 1992. "The Historical Roots of the Modern Portuguese Economy: The First Century of Growth, 1850s to 1950s." In *The New Portugal. Democracy and Europe*, edited by R. Herr, 126–150. Berkeley: Berkeley University Press

Reis, Jaime. 1993. *O Atraso Económico Português em Perspectiva Histórica: Estudos sobre a Economia Portuguesa na Segunda Metade do Século XIX, 1850–1930*. Lisbon: Imprensa Nacional-Casa da Moeda.

Reis, Jaime. 1994. "Alguns Aspectos da História Monetária Portuguesa da Segunda Metade do Século XIX." *Análise Social* 29 (1–2): 33–54.

Reis, Jaime. 1995a. "The National Savings Bank as an Instrument of Economic Policy: Portugal in the Interwar Period." In *The Evolution of Financial Institutions and Markets in Twentieth Century Europe*, edited by Youssef Cassis et al., 163–183. London: Scholar Press.

Reis, Jaime. 1995b. "Portuguese Banking in the Inter-war Period." In *Banking, Currency, and Finance in Europe between the Wars*, edited by C. H. Feinstein, 472–501. Oxford: Clarendon Press.

Reis, Jaime. 1996. *O Banco de Portugal das Origens a 1914*, vol. I. Lisbon: Banco de Portugal.

Reis, Jaime. 2007. "An 'Art', not a 'Science'? Central Bank Management in Portugal under the Gold Standard, 1863–1887." *Economic History Review* 60 (2): 712–741.

Reis, Jaime, ed. 2008–2010. *Prices, Wages and Rents in Portugal 1500–1900*. Lisbon: University of Lisbon.

Ribeiro, J. F., L. G. Fernandes e M. M. C. Ramos. 1987. "Grande Indústria, Banca e Grupos Financeiros, 1953–1973." *Análise Social* 23 (5): 945–1018.

Ribeiro, Orlando.1945. *Portugal, o Mediterrâneo e o Atlântico. Estudo geográfico*. s. l.: Coimbra Editora.

Ribeiro, Orlando. 1979. "Significado Ecológico, Expansão e Declínio da Oliveira em Portugal." *Boletim do Instituto do Azeite e dos Produtos Oleaginosos* 7 (2): 50–54.

Ritschl, Albrecht O. 1996. "An Exercise in Futility: East German Economic Growth and Decline, 1945–1989." In *Economic Growth in Europe since 1945*, edited by Nicholas Crafts and Gianni Toniolo, 498–540. Cambridge: Cambridge University Press.

Rocha, Maria Manuela. 1996. *Crédito Privado num Contexto Urbano, Lisboa 1770–1830.* PhD diss., Florence: European University Institute.

Rocha, Maria Manuela. 1998. "Crédito Privado em Lisboa numa Perspectiva Comparada (séculos XVII–XVIII)." *Análise Social* 33 (1): 91–115.

Rodrigues, Ana Maria. 1995. *Torres Vedras. A Vila e o Termo nos Finais da Idade Média.* Lisbon: Fundação Calouste Gulbenkian.

Rodrigues, Ana Maria. 1998. "A Produção Agro-pecuária." In *Nova História de Portugal. Portugal: do Renascimento à Crise Dinástica*, edited by Joel Serrão and A. H. de Oliveira Marques, organized by João José Alves Dias, vol. 5, 165–181. Lisbon: Estampa.

Rodrigues, Ana Maria and Luís Miguel Duarte. 1998. "A Propriedade." In *Nova História de Portugal. Portugal: do Renascimento à Crise Dinástica*, edited Joel Serrão and A. H. de Oliveira Marques, organized by João José Alves Dias, vol. 5, 83–160. Lisbon: Estampa.

Rodrigues, Lisbeth de Oliveira. 2013. *Os Hospitais Portugueses no Renascimento (1480–1580): O Caso de Nossa Senhora do Pópulo das Caldas da Rainha*, PhD diss., University of Minho.

Rodrigues, Manuel Ferreira and José Amado Mendes. 1999. *História da Indústria Portuguesa da Idade Média aos Nossos Dias.* Mem Martins: Europa-América.

Rodrigues, Teresa Ferreira, ed. 2008. *História da População Portuguesa. Das Longas Permanências à Conquista da Modernidade.* Porto: Edições Afrontamento.

Rodrigues, Victor. 2004. "A Guerra na Índia." In *Nova História Militar de Portugal*, edited by Manuel Themudo Barata and Nuno Severiano Teixeira, vol. III, 198–223. Lisbon: Círculo de Leitores.

Rollo, Maria Fernanda. 1994. *Portugal e o Plano Marshall. Da Rejeição à Solicitação da Ajuda Financeira Norte-Americana, 1947–1952.* Lisbon: Editorial Estampa.

Rollo, Maria Fernanda. 2007. *Portugal e a Reconstrução Económica do Pós-Guerra. O Plano Marshall e a Economia Portuguesa dos anos 50.* Lisbon: Instituto Diplomático.

Romano, Ruggiero. 1962. "Tra XVI e XVII secolo. Una Crise Economica: 1619–1622." *Revista Storica Italiana* 70 (3): 408–531.

Rosas, Fernando. 1994. *História de Portugal. O Estado Novo, 1926–1974*, edited by José Mattoso, vol. VII. Lisbon: Círculo de Leitores.

Rosas, Fernando, ed. 2000. *Salazarismo e Fomento Económico, 1928–1948. O Primado do Político na História Económica do Estado Novo.* Lisbon: Editorial Notícias.

Rowland, Robert. 1984. "Sistemas Familiares e Padrões Demográficos em Portugal: Questões para uma Investigação Comparada." *Ler História* 3: 13–32.

Rowland, Robert. 2009. "Emigração e Contexto." In *Desenvolvimento Económico e Mudança Social. Portugal nos Últimos dois Séculos. Homenagem a Miriam Halpern Pereira*, edited by José V. Serrão, M. de Avelar Pinheiro, Maria de Fátima Sá e Melo Ferreira, 393–403. Lisbon: Imprensa de Ciências Sociais.

Sá, Isabel dos Guimarães. 2005. "O Trabalho." In *História Económica de Portugal. O Século XVIII*, edited by Pedro Lains and Álvaro Ferreira da Silva, vol. 1, 93–121. Lisbon: Imprensa de Ciências Sociais.

Salazar, António de Oliveira. 1997. *O Ágio do Ouro e Outros Textos Económicos*, edited by Nuno Valério. Lisbon: Banco de Portugal.

Salvado, João Paulo. 2009. *Nobreza, Monarquia e Império. A Casa Senhorial dos Almotacés-Mores do Reino (Séculos XVI-XVIII)*. PhD diss., Lisbon: Universidade Nova de Lisboa.

Santos, Catarina Madeira. 2006. "Os Refluxos do Império, numa Época de Crise. A Câmara de Lisboa, as Armadas da Índia e as Armadas do Brasil: Quatro Tempos e uma Interrogação." *Anais de História de Além Mar* 7: 81–105.

Santos, Rui. 2003. *Sociogénese do Latifundismo Moderno. Mercados, Crises e Mudança Social na Região de Évora. Séculos XVII a XIX*. Lisbon: Banco de Portugal.

Santos, Rui. 2005. "The Agrarian Economy of the Region of Évora in the First Half of the 17th Century, 1595–1660: An Exploration of Main Indicators." *Revista de História Económica* 23: 349–378.

Santos, Rui. 2006. "Risk-sharing and Social Differentiation of Demand in Land Tenancy Markets in Southern Portugal, Seventeenth-Nineteenth Centuries." *Continuity and Change* 21 (2): 287–312.

Schaub, Jean-Frédéric. 2001. *Portugal na Monarquia Hispânica, 1580–1640*. Lisbon: Livros Horizonte.

Schneider, Susan. 1980. *O Marquês de Pombal e o Vinho do Porto. Dependência e Subdesenvolvimento em Portugal no Século XVIII*. Lisbon: Regra do Jogo.

Schumpeter, Joseph. 1991. "The Crisis of the Tax State." In *The Economics and Sociology of Capitalism*, edited by R. Swedberg, 99–140. Princeton: Princeton University Press.

Schwartz, Stuart. 1984. "Colonial Brazil, c. 1580–1750: Plantations and Peripheries." In *The Cambridge History of Latin America. Colonial Latin America*, edited by Leslie Bethell, vol. 2, 423–499. Cambridge: Cambridge University Press.

Schwartz, Stuart. 1985. *Sugar Plantations in the Formation of Brazilian Society. Bahia, 1550–1835*. Cambridge: Cambridge University Press.

Schwartz, Stuart. 2003. *Da América Portuguesa ao Brasil*. Lisbon: Difel.

Sequeira, Joana Isabel. 2012. *Produção Têxtil em Portugal no Final da Idade Média*. PhD diss., University of Porto.

Sérgio, António. 1984. "As Duas Políticas Nacionais." In *António Sérgio. Uma Antologia*, edited by Joel Serrão, 74–94. Lisbon: Livros Horizonte.

Serrão, Joel. 1951. "Rendimento das alfândegas do arquipélago da Madeira, 1581–1587." *Das Artes e da História da Madeira* 1 (6): 14–18.

Serrão, Joel. 1980. *Temas Oitocentistas*. Lisbon: Livros Horizonte.

Serrão, Joel. 1982. *A Emigração Portuguesa*. Lisbon: Livros Horizonte.

Serrão, José Vicente. 1993a. "O Quadro Humano." In *História de Portugal. O Antigo Regime, 1620–1807*, edited by José Mattoso, organized by António Manuel Hespanha, vol. IV, 49–69. Lisbon: Círculo de Leitores.

Serrão, José Vicente. 1993b. "O Quadro Económico." In *História de Portugal. O Antigo Regime, 1620–1807*, edited by José Mattoso, organized by António Manuel Hespanha, vol. 4, 71–88. Lisbon: Círculo de Leitores.

Serrão, José Vicente. 1996. "População e Rede Urbana nos séculos XVI-XVIII." In *História dos Municípios e do Poder Local*, edited by César de Oliveira, 63–77. Lisbon: Círculo de Leitores.

Serrão, José Vicente. 2000. *Os Campos da Cidade. Configuração das Estruturas Fundiárias da Região de Lisboa nos Finais do Antigo Regime*. PhD diss., Lisbon: Instituto Superior de Ciências do Trabalho e da Empresa.

Serrão, José Vicente. 2005. "A Agricultura." In *História Económica de Portugal, 1700–2000*, edited by Pedro Lains e Álvaro Ferreira da Silva, vol. I, 145–175. Lisbon, Imprensa de Ciências Sociais.

Serrão, José Vicente. 2007. "Os Impactos Económicos do Terramoto." In *O Terramoto de 1755. Impactos Históricos*, edited by A. Araújo *et al.*, 141–164. Lisbon: Livros Horizonte.

Serrão, José Vicente. 2009. "Land Management Responses to Market Changes. Portugal, Seventeenth–Nineteenth Centuries." In *Markets and Agricultural Changes in Europe, from the 13th to the 20th Century*, edited by V. Pinilla, 47–73. Turnhout: Brepols Publishers.

Serrão, José Vicente and Rui Santos. 2013. "Land Policies and Land Markets: Portugal, Late Eighteenth and Early Nineteenth Centuries." In *Property Rights, Land Markets and Economic Growth in the European Countryside (13th–19th Centuries)*, edited by Gérard Béaur, Jean-Michel Chevet, Maria Teresa Pérez Picazo and Phillipp Schoffield, 317–341. Turnhout: Brepols Publishers.

Shaw, L. M. E. 1998. *The Anglo-Portuguese Alliance and the English Merchants in Portugal, 1654–1810*. Aldershot: Ashgate.

Shillington, V. M. and A. B. Wallis Chapman. 1907. *The Commercial Relations of England and Portugal*. London: Routledge and Sons.

Sideri, Sandro. 1978. *Comércio e Poder. Colonialismo Informal nas Relações Anglo-Portuguesas*. Lisbon: Edições Cosmos.

Silbert, Albert. 1978. *Le Portugal Mediterranéen à la fin de l'Ancien Régime. Contribution à l'Histoire Agraire Comparée*, 3 vols. Lisbon: Instituto Nacional de Investigação Científica.

Silva, Álvaro Ferreira da. 1987. "Família e Trabalho Doméstico no 'Hinterland' de Lisboa: Oeiras, 1763–1818." *Análise Social* 23 (3): 531–562.

Silva, Álvaro Ferreira da. 1997. "A Evolução da Rede Urbana Portuguesa (1801–1940)." *Análise Social* 32 (4–5): 779–814.

Silva, Álvaro Ferreira da. 2005. "Finanças Públicas." In *História Económica de Portugal (1700–2000). O Século XVIII*, edited by Pedro Lains and Álvaro Ferreira da Silva, vol. 1, 237–261. Lisbon: Imprensa de Ciências Sociais.

Silva, Célia Maria Taborda da. 1993. *O Mosteiro de Ganfei. Propriedade, Produção e Rendas no Antigo Regime, 1629–1683 e 1716–1822*. Master diss., Porto: University of Porto.

Silva, Francisco Ribeiro da. 1988. *O Porto e o seu Termo, 1580–1640. Os Homens, as Instituições e o Poder*. Porto: Arquivo Histórico da Câmara Municipal do Porto.

Silva, J. Andrade. 1854–1859. *Collecção Chronológica da Legislação Portugueza*, vols. I-X. Lisbon: s.n.

Silva, L. A. Rebello. 1867. *História de Portugal nos Séculos XVI e XVII*, vol. III. Lisbon: Imprensa Nacional.

Silva, Teresa Rebelo da. 2006. "Drenagem do Paul de Lagos (finais do século XV)." *Paisagens Rurais e Urbanas. Fontes, Metodologias, Problemáticas*, Lisbon, Centro de Estudos Históricos – Universidade Nova de Lisboa, 207–212.

Silveira, L. E. da *et al.* 2011. "Population and Railways in Portugal, 1801–1930." *Journal of Interdisciplinary History* 42 (1): 29–52.

Silveira, Luís Espinha da. 1987. "Aspectos da Evolução das Finanças Públicas Portuguesas (1800–1827)." *Análise Social* 23 (3): 505–529.

Simões, Veiga. 1938. *Portugal, o Ouro, as Descobertas e a Criação do Estado Capitalista.* Lisbon: s. n.

Simpson, James. 2004. "Agriculture and Industrialization." In *Exceptionalism and Industrialisation. Britain and Its European Rivals 1688–1815*, edited by Leandro Prados de la Escosura, 69–85. Cambridge: Cambridge University Press.

Smith, David Grant. 1975. *The Portuguese Mercantile Class of Portugal and Brazil in the Seventeenth Century: A Socioeconomic Study of the Merchants of Lisbon and Bahia, 1620–1690.* PhD diss., Texas: Texas University.

Soares, Fernando Brito. 2005. "A Agricultura." In *História Económica de Portugal, 1700–2000. O Século XX*, edited by Pedro Lains and Álvaro Ferreira da Silva, vol. 3, 157–183. Lisbon: Imprensa de Ciências Sociais.

Sousa, Fernando de. 1978. "A Indústria das Sedas em Trás-os-Montes." *Revista de História Económica e Social* 2: 59–73.

Sousa, Fernando, ed. 2008. *A Companhia e as Relações Económicas de Portugal com o Brasil, a Inglaterra e a Rússia.* Lisbon: Edições Afrontamento.

Sousa, Fernando Freire de and Ricardo Cruz. 1995. *O Processo de Privatizações em Portugal.* Porto: Associação Industrial Portuense.

Sousa, João Silva de. 1991. *A Casa Senhorial do Infante D. Henrique.* Lisbon: Livros Horizonte.

Sousa, Rita Martins de. 2006. *Moeda e Metais Preciosos no Portugal Setecentista, 1688–1797.* Lisbon: Imprensa Nacional-Casa da Moeda.

Souza, George Bryan. 1986. *The Survival of Empire: Portuguese Trade and Society in China and the South China Sea, 1630–1754.* Cambridge: Cambridge Univ Press.

Souza, George Bryan. 2014. *Portuguese, Dutch and Chinese in Maritime Asia, c. 1585–1800. Merchants, Commodities and Commerce.* Farnham: Ashgate-Variorum.

Souza, L. M. 2006. *O Sol e a Sombra: Política e Administração na América Portuguesa do século XVIII.* São Paulo: Companhia das Letras.

Spooner, Frank C. 1983. *Risks at Sea, Amsterdam Insurance and Maritime Europe, 1766–1780.* Cambridge: Cambridge University Press.

St. Aubyn, Miguel. 2014. "We'll Still Be Here in the Long Run. Austerity and Peripheral Growth Hypothesis." In *Structural Change, Competitiveness and Industrial Policy. Painful Lessons from the European Periphery*, edited by A. A. C. Teixeira, E.G. Silva and R. P. Mamede, 67–79. Abingdon: Routledge.

Steensgaard, Niels.1990. "The Growth and Composition of the Long Distance Trade of England and the Dutch before 1750." In *The Rise of Merchant Empires.*

*Long Distance Trade in the Early Modern World, 1350–1750,* edited by James Tracy, 102–152. Cambridge: Cambridge University Press.

Steil, Benn. 2013. *The Battle of Bretton Woods: John Maynard Keynes, Harry Dexter White, and the Making of a New World Order.* Princeton: Princeton University Press.

Stolz, Yvonne, Joerg Baten and Jaime Reis. 2013. "Portuguese Living Standards, 1720–1980, in European comparison: Heights, Income, and Human Capital." *Economic History Review* 66 (2): 545–578.

Strum, Daniel. 2013. *The Sugar Trade Brazil, Portugal, and the Netherlands, 1595–1630.* Stanford: Stanford University Press.

Subrahmanyam, Sanjay. 1993. *The Portuguese Empire in Asia, 1500–1700: A Political and Economic History.* London: Longman.

Subtil, José Manuel.1993. "Os Poderes do Centro." In *História de Portugal. O Antigo Regime, 1620–1807,* edited by José Mattoso and organized by António Manuel Hespanha, vol. IV, 157–193. Lisbon: Círculo de Leitores.

Subtil, José Manuel. 2007. *O Terramoto Político (1755–1759). Memória e Poder.* Lisbon: Universidade Autónoma de Lisboa.

Sutherland, Lucy. 1933. *A London Merchant, 1695–1774.* Oxford: Oxford University Press.

Tavares, Maria José Ferro. 1987. *Os Judeus em Portugal no Século XV.* Lisbon: Universidade Nova de Lisboa.

Teixeira, Aurora A. C., Ester G. Silva and Ricardo Paes Mamede, eds. 2014. *Structural Change, Competitiveness and Industrial Policy. Painful Lessons from the European Periphery.* Abingdon: Routledge.

Telo, António José.1994. "A Obra Financeira de Salazar: a 'Ditadura Financeira' como Caminho para a Unidade Política, 1928–1932." *Análise Social* 29 (4): 779–800.

Temin, Peter. 2002. "The Golden Age of European Growth Reconsidered." *European Review of Economic History* 6 (1): 3–22.

'T hart, Marjolein C. 1993. *The Making of a Bourgeois State. War, Politics and Finance during the Dutch Revolt.* Manchester: Manchester University Press.

Tomaz, Fernando. 1988. "As Finanças do Estado Pombalino, 1762–1776." *Estudos e Ensaios em Homenagem a Vitorino Magalhães Godinho,* 355–388. Lisbon: Sá da Costa.

Thomaz, Luís Filipe. 1994. *De Ceuta a Timor.* Lisbon: Difel.

Tilly, Charles. 1975. "Reflections on the History of European State Making." In *The Formation of National States in Western Europe,* edited by Charles Tilly, 3–83. Princeton: Princeton University Press.

Tilly, Charles. 1990. *Coercion, Capital and European States* AD *990–1990,* Cambridge: Cambridge University Press.

Tirado Fabregat, Daniel A. and Marc Badia-Miró. 2014. "New Evidence on Regional Inequality in Iberia (1900–2000). A Geographical Approach." *Historical Methods* 47 (4): 180–189.

Torrão, Maria Manuel. 1991. "Actividade Comercial Externa de Cabo Verde: Organização, Funcionamento, Evolução." In *História Geral de Cabo Verde,* edited by L. de Albuquerque, M. Emília Madeira Santo, vol. I, 237–337. Lisbon: Centro de Estudos de Cartografia Antiga.

Tortella, Gabriel. 1994. "Patterns of Economic Retardation and Recovery in South-western Europe in the Nineteenth and Twentieth Centuries." *Economic History Review* 47 (1): 1–21.

Tortella, Gabriel. 2000. *The Development of Modern Spain: An Economic History of the Nineteenth and Twentieth Centuries.* Cambridge (Mass.): Harvard University Press.

Trindade, Maria José. 1965. "Alguns Problemas do Pastoreio em Portugal nos Séculos XV e XVI." *Do Tempo e da História* 1:114–134.

Valente, Vasco Pulido. 1997. *Os Militares e a Política 1820–1856.* Lisbon: Imprensa Nacional-Casa da Moeda.

Valério, Nuno. 1980. "Portugal nos Séculos XVIII e XIX segundo Adam Smith e Friederich List." *Revista de História Económica e Social* 6: 105–115.

Valério, Nuno. 1994. *As Finanças Públicas Portuguesas entre as Duas Guerras Mundiais.* Lisbon: Cosmos.

Valério, Nuno. 1997. "Um Indicador da Evolução dos Preços em Portugal nos Séculos XVI a XIX." Working Paper no. 4, Gabinete de História Económica e Social.

Valério, Nuno. 2001. *Estatísticas Históricas Portuguesas.* Lisbon: Instituto Nacional de Estatística.

Van Bath, B. H. Slicher. 1963. *The Agrarian History of Western Europe.* AD *500–1850.* London: Arnold.

Van Tielhof, Mijlfa and Jan Luiten van Zanden. 2009. "Roots of Growth and Productivity Change in Dutch Shipping Industry, 1500–1800." *Explorations in Economic History* 46 (4): 389–403.

Van Veen, Ernst. 2000. *Decay or Defeat. An Inquiry into the Portuguese Decline in Asia. 1580–1645.* Leiden: University of Leiden.

Van Zanden, Jan Luiten. 2005. "What Happened to the Standard of Living before the Industrial Revolution? New Evidence from the Western Part of the Netherlands." In *Living Standards in the Past. New Perspectives on Well-Being in Asia and Europe,* edited by R. C. Allen, T. Bengtsson and M. Dribe, 173–194. Oxford: Oxford University Press.

Van Zanden, Jan Luiten. 2009. *The Long Road to the Industrial Revolution. The European Economy in a Global Perspective,* 1000–1800. Leiden: Brill.

Vasconcelos, Álvaro de and Maria João Seabra, eds. 2000. *Portugal. A European Story.* Cascais: Princípia.

Verger, Pierre. 1976. *Trade Relations between the Bight of Benin and Bahia from the 17th to 19th Century.* Ibadan: Ibadan University Press.

Viana, Mário. 2007. *Espaço e Povoamento numa Vila Portuguesa (Santarém 1147–1350).* Lisbon: Caleidoscópio.

Vieira, Alberto. 1985. "A Questão Cerealífera nos Açores nos Séculos XV-XVII. Elementos para o seu Estudo." *Arquipélago,* série História e Filosofia 1: 123–201.

Vieira, Alberto. 2002. "A Madeira e o Mercado do Açúcar, séculos XV-XVI." In *História do Açúcar. Rotas e Mercados,* edited by Alberto Vieira, 55–89. Funchal: Centro de Estudos de História do Atlântico.

Vilaça, J. Cruz. 2000. "Portugal and European Integration. Negotiations and Legal Implications." In *Portugal. A European Story,* edited by A. Vasconcelos and Maria J. Seabra, 79–87. Cascais: Principia.

Vogt, John. 1979. *Portuguese Rule on the Gold Coast, 1469–1682*. Athens (Georgia): University of Georgia Press.

Wallerstein, Immanuel. 1974–1980. *The Modern World System*. Vols I and II. New York/London: Academic Press.

Williamson, J. and K. H. O'Rourke. 2002. "After Columbus: Explaining Europe's Overseas Trade Boom, 1500–1800." *The Journal of Economic History* 62 (2): 417–456.

Yun-Casalilla, Bartolomé and Patrick O'Brien. 2012. *The Rise of Fiscal States. A Global History, 1500–1914*. Cambridge: Cambridge University Press.

Zamagni, Vera. 1993. *The Economic History of Italy, 1860–1990. Recovery after Decline*. Oxford: Clarendon Press.

# Index

Abrantes, 62
absolutism, 10, 222, 232–234
Acapulco, 105
*Acto Colonial* (1930), 299
Afonso Henriques, king of Portugal, 15–16, 18–19
Afonso III, king of Portugal, 37–39
Afonso IV, king of Portugal, 39
Afonso V, king of Portugal, 49
Africa, 202
  East, 50, 217
  North, 6, 37, 43–46, 48–49, 59–60, 68, 87, 210
  West coast, 6, 43, 46, 48, 51, 79, 87, 104, 106, 149–150, 217
African colonies, 257, 260, 282, 287–288, 300–301, 315, 334
agrarian economy, 26, 40, 66, 292
agrarian reform, 311
agriculture, 5, 8, 10, 208, 291, 306, 330, 337, *See* crops; farms; investment; labor; land; productivity; proteccionism
  animal husbandry, 31–32, 66–68, 71, 139, 180–183, 239, 241–243, 266–267, 312
  arable husbandry, 176
  commercial, 32, 47, 176
  convertible husbandry, 171
  costs of farming-capital goods, 243
  draft animals, 232, 238–240, 242–244
  fertilizers in, 238–240, 244
  first farming revolution, 239
  intensive, 238
  irrigation, 12, 238, 306
  levies on, 29–30
  mechanization, 239–240
  output, 5–6, 8, 11, 31, 52, 67, 90, 94, 110, 133, 152, 164, 171, 176, 181, 184, 229, 240–245, 254, 266, 311, 329–330
  pasture, 25, 32, 47, 62, 66–67, 181, 240

  plantation, 76, 78–79
  second agricultural revolution, 239
  techniques, 31, 62, 67, 70, 171, 175, 184, 238–239, 241, 244
  tools and implements of, 31, 33, 238
  yields, 30, 65, 68, 132, 180–181, 183, 239–240
*aguardente*, 177
*alambéis*, 86
al-Andalus, 1, 14–15, 18, 20, 25
Alcácer do Sal, 20
Alcácer Quibir. *See* Al-Ksar al-Kebir
Alcobaça, 61–62, 64
  monastery of, 20, 22, 31
Aldeia Galega, 75
Alenquer, 34, 62, 188, 250
Alentejo, 20, 34, 39, 54–63, 65–66, 68, 71, 86, 98, 114, 119, 121, 128–131, 133, 139, 141, 167–168, 173–174, 176–180, 182–183, 187, 239–240, 244, 266
Alfonso VII, king of León-Castile, 18
Algarve, 1, 18, 35, 54–60, 62, 64–67, 70, 73, 76, 88, 92, 105, 114, 130–131, 176–182
Al-Ksar al-Kebir, 48, 100
Al-Ksar al-Saghir, 43
Almada, 62
*almoxarifados, almoxarifes*, 38–39, 41, 95, 97–98, 160, 217
Ambon, 106
America, 1, 65, 105, 148, 155, 198, 201, 245
  North, 110, 147, 201–202, 262
  Portuguese America. *See* Brazil
  South, 6, 43, 52, 84, 193, 258, 283
  Spanish, 103–106, 152
Amsterdam, 103, 111, 124
  Jewish community in, 103
  Portuguese merchants in, 106
  sugar refineries in, 103
Andalusia, 59, 65, 238

388